WORKING THROUGH REHAB:
An Inside Look at Adolescent Drug Treatment

By Graeme Daniels, MFT

ISBN: 978-0615944708

Cover design by Don Mathews

CONTENTS

FOREWARD

I am honored that Graeme asked me to write this foreward. We have known each other for sixteen years, but the last several years have pulled us into our separate busy work lives. So reviewing this manuscript gave us time to get together and talk. And it gave me time to think. Graeme asked me to write this because of our experience working together at Thunder Road. I was a staff psychiatrist and Medical Director from 1995 to 2006. Graeme was a therapist in continual development from intern to supervisor ovcr that time. I always enjoyed his quiet thoughtful style and precise, understated language. I appreciated his observant nature and natural skill as a therapist and supervisor.

I relied on him to supervise and support the counselors and staff on our team. They loved him. He was extremely good at teaching and generally invigorating a team that was besieged with challenging clients, families, and a system operating under constant strain. But I had no idea about his quiet compilation of all these experiences, and his ability to write so thoughtfully about them. You are in for a treat. This book is really good. Adolescent residential chemical dependency treatment is difficult and exhausting. The only way to survive it as a clinician is to maintain love. Love for the clients, the staff, and love for the challenge of really helping people.

That's the short version of how I see this book: it's Graeme's very rigorous and personal examination of maintaining love as a clinician in the face of countless erosive forces. And I must emphasize how powerfully and comprehensively Graeme thinks. To the casual observer, myself included, Graeme is just a great therapist and supervisor who is competent, warm, funny, etc. So to read his synthesis of research and theory, beautifully melded with very open disclosures of his personal internal experiences surprised and delighted me beyond expectations. It even helped me integrate and think more deeply about my own experiences and development over those 11 years. And it helped me collect and recalibrate myself in the present. But best of all, the book project gave us a chance to get together and talk. I love talking with Graeme.

We had coffee for the third time a few weeks ago in Oakland. When we have coffee we sit for several hours, thinking, joking, ranting, and bonding. We see eye to eye on most aspects of treatment, which is rare in this window of healthcare, in the context of mental health care in general, and chemical dependency treatment in specific. We are old school curmudgeons, Original Gangsta therapists. We long for treatment that is no longer covered by insurance, and rarely implemented regardless of coverage. We complain and lament. We lose track of time and usually end with a mad scramble back to our offices, always wishing for another fifteen minutes. We can talk for a long time.

But I must help the reader ever so slightly, as Graeme's understated dry wit and almost imperceptible irony may mask his focused passion as a therapist. He is most passionate about reaching his patients' deepest available emotions and thoughts, to bring them to consciousness. The reader that keeps this in mind will understand that his comprehensive review of treatment models, treatment histories, paradigms of treatment theory, etc., are not collected in the interest of due diligence. They are Graeme's personal collection, gathered with the purpose of deepening his own skill as a therapist and teacher. They are gathered in the interest of extending his reach as deeply as possible into the essential workings of his patients' worlds. This book is an insight into Graeme's own "working through" the process of becoming the clinician, teacher, and person his is today. He takes us on a personal tour of his professional development, and very sneakily invites us to help him pause and take stock of himself.

I'll take you back to our last morning coffee. Graeme brought, at my request, the letter I wrote to be read aloud at his farewell party at Thunder Road in 2011. Here's part of it:

Dear Graeme,

You do know, of course, that this time, for real, Thunder Road WILL SHUT DOWN if you leave. I know this has been said before, even by you to me when I left. But this time it is true. Seriously... I've gotta share my last memory of the two of us at Thunder Road. I have a crystal clear recollection of you joining me for a Psych evaluation, as you were preparing to become the new evaluation guy at the time of my departure. We found a new client in his room, sat on the adjacent empty bed (no time for a walk to an office) and flew through our list of questions, trying our best to extrapolate everything possible about his young life. Then we raced downstairs to my tiny disheveled office to dictate into a super cheap, old school, handheld cassette tape recorder many pages of facts, observations, and speculations, and voila—a Psych evaluation!

I remember how we laughed at the ridiculous pace, at the realization of how much we DIDN'T KNOW, but how much we loved the opportunity to convey a story about that young life to the treatment team, hoping for a good outcome. That was really important to both of us, even after two thousand of them in 11 years (TRUE!) I just know that real stories still matter to you and that you care, that you pay close attention and have the curiosity, humor, and love to continue to grow in your work. I am very well aware of how special a teacher, supervisor, and mentor you are. Your interns will miss you deeply. Who will teach the art of Psychotherapy the way you can? The place will shut down! See? Or maybe it will find a way to keep on going—who knows how...

We read it aloud and laughed. The absurd notion of Thunder Road shutting down if any single person left was a legacy of farewell speeches passed back and forth among the clinicians for years. But I really did feel Graeme's departure was of particular significance and concern. The long list of problems contributing to the erosion of thoughtful, long-term therapeutic treatment is far beyond the scope of this foreward. I'll save that for a coffee rant with Graeme. But I will say that maintaining a depth oriented psychotherapeutic approach to treatment in any system, "rehab" included, demands fortitude and perseverance on the part of the clinician.

Graeme has fortitude and perseverance. Look for it in this book. Realize that his skeptical, stubborn, intellectual, intense, oppositional, wry, ironic nature fights wholeheartedly for love. Look for that too, as you "work through rehab" with Graeme. Then picture him with a soft British accent, wearing a soccer jersey, almost invisibly fighting and laughing in equal measure. Got it? Okay, you're ready to jump in…

Michael Wachter M.D.
San Francisco, California May 2013

Introduction (or Orientation)

Check this out: Do you like numbers? Ok, here's a few statistics: according to the Treatment Episode Data Set (TEDS) report, as published online by the Substance Abuse and Mental Health Services Administration (SAMHSA), over 1.8 million people were admitted for substance abuse treatment in 2011 across the United States, and just about 2 million people were admitted for the same problem in 2010. The average number treated over the five years prior to this was between 1.8 and 1.9 million people per year, admitted to just over 13,000 facilities licensed or certified to treat individuals for substance abuse. According to the same data tables, between 7 and 8 percent of these admissions—again, on average—are kids. By kids, I mean ages 12-17, and most of these kids are between 15 and 17. That's about 150,000 teens per year entering programs, in outpatient or inpatient settings—rehab, as the shorthand goes—for the treatment of substance abuse. And by the way, substance abuse is only one of many problems these kids have.

This book is not about numbers. In fact, this book has very few numbers to offer from this point onwards. This book is about the problem of adolescents using drugs; about the serious problems those adolescents have in addition to using drugs; about the problems their loved ones have; about the problems society has with drugs and mental illness. Above all, this book is about the problems mental health professionals have in trying to help all these people. The lens is a little bit macro, but mostly micro, because for fifteen years I was one of these professionals, working in group homes, hospital settings, and sober living homes, sometimes on an outpatient basis, but more regularly in inpatient settings. I'm a psychotherapist by trade and nature, perhaps ill-constituted to comment on some of the broader issues that wrap around all these matters. Not that I don't try. In my time in this business, I took plenty of time to comment, but I was never one of the guys in charge. I was never a medical director, a policy maker, a researcher, or even an outspoken activist. And yet, given the paucity of literature speaking to what really happens in drug rehab programs, I may be one of the better positioned observers around.

My position now is that of looking in the rear view mirror. I left this business-proper in 2011, and have since settled into a quieter working life developing a previously neglected private practice in Contra Costa County, thirty miles east of San Francisco. My departure was serendipity, not choice, and this narrative, filled as it is with personal recollections mixed with exposition and polemics, could only have been written from a safe distance. Despite conceiving this book some years ago, I realized early during the course of my writing that I couldn't possibly be as honest as I'd want or need to be if I were reflecting alongside a direct involvement. That involvement ran a gamut of roles over the years, all along the "front lines" of work with troubled kids, or else in constant proximity to them. The rehab program dominantly featured in this text is that of Thunder Road, a prominent residential treatment center in downtown Oakland, California, and my intermittent employer from 1996 to 2011. I also reflect upon my spell working with the McAlister Institute in San Diego, and sundry episodes outside of these settings. Meanwhile, several chapters in this book contain insights of individuals who have had similar-length (or longer) careers in this field, both at Thunder Road and at several other notable programs.

The focus on residential treatment may disorient some readers. Over 80% of adolescent drug treatment admissions are to outpatient programs. However, when I speak to teens, it is "rehab"—which to them means inpatient (or residential) treatment—about which they hear rumors. Residential treatment is what kids fear: that time-out from life; that *sending away*. For those more familiar with day treatment programs, Methadone, Suboxone, or Gabapentin treatments, or even drop-in Harm Reduction services, the attention given here to such things as Therapeutic Community (TC) Concepts or Behavior Modification may seem secondary to other issues relating to substance abuse. These lesser discussed terms refer to a repertoire of methods that are staples of residential treatment, and I seek to depict them here in vivid detail. The principles that underlie the methods are longstanding and well established; they were developed over time by identifiable sources, and are now under scrutiny—some may say siege—by somewhat less visible sources. Despite my original misgivings, this book goes to bat for the much maligned Social Model, or (alternatively-termed) Therapeutic Community Concepts model and does so quite rigorously, based largely upon direct experience.

The Therapeutic Community Model is hardly obscure. Several books, such as Lonny Shavelson's *Hooked*, Meredith Maran's *Dirty*, and to some extent, *Comeback*, by the mother/daughter team of Claire and Mia Fontaine, have all reported upon the TC approach. Meanwhile, those SAMSHA reports don't appear to have much to say about Therapeutic Community Concepts anymore. A 2009 national survey of treatment services (N-SSATS) tracked use of various approaches in treatment programs, including Cognitive-Behavioral Therapy, 12-step facilitation, trauma-related counseling, brief intervention approaches, anger management, and Motivational Interviewing. My book touches on all of those approaches to one extent or another. But Therapeutic Community Concepts was not addressed in the N-SSATS survey, despite its prominence since the late 1950s, presumably because it did not pass muster as an "evidence-based" approach.

While the Therapeutic Community approach is being diminished in drug treatment programs, the focus on behavioral outcomes in programs seems stronger than ever. In tandem with this development, Psychodynamic approaches to psychotherapy have also been reduced to a backseat role within treatment circles. When I began working in this field in the nineties, Psychodynamic thinking was commonplace among my supervisors. My peers seemed filled with curiosity about unconscious processes. They were ever looking under their own skin and that of their clients, trying to know them as deeply as possible. Nowadays, treatment advocates speak of Cognitive Behavioral Therapy as the established umbrella term for all types of talk therapy—but usually with an implicitly short-term, symptom reduction focus. As a result, the average counselor in a drug rehab program operates more as an educator and symptom tracker for a bulging caseload of lives. The term therapist, applied to many who work in these settings, now seems a misnomer to me. Those thousands of kids, or the 1.whatever million adults in treatment programs: it must be getting harder to know them individually and treat them with any real depth. My main thesis here: when a system (or an individual) focuses so narrowly upon behavioral outcomes—that which is "quantifiable"—it loses track of the unconscious, and then acts unconsciously.

Ironically, my book won't teach that much about the lives of individuals I or others treated. Partly, this is about confidentially. None of the teens whose treatment episodes are depicted here are identified. Names are changed or shortened, as are certain identifiable features; the passage of time alone will obscure some anecdotes. Some former employees of Thunder Road and McAlister Institute are also characterized, but aside from those who agreed to be interviewed, they too remain anonymous. Mostly, the stories are meant to illustrate ideas that I've decided are important for readers to consider. I might have followed any one of the individuals' tales more fully, but this would have taken the story on a much different path.

There is one personal story that is followed throughout *Working Through Rehab*: mine. The narrative presented here is more or less a chronicle of my career working in the field, preceded by some relevant background and dovetailed with commentary on various phenomena along the course of my working life—my "working through" rehab. The personal information about me is not gratuitous, nor is it offered for the sake of transparency, the credentialing of my views. Hopefully, what's apparent is a learning curve that parallels in some ways the evolving or fumbling process of an industry straining to serve millions. The plethora of issues, "approaches", theories, methods, or "tools" described in these pages may be dizzying and circular for those with inside knowledge, let alone those who may be looking in from the outside, hoping to learn something about this peculiar business.

For the veterans of rehab, whether you have been participants or practitioners, I hope to have you nodding in recognition as you read along, and then stir your blood. I will stick you in the middle of treatment planning meetings, and within the circles of hot confrontation groups with ritualistic norms. I will profile the average and not-so average kid in rehab, and cover the scope of problems that programs attempt to consider when formulating treatment strategies. In the denser chapters, I address the bravest of efforts: the attempt to engage kids' families into treatment. Whether confronting parents who undermine their kids' treatment, or teasing out the stories of intergeneration drug use and trauma, those who work with families in rehab chip away at family secrets, the gremlins within closed systems, and they do so more often than not, within the semi-public format of group therapy.

Working Through Rehab is critical of some trends in drug treatment, but none more so than its use of group therapy. Group therapy is the thing in programs, but training in group therapy techniques, or the maintaining of consistent norms for such activities, is not. This is just one of many arguments to be had, and I invite readers to take their pick from the vast menu. Concerned that abstinence may not be the appropriate standard to expect of those receiving services? That topic is covered here. Disturbed by media reports of abuses in group homes and other residential programs? I have stories and opinions. Trauma issues? Some wonder whether trauma must be treated concurrently with substance abuse, or whether it should be treated only after a stabilization of destructive behaviors has occurred. Meanwhile, how does the drug treatment industry continue to reach out to serve more and more people, and are there any drawbacks to this goal? Others still may be more concerned with the entire flavor of drug treatment services: that it furthers a negativistic attitude towards youth and drugs, propagandizing versus teaching truths; or conversely, that the industry is not doing enough to either contain or thoroughly treat the problems of kids and their families.

I have my biases, and the reader will learn of them, of course. I am a TC sympathizer and a rehabilitated therapist. Once that meant I had adapted to life in a drug rehab setting. It meant that I had dropped a slavish adherence to old fashioned ideas and gotten with the program. Latterly, it meant I was grousing for the restoration of some good ideas that should never have been given a pink slip. Some will agree with my opinions, and some won't. Perhaps some will be appalled, hopefully those in charge. Who am I to write these opinions? My reply: Who do I need to be? Now, as a therapist, I must refrain from making lavish promises. It's extremely unlikely that anything whatsoever will change as a result of this book. There. One promise: I will, in the pages ahead, faithfully describe the world in which many have lived and worked. If you have been one of those people, then you might remember or imagine that I was there with you, looking over your shoulder. I am remembering.

Graeme Daniels, May 2013

1
CHECKING FIRE EXTINGUISHERS

So, you're thinking...

So, you're thinking of placing your kid in rehab? Or, maybe you're thinking of getting a job in such a place, as a counselor, social worker, therapist, or whatever they're being called these days. Do you know what it's like being in rehab, or working in one? Have you visited a drug treatment facility, or heard stories from your neighbor who sent their kid to an out-of-state boarding school the previous summer, and later discharged just in time to begin senior year in high school. Are boarding schools the same thing as rehab? You wonder. A doctor outlines options: suggests therapy for a troubled teen, or an assessment at a nearby hospital, which boasts detox facilities and an intensive outpatient program, committing kids and their families to eight weeks of group and family therapy, ten hours a week, not counting the 12-step meetings that counselors will ask participants to attend on the weekends. A residential admission is the next level of care. It is the last resort as far as professional intervention is concerned—the last stop on the treatment ladder.

Do you want this? Need this? Does a kid getting referred to rehab even have a choice: Meaning, is a court presenting rehab as an alternative to incarceration? Or are the parents the mandating authority? Perhaps your kid's best friend has called you up, or texted you anonymously, warning that he or she is drinking or smoking much more than you realize, or "experimenting" with some other, supposedly more hardcore drug—one that will really scare you. You notice the kid's grades are going down, and that more time is being spent with sedentary, seemingly anti-social activities: marathon spells of video-gaming; the vague notion of "hanging out". What happened to that kid that seemed vibrant a year or so before: polite, energetic, and gregarious. Is this normal adolescence? You worry. How long do you wait to see what happens?

Maybe this isn't your story. Maybe you're a parent who has struggled with your own substance use. Maybe you're an addict, and it seems like your kid is following suit. You don't know what to do, or even if, given your own history, you have the aptitude or even the right to speak your concerns. After all, did you listen to adults when you were a teen? So, your kid is staying out all hours, has joined a gang, become a dealer as well as a user. Involvement in the juvenile justice system seems imminent, if it hasn't happened already. You've already had several phone calls from Child Protective Services; one or two home visits. You and a couple of county social workers are on a first name basis.

Maybe you're a fledgling member of the mental health profession, and working with troubled kids seems like a good idea: a stepping stone to a career as a social worker, a teacher, or, if you're really stupid, a psychotherapist. You're a tweenie that's looking for a job while in school. Or you're a journeyman counselor that's just completed requirements for certification as a drug and alcohol abuse counselor. An adolescent drug treatment program, attached, say, to a larger hospital, will offer steady employment, some modest benefits, if not a particularly competitive wage. You're okay with that, maybe…for the time being. You want to reach young minds, work with those who may be more flexible in their ways, feel more hope than the adult addicts you've known. It will be less depressing, you think, working with kids.

Now that you've read the brochures and the websites of various programs, or taken tours of their sterile, hospital corridors and dorm-like accommodations, settle in for a first hand look at what happens in adolescent drug rehab programs, from the ground up, because that's where I started. To do this properly, I have to go back in time to give some history, some context for what is happening today, especially in residential programs, for while some things have changed, others have not. Along the way, there are markers of change, nodal moments in my working life that in my opinion reflect trends in the business as a whole. If by the end of this text, the reader still wants to enter this field, or admit his or her child to a rehab like the ones I worked at, I'll have no complaints. Just consider this the longest informed consent form in rehab history.

Starting with moving on

I recently left the business of adolescent drug treatment. I didn't want to. It wasn't my idea. I wasn't mandated into treatment, but I was mandated to leave. I wanted to stay, continue my work as a teacher/supervisor, leading the modest intern therapist program at the Thunder Road Adolescent Treatment Center in Oakland, working peripherally yet for the most part with affinity for its treatment philosophies and approaches. The areas where therapists needed help were the areas where I could help. That was my stance: one I regularly asserted with peers, supervisees, supervisors, even administrators. I had ideas—ideas about treating kids as though they were capable of things they'd barely considered; about teaching therapists to provide the conditions for a rich and comprehensive therapeutic experience. That may sound a little self-serving; or it might sound a little mawkish, though not especially controversial. Actually, it was controversial.

I saw it coming, my letting go—sort of. Not really. What can I say? Even therapists with a distrusting edge can be in denial. My similarly distrusting wife, who thinks three out of four personal questions are a prelude to identity theft, was unsurprised, and philosophical. It was time, unfortunately: time to let go. I didn't want to walk upstairs on the day I was being terminated. I didn't want to answer the page that summoned me to the clinical director's office. I didn't want to speak to her, or her colleague who'd come in on his day off to help deliver the news. I didn't want patronizing comments about how admirably I'd served the program over the years. I wanted to hide in my office, which was aptly underground, in the farthest corner of the building, and think about drug treatment, therapy with adolescents, so-called Therapeutic Communities from a detached vantage point. So much had changed since I'd first joined the program as an intern. Given the average age of Thunder Road clients, most were being born around about the time I was cutting my teeth as a therapist-in-training. That was during the midst of Thunder Road's halcyon period, and a relative boom time in general for adolescent substance abuse treatment.

On the initial phone call, the director was soft-spoken and deferential. She'd like to speak to me whenever I had time, she said. As this woman had been in her job for not quite a year, and had requested or demanded my presence on about three occasions, the last two of which under unpleasant circumstances, this didn't sound good. My stomach knew before I did. It began a fluttering sensation. My hands went cold. I got lightheaded and fidgety. I knew that many kids had been on both sides of a similar divide: not wanting to leave, or not wanting to be here in the first place. I wondered, as in really wondered, for the first time in years if this was what it was like when kids first sat in the waiting rooms, kicking their heels, worried if their parents would really leave them in a place like this. On the other side, I'd known many kids to sit for hours in their assigned rooms, sweating out the decisions of the treatment team in the wake of some intolerable behavior of theirs. Would they be kicked out, sent back to juvenile hall? Would *they* let go?

Fear.

Perhaps I could come up now, I suggested, adding that this meeting sounded important. I was demonstrating eagerness ahead of a daring mission and she agreed with an air of sympathy. So, I ventured upstairs to her office feeling hurried and compliant. A passing staff member, a guy with whom I shared a single word—"hey"—each day, merely nodded at me, as though he knew something was up. I gingerly knocked on the director's door and walked in. She was clicking away on her computer as she muttered an exchange with another manager who'd been at Thunder Road since the end of the nineties. As he caught my eye, he withdrew his lower lip and gave me a worried look. He was an effete figure, with thin legs ever performing a kind of quick step as he hurried importantly from one meeting to the next. He looked like the type of guy that will have been teased and then bullied about his violin in fourth grade. The director of the moment, a not especially overbearing woman who overplayed compassion, thanked me for coming by—a bad sign—and affected a soothing tone, a sort of mewing that trailed into her prefacing words: "I guess you know this isn't good news." It was hard staying present for the rest. The hospital, they said, was eliminating my position as clinical supervisor to the staff therapists. The hospital to which they referred is Alta Bates Summit in North Oakland. Alta Bates, not Thunder Road, was letting me go after fifteen years of what was reverently-termed "service". The hospital was letting me go, they emphasized, as though distancing themselves from the decision. I didn't know anyone at Alta Bates. My fifteen years will have meant nothing to the Star Chamber making this decision, if that really was what was happening.

They were sorry, they added strenuously, as if they'd just spent the whole morning trying to convince administrators not to make this regrettable decision. I glanced to my right, to a window that was textured in a way so as to reveal a blanket of whiteness. There was a briefing of sorts. I'd have a month to sort out my affairs. This was unprecedented, apparently. The hospital never does this. Ordinarily, an employee being let go would learn of that fact on the day of leaving. Departure day, they call this. Sounds like something you'd hear at an airport, I thought. Anyway, that was hospital policy. I was special, it was implied. For one thing, my position, that of clinical supervisor, was special. I had a responsibility to my supervisees that stretched beyond my employment, to the governing body that regulates the profession of psychotherapy from Sacramento. I'd have to give seven days' notice to the therapists. I'd have documents to sign, Ts to cross and Is to dot, not to mention numerous farewells to make. With administration, these managers had gone to bat for me, pleaded special circumstances. Plus, I'd been at Thunder Road for fifteen years, they kept exclaiming. Hardly anyone stays at Thunder Road for that long. There might have been an insinuation in there, wedged beneath the apologetic front: *really, isn't it time to move on?*

An orientation

I worked at Thunder Road for fifteen years, give or take two or three years wherein I lived in Southern California doing similar work at another group home, albeit a much smaller one.

Thunder Road is a hybrid entity: a group home and chemical dependency hospital for adolescents, licensed by the California Department of Social Services and the Department of Health Services—a once private corporation that transformed into a non-profit public benefit organization affiliated with Summit Medical Center (later Alta Bates/Summit Medical Center) in the mid-nineties. It has an accreditation by the Commission on Accreditation of Rehabilitation Services which expires every three years, and which gets renewed through inspections of its facility, and a thorough review of its procedures. Situated about twenty blocks north of downtown Oakland, about a mile west of the affluent homes that stretch up the Oakland hills, the facility has been a fixture of the community since the mid 80's, the only facility of its kind in Alameda County, but a notable exponent of the so-called Therapeutic Community Concepts Model, or Social Model. In the Bay Area, Thunder Road was a known quantity. Locally speaking, according to a 2004 Bay Area Adolescent Treatment Report sponsored by the Charles Schwab Foundation, only Walden House in San Francisco had a larger capacity for services provided to troubled youth.

It had been a fixture in my life since the mid-nineties, yet things were quite different when I first arrived. My description of a walking tour of the unit in the summer of 96' is a chestnut that I've taxied out on many occasions. Being led along the corridors of Thunder Road's residential component, I remember walking alongside a handful of other incoming staff, among rooms that comprised the female wing of the unit. The area was brightly lit in spaces, with pockets of dark shadows every ten feet. Clean for the most part, there was a slightly musty odor, and a whiff of tobacco coming from outdoors. In the corner of one stretch, there was the faint residue of a cobweb, and tufts of lint tucked in the cracks of second-hand furniture. Stickers, drawings, bold-faced affirmations like "KEEP IT REAL" were stretched across wall space or pinned to bulletin boards. The place had the strained look of an elementary school, with a baseline austerity glossed over by program ephemera. It was as though someone or a set of someones were embarrassed to know that kids lived there. The colors were bland yet varied; a mix of pastels, blue, green, and something close to orange reflected either the indecisive touch of a single designer, or the competing tastes of successive decision-makers. In a place like this one could look around and wonder who decided what about any given feature of the building. Decisions, as well as the names of the decision-makers, are sometimes lost in time.

Our guide was a nervous yet eager twenty-something that worked in the admissions and outreach department. It was part of her job to orient visitors, whether they were new staff, dignitaries, or prospective residents, and she did so with the affected grace of a hotel concierge. Glancing over her shoulder, she gestured towards an outdoor patio in which several truculent youths were seated around a beaten up picnic table, smoking. The group of about six kids, male and female, was concentrated in their task like it was the last supper. "They're allowed ten a day," explained the guide, before adding that things were about to change. "Though, actually, we're going smoke-free next week," she said with a jittery laugh. It was meant to be a point of pride, this change in policy. Thunder Road was to be one of the first programs of its kind to make this decision, and has proudly extolled its Nicotine program ever since. Change: all change is difficult, it was soberly stated. But they can do it, everyone declared. The kids in the program: they expect so little of themselves, and therefore expect others to expect little also. Up front, within the offices of the administrative wing, the smoke-free revolution was being hyped with much self-congratulation. Twenty feet beyond, as visitors entered the realm of the therapeutic milieu, a more palpable tension was evident. Staff and residents were bracing for trouble. One of the kids, a surly youth with a green Mohawk and a tattoo of a dragon on his left arm overheard the comments of the guide and snarled.

With a modicum of political will, the residents might have mounted a protest campaign and aimed it at Amnesty International—such was the outrage with which they protested the violation of their *rights*. Ordinarily, organized demonstrations didn't happen at Thunder Road. Instead, visitors would feel a collective sulk in the air and lock eyes with guides that mustered forced smiles like Soviet technocrats giving tours of Potemkin Village. Another resident, or client as they were more commonly characterized, floated by the tour and murmured the dregs of a more globalized complaint. "I'm gettin' up outa here. This place is bullshit," he said as he thumped his body down on a quite blameless six-foot long bench adjacent to the patio. A time-out, we presumed. He proceeded to sit quietly having summed up the critiques many have voiced about group homes, rehabs, and especially programs practicing the Therapeutic Community Model. He wanted to leave.

Everyone that day wanted to leave, it seemed. I didn't. It was my first day. I'd spent a year, roughly, trying to get in the front door; trying to get a job at Thunder Road. I'd first applied for an on-call position in the fall of 94', but got no response to my resume. The following spring, I answered an ad for what was being called a "Therapeutic Community Counselor" position (TCC), and was subsequently interviewed alongside three other candidates for what would then have been my first full-time job in any mental health setting. I didn't get it. As was common in the era of my early-to-mid twenties, I was wooden and nervous in the first meeting: a group interview with a three-person crossection of what Thunder Road boasts is a multi-disciplinary staff. Anxiety stills my face, unfortunately. So, with a frown masking a smile that I'm told betrays lurking mischief, I flubbed through a forgettable exercise of questions and answers, and watched haplessly as more poised candidates flashed winning smiles and exuded energy. Energy: It's a hot commodity. I know because employers are always talking about it. "I like his energy," they often say. First impressions are what count, especially in an environment of limited time and sparse resources. Perhaps energy implies other qualities: compliance, resilience; a willingness to plunder through no-man's land for the company cause with nothing but a feeble bayonet in hand. Energy is a presumed buffer against burn out, and employers are ever drilling for oil, ever imagining an inexhaustible supply. Parents are often talking about energy, or more specifically, about their diminishing supplies of it.

A year later I had one more chance. Learning of internship opportunities at Thunder Road, I applied with a then clinical supervisor who seemed detached from the hospital's other departments. Intern is a specialized term in medical and social services. At least one definition suggests imprisonment if one checks a dictionary. At Thunder Road it meant that I'd be a student, and that I'd be treated as such, though still as an employee, not a volunteer. I'd be at Thunder Road, if accepted, for what would be termed “a learning experience”, and earning a modest stipend while earning practicum hours that are required before sitting for licensing exams. I sailed through a telephone interview that led thereafter to a refreshingly casual in-person interview within an outside break area adorned with another picnic table (this one a bit rotten) and a rusted barbecue pit.

From the outset of this meeting, it seemed as though my hiring was imminent. The supervisor was relaxed and good-humored, and did most of the talking. The woman spoke of Thunder Road as if introducing its character for the first time. I felt as though I were being properly oriented and welcomed as opposed to scrutinized. It’s a tough place, she asserted like a committed patriot; a great program, but not unique, necessarily. She asked exploratory and then probing questions. Had I heard of something called Therapeutic Community Model, or TC concepts? As we continued our interview, she happily offered me a position, and we made plans for a first day. She knowingly inquired about my feelings regarding the previous process, the failed interviews of yesteryear. Was I disappointed to not get the TCC position? How did I feel about taking a position that offered only a paltry stipend?

I replied that I had been disappointed but would adapt readily enough. Very politic, I thought. As for the money, it wasn’t my priority. That was half-true. I had another two-thirds position at the time, working with developmentally disabled adults, who often acted like adolescents, thus affording what I thought was some relevant experience going into the position. I figured that money, as in meaningful sums of it, might come later, much later. For the time being, I was living at home with my parents, though I’d move in and out for various reasons over the next two to three years. The position I was about to begin was one I ultimately supervised a decade later, funnily enough. I have often said in recent years that my career at Thunder Road had come full circle with my becoming a clinical supervisor. Now those nostalgic reflections have taken on a new and melancholic meaning. Actually, it is only since leaving that life at Thunder Road has come full circle: with rejection.

In the meantime, back in 96’, I needed to learn a great deal about the culture of Thunder Road. I was as excited as I’d ever been about a new job, largely because I thought it my first real job. I was twenty six—about time, you might think, to get a so-called real job, and it wasn't even a real job. It was an internship. I'd languished through my early twenties, working service industry jobs, doing drugs occasionally after having done them prodigiously in my late teens. I'd been a journeyman in the world of retail—a modest and reliable worker, diligent but quite lacking in entrepreneurial gifts. I recall a shift I worked as an usher at a movie theater in 1988. The theater manager laughed at me on my second night. The reason: I volunteered, *energetically*, to check all the fire extinguishers in the building prior to the main showing. I was eager, un-entitled, and patient. I actually stayed in that job, though not as an usher, for almost four years. I was likewise determined to fit in at Thunder Road. As though getting a second chance at adolescence, now as an adult infiltrating the world of adolescents, I was determined not to repeat foolishness. I was determined to prove aptitude, and even among the kids, to be—dare I say—cool.

Thunder Road was cool, though being cool was anything but cool. In fact, for those working in the field of chemical dependency the concept of cool is rigorously turned on its head. Cool is at once prerequisite and ironic in Therapeutic Communities—a term borrowed but then dissembled and repackaged. Cool is a phoenix rising from the ashes of a debilitating addiction. For kids entering treatment, or for kids stuck in an ongoing struggle with adults, the word "cool" has one meaning for peers, quite another for the adults in their lives. For them, "cool" designates a parent who is lenient with rules, "flexible". If they do impose limits, they do so coolly, without judgment. Judgment: it's a bad thing, apparently. Judgment: it's a necessary and realistic thing, I say. Make an appointment at a treatment center and you'll hear words like "assessment", or "addiction", and later, words like "diagnosis". These words denote judgments. What's the real issue? It's about the inflection, and the energy behind the language. Stay cool; that is, try to be calm, compassionate. Above all, get curious and seek to understand.

The first day on the job for me was itself a marathon, though everyone but the disgruntled smokers were saying that Thunder Road was cool. An HR assistant, an officious septuagenarian, started the day warning our group of six newbies that we needed to attend all sixteen hours of a two-day orientation.

This was a blunt instrument the hospital brought down upon newcomer zeal. Energy would be tested. Among other things we had to sign in and out to prove our attendance. Thunder Road was about structure; structure and rules, this woman grimly announced. The orientation, it seemed, would mirror these values, and set the tone for our employment. A sequence of speakers, each extracted from some activity concurrently happening within the facility, and each looking begrudgingly present, went about the job of introducing different aspects of the program: everything from employee benefits, to maintenance department emergency procedures, to nursing practices, and eventually to the aspects that would be most relevant to my upcoming role, the drug treatment and mental health services. The maintenance workers were the best. Something about the righteousness of hard-working men with tools has always endeared me, perhaps because I feel so unlike them. Their grounded yet ardent airs make me feel safe. They stride around seeing the terrible possibilities all around them: the cracks in the vents, the mildew under the carpets; the accidents waiting to happen. They have clear, straightforward answers to problems, and they don't seem to be in denial about anything.

The online or "line" clinical staff was more difficult. Among other things, they were the most difficult to track down. The orientation had been designed as a rotating schedule, with speakers taking over from one another in a sort of tag team style. One counselor showed up, ostensibly to speak of time-out devices, the six-foot wide benches and similar length hallway mirrors, and slumped in a chair, staring at the ceiling for inspiration. He'd not prepared a single word ahead of this exercise, and fumbled through his presentation, speaking in fragments, using vernacular unfamiliar to everyone present. To be fair, the event was hardly intended as a professional workshop. The reader needn't imagine a hotel conference room with speakers wired for sound, orating to a gathering of professionals wearing business suits and badges indicating our names and what cities and states we came from (actually, we wore stickers). This guy—this member of floor staff—had just come from something he called "confrontation group". He heaved an exasperated sigh and shook his head, appealing for space.

The lecture that followed spoke of things like "fast track" (in reference to a resident of a medium-duration component of treatment), of the morning ritual of ITs, which apparently stood for "Industrial Therapy", which meant chores. I smirked inwardly, thinking it audacious that Thunder Road would cast just about every act done under its roof as therapeutic. The man spoke of "monads", a term used by staff and youth to maintain order in a meeting. Its original Greek meaning had an abstruse[1] spiritual connotation, roughly that of "be with yourself". In the everydayspeak of the therapeutic milieu it meant "shut up", basically. Due to the hurried aura of the speaker, most of these terms were uttered without explanation, which meant that we'd have to learn the layered meanings through our own research, or else by osmosis. There would be time enough to learn the ins and outs, we were told. We could have asked. We could have raised our hands like we all learned to back in grade school, and asserted our right to understand more fully.

Next up was a representative from the Continuing Care department, an outpatient wing of Thunder Road that offered free counseling services two nights a week following a completion of the residential program. It was comprised (at that time) of a staff of six part-timers, and provided, in terms of duration, a longer treatment for many kids and families than the residential component. Now, I've never been particularly close to the money side of this business, but even I could tell that this was the kind of arrangement that must have had hospital bean counters grinding their teeth at night. Needless to say, the woman presenting on behalf of Continuing Care said nothing about this, but rather focused on the clinical "flavor" of the department. Sounding as dissimilar as possible to the previous speaker without actually speaking in a foreign language, this woman spoke in amorphous terms, about different approaches "working" for different people, about the importance of creating a unique narrative—she used this kind of language. There were pregnant pauses between statements, hanging ellipses on each succeeding thought as she glanced wistfully over her audience members' heads. Each word was carefully crafted so as to be as benign or cryptic as possible. It was as if the room had been filled with delegates from every conceivable religion on the face of the earth, and she had been charged with the task of not offending anyone.

The next speaker was less equivocal. This was the recently appointed program director, a silky-voiced woman in her early thirties whose sonorous timbre, I would soon learn, was a versatile tool, and sometimes weapon. If you've never encountered anyone like this, allow me to paint a picture. Imagine you're standing in a hallway, roughly thirty yards long. People are milling around, going about separate business, each giving fleeting acknowledgements to one another. You are a bit lost. You're not sure where you are supposed to be, much less what you are supposed to be doing. A woman walks up to you, smiling, and looks into you with warm yet fiercely penetrating eyes. She welcomes you with caramel-like smoothness. The contrivance of her pleasantries is almost too much to take, but you appreciate the effort. It's not even that it feels condescending, necessarily. It's just that you know there's another side to this polish. Beneath the confident, inviting presence is a beast of intimidation, and she can unleash this beast at any moment, turned on a dime. She does so seconds later, as if in demonstration, but not at you. Glancing to her left, she sees that something's not right at the end of that thirty yard hallway. You even see the reflection of the stimulus in her right pupil. "Excuse me," she says politely.

"ETHAN! WHERE ARE YOU SUPPOSED TO BE RIGHT NOW?" she bellows past your ear. Shaken, you follow the sound, and are reminded of analogous treatment modalities and spiritual philosophy: *lean into it, be mindful; watch these thoughts and feelings go by*. Following this mental Aikido, you look in the direction of the sonic boon, which deflects off your cheeks, thus softening the impact. Down the hall, a stilled teenage male with a doltish expression gestures to the black hole of his chest, bewildered that he is the source of attention. "DON'T EVEN TRY THAT ON!" warns the director, fixing her glare. The boy's face flattens. A flat tire—that's an expression I learned at Thunder Road—farts its way from his mouth in abject defeat. In the moments leading up to this, he'd bullied just about every living being away from his vicinity. Reasonable-sounding adults had been told to leave him alone. A gentle-spirited nurse had been snapped at and hurried into dispensing some manner of painkiller.

Frightened peers had been stared down, told to fuck off, and even I had received a malevolent glance from this boy. Actually, it wasn't so much a look of devaluation, or hate; nor was it a predator's warning to not get too close. It was more cursory than that, a fleeting curiosity. I was a life form, it seemed, but of what level of significance? That will have been unclear.

During the afternoon portion of the orientation, the leather-lunged program director stepped up and presented her lesson. Rehabilitation is about rules, she asserted, picking up from where the HR assistant had left off. Of course, rules against smoking were only the tip of the iceberg. As I was presented with a list of house rules, I was astonished at the breadth and detail. Welcome to group home reality, evinced the woman whose aloof, yet indomitable quality washed over newcomers, clients and employees alike. There were rules about getting up, going to the bathroom, not talking to the opposite sex; rules about when you could do your laundry, when you could shave, how you *had* to shave if you had facial hair; rules about make-up (as in not wearing much of it), clothes that eliminated the prominence of red or blue because they were rival gang colors; rules about the necessity of talking in groups, about not talking outside of groups, about not talking at all in some circumstances. Her orientation spoke of all these matters, girded with an impressively driven social context.

These kids, she gravely intoned, come from harsh backgrounds, where there have been no rules. Their homes and upbringings have been saddled by neglect, substance abuse, mixed messages about all manner of things; physical and sexual abuse. They have no boundaries. As for drugs: they were tools of self-medication, she said definitively; the means of escaping pain. Kids ended up at places like Thunder Road because their drug using lifestyles had bottomed-out for them. The habit of avoiding pain had in fact led to pain. Disoriented and angry, kids arrived at the treatment doorstep knowing, whether they admitted so or not, that the lifestyle they'd been leading had been a lie; that it had promised so much in terms of freedom, yet ultimately failed to deliver. The woman was quite convincing. She continued: as an employee of Thunder Road, our job is to help these young people adjust to a new reality, a caring reality. But we would not be their friends. Then she broke down the job descriptions, ours and theirs, speaking next with an ambiguously flippant air. The kids' jobs are to act out, break rules, cuss at us, call us names, put us down, reject us, disregard us; use us even as they relentlessly deny or else test the promise of our alternative yet healthy way. Our job is to hold structure, that of the program and (implicitly) our own, and understand that from structure proceeds safety.

She softened. Rehabilitation is also about bonding and fellowship, she pronounced. Unwittingly, she was paraphrasing systems theorists, cyberneticists, who characterize dysfunctional families as those mired in feedback loops: an angry child protests, acts out, and induces crying and outrage—controlling responses—from anxious parents, which further amplifies child opposition. The Therapeutic Community would not repeat vicious cycles, the director proclaimed; at Thunder Road staff would introduce, or re-introduce reality, exude calm and compassion, yet contain in numbers. The stacked ratio of staff to clients (variously 1:8, 1:10, 1:6), the absence of privacy in the building; the fact that most activities happened in groups—it was all about maintaining proximity with caregivers and peers, reducing isolation, and ultimately, shame. What about autonomy? someone asked with a whiff of skepticism. What about fun? asked somebody else. These questions foreshadowed the kinds of questions that would become more prominent in later years. Meanwhile, the director cautiously replied that there was time and space for both, but offered that it would not be felt in the short-term. Fun, she said, had been a distorted promise of addiction. *Fun in recovery*, as the saying goes, would be a different animal. The existing promise of fun, or what would be more accurately described as license, represented one of addiction's lies. I remember feeling quizzical as I heard this personification of the problem. The addiction: it speaks. It has a personality. She brightened again, to offset her solemnity and convey hope. As for autonomy, that would increase over the course of the program. It was conditional, she implied, unlike love.

A background of feelings and impulse

Well, ok then. Welcome to Thunder Road, and welcome to the TC model of rehabilitation. I was in for a rollercoaster ride, I thought. I was an intern—that is, a student therapist—for about nine months. That was the norm, the typical tenure of that particular position. I worked three, sometimes four days a week, sitting in on large group therapy sessions, co-facilitating others, mostly in quiet participation, with sporadic remarks that invariably took onlookers by surprise. *Oh right, he's part of this group*, they seemed to be thinking, clients and other members of staff. It took me about three months to learn all the rules, or more accurately, to learn them to the extent that I might competently enforce them with kids. It was a truly difficult assimilation: I'd feel alternately connected and disconnected; intimately involved and knowing on some occasions; bereft and inadequate on others, a spare wrench in a large and congested toolbox. Regardless, I stuck it out like I'd done all my previous jobs, whether I'd liked them or not.

I'd had my own experience with drugs and alcohol in my teens, though by the time I began my internship, I was clean from everything except cigarettes. Well, almost. I drank on occasion, carefully, and with a bashful conservatism. This bemused some who thought me a kind of prude. I wasn't saying much. Only those closest to me learned that I'd had anything like an alcohol problem in the past, and even they were undisturbed. To some, I had characterized past blackouts as fugue states, implying I was benignly crazy, but nothing as serious or unseemly as an alcoholic. For the record, I don't identify as an alcoholic, though I went back and forth on that question in my twenties. I've abused alcohol and drugs in the past—use socially today—and I've certainly been nicotine dependent. If this must be an "are you or are you not an addict?" discussion, then I suppose I'd say yes, but in terms of severity, I'd say that I'm on the lower end of the spectrum. Anyway, back in the day, friends were unimpressed by my reticence. After all, I'd not killed anyone in a car accident, or date-raped anyone in an alcohol-induced fit. Though I'd hosed down the rims of a few friends' toilets with the odd esophageal purge here and there, I'd not gotten close to a hospital because of alcohol, and was surely years away from anything like heart or liver disease. What's the problem? asked later friends who yearned for me to lighten up and have a good time.

Well, at least until entering graduate school in 1994, I was depressed. Very depressed. Not depressed as in imminently suicidal, but depressed as in flat, fatigued, uninterested in life; not liking myself, not thinking I was good at anything, thinking I was a loser—that kind of depressed. I did talk to some people about all this: professional people. One or two therapists were visited in this period—one around the time of my second stint at college, at San Jose State University—the second nearby my parents' home shortly after my dog died in the early nineties. I spoke to therapists about drinking episodes and about smoking. The therapists suggested I go to 12-step meetings, which I vaguely knew to mean Alcoholic's Anonymous. Though I nodded in compliance, I didn't go, at least not at first. I'm not sure why I went ultimately. I just about recall the first meeting, which I attended during a period of nearly two years when I was hardly drinking at all. I somewhat fancifully thought I'd talk about depression instead of drinking, or find free therapy within a peer-based fellowship. In retrospect, I think I was just lonely, and needing somewhere to go on nights when others were at parties I was too shy to attend.

I hadn't any money for therapy. The University offered free counseling, but it was crisis oriented, and after a few sessions I felt I was being shuffled out the door with brochures pressed into my hands. I was told to exercise more, and eat right. They taught me breathing exercises, and called them "coping tools"; they asked with penetrating sincerity about the feelings I was having in my chest as I spoke about my dead dog. They didn't seem interested in my life as a whole. I could have asked my parents to subsidize a more substantial therapy, or taken advantage of their Kaiser coverage and gotten a few sessions with one of their therapists. The same problems would have arisen, I think. It's strange, but I think these experiences fueled my later distrust of brief therapy models. These people were interested in helping me feel better, but they couldn't help me feel better about myself, and the distinction, elusive at that time, was and is crucial.

What can you tell people about depression? If you've never had a serious depression, I can't describe it to you. I can come close with respect to the physical sensations: there's a weight, a palpable weight that hovers perpetually about your shoulder. Your appetite goes. Pleasure absents itself, and nothing is funny except the blackest of thoughts, which more often than not leave you laughing alone. Misery loves company, and it abhors the opposite: other's happiness. Alienation and envy. When you wake up, you get out of bed and you move around for a while. Diffuse thoughts of what to do that day dizzy your mind. Eventually it stops. If your mind could talk it would say in these moments, "Um…short circuit here!" If it were a computer an error message would appear, coupled with a disinterested link to online support. *Don't send*, you end up clicking. You think and feel as though your mind is full. In your imagination—your delusion—your mind *is* full, and you're working hard, so hard. But in truth you've stopped; you've fallen down, and as that oft-mocked old woman in the commercial once said, you can't get up. But you can go back to bed.

In 12-step meetings, in therapy, and at places like Thunder Road, you're supposed to talk about this kind of stuff, and in theory receive empathy[2] as well as some other, more diversely prescribed palette of nurturing. As a provider of services, you're supposed to have experienced such suffering, and worked through it, because if you haven't experienced it, I can't describe it to you. I couldn't, or wouldn't describe my depression to people in my late teens and early twenties. Shame kept the reasons at bay. There were rules governing the teen cliques that I hung out with in high school: you weren't supposed to ask questions about each others' lives, such as information about each others' families, or about our future goals. This used to bemuse my parents, who would ask after my relationships and facetiously say things like, "aren't you full of information", in reply to my terse, shrugging responses. I couldn't explain the rules to them. I couldn't explain how listless mutual disinterest protected me and my friends from feeling like losers. I couldn't explain why the phrase "that sucks" constituted optimal empathy between peers. The rules said, *don't talk about it, you'll only make things worse*. Shame: both before and after my friends' deaths, shame stopped my tongue.

I bonded with some friends over depression. That doesn't mean we helped each other necessarily, but we did help each not feel alone. Originally, bonding moments came naturally, and unconsciously; they were like beta elements, seeds planted that might later make sense. Bonding emerged as a problem in my life, especially during latency when I first emigrated to the United States from the UK. As a young child, I'd done well at bonding. I recall being confident and playful; my supposedly impish smile made spontaneous appearances, and is well documented via the photographs of that era. Adolescence seemed to change things, re-ignite some unknown rapprochement crisis. Fitting in had long been a problem: in middle school, then high school, in college, within the post-high school milieu that was retail culture.

Fitting in

I worried about fitting in at Thunder Road, and failing at my first two attempts to get employed hadn't helped. Upon completing those arduous orientations, I began attending regular meetings, sitting in on groups, even being assigned a client or two to counsel one-on-one. Strange, but the word client didn't seem to fit. I'd actually had some experience as a therapist already, having finished three semesters of practicum work at my graduate program's training center at JFK University in nearby Pleasant Hill. There the word client seemed to fit. Based upon guidelines outlined by the likes of Carl Rogers (1951), Heinz Kohut (1971), and attachment researcher John Bowlby (1969; 1973; 1980), instruction was comprised of individualized supervision to the student therapists as well as didactic lessons. The term client seemed appropriately Rogerian given the fact that most who came to the center were self-motivated (if low on income), eager to collaborate, and seemed psychologically-minded[3]. At the training center, the ambience of egalitarian values, diminishing the power divide between expert and consumer of services, seemed apt.

At Thunder Road, as in many group home or hospital settings, most of the kids were mandated; that is, there because of a court order, a social services referral, an academic requirement that may forestall expulsion, or a parental tough love maneuver in the wake of a series of misadventures. Though many kids paid lip service to the need for change, the truth lay in a pattern of opposition, subdued and then exploded rage; freedom thwarted, and then seized. In graduate school, many instructors commented on the profile of the average consumer of psychotherapy. I recall them reassuring us (the students) that we'd not encounter anti-social or schizotypal personalities in our subsequent practicum placements, as those people tend not to seek out psychotherapy. I later realized, with a blinding flash of the obvious, that they were not talking about places like Thunder Road, but rather private practice settings. Furthermore, they weren't talking about adolescents, or pre-teens, as few in either of these categories tend to pick up phones and say things like, "I think it's time I worked on my issues."

At Thunder Road, few of the clients seemed motivated in the fullest sense, or even psychologically-minded. Rather, they tended to divide their worlds into camps of victims and perpetrators, with themselves as victims typically. Graduate school hadn't prepared me for this. Instructors had little to say about working with people who didn't really want to participate in therapy. In fact, the language—that working *with* people idea, versus working to resolve problems—would only later seem meaningful. Instructors offered flat, sympathetic expressions, and privately mulled over the opportunities for those entering their jealously guarded profession. I suspect that many knew but kept secret a rather worrying idea: mental health was a growing industry, but the jobs on offer would be of varying quality in the future. In the staff meetings that first introduced and discussed Thunder Road clients' programs and lives, staff members, some jaded, some not, appeared to play out roles of sympathizer or would-be oppressors, with another faction, quieter than the others, straining to find a middle ground. Sitting in on those first few meetings, I listened to veteran counselors speak of the clients in ways that ran a gamut of perspectives; meanwhile, Carl Rogers' famous notion of "unconditional positive regard" seemed tenuously represented.

Listening to mental health professionals talk about their process is a fascinating experience. It can also be a highly frustrating experience if what you want is to find out what's really happening in a therapeutic process. The reason for this is that counselors and therapists in many community mental health settings aren't really compelled to demonstrate what they are doing. Meaning, there are no transcripts of sessions, taped recordings, or two-way mirrors such that a counselor's technique might be rigorously assessed. This is both a problem and an advantage. When I was new to drug treatment, it certainly felt like a disadvantage. I'd listen patiently and attentively, hoping to get a sense of what was happening in the therapeutic exchanges that were being characterized but not detailed. I was eager to learn about the inner worlds of the kids; the outer world that was their family constellations, the realities of their neighborhoods and schools. I particularly wanted to know what kids did with the forum—the opportunity—that was psychotherapy.

Though referenced interchangeably in this text, the terms counseling and therapy have distinct meanings, and while it may be unfair to generalize, counselors tend to be directive, encouraging, and educative. In concrete terms, counselors encourage specific behaviors, exercise and abstinence, time-outs or breathing exercises when upset; even proper attention to diet. They start sentences with phrases like, "have you thought of…" and sometimes speak at length, because the task is to impart information, not so much stir in clients an exploratory sharing or an inner contemplation. In a residential setting, working with minors, the tendency is to become parentally directive. Usually, it's not long before a fledgling counselor is in full stride giving directives on mundane, day-to-day matters, such as asking young men to pull up their pants (in reference to the sagging habit that is inexplicably still in fashion after about twenty years). Therapists, on the other hand, are prone towards neutral positions regarding problems: they emphasize listening, reflection or interpretation, or circular questioning. They confront negative patterns, but tend to be less specific: "What might be a more constructive way of coping with your feelings?" expecting clients to figure out the details. Therapists at Thunder Road would learn to "pull up" (no pun intended—that was TC slang for redirection) clients who let their pants sag, but they'd do so reluctantly, with a slightly discernible whine, as though the task was beneath them. The differences between the factions were real, largely because the premises of care were understood differently, and within Thunder Road, for example, the differences between therapists and counselors were perennially misunderstood by a lot of people.

This brings me to a term that is often used in a mental heath context, and certainly throughout this text: feelings. Feelings are ambiguously distinguished from emotion in literature that informs the mental health profession. According to LeDoux (1997), emotion is comprised of bodily responses originating in the limbic system. This system is ill-defined in terms of where it begins and ends, but is part of an interconnected mental structure specialized to appraise meaning of stimuli, according to Siegel (1999). Feelings, so-called, are mental representations, with meanings assigned to emotions that enhance learning and stimulate anticipation of future events (Damasio, 2001). That idea would seem to bring into question whether such meanings are distortions, which would in turn lead to discussions of mental dimensions relating to addiction and trauma. Mental health workers, whether they are counselors, therapists, or medical professionals, are frequently referring to "feelings" as a catch-all term for a cognitive and emotional process that entails both distortions and "real" expressions. When they do refer to feelings and emotion, they often do so interchangeably, and it is further unclear whether they are referring to a conscious or an unconscious process; reactions borne of thoughtful reflection, or just impulse. As a result, the term "feeling", plainspoken as it may be, seems responsible for a great deal of confusion, both from the standpoint of practitioners as well as consumers of mental health services.

After lengthy treatment planning meetings, I was often left confused and bombarded by staff discussions: their references to, among other things, thinking, emotion, and feelings. These meetings recalled Wilfred Bion's theory of beta elements, those seemingly meaningless fragments of dreams and everyday life; things that have meaning, actually. I picked up the emotion, at least. There was restless energy in those rooms, and impatience: someone's coffee would spill over a treatment plan. The clock would forever be ten minutes off. A person leading a discussion would be half-attentive, with one ear primed for the sound of an announcement over an intrusive paging system. Anyone speaking would have to tolerate several interruptions, the comings and goings of people filing into and out of meetings. If new, one could tell who the managers were just by the way they were able to speak past disruptions with relative aplomb.

There was much generalizing of events, of exchanges. Counselors described the "attitudes" of the kids, declared whether or not they *wanted* recovery. They described their interventions with abstractions: they offered "support", or else encouraged clients to seek support from the community. Regarding a listed set of negative behaviors, one staff member asserted with conviction that he'd helped his client "explore options as far as coping skills," which meant finding someone to talk to, basically. I nodded like one is supposed to in these discussions, but none of this was telling me much. The terminology wasn't lost on me, necessarily. I knew from my own experience that "recovery" was a 12-step term, referring in this context to a client's commitment to his or her program. I gathered that "community" was a reference to the residence of Thunder Road, which at this time in history consisted of fifty beds, housing on average forty plus youths with a three to one male to female ratio. The program was further split into two factions of clients: so-called "Hospital" or short-term clients, whose treatment revolved around a 28-day model, and a second half or two thirds, variously termed "Group Home" or (strangely) "Fast Track" who would be in residence for months, or upwards of a year; in rare cases, sometimes longer. I further understood that this idea of community was a value-laden concept; an attempt by Therapeutic Communities to introduce some worthy notions: interdependence, wholesomeness, even charity.

These ideas were compatible with the 12-step ethos, the dominant philosophical underpinning the program, and of most programs still. Staff explained that the cultural term addiction, as opposed to the medical construct of dependency, proceeded from a three dimensional problem: behavioral, mental, and spiritual. The spiritual dimension, most notably articulated by the 12-step community, asserted that those caught up in an addictive lifestyle are hindered by an ever increasing isolation. They lie, they cheat, they steal, and they manipulate. They are self centered, either by predisposition, or else as a result of development arrest, and these qualities lead invariably to destruction. Thus it was a given that teens in the program were addicted to drugs.

That was then. Latterly, it seems as though this position is changing somewhat, and not for the better in my opinion. Why? Well, I think it one thing to not "label" clients entering a treatment program, thinking that the stigma of identification will be an obstacle to progress rather than a facilitator, as the 12-step community suggests. It's quite another thing for mental health professionals to become squeamish around language and thus minimize the risk to drug abusing individuals. The issue is not so much whether to use words like “addict” as a short-hand when directly addressing clients. Rather, the concern is that treatment providers, in their zeal to keep things “positive”, will quite simply miss that which is important, and therefore inadvertently place those in their care at further risk.

I’ve rarely been a subscriber of the you’re-making-me-feel-bad-therefore-I-shall-have-to-act-out-destructively argument. However, I have tried to understand why some resist the addict-identification factor, especially as it might be applied to youth. It’s about personality and hope, I think: I mean that words like “addict” connote something pervasive, enduring, and inflexible. It suggests something long established, or something that cannot be unlearned—“it’s how I am”, some say to comfort themselves. For others who deny addiction, it’s a defiance of treatment’s insistence on change. For the culture at large, I think ideas of addiction, of being an addict, imply a loss of hope, which is at least an uncomfortable feeling to have when regarding the young. We want instead not to lose hope in them, and for them not to lose hope in themselves.

As a result, I hear many therapists and other mental health professionals employing variations of the “hate the sin, love the sinner” principle that a pastoral counselors might promulgate. I hear interventions like, “it’s the behavior, not you” being used so as to downplay the problem of stigma, the potential loss of hope or self esteem. The thing is that many would-be admits to programs see through this sensibility. They sit through assessments with admissions counselors, endure tense negotiations with parents or legal authorities, or else they have tantrums as the reality of adults’ referral decisions is sinking in. If asking why rehab is necessary, they are reminded of the bad decisions they have made, and the consequences that have followed as a result. They are told that people no longer believe them when they say they’ll not do drugs again, or that they’ll cut down, focus on doing better in school, or whatever. They are told that they are “out of control”, and therefore need help. They need a time-out, even, from their regular life and responsibilities, even if that time-out further disrupts that regular life and those responsibilities. What are admits to hospital-based programs meant to infer from this if not that others believe that they are indeed addicts?

Back in the nineties, the program director of Thunder Road, at times quieted after a prolonged bark at clients during afternoon sessions, would scan the treatment planning room wherein those team meetings took place. She'd look over her staff with a proprietary gaze. Typically, she'd wear a satisfied expression as she oversaw the discussions: the back and forth strategizing; the plainly spoken pronouncements as to who was progressing in treatment, and who wasn't. Everything seemed in control. There was cohesion amongst the staff and I think treatment will have felt integrated from her point of view and that of program administrators. We were treating addicts: period. Not that everyone felt a part of this: I knew colleagues, especially fellow interns, who felt alienated from the general ethos of the program, and thus left out. Not me. Not then. At times the director would direct a glance at me and offer a warm, inviting smile. From the outset, I thought she liked me, thought I was *part of,* as some in the 12-step community say.

Still, I was sometimes frustrated by what was missing in treatment planning. I wanted to know what was being said, how kids responded to what was said; what it revealed about their thinking; what the staff's responses suggested about theirs. Listening to the talking points, I felt lost as to the processes of intervention, and I'd feel retroactively pleased by the comparatively rigorous training experience I'd had at my previous therapeutic placement. In my graduate program at JFK, students were required to tape sessions, or portions of sessions at least, and then present those taped sessions to individual clinical supervisors, as well as in group consultations with didactic instructors. These were tough assignments that generated much anxiety amongst students, as the tapes were subject to much critique. It was dreadful listening to sound of my own voice. I cringed as I heard the awkward attempts at clarifying questions, the remedial stabs at mirroring, and I'd spend ages searching through sections of audiotape, craving a suitable ten minutes that wouldn't expose the mistakes of a novice. At the training center, the dominant philosophical orientation being taught at that time was that of Self psychology, whose most famous exponent, Heinz Kohut (1971), spoke and wrote of concepts like mirroring, transmuting internalizations, and corrective emotional experiences. Nice things, I thought.

According to graduate school instructors, students were meant to refrain from confronting or directing people, as well as elaborate interpretations as to the depth, purpose, or destructive potential of clients' behavior or defense mechanisms. I don't recall intervention strategies that were directive—nothing specific about sagging pants, for instance. I do recall one teenager providing a preview of my later Thunder Road experience. Attending therapy at the insistence of his mother, the young man had several visits with me and managed to conceal his eyes for almost the entirety of his treatment. The reason: he always wore a hood over his head; a "hoodie", as they are still called. Through my delicate interpretations about his "not being seen" (my supervisor's words), the hood would be removed from time to time. At Thunder Road, this issue would have been dealt with in no time, with a blunt command: *remove the hood.* Case closed.

Mirroring, that technique or more or less echoing back what the client says, with further words intended to amplify the importance of the client's feelings (to themselves), was the prescribed intervention at the training center. Kohut's notion was that afflicted individuals are those who have been denied experiences of healthy Naricissism: a mirroring of needs in early development. Psychotherapy, from this perspective, is a kind of restorative exercise; a rigorous feeding of that which has been previously missing. Orcutt (2012) writes that mirroring alone, without interpretation (of defensive purpose) may be necessary at times when the patient feels especially vulnerable. I remember hearing a version of this argument many times at the training center, and have been hearing variations of it ever since. Yet it seemed a point of contention, this paradigm, because all clients at the center or in treatment seem vulnerable. The argument seemed indiscriminate to me.

I spent a year at that training center, working with just a few cases that presented with substance abuse issues, even though it was my chosen specialization. Most of my peers spent two years there, as that was the norm in what was termed the "family program". Addiction work was different. Private practice wasn't really the ideal model for it, my then supervisor commented.

Working with one or two cases, I was advised to remain alert for continued use of drugs, and be ready to give referrals to higher levels of care, either outpatient or residential levels of care, in hospital-based programs. One early twenty something, identified at intake as a marijuana user, came to sessions regularly, but often late, and with heavy eyes and a perpetual stupor. My supervisor asked if I thought he was still using, and I said yes. But the man denied using or rather he laughingly minimized his use, and wanted to speak of his cheating girlfriend instead. I'm glad he admitted using, at least. Otherwise, I'd have to deal with his lying, which would have meant not mirroring him, which in turn would have annoyed my supervisor—I think. Then one day he—the marijuana user, not my supervisor—stopped showing up for meetings. "In relapse," my supervisor gloomily concluded.

Meanwhile, another case was that of a single father who presented with a truculent and secretive daughter. "She won't talk to me," he complained, referencing her shrugging shoulders and repeated "I don't know" answers to his inquisitions. The girl asked after her mother, who was absent, and according to the father, prone to drunkenness. But he didn't like speaking of that, or his own drinking, which he said was minor, social, and by implication, not on the table for discussion. The girl didn't comment, but her eyes shifted elsewhere. With them I did about a dozen sessions, as the father pressed for information about his daughter's drinking, allegedly prodigious. But the girl wasn't talking. While she didn't issue injunctions the way father did, she could passively stonewall as well as anyone, and in so doing prove equally effective at blocking discussion.

"Refer them to Thunder Road," said that same supervisor, indicating its behavior modification system and family program. A residential program, he argued, would contain the drinking and other acting out that was undoubtedly happening, but it would also allow space for the kind of conversation this father and daughter weren't yet ready to have. Thunder Road was one of the places I learned about in this period. Actually, I'd first heard of the facility when working a night shift at the county crisis hotline about a year prior to this. I was a volunteer at that service for two years, beginning around 1993. One night I was talking to a fellow volunteer in between calls, about a woman who had called in feeling anxious about her teenage son who kept coming home in the middle of the night, drunk. "Call her back and give the number to Thunder Road," that colleague said. By mid-94' I'd gotten the message as to where kids from Alameda or Contra Costa counties went for drug rehabilitation.

Behavior Modification: confrontation

As I transitioned after three semesters to my "external placement" in the form of Thunder Road, I made a few assumptions. Firstly, that Thunder Road clients would be lesser motivated, because therapy is dominantly an adult's idea. Secondly, because adolescents tend to be less politically savvy than adults, they'd be more likely to say what they really thought at any given moment. I figured I'd be in store for some refreshing honesty, or at least a few clumsily revealed truisms. Reciprocally, I imagined the program would be largely didactic, due to the premises of treatment: the teens had problems with drugs, and generally behaved in ways adults thought were bad for them. I figured that the line between teacher and therapist, if not parent, would seem thin, especially with lesser experienced therapists, though I was wary of becoming a teacher, much less a parent.

Regardless, I also thought that good humor, hand-wringing sympathy, and an underlying gentleness, ultimately in keeping with the Kohutian/Rogerian way, would prevail, if only because of the presumed fragility of adolescent egos. As I took part in my first few therapy groups, I watched to see whether the counseling would reflect the hard-line attitudes I'd observed during orientation and those initial staff meetings. The first experience I recall took place in a large, dull room in the basement of the hospital, flanking the office that ten years later would become my private office space. The "Family Room", so-called, was the largest room in the facility; or the largest room used for the purposes of anything like a therapeutic exercise. It was also the least cluttered, which meant that it offered the fewest distractions in terms of decor. Harsh fluorescents buzzed overhead as I walked in, following a silent trail of subdued male clients. "Monads" said a counselor thickly. Kids hissed air at staff in the gesture nicknamed "flat tire".

"Take a seat on the bench," said the program director, determined to oversee a correct spirit to the exercise, and not missing any infraction, big or small. One youth sullenly complied. Had it been any staff other than the director, he may have debated the moment, insisting that simple vocalisms do not violate the sacred Monads rule. Stepping into the room, I looked about and regarded a circle of chairs. A colleague, a woman whom I'd been asked to "shadow", motioned for me to step away from the chairs, stand against the wall and observe quietly. The kids took their seats but stayed on Monads. Feeling detached and bookish, I made a mental note to research the etiology of the term, though I'd asked earlier and received uncaring guesses in response; another fire extinguisher moment, I realized. My colleague stared at me in a glassy-eyed way, confused. She reminded me of that scoffing manager at the movie theater, the one that ridiculed me for being concerned with unnecessary details.

A client was asked to read out a list of rules to the exercise, which was called "confrontation group". A boy of fifteen, with a malnourished, scrawny frame but an oversized head, suggestive of fetal alcohol syndrome, spoke out in a robotic voice. Glancing up from a paper that listed the rules, he nonetheless spoke with confidence, not needing to look down and remind himself of the words. Raul, the boy, had been in the program for ten months, and had done this activity, listened to these rules, or else spoken them out loud, three times a week, every week, since he'd arrived at Thunder Road. As he concluded the list, a facilitating staff—not the director—asked Raul to read out who was due to have business in the present meeting. The staff sounded and looked a bit like a collection of judges and bailiffs holding court. Three names were read out. Three young men were due to receive what were called "hot seats" from the Therapeutic Community.

I was fascinated by the structure of the exercise, and drawn to a memory of academic instruction. In our group process class in graduate school, students were asked to simulate an ongoing group process, with students taking turns leading the exercises. Several things were obviously different about Thunder Road's group therapy program. That group participants were required to take part, as opposed to being advised that they could leave without pressure to remain, was one clear departure from group therapy standards (Corey, 1995). The circular format of the group was at least familiar. Though I recall nothing in particular declaring its necessity, I later fashioned reasons that I have by now delivered to hundreds of unquestioning listeners. Additionally, I had earlier learned that group participants ought to be sat facing one another. This fosters interaction, which is encouraged in group process, as opposed to, say, a classroom, wherein interaction between class members is deemed less essential. The interaction is personal in nature, both in terms of the content and the non-verbal elements.

In Thunder Road's confrontation group, it was the non-verbal elements that were at issue, and therefore painstakingly controlled. In the exercise that followed, a young man was asked to stand and place his hands at his side. He was not to clasp his hands or otherwise gesture or flail with them. He was next directed to hear the observations of his peers, who would deliver them in terse sequences, going around the circle, and not respond; that is, not comment, argue, roll his eyes…anything. "Take it in", is what he'd hear should he dare to contest any feedback. An assenting reply—"that's valid"—was allowed after all confrontations were issued. I observed from the back of the room with an intent, stoic look. As the young man "took in" one confrontation after another, from peers whose apathy was all too obvious in many cases, I noted the defensive posture of the "hot seat" client. His chin was raised to a steady thirty degrees incline. The shoulders were pinned back, the arms swinging gently for balance. The chest, well-exercised, as if in preparation for events like this, was shoved outward atavistically. When asked finally to respond to the barrage of criticism—"concerns"—that he'd received from his peers, the young man didn't say "that's valid"; he quite predictably shrugged.

Some things said were valid, he ultimately conceded: mostly the generalities, delivered by peers conscious that they'd be sharing a room later with the targeted boy, or else receiving a hot glare from him across the pool table in the room named after that game. Yes, it's true he isolates, he pronounced. Yes, it's also true that he keeps his feelings to himself. The young man swayed back and forth, obeying an inner rhythm. "Keep still," said a counselor behind him. Another staff pointed out that nothing had been said of the most damning confrontation, that of being "focused on females". Of those hard-line attitudes I'd heard earlier, some were carried over into these groups, but not all. In front of clients, some staff members lost their edge and betrayed their diffidence. Certainty in staff meetings was replaced by uncertainty on the floor. Knowing the limits of groupspeak, one staff member, an unswerving sergeant of the milieu, shot fierce eyes into the hot-seated client and asked for specifics, the verboten details. The young man averted his eyes. Fleetingly, it seemed as though he may have been scanning the room, trying to recall which of the twenty other clients had opened the can of worms, betrayed him. He shrugged again and denied knowledge of this supposed pattern, but asserted he'd "take a look at that". I was bored. This activity was about a half hour old at this point, and so far I'd witnessed not so much the intense therapeutic value of confrontation that I was led to anticipate, but rather the familiar deadness of stonewalling.

The program director stepped into the mix. I mean literally, she stepped in, penetrated the circle with a militant stride and ran her piercing gaze over the assembly of young men. A blend of ardor, warmth, and faint disgust flavored her stance. Her briefly held glare aimed at specifically chosen clients—the more senior boys—was meant to convey a collective responsibility to the community. Were they really supporting this young man? Were they colluding with his secrecy by tepidly confronting his behaviors? Then she turned back to the young man receiving the hot seat and ran down a list of household crimes, none of which touched upon themes of isolation or "not talking about feelings". Instead, there were more concrete charges: the passing of notes which matched his handwriting; staff reports of "gender splitting", which meant communicating with girls; allegations that the client had stolen staff keys, keys that were still missing; finally, an insinuation that contraband—lighters and a pipe—had been smuggled onto the unit and that the boy on the hot seat was responsible. The boy stiffened visibly at this last announcement, and once again ran his eyes over the room.

"Who are you looking at?" challenged the director, having noticed the not-so-subtle movements.

Having presented the multi-pronged rap-sheet, the director stepped back, folded her arms, and waited. Staff members outside the circle solemnly nodded, affirming the confrontations leveled. All eyes were now heavily upon the young man, and there was a thick righteousness in the room, this "family room". I looked away towards a mural that wrapped around one-fourth of the wall space. A depiction of a highway—the *road*, I figured—snaked its way through rolling hills and over a horizon, towards a land of omniscient hope. The fluorescents continued to buzz and their sound was accentuated by the seconds of silence, that waiting. The eyes of the client receiving the hot seat peered over the shoulder of the director, onto a safe, indistinct spot upon the blank wall, as though hers were the eyes of Medussa. By this point I was no longer bored, but I was uncomfortable. I didn't care for the interrogatory tone of the exercise, the generally oppressive air. I could breathe alright, but the air nonetheless seemed thin. I wasn't sure what I'd expected, but somehow, being part of something a bit like hell week from football camp wasn't it. The room was hot. I noticed that my mouth was dry and my skin was cold. I'd been advised not to say much during this activity, as it was my first month still and I was meant to be just observing, but it was only implicit that I keep quiet. It was more in the thin, unconvincing delivery of my colleague that I perceived anything like a gag order. "By all means, say something if you feel like you have something important to say," she said. "We encourage you to find your voice here," she added. I noted that staff tended to use this word—"voice"—to signify an indigenous brand of growth. But no less than a sensitive child given mixed messages about what to say about the family situation to the extended family members visiting temporarily for the holidays, I divined the underlying caveat. Monads.

The stand-off continued for another several minutes before any kind of relenting occurred. When it did arrive, it did so in the form that clients had wanted all along: with disingenuous, rhetorical warnings circling the facts, but keeping a safe, centrifugal distance. After several minutes, the director seemed content to have announced all that was known or suspected of the young man on the hot seat. She, or Thunder Road, had meager evidence of the misbehaviors attributed to him, so his stubborn silence, perhaps calculated to withstand a marathon of confrontations, would hold firm for the time being. A summing up, directed at the whole male community, reiterated the director's belief that the young man was not working his recovery, but rather on his addict. This was a common enough turn of phrase, again used to signify a personification of problems. He was, in the director's estimation, "working his next relapse". "If you're not heading out of the woods, you're heading into the woods," she added. Faint nods from some of the boys suggested that her metaphorical flourish was one they'd heard before. I noticed that the kids liked many things that skirted concrete reality. Ideas, metaphors, weren't real. Understood or not, they were just words, abstractions; and abstractions can be agreed upon with relative impunity.

Clients appeared to appreciate the metaphor of the road, of sayings like "bridges to their future". These lessons carried hope, but left the integrity of current fantasies—their baseline isolationism—largely untouched. They were guessing, also: observing what words, phrases, and ideas appealed to adults; what placated them, kept them out of their business. Details, the concrete, hidden realities that determined the guilty or not guilty verdicts, would be more elusive. They had to be kept secret, those uncontestable elements of reality—the behaviors that happened out of sight, with few and thoroughly censured witnesses. In general, specificity was to be avoided at all costs when clients spoke of their negative behaviors, especially those not yet understood as factual events.

At times, it felt as though the kids held training sessions after dark, coaching one another with stock phrases to give in response to inquisitional staff. I was often reminded of the way athletes give interviews to journalists, with sweeping banalities that conceal the secrets of the playbook. This may confuse many who assume that kids, especially kids with arrested developments, are largely concrete in their thinking; that they relate only to that which is specific and actual, as opposed to relating to ideas. This seems true, but it doesn't mean that kids can't use ideas, co-opt or parrot them, and become glib, especially when they feel the spotlight is upon them. Concrete in their thinking and understanding, yet abstract in their delivery: that's what I observed as often as not. That client receiving the hot seat had not yet been caught. He was not yet in trouble, and so this warning from the director, heatedly theatrical though it may have been, had been anti-climactic. Yet he could nod his head and agree with the principles.

Still, the director had one more ploy, after which she'd start again with the next hot seat, with the same drive and determination; the same *energy*. As the boy poised to sit down, as indicated by someone's gingerly announcement that other hot seats were on the agenda, the director made a "just a minute" gesture and approached the client just as his knees began buckling towards a seated position. Now she was standing less that a yard before him and once again staring into his eyes. She raised her right arm and brazenly placed it on his chest. The young man flinched, taken aback by the woman's closeness.

"Is this ok that I'm touching you?" the director asked microseconds before stretching out her arm. The boy nodded uncertainly. "We're here to help you," she said evangelically. "Take a look around, at your peers and at the adults in the room. Everyone here—everyone!—is here to support you, if you let us." The boy gulped. The whole room will have seen his adam's apple pistoning up and down, fearful of this kind of intervention. This maneuver was the bone being thrown to the topic first raised by the group. Though not entirely surprised, he'd hoped to avoid this part. The rest had been familiar territory: the suspicion of a frustrated adult; the indignant cross-examination—he'd found none of that especially intimidating, much less unfamiliar. This latter moment, however, called for the blocking of isolation, of *feelings*. I've observed plenty of these kinds of interventions over the years. I've seen clients, boys and girls, crumple into tears with relief, enfolded into hugs whilst their bodies released oxytocin, the so-called attachment hormone, to stimulate arousal. On this occasion, the boy looked back at the director, and by his shaking demeanor appealed for this ordeal to pass. This was leading him beyond an intellectual exercise; this intervention was in pursuit of intimacy. His defenses dug in. He steeled himself and tried to hold on, trying so hard not to let himself experience that new and old kind of relief.

After two more such exercises, both similar in content and tone, that peer leader from the outset of the group, the one who had read out the rules, was again summoned, this time to give closure.

He stood up, unfolded his crumpled list of announcements, and began calling out instructions with a hesitant bray, a bit like a circus ringleader closing a show. The final act of ritual featured an elaborate version of a clap and chant. Everyone in the room was meant to enter the circle, abandon their chairs, and then sit in something like a lotus position and shout out responses to a series of affirmations. At the end of each chant, everyone slapped their knees and shouted "support", and then "keep coming back, it works if you work it" as a tautological[4] closing phrase. After my first experience of watching this, as the boys moped out of the room in a languid march, I felt disturbed yet properly energized. Some thoughts came to me in a mischievous spirit: unnecessary, trivial questions, like why was it called a hot "seat" when the people in question were directed to stand up?

Contract Breaking

My adaptation to what was (and is) called TC concepts, or the Therapeutic Community Concepts model, took quite some time, and stirred, or triggered as some call it, many conflicting feelings. I sat in and gradually participated in activities like confrontation group over the next several months, the period of my internship. For quite some time, I was bothered by the heavy-handed tone of the groups, the almost playacting style of some facilitators. Some among staff seemed to delight in having an audience. For those without professional credentials as either teachers or mental health professionals, forums like confrontation group would represent the biggest stages they'd ever seize for the exercise of their frustrated ministerial skills. With the kids ever a captive audience, a confident and outspoken leader could easily step to the middle and begin orating at will, sometimes raising their voices, sometimes openly mocking the clients, while creating a quasi police-to-suspect atmosphere. Early on in my career, I found it hard to imagine that I'd ever take part in a like-fashion.

When time came for what was called "contract breaking" (the revealing of rules broken in the program), which was a variation on confrontation group, the clients were directed to face outwards so as to minimize eye contact with one another. This was a fascinating nuance to the technique of confrontation, and beyond that, another telling departure from all the norms of group therapy that I'd learned in graduate school. Back then the idea that group members are meant to face one another had seemed inviolable: that was and is the point of group therapy, to among other things distinguish it from an academic exercise in which everyone sits in rows. This latter set-up recalls for us the experience of the classroom, with all its attendant hierarchies—the teacher is in charge; he or she knows, and you don't, etcetera. In graduate school, we learned that group therapy was an egalitarian exercise, with a group leader fixed ambiguously within a circle whose possibilities were eclectic and far reaching. The point of the group was to facilitate communication, interaction; perhaps an interaction that would filter through a leader figure, but one that in theory could move in various directions, with group members entitled to speak to one another without craning their necks to look behind them.

Well, the secret-breaking exercises of the Therapeutic Community were designed with almost an opposite purpose. Mindful of the power of non-verbal, so-called right brain-to-right brain communication, the contract breaking group was designed so as to minimize communication, and to limit discussion. Discussion was tantamount to obfuscation, it was implied—a waste of time. Therefore, a more terse facilitation was called for: "break your contracts," a staff (or a designated senior client, seemingly allied with staff) would direct. Clients would then raise their thumbs and then be directed to stand and announce their misdeeds in the program. The raising of thumbs was a norm of both groups and the general milieu, designed to contain interruptions or maintain silence, but again, exist as an alternative to the norms of a classroom: the strident hand-raising convention we all learned in grade school.

2

PLAY GONE WRONG

The TC Model

Consider the following scenario: a mother is at a playground with her two kids. Her five year old son jets off towards a play area. He is excitable and single-minded, and the mother calls out, "stay on or near the handlebars. I don't want to come after you." The boy looks back, grimaces, and says, "why?" He wants to explore the whole playground, not just the handlebars.

"Because I say so," the mother sternly responds. Inside, she's thinking something like, *because I have your nine-month old sister with me and I can't put her down to chase after you, or come after you with her in my arms. So, can you please consider these things and give me a break*? She likely doesn't say all of this, partly because it would take a lot of energy, but more importantly, because of the narrow-minded focus and limited capacities of her son. Therefore, she is blunt, directive, and for the time being, at least, non-explanatory.

Think of the kids in drug treatment—many of them, not all—as being rather like that five year old. They are narrow-minded, and limited in their capacities. They want what they want: to explore that playground, not just the handlebars. But if you're bristling at this comparison and wondering if or when teens in treatment are treated like the up-and-coming adults that they are, then know that for them a fuller discussion will be coming later: a therapy session, either one-on-one or in group, wherein all the thoughts and feelings, theirs and others, might become understood.

Obviously, a different style of communication—a kind of mini-culture—was being introduced to me at Thunder Road. I'd learned none of this in school, so it was all on-the-job training as far as I was concerned. I felt as though I were learning an entirely different set of rules, as though someone were intimating that eighty percent of what I'd learned in my graduate school classes ought to be thrown out. The biggest reason for having clients not face one another, I was told, was to deter non-verbal threats in the form of *mad-dogging*—threatening eye contact. Kids adapted, basically. Therefore threats of other kinds were restored. Vocalisms suggested recognition of someone's voice. Aggressive body postures seemed to radiate around circles. A muttered hostility would follow. I wondered how much of the ritual flavor, including the chants and the clapping, concerned the fact that Thunder Road served adolescents and not adults.

It all had a very masculine air about it—the echo of the gridiron, or of a hard-line boarding school. The style of intervention seemed paradigmatic. Staff addressed resistance directly, head-on, like lineman butting heads at the line of scrimmage; they were more or less encouraged to act like coaches of a football team, with aggressive tones in their voices, an inspirational 12-step-derived slogan ever at the ready. In later years, this style would transition into a more Tai-chi-like position, one in which counselors increasingly *leaned into*, rather than confronting oppositional attitudes directly. That was the price of war, that later, softer approach: a war that adults were losing, and not just with drugs. Still, for the time being, what I observed within the milieu—what seemed to prevail during the nineties and well into the new century—was this more aggressive approach, only I wondered: were we heavyhanded with kids simply because we could be that way, because of the power differentials?

I soon learned that Therapeutic Communities were originally aimed at adults, in programs like Synanon[5] and that, if anything, the application of similar strategies towards youth was more or less in keeping with an adult model that had gotten its start back in the late 1950s. By the mid-nineties, rehab, as it is plainly referenced, or substance abuse treatment specific to adolescents had only been around for little over twenty years, with the first program exclusive to adolescents opening at St. Mary's hospital in Minneapolis in 1974 (Wheeler, Malmquist, 1987). Prior to this, even psychiatric wards specific to youth were rare: group homes, orphanages, governed by religious institutions as much as anything, were the traditional placements for disadvantaged or troubled youth (Pazaratz, 2009). Reading the operations manual and the program descriptions of Thunder Road, I detected an eclectic array of influences upon program design, but the language of the program seemed to have a mysterious pedigree. Little was referenced as to where its philosophy had come from. It all seemed like a work-in-progress; an experiment.

According to Randy Snowden, one of the founders of Thunder Road and now an administrator with the department of Health and Human Services in Napa County, the Oakland program was indeed influenced by the Social model, which is the umbrella term that describes programs such as Synanon, which operated at various locations in California between 1958 and 1989. The specific model for Thunder Road was a program in Napa called Our Family, which was in turn modeled on a program called The Family in Mendocino, which had been staffed by former Synanon members. The idea, Snowden recounted, was for troubled youth to be placed in controlled social systems that espoused behaviors and values that ran counter to a drug using lifestyle. Clients in these programs were expected to conform to not only the rules of a residential rehabilitation community, herein termed a Therapeutic Community, but also its values. The primary architects of the Thunder Road program were Marc Rosenbaum, then executive director of the Our Family program in Napa, and Doug Smith M.D., a psychiatrist who was the medical director at Our Family. With a modest air, Mr. Snowden reflected on his years with Thunder Road, from the early days in 1985 assisting in the design the program, to his tenures as program director, and subsequently, senior administrator, to his departure in the mid-nineties. He recalled that few in the industry seemed to understand what effective treatment was back in the eighties. With a dual license, Thunder Road was able to incorporate a psychiatric component, and provide clients with a "hybrid" model of medical care and social model elements.

Armando Corpus, a manager at Thunder Road and one of the few whose employment with the program dates back to this era, recalls that meaningful differences existed between staff informed by TC Concepts versus those primarily influenced by 12-step principles. TC counselors, he asserted, cast treatment as a process of "beating the dragon"—seeking to conquer the addictive impulse in individuals. The aggressive language was telling, and the methods were hardline. For example, TC counselors avoided individuals that were in relapse or "on the shine" as it was called.

Accordingly, they encouraged discharge of clients who relapsed, and resisted their readmissions. This thinking bristled with those who drew from 12-step principles slogans such as "relapse is part of recovery"; who prioritized work with newcomers ("the newcomer is the most important person"); who insisted that addiction is a disease that is never cured. Corpus recounts that as long as he could remember, treatment strategies were divided along philosophical grounds, and that Thunder Road and likely other Therapeutic Community Model programs have ever been in conflict over who calls the shots of treatment.

In that first year of my internship in 1996, I was aware of such tensions, and I listened intently to numerous arguments between staff members who, facilitated by management, warred over the prospective expulsions and/or program punishments that were imposed on clients. Initially, I was fascinated, if bothered by the severe tactics I witnessed in the milieu, though mostly because I wasn't sure I could measure up to them. Meanwhile, some of my own peers were more than somewhat bothered; they were shocked. I mean, other therapists at Thunder Road, especially my hippyish colleagues within my then supervision group, bemoaned what they believed were the "shaming" interventions, particularly those that compelled kids to stand up and face a crowd as though they were being put on trial before tribunals. The zealots among staff thought these tactics healing. They were public moments ultimately serving the unity of the Thunder Road family. These staff members were Dickensian heavies defeating of toxic secrets of a diseased underworld.

Intuitively, I was in agreement with my therapist colleagues, but only mildly. While acknowledging that some counselors and managers seemed over the top in style, I disagreed with those who thought that staff were exaggerating problems, or being melodramatic in their pronouncements. I actually loved the fact that people would come right out and say that kids' lives were at stake, and more specifically, that their lives were at stake because of the behaviors and attitudes they were showing in the milieu, not just outside of Thunder Road, prior to admission. Secrets and lies in the here and now: the boldest counselors asserted that these were the ingredients of a spiritual disease, and were a matter of life and death. Though jolted, I soon joined this point of view, and was invigorated by its fervor and essential correctness. In the meantime I was resolved to keep a reverent tongue and have that neutral learning experience that I'd been promised. I stilled my judgments of either side in the argument, wanting to fit in above all. I wanted to observe more, be open minded and let my mind wander on all things Thunder Road.

Contract Breaking: the process

I remember thinking, for example, that the concept of "contract" in the context of the residential treatment program had some interesting implications. Outside of a Therapeutic Community Concepts model, yet still within a clinical context, the meaning was singular. Behavior contracts, between therapists and clients, establish agreements about contingency plans in the event of emergencies. Behavior contracts are meant to establish that clients will not engage in things like suicidal action without first reaching out to an identified helper. It took time to learn the layered meanings because there were few at Thunder Road who had either time, inclination or the ability to express what the underlying meanings were. I'm sure that in my first year at Thunder Road I annoyed several people with noisome questions about things that didn't really matter. I'll just go check that fire extinguisher then, I was poised to say at times. When I did get a solid response as to the layered meaning of contracts, it came from an unlikely source—a cook who one day joined me for a midday smoke break.

"It's about agreement at all levels," he said about contracts. He affected surprise, as though realizing he was speaking to what was obvious. "Mutually assured destruction," he added with a self-satisfied laugh. It was a hearty, almost sadistic humor, quite removed from the droll flippancy I later became known for. The desire to help kids seemed to compete with raw distaste for their delinquency. Staff's shadowy reactions belied the heartfelt activism that sat within the core of the work, so staff acted out: lounging before meetings, they'd regale one another with gallows humor about their clients' latest misbehaviors, their relentlessly testing ways. One staff member summed up the love/hate divide with a stock confrontation she called her own: "We love you, but you're shady!" And it wasn't just about targeting the addict in the midst. On another level, it felt more personal, this desire to not be hoodwinked by clients' lies and other caprices. On the spirit of contracts and agreement, secrets and lies, I felt less protective of myself, as I was then prepared to defer the *knowing* to others. Instead, I played the role of student. I stood back and made links, believing there was something crucial to this idea of secrets as a means of bonding.

Secrets are a kind of contract; a tacit agreement bringing social order. Secrets and gossip disseminate important information for a community, alerting the group as to who is a danger; who fits in, and who doesn't. All communities keep secrets. All families, or any unit of society, including cliques of teens, competing departments within a hierarchy, keep secrets in order to protect the unit, to keep out the unwanted, and to maintain control from within. The concept of "contracts", I realized, was a sort of gift supplied by the founders of Therapeutic Communities. It was a concept, an element like fire, granted by a higher power and made available so as to provide an ongoing learning experience, with parallel meanings spearing out in all directions. Parallel process, a term introduced to me in graduate school, would revisit me again and again at Thunder Road. It means the following: Whatever happens between clients in a system, or between clients and staff, is replicated between adults in that same system.

The kids at Thunder Road made up their own rules. They seized upon the terms offered via an oral tradition, took in the basics, such as the "secrets keep you sick" slogan disseminated by staff, with deceptive cooperation, because they crafted alongside their experience a parallel value system. And they would defend this value system, transmitted via their own oral tradition, with fierce protectionism, regardless of what was intended by presiding adult authority[6]. Contracts created order. Contracts kept everyone in check. *If you reveal my secret I'll reveal yours*, was an implied warning to peers. *If you tell me your secrets, I must keep them secret*, was a sub-clause in the arrangement. *I will take them to the grave*, was a semi-street/gang variation. And this was where the rebellion lay. Secret-keeping constitutes loyalty. Of course, kids aren't the inventors of this moral stance, but they are remarkably adept at policing one other. "Snitches get stitches", was a kind of shadow slogan, in answer to the 12-stepism, "Secrets keep you sick", and there are items within the Ten Commandments that don't match the severity of this warning. The founders of Thunder Road intended that secrets pertaining to the breaking of house rules would be revealed as soon as possible, by either the person breaking the rules, or by those who, in the program's parlance, "had knowledge of". This meta-rule carried with it the notion of community, or of family. By implication these entities were interdependent, and everyone, it was suggested, was meant to help everyone else do the right thing. I think the conflict is likely broader than that of youth versus adult. It feels primal, somehow, or rooted in ancient and then modern history; something like the edicts of the Old Testament versus the Communist Manifesto.

The problem was that many kids hadn't experienced much of family life, much less community, in the way that Thunder Road was proselytizing, so the standard pedantries flew past many kids' ears. These kids formed cliques that ardently defended against adult intrusion. Those in rigid opposition to program goals clung to victimized personas; they braved "bans" of one another that were imposed by staff members who correctly identified, for the most part, teen dyads that were toxic. On the one hand, this ability to find kindred spirits spoke of resilience and adaptability, or at least street smarts. On the other hand, the prevalence of oppositional clients finding allies in defiance created real problems for the cohesion of the program, not to mention parents who worried that placing their kids in treatment with other troubled youth might "make them worse".

Those oppositional dyads sometimes adopted, or co-opted political causes, mostly for self serving purposes in my opinion. Prejudices of one kind or another—racism was the most popularly imputed charge—were often thrust at staff in response to program restrictions. The dyads formed larger bands, and budding demagogues—or merely shrill opportunists—cut their teeth in the therapeutic milieu. Staff-bashing, this was summarily dubbed, though over time, these outcries took their toll. Meaning, staff seemed to become more passive in later years by my observation. They became more conscious of their vulnerability: not wanting to be accused of anything that might compromise their employment, or the facility as a whole. Among the clients, at least, defense of sexual minorities was an under-represented cause, possibly because many clients were themselves homophobic. At times, the atmosphere of the milieu—that "us versus them" dynamic—seemed to worsen problem behaviors, creating a *Lord Of The Flies* ambience and realizing many parents' worst fears concerning the problem of peer influence.

The kids viewed the issue of contracts like a collection of self-governing orphans would: grafting their own amendments, including those tailored for those who wanted not to sign up. They included get-out clauses: "I don't want to know any contracts," was an oft-expressed example. If a client didn't want to hold any secrets, he or she had to be absented, or else insist that they not be informed of secrets, if that was possible (and few regarded that it was). For some, this was alienating to even try; an ostracism from gossip, and therefore, in the figurative sense, from the group. For anyone who has traversed adolescence, few things will seem as sad as a lonely, abandoned teen. They hang out in packs—date, even, in groups. More so than any child, adult, or even senior, a lone adolescent is one who is visible, exposed, and reliant upon fledgling ego strength. However, for those sufficiently jaded with the crowd, and with enough determination to get through the Thunder Road maze, sheer pragmatism was the call to order: to avoid trouble, they had to avoid—well—everyone.

The backdrop of this strategic system was once poignantly described by a girl who was a client in the program for about three weeks before running away from the facility. Though not making links with her peers' informal set of rules, she had long employed versions of them in her own life. Her description of her household environment was nothing less than an argument for avoidance. She told me a story about her abusive father, who was prone to drunken fits of rage, mostly indoors, away from the view of neighbors. For years, the reasons had seemed inexplicable (and therefore not meaningful), until her early teens, when a characteristic pattern appeared to take shape. "He couldn't stand us doing anything by ourselves," she complained, referencing herself and her four siblings. It was the siblings, however, that had let her down by suggesting an ancillary consequence of defiance: sibling withdrawal. One day, the girl recalled, she was readying herself to go out with friends on a Friday night. She'd been invited to a party in another neighborhood—the first such invitation she'd ever received, she excitably reported—but her father had refused permission. Nervously telling her older sister about her plan to sneak out, she appealed for support. But the sister covered her ears. "Don't tell me this, I don't want to know," the sister moaned, anticipating an interrogatory father later that evening. "In fact, make sure I'm not around when you do it," she added.

The spirit of contract breaking was meant to break this kind of legacy. It would be a tall order, both helped and not by the structure of the exercises. Contract breaking on a group level was a major stand-off; a studied illustration of stonewalling with strange norms that buckled all the remaining standards of group therapy that I'd learned in school. Besides the question of whether members could face one another and actually interact, other boundaries were relaxed. For example, kids could be extracted from groups for various reasons, violating the principle that group members ought to remain in groups for the duration of activities, thereby creating a safe environment for disclosures. Even the stipulation that groups have consistent beginning and end times was expendable. This was especially true of groups like contract breaking which would (within reason) last as long as they needed to, like a lot of conversations between adults and kids: until resolution, as determined by adults, was achieved. Clearly, though technically a treatment exercise (and perhaps documented as a therapy group), contract breaking was more of a group inquisition than an example of group therapy; an echo of stalled exchanges between parents and oppositional teens; a verbal shakedown between authorities and suspects, or management and union leadership. Watching these activities was like watching a drama unfold, like being a fly on the wall of a tense, midnight negotiation in a dilapidated warehouse.

The initial phases of contract breaking involved a jockeying for position, a kind of testing of the Thunder Road waters. Kids would raise their thumbs, stand up, and meet the minimum requirements: tread the path of least resistance and reveal those contracts that would be met with lesser punishments. Chip-stealing-from-the-kitchen anecdotes would dominate early proceedings, to be followed by affected acknowledgements that "new" staff had been manipulated to give out items from the personal belongings closets at inappropriate times. The middle-ground material pertaining to the smuggling of cigarettes, the so-called "cheeking" and subsequent peddling of medications, or the tired attempts to make alcohol out of orange peels, would be revealed next. The major stuff, the headline revelations about sex, violence and *real* drugs, would take even more time to draw out. The kids understood that some disclosures were necessary. It was foolish to say "I've got nothing," when staff inquired. Even amidst the "got your back" ethos of the milieu, anyone uttering this kind of phrase would be scoffed at, perhaps rejected as someone who lacked basic institutional skills. Either they were brand new and needed to be schooled; or they were too obstinate, too street-like, and thus destined to fail the program. Like wolves segregating the runts, the kids actually judged harshly those who didn't learn to adapt.

On the big stuff, the more astute kids knew how to hold out and keep their secrets, and the parallels with police interrogations would become palpable. One typical staff strategy was to create a second contract breaking group (often, say, a group for the girls on their wing of the unit), and elicit separate contracts from that activity. Like someone entering to deliver a subpoena, a staff member would walk into one activity and show to its leader a list of contracts revealed in the parallel contract breaking group. Together, they might look up and cast a disapproving scan over the room. A couple of thumbs would be hastily raised. *Do they still have time to make a deal*? some would be thinking, reliving experiences of courtrooms or before that, of dangerous caregivers. Then someone would be pulled out of the room, and ushered to separate office for a more intensive question and answer session. There were contracts, about violence, about sex, and about drug use, that were taken very seriously, and rightly so. But in retrospect, it's not clear to what degree Thunder Road's observing ego noticed how much it had mirrored the roles of police and parent.

Good cop or bad cop: which one do I want? These were counselors thinking, once resigned to the roles with good humor, and without internal conflict for the most part. The so-called online staff, called Therapeutic Community counselors in the nineties, or those called Recovery Counselors in later years, seemingly accepted or even welcomed the blurring of boundaries between clinician and caretaker. Staff members enlisted into these positions drew their knowledge and beliefs from either TC Concepts or the 12-step community. Some had a vast history of working in group homes, or foster care facilities; many were parents themselves. Successfully treating the addicted individual meant providing a safe environment above all else, they would insist. That means not only the imposition of rules, but the implementation of them; the assigning of punishment (or, in euphemistic terms, "consequences") in response to the breaking of rules; the necessary detective work that roots out the secrets in the building like an exterminator searching for every last termite in the cracks. There were staff members at Thunder Road who specialized in this activity. They had a nose for contracts, and a taste for interrogation. If looking closely, one might see them salivating as they contemplated the shady underbelly of treatment. There was righteousness also: in order to discover who has broken rules, when and how often they have done so, requires a strong, firm hand, not to mention "voice", and if the roles of counselor, parent, and policeman are blurred in the process, then so be it.

Problem, retorts the average therapist—sometimes quietly. Therapists are not supposed to act like parents, much less police officers, so a conflict exists. Therapists are trained to exude qualities like neutrality, the aforementioned "unconditional positive regard"; to intervene with Kohutian-like mirroring statements, or else they make confrontations with calm, subtle skepticism, as opposed to a haranguing. For the therapist, the prospect of taking part in clearly adversarial activities like contract-breaking, or confrontation group, or even room searches, brought with it significant problems: the possibility that therapeutic rapport or therapeutic alliance[7] with a client may be irrevocably damaged. In the years since becoming a clinical supervisor to therapists, I have coached many to adapt to this problem at places like Thunder Road, and to more or less accept that the conflict comes with the territory. The problem, I'd say, lies not so much in the attitudes of so-called recovery counselors versus the ethics of psychotherapists, or even with the needs of management versus those less responsible for the overall disposition of the facility. The conflict lies in the nature of the setting itself, and also within the psyches of everyone involved.

A parent/therapist mesh

In classical psychoanalysis, consumers of analysis (versus what is more popularly termed "therapy" these days) are supposed to participate in treatment several days a week, with some variance in terms of the number of days. The latter day standard of one visit per week is insufficient for the level of symptom reduction and later deepening required for a comprehensive treatment. Transference, the concept whereby attributions of characteristics are unconsciously made by an analysand towards an analyst, are intensified as a treatment episode is entered into and then deepened. Schore (2005, p. 845) writes that transference is the expression of a patient's implicit perceptions and memories, "communicated" (versus spoken) via tone, prosodic vocalizations, body gestures, and eye-to-eye contact. Breaks occur in the transference as an unconscious process becomes conscious, and patients are able to reflect upon how they are engaging with others. For all intents and purposes, these "breaks" represent progress in therapy, a development of an individual's "true" or "real" self. However, in the world of treatment, or rehab, this layer of treatment is shelved at the outset of care. The reason: treatment observes first what brings people to the attention of mental health providers in the first place: namely, the behavioral symptoms.

In his paper, "Remembering, Repeating, and Working Through" (1915), Sigmund Freud offered that patients "repeat" rather than remember. Children play rather than put words to thoughts, or feelings. They entertain a dialectical process between internal and external reality, self and other, and they seek caretaking and direction before they learn to separate and understand. It is understood that Sigmund Freud went to great lengths to treat many of his patients, even feeding and housing those that he felt needed extra care or containment. In Therapeutic Communities like Thunder Road, hardly any professionals are practicing psychoanalysis as it is classically understood. These days, only a fraction of therapists, even, are trained in this highly specialized orientation. However, the background specter of psychoanalysis, reflected in the assumptions of treatment providers, and in the lexicon of terms that comprise residential treatment, is there for anyone who cares to look closely enough. Likewise, the anecdotes of Freud's "analytic" yet directive-giving attention to the feeding, shelter, and containment of some of his patients, is relevant to the prevailing principles of a group home environment.

It isn't necessary to become a police officer in a Therapeutic Community Concepts model, but it's damned near impossible to separate the roles of parent and therapist in such an environment. It was in the nature of the arrangement: within the inevitable associations kids would make as they noticed that the people getting them out of bed each morning, directing them to brush their teeth, make their beds, go to school and thereafter to a structured treatment program were not their parents. But they were sort of acting like them. The staff at Thunder Road or the staff of any group home or hospital is a stand-in—subject to all manner of attributions. Psychoanalysis adds the term projection[8] to mark these attributions, and to understand them as being unconsciously made and manifested throughout a therapeutic relationship. Denial of feeling: kids in the program assigned feelings to others that lay within themselves; otherwise, they embodied feelings through tone, posture, and facial expression, or finally, and even more primitively, they induced these denied feeling states in others. From the moment an adolescent is brought to a Therapeutic Community, either through legal mandate or through the desperation of a parental tough-love maneuver, a parent-like dynamic ensues, one in which clients radiate their emotional states, and vulnerable others, staff included, absorb. Clients are likewise absorbed into the new reality. They are oriented to the fact that someone else other than family—the staff at TR—will be responsible for providing basic needs: food and shelter; and for thereafter delivering what will ominously be called *structure*.

Staff in a therapeutic milieu oversees clients' days, directing them from one activity to the next. Staff members orient clients as to the rules and privileges, and determine whether or not they have broken rules, and therefore still merit their privileges. In my early years, for access to their personal belongings, kids had to ask for permission. Specifically, for access to certain belongings, they had to ask therapists for permission. In order to contact a family member by phone, they had to request permission from staff. In order to make contact with an extended family not obviously involved in an ongoing care-giving capacity, the kids had to again ask permission from their therapist. In order for them to progress through the program, their compliance had to be sanctioned by their therapists, as well as a treatment team consisting of people whose credentials cut across a variety of disciplines. In order to placate an admitting authority, be it legal or parental, they had to again solicit the approval of this team, including their therapist.

Furthermore, kids in residential programs see their therapists practically everyday, and in multiple contexts. It's not like they only see them in the haven of their private offices, and thus get to imagine that they live there because that's the only context in which they are seen. At Thunder Road, therapists could be seen by clients in the hallways, in the dining room, waiting in line to get lunch; disappearing into the staff toilet to perform un-idealized acts that might stir or belie client fantasies. It further strikes me that those who have never worked in a residential setting, including experienced theorists who are quite mindful of transference phenomena, will likely not appreciate the degree to which the parental specter contaminates the work of a residential therapist. What is broadly termed the transference, and corresponding countertransference phenomena, manifest on another level of intensity, creating potential for therapeutic bonds that are surely unparalleled across the spectrum of mental health services. Given the relative inexperience of most therapists working in Therapeutic Communities, these bonds are quite remarkable events.

A busy therapist could be troubled for one of those phone calls anytime they were spotted—going to their car after work, for instance. Once I was asked by a client to call his mother while I was wearily heading towards my car in the parking lot (This was some time after my internship period, after I'd been hired as a full-time case manager/therapist). It had been a long day and I was leaving at least an hour after my shift had officially ended. I heard the voice of the client before seeing him and inwardly groaned. The kid in question was about the most demanding youth I'd ever been assigned to work with, and was almost single-handedly burning me out, or so I felt at the time. I turned thinking that the only surprising thing was that he wasn't asking to make the call himself, with my assistance, since use of staff phone codes were required for all outgoing calls. Then, as we made eye contact, the reason for his appeal crystallized. This time he needed me to make the call for him because he couldn't, and because didn't want his mother to worry. He had burst through the unlocked but heavily alarmed double doors at the back of the facility and was jogging towards the lip of the lot's entryway. He was AWOLing; that is, running away from Thunder Road.

For a therapist in this kind of setting, there is simply too much authority, and responsibility, not to mention sheer presence resembling that of a parent for this dynamic not to play out. Despite this blurring of roles the task of maintaining neutrality remains, with paramount and paradoxical importance. As a result, I have both experienced and observed in others the dilemma of walking an ever shifting line with the clients: ever approaching, seeking to connect; ever distancing, needing to assert boundaries and create space. Like a parent in desperate need of a babysitter, therapists at Thunder Road would crave their weekends, and dream of pastoral escapes (mountains and/or beaches, usually) during the working week—settings as removed from the urban landscape of the facility as was possible. Separating from the workplace was a real challenge. Among other things, the mind kept being called back. The bond, the fusion, the enmeshment, the—whatever it was being called at any one time—compelled a lingering, and often disturbing attachment. Therapists struggle to separate. I struggled to separate. Ruminative about therapeutic impasses, obsessed with fears about inadequacy, therapists persevered at Thunder Road with thoughts of clients taking them over, overwhelming their defenses like some ruthless hurricane battering a Cajun shoreline. Resentful of the mental space being occupied, clients' faces would morph onto those of loved ones, engulfing therapists as in some Ingmar Bergman film from a bygone era. Then there were dream-climaxing questions, the sometimes agonized, "will they make it?" thoughts. Would we?

Becoming invested in treatment outcomes feels normal and human, but it can be demoralizing if professionals in a mental health setting cannot consistently, as management routinely advises, "take care of themselves." A kid that revealed in one of those contract breaking groups that he or she had relapsed on a drug, or else lied about having sex on the unit while overnight staff was distracted, or ran away from the unit on a Saturday night to get drunk, only to return at four in the morning after getting beaten up in the streets of Oakland, would break the hearts of some therapists, or bring out dark feelings of betrayal in others. After their weekends, therapists would return to work, eager to renew the sudden deepening that their client had seemingly achieved in the last session, only to learn that said client had been discharged from the hospital for non-compliance, or run away. The effect was personal, a knife in the chest—that kid that would not be seen again. Sympathetic eyes were cast upon therapists and other staff members who betrayed these feelings, but it wasn't long before they were solemnly admonished, "it's not personal," urged to carry on, and to seek support for their countertransference feelings.

The feelings typically inspired by contract-breaking sessions were a more commonplace imitation of parenthood. Each therapist learned, at some point, that *their* kids had broken rules, and it was the job of therapists to address their clients on the breaking of these rules, or at least be a liaison to the kids' parents or probation officers about the issues, those broken rules. As a result, a therapist in a residential setting is not so much a trusted confidante as he or she is a conduit between different points of a system. I wonder: when kids looked up from their supine positions, and saw adults poring over lists of contracts, wrongdoings, and then looking back to fix eyes upon them, did they consciously think *parent* in those moments? Did they assign other familial roles? Probably not, but as I discovered at places like Thunder Road, the thoughts to which I'm referring weren't really thoughts in the purely cognitive sense.

Attachment

Science and theory. In the mid-nineties, as I was finishing a Master's Degree in clinical psychology, one on my courses introduced me to attachment theory: the research into secure and insecure attachment by John Bowlby in the mid-to-late sixties; the

Strange Situation studies of Mary Ainsworth in the seventies; the development of assessment tools, such as the Adult Attachment Inventory (also used with adolescents), by her prodige Mary Main and her partner Ruth Goldwyn. Conducting their studies at UC Berkeley beginning in the late seventies, their child subjects might have been future Thunder Road clients.

The work of neuropsychologists like Allan Schore has drawn attention to the theory that brain and personality development are largely experience-dependent. According to Schore (1994), the brain of an infant will increase in weight from 400 grams to 1000 grams during the first year, suggesting that life experience plays an enormous role in influencing postnatal brain development. He cites research indicating that the human brain myelinates in the first year and a half, and that the mechanisms for attachment are embedded within the right hemisphere of the human brain. His research, as well as that of others, increasingly asserts the significance of right brain functioning in the service of affect, attention, and implicit (subconscious) memory, and left brain functioning in the service of declarative, explicit and semantic memory, the structures of language.

Such research has considerable implications for psychotherapy, especially for those who note that it is the non-verbal, pre-"cognitive" elements which are keys to therapeutic intervention. Increasingly, science informs practitioners of affective experiences, bodily-based experiences, which can be objectively measured, but which exist below levels of awareness. Schore (2005) writes that the implicit self system of the right brain that evolves in preverbal stages represents the biological substrate of the dynamic unconscious. Siegel (1999) writes that experience—especially interpersonal experience—directly influences how neurons in the brain connect to one another, affecting the "pruning" process in which neuronal pathways that are not stimulated through experience become inactive, and therefore unresponsive. Psychotherapy, in Siegel's opinion, consists of a dialogue of non-verbal elements, of communications that occur outside of consciousness which depend not so much on what individuals do or say, but upon who they are.

Steeped in neurobiology as well as psychology, a full history of attachment theory is beyond the scope of this text, not to mention my level of expertise. However, as the subject is the care of disturbed youth placed in either residential settings or intensive day treatment programs wherein strong attachments are undoubtedly made, some discussion of attachment disorders is surely necessary. As the director once said during that three-day orientation, the kids at Thunder Road were from harsh or neglectful backgrounds. Their lives had been marked by abuse, as well as persistent, yet habitual, and unintended patterns of misattunement in early development. They had no boundaries—consistent rules, structure, she meant in one sense. Containment of affect, the consistent regulation of feeling states through caregiving: this had also been missing—as a secondary result of caregivers' drug use, depression, or protracted anxiety. Reminders of these observations, presented as if factual, were driven home in meeting after meeting, supervision hour after supervision hour, during my early years at Thunder Road, by thoughtful, impassioned trainers. The statements, like dire warnings, informed staff as to the problem. The program structure, with all its means of implementing rules and containing disorderly behavior and emotions, spoke loud and clear of a proposed solution, or at least a first line of solution.

Had they been subject to the Strange Situation studies, the kids at Thunder Road would have likely emerged with one of three designations of insecure attachment: avoidant, ambivalent, and disorganized. For each of these categories demonstrated by the Strange Situation studies, attachment theory suggests that the pattern of communication between parent and child has shaped the child's attachment system. Thus, parents who are emotionally receptive, and responsive, are associated with securely attached children. As part of Ainsworth's earlier research (1972), she tellingly observed that securely attached, crying children responded positively when picked up by parents; that action terminated the crying, attachment behavior. Also telling was the observation that securely attached children did not resume crying when subsequently let go. However, parents that were unresponsive and imperceptive were associated with avoidant-attached infants. When an attachment behavior, such as crying, is repeatedly activated, but repeatedly not terminated, or un-terminated for extended periods, an avoidance pattern—what

Bowlby termed a defensive exclusion of material from consciousness—becomes likely. Alternatively, parents that were inconsistently responsive, or else intrusive with their own states of mind tended to generate ambivalent-attached children. These children were continuously activated, anxious and preoccupied with the contingency of caretaking. They cling or else resist attempts to have them settle and calm down. Finally, parents that are frightened, frightening, or confused in their communication with children, tend to nurture a disorganized, or disoriented attachment in their children. Such children become confused figures in relationships: detached, frozen, perhaps chaotic.

I think the term "defensive exclusion" bears further comment. The assertion that clients are experiencing feeling states, despite clients' denial of said feeling states, or the lack of outward appearance of those feeling states, seems so common in treatment settings that the lesson seems axiomatic. Instead of deterring concern, these clients bring attention to themselves through their behaviors, their embodiments, and less understood perhaps, through their inducement of denied feelings in others. Tacitly, observers make empathic interpretations as to an internal ordeal that commands a protective avoidance. But there are problems with these observations. "How do you empathically relate to an unexpressed emotion," writes Maroda (2005). This is a fascinating question, and one that begs another question: can one empathize with a feeling not expressed, but inferred? On one level, after hearing countless clients "relate" to each others' attempts to ward off feelings, I could answer yes to this question. But that "relating" often seemed more a collusion with a defensive posture than a truly empathetic act. I'm referring to an experience that is concealed; that is fleetingly experienced, and not uttered. Feelings not so manifested are readily denied, sometimes aggressively. "You're analyzing me, trying to tell me how I feel," some kids complained, as though the autonomy of their true selves were at stake. Others became or affected confusion, and then projected that state onto counselors: "You're trippin'," they'd say.

I think it fair to say that most schools of thought pertaining to psychotherapy or social work have been influenced by advances in attachment theory and neurobiological science. The writings of Schore and Seigel, and the categories of secure and insecure attachment, as originally described by Bowlby (1969), help us understand the psychology of individuals afflicted with problems relating to developmental problems. Bowlby's studies with infants, in association with clinics such as the famous Tavistock clinic in London, were landmark in so far as his subsequent conclusions departed from the prevailing views of then contemporary psychoanalysts. Bowlby's assertion was that the origins of patient difficulties were rooted in real life difficulties, especially early separations (as a result of war, for instance), as opposed to infantile fantasies, which was the prevailing theory of Freudian treatment models, the Melanie Klein followers mid-way through the last century. Bowlby (a one-time Klein supervisee) rejected drive theory as a primary determinant of development. In his theory, maternal deprivation obstructed healthy development; attachment to caregivers is a contingent series of events, as opposed a stage-driven process as contemporary Margaret Mahler theorized (Coates, 2004). Based on his research, he proposed paradigmatic guidelines for psychotherapy: 1.) that a first task was that of fully understanding of patient's present difficulties, 2.) that therapist and patient form a secure base; that is, a trusting relationship from which separation can proceed, 3.) that the origin of difficulties is understood to be linked to real life experiences, and 4.) that the ongoing task of therapy was to help individuals link past experiences to present conditions; and in particular, to highlight interpersonal expectations that were once appropriate, but subsequently obsolete and self-defeating.

The range of problems stemming from chaotic nurturing environments are wide, but what seems important for the purposes of this book are the pervasive deficits that present in day-to-day behaviors, interactions, which are speculatively linked to problems of early childhood attachment at least as much as they are genetic causes. The problems that consistently afflict kids in places like Thunder Road include the following: poor reality testing, poor impulse control, low frustration tolerance, poor ego boundaries, so-called alexithymia—the failure to access or articulate feeling states. Add to these deficits problems of hyper-arousal and hypo-arousal in response to stressful situations, then life difficulties become pervasive, resulting in failures to access what Masterson (1980) termed "the capacities of the real self". These include the following: creativity, spontaneity, self-assertion, or continuity of self experience, a sense of cohesion, of identity. Most of the kids at Thunder Road held some motivation relating to drug use. Would they contemplate other facets of their lives?

A primary function of attachment, according to researchers, is to provide a child with an environment within which an understanding of mental states in self and others can develop (Masterson, 2006). Those without this capacity cannot sustain rewarding personal relationships. They are ever focused on others, though not in a manner that is empathetic or curious. Rather, an underdeveloped capacity for what Fonagy (1996) terms "mentalization", or what Siegel (1999) similarly terms "mindsight", leads to chronic suspicion, distrust, hypervigilance, and misunderstanding. It was relatively easy to see that kids who lacked understanding of the dynamics between themselves and others suffered feelings of emptiness and paranoia. They were preoccupied with defending themselves, either beseechingly or else with aggressive attitudes. They were paradoxically self- centered: concerned with their own needs, yet focused upon external cues, and without a compass for their own internal processes. They generally struggled in their relationships with others. They lacked not only words. They lacked what is commonly termed reflective function in mental health circles.

Assessment of mental health and substance use histories

At the outset of drug treatment, an intake process outlines the presenting problems affecting a client's life. Conceivably, this process seeks to identify both external and internal conflicts, though for the purposes of initial planning, the first observations tends to focus on known events, or the obstacles presented by the client's living environment. Either in treatment team meetings, or else via reports made available by an automated data base, a series of precipitating events, recent and historical, should be made known to staff. Substance abuse is typically (or even requisitely) the presenting issue for treatment, though a variety of complaints might also become a focus of treatment. A rough history of drug use would likely be collected up front, with lists of drugs that had been used; frequency of use, the method of use, as well as attempts to cease using that had presumably failed.

I frequently noticed that kids in treatment seemed quite disconnected from their feelings about their drug use, and this disconnection took several forms: one of which was the pastime known as *war storying*, which occurred when kids recounted their drug using histories. When conducting assessments myself, I often heard clients speak candidly about their pre-treatment drug use. While often dismissing the notion of "problem" drug use, many seemed to enjoy the telling of events related to drugs. The kids would become stimulated and pleased at the opportunity to share their stories, like toddlers sharing make-believe born of play. They often drooled out these stories like they were spewing vomit over the group home floor, or else spilling toys for others to tidy up. On the one hand this wasn't especially surprising. These were defensive selves on display, without apology or apparent shame. I'd known myself to be glorifying of intoxication in the past, though it seemed to me that Thunder Road clients took this habit to a new and much more primitive level, hence the infantile quality. Over the course of hundreds of interviews, I just about managed to keep a stoic face listening to some quite ugly tales—attempting to neither collude nor shame—while maintaining a fixed intrigue. "Distance", intoned a former supervisor: the testimonials were designed to keep distance and to enable separation—among other things, the essential task of adolescence (versus attachment?), though it would be overstatement to attach normalcy to war stories.

Inquiry into circumstances prior to admission would often touch upon related problems, though histories might become less reliable as the process expanded through direct questioning. Kids might have recollections about traumatic events, like instances of physical or sexual abuse, or the witnessing of shootings and other violent episodes, but be unwilling to share details, or else they might proclaim loss of memory pertaining to these events, or worse still, they'd recount the events without emotion. That was often a problem with the tools used, the number "scales", that were meant to track traumatic symptoms or accounts: they were strictly language-based exercises and therefore missed affective information. Denying instances of startle response, even if examples were given, kids would later be observed twisting their necks spasmodically at the sound of a passing siren. Or they'd flinch and overreact to the compromising of space: the unwanted touch of a peer, such as the jostling of bodies when boisterous youth is gathered in groups. Dissociation[9]: the phenomenon of disrupted consciousness and memory is common to those who have experienced either episodic or chronic trauma. Benignly, this might manifest as day-dreaming during a lazy mid-morning after a disrupted night's sleep. More problematically, such symptoms, the blank stares and flat deliveries, killed therapeutic moments, and stalled progress in treatment for months.

Background documents might fill out the picture of an insecure attachment history. So, too, would reports from intake staff members who passed on nuggets of information from collateral sources. Delicately posed questions might elicit a coded recollection of acting out history. Alongside the near pharmaceutical factory volume of substances that kids had ingested, smoked, or else speared into their veins, incredible measures had been taken in the cause of the lifestyle. Kids on streets had worked internships of their own, as runners for the local clique of a statewide gang, working *hand to hand,* as many described it. In the hills, parents' bank accounts had been drained with pilfered credit and/or debit cards; their cars had been repeatedly stolen until finally crashed and destroyed. Elderly and disabled citizens had been assaulted, or perhaps killed, in the interests of winning the approval of overseeing gangstas. Homes were vandalized; friends' sisters were raped, and villainous drug dealers had been routinely felated instead of paid. Flesh had been burned in acts of intoxicated self-mutilation; tattoos were self-applied. Bones had been broken, and scars had been left following daredevil acts of what adults please to call "risk-taking behaviors". The kids often shrugged, laughed and then remarked that such behaviors were "stupid". They'd even seem persuasive in promising that such things would never happen again.

I marveled at the resilient physicality, the otherwise untainted perfection of many of their bodies, wondering how it was all possible given the scale of chemical contamination. I marveled at nature; at time, and the precious split-second of life that is youth. Youth is wasted on the young, says a cliché. Certainly, youth seems to go unnoticed by youth; they're too busy living it, and toying with its fragility. Talking to a lean seventeen or eighteen year old, whose proportion of body fat would likely treble in a decade, it was sometimes hard to see into their self destructive histories. How was it that these kids were still alive? I often thought. For those who didn't delight in sordid stories, reticence might also be attributed (by others) to shame, or perhaps to dissociation, and either presentation might serve as criteria for a diagnosis of Post Traumatic Stress Disorder. It was often presumed that drug use was a concomitant to this malady, serving the functions of "numbing"; parasympathetic, reptilian (as in "hiding") come downs if not a more conscious and mundane version of escape.

Meanwhile, these intake assessments would seek to assess other factors: client motivation, the stability (or not) of their former living environment, the potential for a meaningful inclusion of the existing family system; the influence of a development history, often accrued in a piecemeal fashion, through (again) checkered recollections. Factors such as ego boundaries—the patterns of self and other perceptions—were harder to determine at the level of intake assessment, though I think levels of mentalization were observable, even if staff weren't familiar with that particular term. Kids could be asked, for example, how their behaviors—the ones admitted to—had affected others, how others might think or feel. Assessments could determine to some extent what capacity a client had for contemplating another's experience, and whether they could even reflect upon their own.

Unofficially, I'd try to observe a client in the milieu in the days following an assessment, in order to see if I might notice something not evident in an interview. I remember a boy named Eddie who, when talking privately to me, asserted with righteous conviction that he never started fights, largely because he was a respectful person who merely expected reciprocal treatment from others. The next day, I saw him poised to enter a room when situated in one of a pair of line-ups heading through a narrow doorway. When the moment arrived for Eddie to enter the room, he and another boy moved simultaneously into the open space. Appearing to anticipate a collision, Eddie preemptively flailed his left arm, striking the other boy from his path and causing him to hit up against a wall and bruise his shoulder. "Why are you trying to invade my space?" Eddie spat viciously as the other boy recoiled. When later chastised over the incident, Eddie proclaimed his innocence, insisting that he'd been victimized by an interloping peer, and later by an unjust, misunderstanding staff authority.

Regardless of whether assessments or prior placement reports anticipated such incidents, those patterns of not only violent behavior, but also poor ego boundaries and arrested reflective function, were often left to chance, meaning that staff would work with deficits in these areas as best they could. I found that there was information in those interviews that was subtle, yet significant, or else patterns that might be inferred from impressions forwarded from previous placements, such as the oblique comments of a former counselor that had concluded a discharge summary. While supposedly admitted for treatment of a drug problem, some kids' precipitating events hadn't involved drugs necessarily. Instead, the criterion factors may have been assaults, thefts, binges of sex; lurid stories with sometimes random elements, behaviors that kids might recount but not explain. Whether or not clients could even speak of these matters, the intakes and later assessments were previews of all that would follow.

Diagnosis of depression was often inferred from a description of behaviors or feelings, none of which needed to entail the characterization of depression from the kids themselves. Depression might be evident from a client's affect—a concept similar to tone. In the client histories, sleep problems, appetite problems might be attributed to drug use, but might also be presumptive indicators of depression. So, too, would suicidal ideation, or a history of suicide attempts. Irritability would also be an indicator of depression, or boredom. Hospital-based programs, as licensed health facilities, offer psychiatric observation, and as a result, many admits are placed on a variety of psychotropic medications over the course of their programs: Abilify, Wellbutrin, Paxil, Lexapro, Haldol, Concerta, Seroquel, to mention just a few; all for a variety of presenting problems: not just depression, but also anxiety and impulsivity; distraction or psychotic symptoms. In theory, these medications were reserved for lower functioning clients, who were assessed in terms of symptoms that placed them at imminent risk. Other clients, deemed more stable in outward appearance, were perhaps thought of as neurotics, kids whose symptoms may seem pervasive over the course of treatment, but nonetheless—not medically acute. By my observation, many who were diagnosed as being depressed or anxiety-disordered simply did not perceive themselves this way.

Of course, many didn't perceive themselves as having a problem with drugs either. They tended to normalize their drug use, especially their use of marijuana and alcohol (normalizing of prescription drug abuse seemed an era away in the nineties), thinking it a substitute for therapy, if anything—not a reason for it. Suicidal impulses might be dismissed as aberrant and violent behaviors, or criminal associations, which brought with them legal consequences, were either blamed on others or somehow justified as part of an established and accepted self-identity. Drug use was and is fun or stress-relieving, and with respect to certain drugs at least, ought to be legalized, thought many. Violence, they'd suggest, is a necessary response to a hostile living environment for which individuals do not bear responsibility. As for the accomplice that is sex: only if they'd done something they thought abhorrent, such as—as one kid put it, "suckin' dicks for drugs"—might they think themselves "addicted". Many of the kids had experience living on the streets. They spoke of street values, street rules, with an air of virtue. Much of what attended the use of drugs was essentially ego-syntonic; that is, consistent with an established value system. Those that didn't make virtues out of self-reliance did so of neediness, or a version of neediness: the demand that others' meet their needs, or that drugs serve that purpose. They made demands for admiration, and dressed this need with euphemisms, the call for *respect*. In my opinion, this normalization trend has increased over the years, and not just among adolescents. This surely makes "rehab" an endangered entity, living on the margins of society's motivations.

Motivation

The staff of Thunder Road commonly observed that most kids in the program simply hadn't suffered enough at the hands of a drug-using lifestyle; at least, not enough to motivate real change. Unlike adult Therapeutic Communities, wherein desperate addicts make, and persistently make, impassioned appeals for treatment in attempts to save their own lives, the adolescent treatment milieu tends to lack a dominant core of youths who have experienced depths of despair related to substance use. Maran (2003) cites professionals in facilities similar to Thunder Road who echo this observation. Few die of lung cancer or liver disease at the age of sixteen, and fewer still would compare their lists of rap-sheets and broken relationships with those of their elders and say they'd wrought as much if not more damage. The chorus of warning said, *look where you're heading*, but the rub was and is that the actively addicted frequently exalt the present, deny the past, and anticipate a future of immediate gratification. These kids' bodies were stronger than they would ever be again, observed those warning of the problem. Staff members at Thunder Road, the 12-step or TC Concepts veterans especially, ardently told their stories, but knew they were fighting an uphill battle.

They offered the paternalistic perspective of "I wish I'd gotten this at your age" with melancholic airs. They drew attention to physical deterioration as a principal consequence of unabated substance use. Others may have cited constant legal difficulties, a series of relationships destroyed by bad decisions, or the tragedy of estrangement from their own kids. Many clients had experienced these events from the other side, as witnesses: they had parents with disease; parents that were separated or divorced. Some knew what it was like to be removed from a home by a social worker, or to have known or even witnessed a caretaker's death. The cautionary tales of staff resonated with some kids, but often missed the mark with others, sometimes because kids were not ready to cope with painful histories, but also because staff caveats often failed to connect the projected results of an unresolved problem with the intrinsic problem of a disturbed self. "I've got problems because I'm messed up," said the recovering addicts, reflecting on past damage but a chronic condition. "I wanna learn what to do so I can avoid this stuff in the future," the most motivated kids would answer, thinking concretely of action steps and therefore missing an important point. The slogan *One Day At A Time* seemed designed for them, for their myopic ambitions and short attention spans.

Motivation for treatment is a precious resource, something that is scrutinized, asserted, speculated upon, and sometimes discovered. *Flight into health*, a phrase used by relapse prevention specialists, is often used in rehabilitation programs to describe those who are not so much defiant of treatment, or even normalizing of their drug use, but instead proclaim themselves prematurely clean, sober, and cured, and therefore do not require further assistance from intrusive helpers. They elicit skepticism, basically: smirks from staff (and senior clients) that see through their gamey intentions. These clients behave well, confront their peers, say all the things that staff members appear to want to hear, and diligently read their recovery literature. When sharing in groups, they speak of the "new" me versus the "old me", even when reflecting upon behaviors that may be days old. They seem oblivious to their own absurdity, exhibiting what might be characterized as a dismissive style through an attachment lens. They lack reality testing skills. In another sense, they are testing the reality of treatment: gauging the gullibility of treatment teams, angling for an advantage. Mandated into treatment as a pleasant alternative to jail, they seek to just get through their programs.

Navigation versus Engagement. In their ethnographic study of twenty one adolescent residents in a Therapeutic Community in Australia, Foster, Nathan, and Ferry (2010) observed that programs must consider whether clients are truly engaged in the change process of treatment, or simply navigating their way through treatment in order to meet others' requirements. Conducting interviews with clients and staff over a period of four months, the authors noted the problem of client boredom—the tendency to make statements like, "I hate this place. All we do is the same shit each day"; frustration with rote activities like journaling; the need for adjunctive therapies that incorporate art; recreational and vocational outlets. While focused upon what captures the interest of adolescents in Therapeutic Communities, the study offers little on the matter of containment of self-destructive behaviors, but concludes that program "completion"—a commonly referenced marker in outcome studies—may be too blunt an instrument to measure success, and that Therapeutic Communities in general require an in-depth exploration of their treatment methods.

For those that have observed adult Therapeutic Communities, such as journalist and physician Lonny Shavelson, this disengaged navigation position, as well as the accompanying dynamic between provider and patient, is a contamination of treatment goals, undermining the integrity of programs and leading to the impression that drug rehabilitation (perhaps narrowly defined) simply does not work for those coerced into change (Shavelson, 2001). Indeed, motivation did seem like a commodity to many clients at Thunder Road, inpatient and outpatient, as well as a residential program wherein I worked in Southern California. Perhaps this is true of most programs, residential or not, that are dominantly comprised of mandated referrals. Motivation seems like something to be played with, used and sold, for as long as treatment will last. The consumers of this sale are the clients as well as the concerned onlookers: the treatment staff, the extended staff of probation officers and court officials; the suffering family members. For all of these players, motivation seems paramount. "Motivation may be the reason for substance use improvement as opposed to the substance use treatment." (Tripodi, 2009, P. 290). The true motivation of clients is always difficult to assess, and yet despite all this, and despite what treatment outcome research may indicate, it also seems the most important factor in a successful treatment outcome—more important than psychological mindedness; more important than reflective function; even more important than impulse control or reality testing.

So what is it that kids are signing up for when they enter treatment? Assuming they'd understand all that was being asked of them—all that was possible—what would they be motivated to achieve? Firstly, do they agree with that one-time program director of Thunder Road, the woman who determinedly argued from personal experience that drugs, the "lifestyle", promises much more than it can ever deliver? Before engaging the proposed solution, do they see the problem the same way? Some did, in my experience. Perhaps many did; it was hard to tell given the play-acting that perpetually transpired. Some pretended; that is, they nodded reverently at staff pronouncements, while internally plotting their next using episode; their next *run*. Some understood the consequences of drug use: the legal, health-related, emotional and relational consequences; the guilt and shame. They actually feared those consequences, even if their caprices told them that getting high was worth the gamble that such things may or may not come to pass.

Can such kids imagine a life without drugs, or violence or even sexual acting out? Do they fear the consequences of *not* acting out with drugs, violence, or sex? I wondered. Again, some did. Some thought of violence, for example, as a secondary disease, one that afflicted their families, communities, and therefore themselves. To not be violent was tantamount to capitulation, perhaps suicide. Ask an average kid in treatment—not just Eddie—about their propensity for fighting, and they might reply with something like, "I don't like to fight, but I'll do it I have to." Or, a counselor might hear something mournfully justifying like, "It's how I was brought up," in response to a query about why violence seems necessary as a solution to all problems. Among clients in treatment, problems of all kinds were normalized, and futures were often characterized with flat hopelessness. Above all, choice was often presented as though it was illusory.

Could these kids consider consequences for drug use, physical and sexual violence, and make decisions to pursue a different way, and possibly come to understand what treatment would be about; what something like psychotherapy might offer? In my opinion, hardly any of the kids admitted to treatment in my fifteen years, or their parents, truly knew what was in store for them should they last the distance of the program. Like desperate addicts who bang on the doors of treatment facilities in need of a bed and a second chance, some may have felt "down" for anything—at least when coming down *off* something and feeling their worst about themselves. Those who had taken their altered states to points of psychosis, or had truly experienced crisis of another kind, the "bottom out" experiences that 12-step veterans speak of, may have felt prepared for interventions they would later not understand. But even they couldn't have known what it was like to live and work through the Therapeutic Community process.

Reality testing

Reality testing was always first order of business at Thunder Road: the reality that clients had serious problems; that safety, proceeding from structure, was a necessary antidote. Assessed (and confronted) upon admit, reality testing was a likely area of deficit among clients and was thereafter addressed repeatedly as a client's program unfolded. The re-orientation to reality, as well as the questioning as to what *was* real, was exhaustive and ongoing. Building upon the writings of Freud, other psychoanalysts have described the process of repetition in treatment. Fenichel (1945) wrote that "working through is working on the ego; it is a process of 'confronting' the ego, and the abolition of the isolated or warded off instinct components from the total personality." He further wrote of the inertia of human beings, the tendency to become less elastic, more rigid; more habit-based. Of the resistant patient, he wrote: "repetition persuades him finally that in the future things no longer need to be the way they had always been previously; a new state of affairs can come about which need not be frightening."

At Thunder Road, staff echoed this hopeful and strident stance. The re-establishment of structure, through a system of rules, and the attendant containment of affect states was a major task of treatment, and was highly repetitive. All kids play, and some adults remember what it was like to play, or still do play, sometimes recklessly. In play therapy, the therapist begins with a delineation of the limits, and then proceeds with the therapy, knowing that children, especially children with poor attachment histories, will test these limits—test them unconsciously. All games have rules, we learn at some point. Games that don't have rules, or don't have consistent rules, are games that break the rules; they are games that have become unreal and become play gone wrong. For many staff members at Thunder Road, this was exhausting, this task of delineating treatment's game. The job was, broadly speaking, to educate: to begin working with clients whom Prochaska, Norcross and Diclemente (1983, 1994) designated as "precontemplative" of change, and proceed to undo, as methodically as possible, all the obstacles that stood in the way of clients' understanding of their problems.

The ubiquity of poor reality testing was why the Kohutian technique of mirroring, so rigorously taught at my initial practicum placement, seemed to me an insufficient intervention for most kids in the program. The virtues of mirroring presume an orientation to reality on the part of the client; but to make affirming noises, or else paraphrase back and amplify the feeling states (perhaps accurately) connected with someone's versatile denial patterns seemed to do little more than reinforce those denial patterns. Instead, the first task with mentally ill and substance abusing clients is to review the events leading to admission, and to sort through what has resulted from clients' behavior; their "negative" choices. Once these things are understood and a system of limits is established, a therapy proper can ensue. However, clients with closed minds or limited capacities can become fixated upon callow understandings. For some, an entire year's worth of treatment might attend to the issue of motivation, but still not traverse the opening bullet points of a resistant argument. "My P.O. sent me here because the judge didn't like me." I once had a client named Aaron who believed this the first day I met him, and appeared to still believe this eleven months later.

Aaron did what he needed to do, and said what he needed to say, like many who are coerced into treatment. That is, he remained abstinent, as far as anyone could tell via semi-regular urinalysis: compliance as defense. He agreed, in principle, to some roughly associated goals, and parroted back to staff the necessary rhetoric when interviewed at regular intervals. He agreed to go back to school upon discharge. He even agreed, sort of, to disavow allegiance to his chosen gang, a local strain of "northerners" as he put it, also known as Nortenos. Actually, the position he held was a commonly seized compromise, a contextually-based characterizing of his associations. To peers or a sufficiently entrusted adult, he "ran with northerners". To authority or to the untutored in gang culture, he was evasive and terse: "I'm not a part of that no more." He, like many others, before and since, agreed—even promised—to behave in the future, but never properly accepted that he had a problem in the first place. His gang affiliation, like his motivation to stay clean, was something to proclaim to some, but protect amongst others. He walked this thin line and played his game, and ours, as well as anyone. He was motivated to stay out of trouble, and perhaps thinly interested in staying clean from drugs. As to the associated problems—gang affiliation, his internal chaos—he was stuck in old patterns of behaving, thinking, and feeling.

This question of reality testing was, for the most part, not a question of psychosis. Though some may have fallen through the cracks over the years, the programs I worked in had policies of screening out those with a psychotic level of reality testing, at least until the end of the last decade. Therefore, the poor reality testing to which I refer is therefore a more commonplace pattern of self-deceit, as well as a deep-rooted incomprehension of one's self in relation to others: it is the poor assessment of the individual who does not perceive danger in a pattern of destructive behavior; it is the denial of someone who blames others for his or her problems, or who conversely takes on blame for a what is truly a systemic failing, often because of a false need to assert maturity. "Nah, this is on me," complains the client anxious to protect the parent whose drinking staff threatens to confront.

The former realities, such as the insecure attachment histories of these individuals, train quick assessments, accompanied by rigid beliefs. Impulses govern decisions, as well as flash-point associations. These are the people who, in the midst (or even the aftermath of a conflict) are convinced as to their own intentions and those of others. "I know for a fact that she hates me!" insisted another client with respect to that omniscient director. Reality, that client's reality, and that of others like Aaron, is fundamentally distorted, but nonetheless presented with defiant certainty. The strongest of Thunder Road staff: those who had experienced pain in their own lives yet worked on themselves so as to exude conviction blazed fierce eyes through the denial systems of clients. The most gifted of caregivers often didn't need to put words to their stories. The way they carried themselves, maintained an unshaken pitch to their voices, at once saw through defenses and held the crumbling children behind the facades.

With respect to the director, Aaron was responding not so much to explicit verbal content, and much less to any behavior that could have been objectively observed. There was no "I hate you," on which he could pin his assertions. Had the instructor of my one-time Rational Emotive Therapy course been present, he might have assigned an essay headlined with the question, "If there had been a camera on this scene, what would it see?" Aaron would have persisted with his reality, speaking past my instructor's teleological (inferring reality from what is observable) argument; utterly uninterested in its common sense philosophical center, and insistent upon the other's enemy intent. His point of view, like that of many in the program, seemed impervious to either insight or so-called cognitive reframe. I think this because I tried things like cognitive reframes with kids like Aaron over and over again. All too often they failed to penetrate clients' defenses.

Aaron's experience was in all likelihood, as researcher Daniel Siegel (1999) has written, a product of procedural (that is, implicit) memory. The micro experiences of infant-mother experiences aggregate into enduring structures: in tone and prosody, facial expression, body posture, and eye contact. Scientific researchers find that the brain's production of axons, dendrites, and synapses in early development far exceeds needs, and that synaptic connections are pruned away through lack of use. Reflective function is lacking in troubled teens because the conditions for its development have not been cultivated—a sort of *use it or lose it* principle, proceeding from the theories of patterned neuronal organization proposed by Donald Hebb in the late 1940s. Fonagy and Target (1996) further speculate that because children of abusive or neglectful parents must ever be wary of those parents' states of being, or how they seem, a corresponding neglect of self-states, and therefore reflective function, is developed.

The person presenting with a distorted interpretation of reality is inattentive to his own thoughts and feelings in any truly reflective sense, but rather preoccupied with self-states of another in a way that does not accommodate the separateness of those others, and therefore such people lack empathy. Kids like Aaron were paranoid; frightened, yet taking leave of themselves through a readiness to fight—a commonly chosen (if choice can be applied here) means of dissociation for troubled kids. This made the task of connecting with some kids extremely difficult, and I was often at pains to persuade these disturbed youths that I had worthy intentions. But this often fell on deaf ears. Or rather it lodged only in those clients' left brains, and was therefore unconvincing. As one mentor once put it to me, "Your clients are not in relationship with you. Not really. They are in relationship with you plus the aggregate of everyone who has ever entered their lives, beginning most prominently with those early caregivers." So, my clients would not perceive me as a separate person, individualized in my own right—at least, not for quite some time. I had to be patient and consistent if I were to gain trust. I had to learn to accept this as they projected their needs and frustrations onto me.

I learned this quite pointedly with a spiky-tempered kid on my caseload nicknamed Ray Joe. I privately conjoined the names, emphasizing the *rage* in my pronunciation, for it seemed to me that hate formed the basis of our therapeutic alliance: his feeling of hate, and my wariness of that hate. In meetings, he'd avoid eye contact with me, and snarl if I asked him a question. In one-on-one sessions his hands would fidget and his teeth would grind. I recall that his thumb and forefinger did this repetitive action, suggestive of muscle memory, which simulated the flicking of a Zippo lighter. "Can I go now?" was his most consistently asked question. A physically nondescript young man from Santa Rosa, his antipathy towards me was mostly inexplicable; that is, until he decided one day to inform me as to the reasons for his attitude. It was in a public setting, surprisingly: during the weekly therapy group facilitated by the head psychiatrist of the group home track.

Ray Joe declared in an even, unemotional voice that my manner, posture, and general appearance reminded him of his hated step-father, a man who had relentlessly derogated him since he was four years old. His biological father was both a criminal and a chronic absentee. Ray Joe had never met him and was by this time sixteen. He was graciously sharing with me the context of his hostility, and more or less apologizing for any offense, and doing so with witnesses. But he did not promise change, and his revelations still implied a warning for me to keep away. Change, it seemed, would not be on the table for discussion, no matter where his insights might take him. So far, he seemed aware of only half of his projections, and so it seemed that a huge piece of his story was still missing. The exchange with him was eerie; Ray Joe's creepy menace left me still feeling wary, even as I thanked him for his seemingly honest words. He had exiled feeling, assigned to me not only the role of would-be critic, but of distant father. He was preemptive in his defenses. In his life he had sought to make himself invisible and dovetailed alcohol abuse and runaways as his principal methods of coping. Basically, he and others like him would not *do* feelings; at least, not as I had come to understand them. They might talk about feelings; might even theorize about their feelings, or explain why they didn't do feelings—why they were *chill*—and why they should therefore be sort of excused from things like therapy, and from emotions in general, except those that erupted impulsively, chaotically, and necessarily, like rage.

Sometime later, the invisibility of Ray Joe was rudely shattered. Called up for a hot seat in a confrontation group, Ray Joe was asked to explain a host of contracts suggesting he'd been responsible for the smuggling of alcohol onto the unit. From the moment that he rose to his feet, I watched intently and studied his body language. He stood gingerly with his arms slung unevenly. Another counselor performed the obligatory "stand up straight" directive and Ray Joe twitched, jolted only slightly into correct position. His eyes betrayed regret: he should have run while he had the chance, his eyes said—while he was on the field trip? That's where he'd gotten the alcohol, said other kids. On route to a river in West Marin for a kayaking excursion, staff had inadvisably stopped at a grocery store for reasons that were never entirely made clear, though sideways glances suggested that a staff-to-staff hot seat might proceed from that decision. Ray Joe was taken into the store along with two other boys, supposedly to help carry items purchased. Ray Joe cooperated with that task, but also helped himself to a bottle of Hennessey, and somehow managed to slip it past the watching eyes of store clerks and monitoring staff.

The hot seat lasted nearly an hour. Firstly, it pored over the details of the incident, with staff leading the inquisition, with ambitious, mostly approval-seeking peers chiming in with challenging remarks. As the process transitioned from a deconstruction of the event to an exploration of "why", the more experienced inquisitors pushed the envelope, speaking past the glib explanation—"because he's an addict"—that all too often blunts these kinds of conversations. The process softened, partly because Ray Joe had lapsed into a taciturn whisper, and many in the room had become weary of asking him to speak up. But something else was also happening: an unspoken sense of Ray Joe's vulnerability, even as his shoulders performed metronomic shrugs every thirty seconds—his unconscious attempt to "shrug off" (that is, get rid) of pain. The program director stepped forward, ready to do what she'd done effectively on other occasions: use herself, her body, her demeanor and presence, and absorb the youth into an emotive experience.

To both hear and witness all that was happening, one had to be situated within a few feet. The room got quiet and the director matched Ray Joe's volume. Though it was a public moment, with another twenty or so people in the room, the moment got private and felt somewhat dangerous. From behind the director's right shoulder, I caught fragments of sentences, words like "father", "pain" mixed with phrases like "you've suffered so much." Ray Joe's eyes were fixed upon a space on the floor, to the right of the director's thigh. As the minutes wore on, the occasional yawn could be heard in the room. Time was scarce, and many sensed that the process was nearing an end. For the most part, Ray Joe's affect, his expression, even his line of sight, hadn't budged throughout the hour. The director persisted, however, with a kind of mirroring soliloquy that meandered, stopped, and then aimed to strike at decisive moments. At about the fifty minute mark, something broke. Ray Joe's face—it broke, as in collapsed—and his body went with him. His features crumpling, he fell forward and let out a deep whine that lasted several seconds. He paused, looked up and perhaps panicked over the fact of his visibility. Witnesses! Uncontrollably, he resumed his sobs, and the director invited peers and staff, including myself, to enfold the young man in a group embrace.

Ray Joe didn't escape consequences for his transgression, and sometime later he was discharged due to a separate incident of drug-seeking behavior. A few disgruntled voices would decry the kind of tactics used in his and others' hot seats—the director's seeming intrusiveness, for example, which may have been ill-advised considering Ray Joe's likely abuse history. Orcutt (2012) writes that therapists should not touch sufferers during what psychoanalysts call abreaction, as touch can be misunderstood as part of the traumatic re-experience, the "emerging scenario" as she puts it. She may be right. From my point of view, however, the impression of shaming or intrusion was offset by the sense that something momentous was occurring; that Ray Joe got to experience nurturing before he left. As staff, we felt held by the notion that we were providing an experience, or at least an opportunity for a corrective experience, that few of the kids would receive elsewhere; that it was rare and memorable; painful, yet worth the struggle…maybe?

Impulse control and powerlessness

Regarding the back-stories of substance abusers, a 12-step counselor or a social psychologist might agree that disturbed kids were afflicted with poor attachment histories, manifest as poor reality testing and deficits in reflective functioning, or observe with interest scientific discoveries about the unparalleled value of right brain to right brain communication. Asserting a more plainspoken argument, they might apply the word powerlessness to the mix of explanations for what is termed the disease of addiction[10]. The word powerlessness is central to the 12-step movement: those accepting powerlessness over addiction are afforded hope because such an acceptance is said to diminish denial patterns that thwart recovery. That's the paradoxical value of powerlessness, and the implied rebuke to those who suggest that terms like addiction are merely stigmatizing. One is empowered by the surrender of self-will: that's the idea. For the concerned observer of social problems, the concept of powerlessness is less a prescription for disturbed individuals as it is an explanation of their plight. Those marginalized by society, who cannot find jobs, who are ignored or feel rejected by teachers, abused at home, and without hope for the future, are sensitive to transient, seemingly trivial provocations because their spheres of empowerment seem constricted around such events.

On the surface, it seemed to me that kids got into fights not so much because of gang rivalries or social marginalization, but instead because of more plainly interpersonal conflicts, such as that incident with Eddie and his hapless rival. Someone gets looked at the wrong way, and feels disrespected; someone's shoulder gets bumped, and feels threatened, at risk of being a *punk*. For those feeling a surfeit of frustrations or humiliations in their lives, and without a place, the aptitude, or even the permission to speak openly of these stressors, "stupid stuff" becomes inflated in meaning. Seemingly trivial stressors are the proverbial straws on camels' backs. As a result, thousands of clients have struggled their way through Therapeutic Communities walking a knife edge.

Add to this low self esteem, short attention spans, underlying insecure attachment styles, genetic codes, and who knows what else—perhaps an excess of soft plastic and corn syrup in our supermarkets. In the space of a year-long program, the idea of treatment was to attempt a thorough re-socialization of kids, with appeals to client motivation girding the unsteady, unknowing path through a diffuse treatment plan. Again: through repetition. Clients, it was ever believed, actually wanted the promise land that is relief from chronic difficulties. Even if they didn't understand the obstacles that stood in their way, most wanted what was promised at the finish line: pride, self-esteem, aliveness; acceptance, both of themselves and from others—that deliverance from fear of which Fenichal wrote. But they wouldn't achieve those ends simply because they wanted them; and they wouldn't get there via fantasies of fight or flight, and certainly not by proclaiming themselves precipitately cured.

The tertiary arm of reality testing was limit setting, featuring a system of punitive assignments ("learning experiences"), particularly in the early stages of a client's program: limits set on poor impulse control in response to acts of sexual acting out, or violence. (instances of relapse, or "drug-seeking" were comparatively fewer, largely due to relative lack of opportunity) Drug use, or sexual acts (or sexualized behavior, including the writing of notes to opposite sex peers) were to be met with a special assignment called *Reassessment*. Reassessment, understood literally, meant that a client's placement in the program was under review; that is, under threat. Resumption of normal participation in activities would be contingent upon the client's completion of a rigorous set of tasks (typically written essays plus household chores), as well as the determination of a sufficiently remorseful attitude. At any given time, at least one kid in the program would be on reassessment for breaking the weightily termed "Cardinal" rules (which included instances of drug use and among other things, violence, stealing, or sexual acts). But reassessment was rarely as cutthroat as the term implies. Some kids would accrue nearly a dozen reassessment episodes before management would proverbially show them the door. Ray Joe, for example, had about five or six reassessments before he was discharged.

Relapse in the program sometimes merited a discharge from the program, but rarely upon a first offense, unless the episode was egregious. Once a client absconded in the dead of night, climbing onto the facility's roof via its outdoor patio, and then abseiled down to the ground beyond the building's perimeter with some rope pilfered from the maintenance department. The kid then strolled down to a neighborhood liquor store, somehow procured a slew of forty ounce beer bottles, and then sneaked back on to the unit to share his spoils with other Thunder Road peers. I know. I write "somehow" as though these behaviors rivaled magic tricks performed by Vegas headlining acts. Well, they might have. The boy also managed to elude the attention of the program's nocturnal staff, both when leaving the facility, and again upon his return. Aside from being impressed with the young man's athleticism and ingenuity, the program leadership was unimpressed with the behavior, and even less so with his attitude, and so the kid was soon returned to juvenile hall, but not before receiving a hot seat in front of the male community. Staff reviewed the incident in front of everyone: as the group leader spoke of alcohol reeking through the air vents of the group home, a smirk emerged on the face of the offending boy and rippled briefly among his peers. That triggered an onslaught of confrontations, some from his peers, but mostly from staff.

What followed were hot diatribes declaring that the young man had not only placed his own life in danger, but those of others also. Had he not so blatantly shared his ill-gotten gains with his peers, or shown just the slightest bit of remorse during his hot seat, a second chance might have been afforded him. In other words, he might have gotten a reassessment and stayed in the program. Unfortunately, the mischief of his initial act was followed by a well-practiced shutting down of emotion and—smirk notwithstanding—not without some justification. He was plainly berated in front of nearly thirty people. His defenses dug in. He fell silent and affected a stolid demeanor. Then the group became frustrated. The hot seat deteriorated, became an unwieldy, ungoverned exercise with multiple voices from staff and clients alike all thrusting interventions like darts. Everyone seemed determined to ask the golden question or make the decisive insight—anything to penetrate the client's wall. It was like watching a flogging. Flanking three ardent-looking members of management, I issued some feckless words as to how the client was feeling. Then someone else threw a question out as if I'd not said anything. I faded into the background, intimidated by authority, the groupspeak. I wanted someone to step forward, observe the quieted young man and check his pulse to see if he was still alive. Eventually, someone called a halt to the ordeal and he was escorted from the room, and he was not seen in the facility again. Unfortunate. The confrontations, taken in terms of their content, seemed necessary, but this episode seems an example of how our methods sometimes got away from us.

Not all confrontation groups were this intense, or interrogating. Many were simply deadened exercises, while others still were warm, truly heartfelt explorations. The divisions were observable: the kids who were either uninterested, well-defended, or both, slumped over, straining against the pull of sleep. They'd look up just long enough to cast bemused sideways sneers at those who seemed more engaged. Some kids were more compliant, sitting wide-eyed and nodding. Then there was one other faction, of kids who really did want something else for themselves, who spared staff members from their cynicism. They were perked up, interested in the process, and were often thrusting their thumbs forward in order to speak their minds. These were the rich times, these heavier groups. Time seemed to stand still on these occasions. The room would heat up, but not so much with tension as with meaning. At the end of such activities I felt as though I was part of something important—that I was helping people in this world of adolescent drug treatment—and I'd leave for home with a smile on my face.

Due to the structure of the program—its capacity to limit some behaviors better than others—drug use wasn't even the biggest source of concern within these hotly contentious groups. Acts of sex and aggression were. Officially, acts of violence were supposed to be met with expulsion from the program. To be violent or sexual was to violate two of the so-called Cardinal rules. This seemed politic if parents of non-legally mandated kids were to be convinced of program safety. In reality, I think that hundreds of couplings and beatings, some minor, some severe, have occurred over the years with varying degrees of punishment being meted out. The truth is that not every kid that got serviced, or bled another's nose or bruised another's rib with so-called "body shots" got kicked out, not by a—excuse me—long shot.

Behavior Modification: "consequences"

Emotionally-driven confrontations groups were one thing; the more common and mundane confrontations of negative behaviors were another. The kids with significant ego deficits reacted badly to the day-to-day imposition of "consequences", whether they were assignments to write one-page essays, three-day bans from the rooms containing the video games, or else more spontaneously, the frequent commands to take a seat upon one of the Therapeutic Community's iconic wooden benches. Alas, the bench. Along with a set of mirrors lining the hallways, the bench was one of two devices commonly used for on-the-spot containment of client acting out. The bench was a half time-out device, half a place for quiet rumination, at least in theory. Drawn from adult Therapeutic Community programs, the bench was one ten "key treatment concepts" as outlined in a Thunder Road-produced manual in 2003. While a previous generation might have associations with the "go stand in the corner" clichés of severe classrooms, I think that latter day kids will have thought of the bench as a kind of penalty box—sometimes welcome, usually not. It was the kids' school requirement that triggered the most number of benchings. Hitherto, at nine in the morning of an average day, most Thunder Road clients will have practiced truancy with evolving sophistication. The typical Thunder Road kid had experienced numerous suspensions, and a fair share of expulsions, with truancy being cited as the least of their offences. Walking out of a classroom, either out of boredom, disgust, or else at the insistence of an angry teacher had been a common enough experience for many. However, being told to leave the room and then sit quietly on a wooden bench for twenty minutes will have been unheard of.

The intent was for the bench to serve as a place to reflect; that is, for youth to consider the inappropriateness of their negative behaviors; to reflect upon the distress brought to a teacher, the disruption brought to a classroom (or a group, if that was the case). The benches lined the hallways of the milieu, sometimes situated opposite one another, otherwise at intermittent intervals. Staff were meant to monitor a client's "bench time": to maintain the correct standards, which included silence, proper posture (hands on knees, back straight), and appropriate signals for attention (that versatile thumbs-up gesture). Bench time was meant to last in 20 minute increments, but could conceivably last for hours during marathon group sessions, with stretch breaks woven into these 20 minute segments. Over the years, the bench has been the source of many debates—some private, in management circles—some open to an all-staff contribution. Controversial yet oddly beloved, the bench was a device, a therapeutic tool, deemed cruel and unusual by some, an inspired proto-meditation device by others. The accurate view is somewhere in between, I think. At least when utilized properly, the bench was a tool that saved many kids from themselves. It enabled, gave an opportunity, to suspend action long enough for an impulse to abate, even if fixed beliefs, levels of frustrations did not. A wooden bench of about six feet in length and about a foot deep was therefore situated outside just about every room used for a therapeutic or educational purpose, save for the assessment rooms used for intake interviews. The bench was an instant reminder of impending consequence: a gloomy symbol of infantilization, of the shame of expulsion, and an artifact of both an individual and systemic need for control.

It's difficult to say whether Therapeutic Community tools like the bench are an effective intervention device in a treatment setting. Researchers like Wilson, Gottfredson, and Najaka (2001) have studied techniques in treatment settings and determined that restraint measures, isolation techniques, or lecturing are ineffective in eliminating unacceptable or concerning behavior (cited in Kalke, Glantaon, and Cristalli, 2007). Interventions may be considered effective when clients exhibit measurable changes in behavior, for example, but in a milieu wherein multiple interventions of different types (even different pedigree) are evident, how can researchers track that which might be responsible for change?

At Thunder Road, the bench wasn't the only tool of intervention at staff's disposal, just the most commonly and most spontaneously used. Otherwise, the behavior modification system consisted of an array of jobs assigned to clients, formed in a hierarchical order (rewards for progress), and a process whereby clients and staff would pass out what were called "bookings" for negative behavior. These bookings, paper slips with infractions curtly scribbled upon them, were passed out like parking tickets by kids assigned a monitoring role called "team captain". The team captain would book a peer for breaking a rule such as "respecting staff and peers", write something like, "disrespecting staff" across the slip, and then approach the offending client for a signature upon the slip, signifying acknowledgement. At this stage, contrition wasn't required—only compliance was. Then, at a later date, bookings for the week would be gathered by staff from a box wherein team captains had been directed to deposit their quotas. Staff would then review the bookings and from that point onwards give assignments based upon the patterns indicated.

Sometimes the assignments were tongue-in-cheek and intended as fun, sort of. I remember a veteran staff member named Bobby, a fixture in the milieu during the nineties, who was known for his gruff approach and somewhat un-PC assignments. Standing beside a six-foot wide mirror, he'd preside over a girl staring into the glass and repeating the supposedly affirming line, "naughty girls don't cuss" as her post-booking assignment. Otherwise, he'd assign what were called image-breakers to especially tough-minded boys: a clothing change involving pens in pockets, a bow tie, and most importantly, a pair of bright red suspenders. This was nerd insertion: emasculation, driven with gentle humor, and for the most part it was received that way. The sexism of these chores was coyly indulged. So called "mirror time" and image breakers were standard repertoire, though any given assignment might reflect the idiosyncrasies of the overseeing staff. The idea of any assignment, whether it was verbal, written, or even performance-related, was for day to day and moment to moment infractions to be identified, and then be subject to a learning experience. The spirit was punitive, but it wasn't malevolent. It was an opportunity for clients and staff to practice this oft-promoted idea of community: of negotiating conflict, the demonstration of leadership and cooperation.

Of course, there were all different kinds of responses to the bookings dispensed, and the assignments later given. Often kids would create a scene over the initial booking, and compel staff intervention because of a seeming escalation of tempers. This especially happened when clients received bookings from other clients, as many were unaccustomed to being subject to a peer's authority, even those kids who came from families with multiple siblings. Many kids displayed their avoidance patterns, especially if booked by adults. These were the kids that walked off back to their rooms, and shouted insults from beneath their pillows. The will to aggression, towards revenge, competed with self-loathing, the desire to hide and be left alone. These kids perceived confrontation as a kind of assault—threats tantamount to abuse, abandonment, or simple disregard, because those were the associations that were downloaded earlier in life. Those parental limits that had been set—those ancient "don't do that", or "what are you thinking" remarks, and punishments meted out—limits we might ordinarily associate with parenting, had accompanied a range of preoccupied states and sometimes disorganized states. Some parents had been abusive. Some were merely distracted. Some had simply not been around.

Being there. For many, this was and is good enough. Being present, consistently, is as good a characterization of caring as any other. Scott Peck wrote of love in *The Road Less Traveled*, the philosophical gem adopted by the 12-step community after its publication in the late seventies, and commented that love entailed above all else the giving of one's time and attention to another. Implicit at Thunder Road was the understanding that being consistently present in every sense of the word was the most important quality of any staff or peer within the community. As one oft-rejected yet resilient parent once put it to me, "it's all about showing up." Predictability, over time, was indeed soothing for many; it provided safety, and in some cases, was sufficient in and of itself for the containment of negative behaviors. This is why consistency of rules, and of structure, seemed so important: the predictability of the treatment experience came to represent an antidote to unpredictable lives. It's just unfortunate that while rules and structure may have been consistent for clients, the same could not be said for staff composition. Most clinical staff members outside of management came and went within a year, let alone several.

Clients in the milieu soothingly focused on the external, upon what they observed, and much less upon *what* was explained to them. What they observed was filtered through past experience, through the bond with the person engaging with them at any given time. Fonagy (2006) argues that insecurely attached children come to experience their own arousal as a danger sign for abandonment, which triggers a crudely teleological, non-mentalizing function; one that makes quick judgments as to others' intentions. The securely attached individual may feel safe in making attributions of mental states, thoughts and feelings that are not immediately apparent, to account for others' behavior. The avoidant person shuns the mental state of the other to a significant degree, instead condensing it into a simplified package. The resistant or ambivalently attached focuses on the state of distress, to the exclusion of others' thoughts and feelings. The disorganized, meanwhile, represent a special category: hypervigilant of caregivers' behavior, they use all cues available for prediction and may be acutely sensitized to intentional states, and thus prepared to construct a concise view of others' feeling states, but remain uncomprehending of their own.

Fonagy goes on to argue that while the faculty may be underdeveloped in some due to lack of repetitive neuronal activity paired with it, it may be further arrested in neglected or abused children because for them recognition of the mental state of oneself or the other can be dangerous to the self. For example, the child who recognizes the hatred or murderousness implied by the parent's act of abuse is forced to see him or herself as worthless or unlovable. Put another way, the child is rendered unsafe by an acknowledgement of reality. Reassurance of safety in defiance of historical experience seems false, which further undermines the capacity to trust inner reality[11]. Abuse trains the individual to attend primarily to the physical world, to be hypervigilant of external cues, but distrustful of playfulness, disregarding of internal worlds, feelings that may disorient, shame, or persecute.

This person is arrested at a point wherein all that matters is sensation, and appearance. I've heard clients allude to this strategy when questioned about family history: "I thought if I did what was right, that would keep him from being mad," reported one teen, explaining a history of seeming compliance with a violent father. Did? Behavior: not thoughts, and certainly not feelings—what he *did*. As for those clients who insist that therapists, program directors, and judges do not like them, they are convinced of such realities because the external cues tell them such things are true, and ironically, because they *feel* it. As to the true significance of their own feelings—of their history, or its layered meanings—they are not only uncomprehending, they are dismissive. These things simply do not matter. Perception in the here and now was what mattered.

But what strikes me most about the compromised reality testing of these clients was not so much their distortions, but the strange way in which surrounding adults—parents, collateral professionals, even staff—at times mirrored these patterns. The reasons: either because they had developed that way themselves, or because they had surrendered to the chronic nature of the problem. About countertransference: there was never enough time, it seemed, to give it the attention it was due; never enough time for a parallel reflective function across all the divisions of staff, or the divisions beyond even. Therefore, it was easy to act on automatic pilot: to focus upon clients' behavior, the broad and troublesome question of "how to keep kids off drugs" that was overly directive and pragmatic. It seemed expedient to focus on behavior, or thinking instead of underlying affects; to be didactic or even heavyhanded; to reassure escalating teens that treatment was safe when sometimes it wasn't and in the process disregard subjective experience. Alongside the overall cohesiveness of the program, the air continued to seem thin, and space for real movement seemed tight.

3

A TYRANNY OF NUMBERS

A teleological process

Step back even and consider teleological process in industry, and within society as a whole, and one can easily see how treatment becomes a numbers game. At Thunder Road, there are fifty beds to be filled within the hospital unit. Now, rarely has all fifty beds been filled at any given time. In fact, over the last decade of my employment, the hospital rarely filled over forty of those beds for a meaningfully sustained period. However, a certain minimum census had to be maintained at all times. The success and/or failure of the program similarly rested upon this idea of numbers. From 2001 to 2004, when my role was that of a coordinator of Thunder Road's modestly-sized outpatient program, I was charged with the task of maintaining a minimum caseload over a period of months lest funding be thereafter cut as a result of failing to meet a numerical threshold.

I could cite the examples ad nauseum, which may seem unnecessary. The economic realities that govern our lives needn't be bludgeoned into our minds. Or, perhaps they do: those are the ingredients of another kind of reality testing after all. But on this question of reality, I'm not only referring to money, but rather to a more fundamentally economical, and physical way of perceiving reality. Those who study outcomes in treatment programs, psychotherapeutic practices: what are they really looking at? In science, this process of assessment might be referred to as empiricism, versus the more philosophical construct of teleology. What is the baseline barometer at which we are left staring come the end of the working day? Fancifully, I might argue that our community, our politics, seems rife with crude, teleological observations, blunted reflective function, lack of empathy, and a resultant failure to bond.

Our society seems reductionist on many levels: its thinking is black and white, dualistic. And so it is with adolescent residential treatment. Is the client doing well in the program? a parent or probation officer will ask. Yes or no: fit that square peg into that round hole, leaving just enough room for a cursory mention of context. What's the progress on the treatment plan? asks the referral or funding source. How many instances of "negative" behavior, as outlined in goal item #2, have occurred since the last report? Has the number dropped, from behaving aggressively on 8 out of 10 ten instances, to 5? Cue the legal representative: has the client relapsed? Are they doing their homework? Or has he or she had any more episodes of stealing or disrespect towards staff since the last team discussion? Are they still disrupting groups, passing gas while others are sharing; reclining on the sofas, eyes closed, arguing about whether this constitutes acceptable participation? Do we have charts on this stuff? Based on all this data, when do you think he or she should be honorably discharged, and can the discharge report be faxed over by noon? Note here the tyranny of numbers, the sheer omnipotence of economy.

Parents of troubled teens are left with a similar lens. Has my son or daughter been expelled from school? Have they been arrested? Are their grades dropping, or have the number of classes cut this semester gone down or up? More ambiguously, they might ask, are they respecting me and my household? Regarding the need to follow rules and follow structure, many parents resonated with Thunder Road's strict regimen of rules, having experienced firsthand their kids' resistance to their own limits. Others seemed oblivious as to how they'd contributed to their kids' problems, or else they were painfully aware of their contribution yet quietly protective of homeostatic lies. After all the tangible gauges of reality had been checked, parents would consider a climactic deprivation: the denied access to their kids' interior lives.

Regarding the inner lives of humans, we know that we can utilize brain scans and demonstrate that the brains of alcoholics are markedly different than those of the general population. Empirically, we can demonstrate that dopamine levels or numbers of serotonin receptors are greater in those with secure attachments. MRI, or magnetic resonance imaging, examines brain activation during standard cognitive tasks that excite attention, perception, or memory. Electroencephalogram technology has implicated anterior regions of the left and right cerebral hemispheres in the expression and/or experience of emotions. Through skin conductance technology, measurements of heart rates can offer objective assessments of stress, sometimes contrasting with subjects' self reports or outward appearance. So can assessments of Cortisol levels drawn from saliva samples. To this extent, we can see what's happening inside, to measure cognitive activity, stress reactivity. None of this stuff is available to teachers, therapists, counselors in and out of group homes, or parents. Meaning, the day-to-day assessments—those ordinary judgments made by parents, legal officials, and mental health professionals as to the functioning of kids at places like Thunder Road: this is guesswork; subjective guesswork that moves circularly and settles back upon a default position. What is it that we're observing? What is reality?

Therefore, it seems problematic to urge troubled kids not to "judge a book by its cover", as we commonly teach kids, not to mention clients of all ages; to ask them to observe not only the external cues of a situation, but to imagine what may be an alternative explanation, an unseen reality—the opinions and feelings of others, as well as the hidden feelings of one's own self—when adult systems are judging by covers also. How can we fault those who in closer quarters, on the back of a lifetime's experience, robotically employ a similar principle? This was the kind of conundrum that perplexed me as I worked through different levels of drug treatment. I was developing that "voice" as my one-time co-facilitator had called it, and realizing that this voice had two dimensions, an outside and inside reality. On occasion I'd watch from the wings as clients were escorted from the facility in the care of stolid police officers. The reason for police: The clients' breaking of Cardinal rules. From those trespasses motivational interpretations were made and decisions were lain down. Dishonorably discharged kids left with a two-fold purpose: to accept what was happening externally, and to live with *that* reality. Then, an internal process: what is the truth?

A blocking of reflection

I wasn't always watching from the wings. Sometimes I followed clients as they were being led out of the building, or else sat with them as they collapsed into corners of their rooms, emotionally falling apart at the sight of uniformed officers dutifully poised to lead them away. I once followed a male client from the milieu to the back seat of a police car. After taking a moment to take in the strangeness of the compartment, I looked into the kid's tear-stained eyes; his look of betrayal, and the wincing expression caused by handcuffs that were chaffing at his wrists. He'd been repeatedly implicated by staff in attempts (partly successful) at so-called gender-splitting: flirting and other sexualized activity directed at the girls on the unit. Cardinal rules: he kept breaking them. The young man had denied all the allegations, which had been reported persistently since the beginning of his program. Flat denials, coupled with epithets directed at his accusers. I wasn't one of the accusers, but I wasn't his advocate either. Outwardly, I was neutral, yet implicitly I supported the treatment team's decision to discharge dishonorably, sending him back to a detention camp. And this kid understood this. As strange as it was to sit in the back seat of a police car attempting a "one-on-one" with a troubled and expelled youth, it was stranger still to sit with him offering trite encouragements while listening to his persecutory diatribe, and believing the whole time that he was lying through his teeth.

After being an intern for several months, I became a full-time employee of Thunder Road, a case manager. Case manager was and is an ambiguously-defined position, a term interchangeable with the term therapist or counselor in a hospital-based program, just as client, teen, youth, or "kid" may be referenced alternately. One definition of case manager was that of a therapist to a caseload of typically six kids and a principal point of contact for what are collectively termed collateral contacts: parents, social workers, probation officers; sometimes lawyers. For management, therapy, counseling, and case management are more or less conflated concepts. In my full-time position, I was often situated to make a decision, and do so upon a hazy congealing of observations: some of them external—the so-called "behaviors"—others based upon my insights, my tentative insights, contaminated as they may have been by fantasies, projections; my wishful thinking. But in general, there seemed to be little incentive for counselors at Thunder Road to focus upon the inner worlds of clients.

Meanwhile, the inner lives of many clients and their parents—some might say most clients and their parents—were largely concealed by opaque fronts. Most of the kids struggled to identify feeling states, and as a result resisted doing so, the way most people resist doing something they don't think they're good at. Many kids would pay lip service to reflection because it appeared to be what adults wanted to hear; the path of least resistance. In the first week of a client's program, they'd be given a packet of assignments, filled with open-ended questions designed to stir later conversations, the grinding of the therapeutic wheels. This was the welcome packet to the first stage of treatment, designed to last roughly ninety days for those in the long term program. The main task in this first stage of treatment was to adhere to structure and assimilate reality: get used to living at Thunder Road, and consider the impact of drugs upon one's life. Within those work packets were also sheets of words: a vocabulary cheat-sheet. Attached were cartoonish renderings of dozens of faces, matched to the list of words. The somewhat remedial task was for clients to use these sheets and develop a tongue for the therapeutic process.

Those packets, returned within days by clients and filled with brief replies to involved questions, reflected a two, sometimes three-fold problem: sub-literacy (or English as second language) married to limited motivation and habitual emotional thwarting. Clients railed against these assignments. In seeming advocacy of their own poor reflective function, clients mustered strong arguments against the psychotherapeutic basics. There would be a catalog of rationales, defensive patterns of thinking that could be summoned at will: "Time to move on"; "It's no good dwelling on what you can't control"; the especially insidious "what's the point? It won't change anything"; and finally, even the co-opting of 12-step isms like "letting go", as in "let go of those feelings", for the more sophisticated of prevaricators. "I don't give a shit!" was the less sanitized version of this defense. This was the kind of language invoked in the devaluation of talk therapy, to indicate the utter futility of symbolic (as in use of language) expression, and to assert that the problem is not so much one of "not talking about it," but rather one of "talking about it".

I had issues with the standard two-page essays that were assigned to the often sub-literate clients in the program, though the problem wasn't really one of literacy, in my opinion. As indicated previously, many of the clients struggled with the whole concept of reflective functioning. They seemed unwired for the task that was routinely asked of them. "Write a 500 essay on how your actions impacted the community," was a typically-worded assignment. Ideally, such assignments would link back to initial interventions wherein the groundwork will have been laid for the later essay. A staff member's interruption of disruptive behavior might be followed by a benching, and after a period of twenty minutes or so of time-out, perhaps a thoughtful deconstruction of the incident in question. That would give the intervention a chance. Then the written assignment could build upon an initial understanding between client and staff.

All too often it didn't happen this way. The bench might be used appropriately enough as a time-out device, but then misused if no follow-up exchange occurred. Sometimes this happened if clients seemed too agitated to engage in proper reflection, even after a half hour or so. As a result, staff members might precipitately disengage, not wanting to inflame a fragile situation, or else be blamed by management for an escalation of mood and negative behavior. A booking might follow, but with little explanation, so the subsequent essays were inevitably vapid. At Thunder Road staff accumulated such a mass of dead literature that no one really knew how to process. Honestly, the amount of paper that has been used to write the above-described essays, print rote repetitions of 12-step slogans, or to make perfunctory amends over behaviors whose meaning to clients was thinly understood, should astound. Once I was told that client records that were more than seven years old were archived in a locked vault, embedded within the side of a mountain somewhere in Colorado. In my view there should be another vault, embedded in a separate mountain, filled with the written work of clients from Thunder Road and places like it, and then emptied for a thorough recycling of paper.

I think the preference for assigning essays was about a couple of things: first of all, about faith in the written word as an organizer of thought; and secondly, the norm of giving assignments is borrowed from the academic model—school as a reference point for those in the learning process. On the first point, a colleague of mine in private practice recently offered her rationale for giving "homework". "Addicts are notorious for their distortions," she argued pleasantly. She was speaking of their tendency to filter out unwanted information in a verbal exchange; the "that's not what you said" phenomenon that so often occurs between addicts, helpers, and loved ones. Fair enough, I think, though I'd add that drug addicts aren't the only ones prone to this behavior. Secondly, if the written word—meaning written assignments, rules sheets, informational handouts—are more effective in containing memories, can this be proven? That is, are we sure that the written word fosters retention, versus an oral tradition? I'd wish for someone from an ancient druidic preservation society to enter that discussion.

As a case manager, it was my job to read these clients' essays, most of which turned me off for good from teaching in the public school system. Peers of mine sometimes made patronizing comments about clients' written work; others still appeared to be impressed by the thoughtfulness of the kids on their caseloads. I thought there was a self-serving side to this: case managers, invested in the progress of their clients, would sometimes engage in a little promotion on their behalf, with a sideways implication that said case managers' diligence and open hearts had been the stokers of recovery. There were jealousies between counselors, I thought. I believed this because I felt the jealousies myself, and projected those jealousies onto others. Nonetheless, I detected real competition at times, over whose caseload was the most stable; who graduated the most kids from their caseloads; who achieved the most meaningful bonds with their clients, and so on. With respect to clients' progress, I was ever skeptical. Cynical, you might think, but I don't think: the limitations of the kids were not their fault, and as a result, I was rarely indignant. But neither was I saddled with false hope, or false expectations. I wanted kids in the program to get better, but more often than not, I didn't need them to. I believed the kids at Thunder Road were not only limited in their capacity, they were deeply wounded. That program director was right about this, and what the kids needed, in my opinion, was a rigorous, conscious, here and now attention to their long-standing problems.

The assignments routinely missed their marks. I guess I think that the written word, ultimately, misses the mark. But specifically, writing an essay about an event twenty four hours in the past, when the client had by that time moved on to another half dozen or so equally misunderstood stressors, was a near-meaningless exercise as far as I was concerned. Moreover, as they were meant to be two-pages long, little follow-up was done on such essays, owing to the belief that writing two or three pages was sufficient work for any client. This process allowed for little feedback, little room for response. If the client wrote something in an essay that didn't make sense, or else begged further exploration, it didn't matter. The exercises were over upon their half-hearted completion. To request further writing would have incurred the clients' wrath, for in writing the essays, they had already done what had been asked of them. Who cared whether or not there was an incipient example of reflection in a client's paper? The clients didn't, for the most part. What they cared about was being compliant, and thereafter receiving the credit for such compliance.

"Secrets keep you sick" reads one of the most notable slogans of the 12-step community. Broadly speaking, the ethic is meant to chastise the toxic silence of an isolated, addictive system. Those tethered to the lifestyle, or as yet unconvinced by the promises of an alternative, rebut forcefully that the reverse is true. As a result, therapists at Thunder Road were often a source of irritation for clients, because therapists, above all, embody this invitation to open up and emote truthfully with feelings other than those along the continuum of anger[12]. Talking about (as in around) feelings was fine, or talking about not having feelings was fine. Bright kids like Ray Joe could easily catch on that a theoretical referencing of feelings might suffice for many who were scrutinizing their process, hence the acceptance of abstraction and a baseline accommodation of metaphors. But some things crossed the line of comfort and adaptation, like those moments when the director approached kids in confrontation groups and used touch, eliciting catharsis, sometimes abreaction. At those moments, words might not have been necessary, even. Thunder Road's most formidable and present personalities may have burdened some, but they bonded and held many others, modeling strength, the promise not to abandon. They exuded knowledge—implicit knowledge, if you like.

The discomfort with the basic assumptions, techniques, and goals of psychotherapy was a big reason why many kids at Thunder Road didn't readily attach to their therapists, but instead to other staff members, such as cooks, maintenance workers, or even receptionists. On the one hand, this may seem counter-intuitive. Surely, clients would gravitate towards those whose primary job it was to be empathetic, compassionately listening, and suggestive of ways to cope best with stressors. Well, not necessarily. For those kids who had already experienced intrusive or anxious care-giving, or who were not readily motivated for treatment, the eagerness of therapists looking to get in touch with their clients' inner lives was off-putting, if not frightening. These distrusting kids would be the ones who would experiment in their mingling, much as they had done in their families and peer circles. They might attach with a seemingly peripheral, yet consistently available figure amongst staff, and ask after ways to help out with physical tasks so as to keep out of trouble and away from the spotlight. They might pretend to go about a manual chore with resentment, but later confide that such activities were far more preferable than taking part in anything therapeutic. This was also the reason why demarcations between clinical staff and other departments (save for administration) were illusory. Often, the first person to hear of a family secret, or a troublesome contract, was a member of the kitchen staff, or a nurse, or the art therapist who visited only once a week but was otherwise separate from the treatment team. The reason: Because for many kids they will have seemed the least intrusive; quietly interested and concerned, perhaps, but the least agenda-driven.

I'm sure that many of the lesser experienced non-clinical staff will have been surprised by these curious intimacies, and perhaps rendered anxious about what to do in such situations. In later years, when I became a clinical supervisor and held the image of a consulting expert, staff members from the periphery of the treatment team would sometimes approach me and ask after my advice about these typically unforeseen events. In quiet, sheepish voices, they'd fret over what they should be doing, or what they should have done better whenever a kid addressed them with a confidence. With rare exception, I'd reply that they should continue doing what they were doing, offering that kids were approaching them for reasons that were likely complicated, but largely positive. Whether the staff had embodied quiet strength, the right balance of concern and aloofness, it didn't matter. The point was that a Thunder Road client had made healthy use of another human being, and this ought to be reinforced[13].

Trust

There are some who would perceive this trust phenomenon differently, and posit that kids, especially kids from minority backgrounds, approached a variety of staff members with their secrets because of a distrust of systems. The problem, they'd say, had a bedrock cultural flavor to it: that kids mandated into treatment had already grown accustomed to earnest social workers, mostly white, instructing them as to their lives, and figuratively wagging their fingers at self-destructive behaviors. Therapists, especially, were agents of probation officers, social workers, or else were direct reporters to parents and judges. Alternatively, they might ally with family courts, and betray a family loyalty by intruding into clients' secret home lives. Intuiting that holding secrets does indeed create problems, some kids experimented with the options, and at times sought out seemingly inconsequential recipients to absorb their burdens.

In working with addictions, especially when addressing a family system about addictions, it is common for all concerned to focus upon the broken trust as created by the drug-using person, the would-be addict. Meanwhile, what is concurrently processed, especially in private, one-on-one counseling, is this person's corresponding lack of trust in others. The problem of trust is invariably mutual between the clients and the array of adults that support them. Clients are the identified patients, the IPs, as they are sometimes dubbed. This is a common term, but an ironic one, designed to call attention to scapegoating: a system's defensive congealing of problems onto a single person. The purportedly affected party, the family, understandably distrusts the person locked in an addictive or otherwise self-destructive pattern. As parents or siblings, they have heard the promises many times before; they have felt duped.

The client/addict hangs his or her head, confirms the reasonableness of these feelings when they are discussed soberly in the light of day. What is driven momentarily underground, only to reappear in fitful spurts, is the ever lurking counter-distrust: the fear of judgment or the compromising of anticipated freedoms that may follow disclosure of negative behavior, or the retrospective disclosure of past unhealthy acts; the implicit rejection of scapegoating that at some point emerges. Drug histories, clients' reports from the front lines of addiction, comprised the early processes in family therapy activities at Thunder Road, with good reason. But parents or other family members who are too full of their own virtue can hinder this process as much as any stonewalling teen. They can become judgmental, overly reactive to that which has been previously withheld; otherwise ashamed for having believed earlier lies. It's a tense dynamic. The client as well as the afflicted other, questions whether they are ever hearing the truth, and further questions whether to report their own.

Therapists and counselors, more so than staff members from other departments at Thunder Road, were placed in the firing line of this precarious dynamic, and as the feelings, assumptions, and secrets started flying, it was easy to get tagged if standing nearby. And that's the life of a therapist: we stand nearby, moving amongst emotional shrapnel, dodging projections and seeking to fix our positions so we can help. Clients either begrudged or idealized their therapists for a plethora reasons. Some therapists would be dismissed for being incompetent, which usually meant they were deemed intrusive, unresponsive or unavailable. This mirrored the persona of the absent or preoccupied parent, who would forget to bring favorite clothing items on a Saturday visiting; who failed to call school officials and request a transfer of records for Thunder Road's school program. Entering the back doors at a place like Thunder Road to begin a workday is a bit like being a father coming home from work. You plug in your keys, disengage the alarm, walk in and hope to make it to the elevator twenty feet away without hearing your name bellowed out from across a hallway. If you make it, you're in. You're safe. Downstairs is where your office is, and once ensconced in your cave you can, as a case manager, get some work done—that is, paperwork done—without being troubled by the needs of youth. If feeling present enough, a conscientious therapist might dwell upon the parallels, and consider that avoiding clients' demands, and thus reenacting those kids' histories, is both insidious and cyclical.

I think my own reputation as a case manager was not so much one of unavailability or unresponsiveness (I may have been intrusive). I was often thought to be unfair, or misunderstanding, and it was during these instances of mis-attunement that I would be rejected by a client; my professional credentials questioned, and my right to open my mouth actively challenged. My denial of client privileges was often interpreted as a rejection of a client's core existence. The language used to illustrate the divide, or else appeal for connection, was often strewn with the "f" word. *You feel me*, the kids often said/asked, without intending irony. Some of those kids might have preferred that I make it to the elevator, lock myself in my office, and not come out. Others were more cunning, and were actually needy of my attention. They figured out how to make use of me; how to flatter or otherwise manipulate me into meeting their needs, and in turn make me feel good about myself and my role. These clients weren't necessarily more motivated than those who wanted none of my attention. Some of them thought of me like the genie from Aladdin; I was to be summoned when needed, and then stuffed back into the bottle when finished with.

Also, this critique—of being strict or unfair—was one that followed me into other positions and was echoed (though only sometimes as a critique) by supervisors during this and later periods. I was sometimes challenged to be more flexible with kids, to *meet them where they're at.* And sometimes I did. A good example was in the case of Katy, a hyperkinetic girl diagnosed singly with attention deficit/hyperactivity disorder, and assigned to my caseload during the era when client caseloads at Thunder Road were still coed. Katy had a problem meeting with me one-on-one. Whenever we met, typically in a room not specifically designed for therapy (hardly any rooms at TR were actually designed for therapy), she'd start pacing, and if irritated, would grab items and assert her prerogative to abuse them in one way or another—sometimes throwing them against the wall. Management agreed that I should set limits on the throwing of objects, but felt I should indulge her other requests. I should take her for a walk, play basketball with her, let her lie on the floor and roll around…whatever. Katy was clearly arrested in her development, though it was difficult collecting a reliable history. Whenever I tried asking after her upbringing, she'd roll her eyes and mock me for dwelling on the past. My therapeutic team agreed with her, sort of. I should meet her half way, they thought. I should strike a rapport, *work* with her.

I was confused and skeptical. Among other things, the feedback seemed backward. What had happened to safety proceeding from structure? What had happened to the idea that rapport proceeded from alliance, the reality-based understanding born of limit setting. Secondly, why should her deficits mean that she couldn't learn to sit still and talk about her feelings, and why should she learn to do so if not subject to limits? Katy was seventeen, I asserted, not a twelve year old. Within six months she'd be a legal adult, and told to go on passes to look for a job. Should I be coaching her on how to pace respectfully during interviews, or to wait until afterwards to begin throwing things? Knowing that therapy is not really comparable to job interviews, I challenged about more intimate relationships: how could she take part in anything like that if she couldn't sit still or look at anyone.

I took in the redirections of directors, who seemed impatient and unconcerned with these concerns. I made note of their pronouncements: "she simply cannot self-regulate in such a stimulating environment, either in group, or one-on-one," they insisted. Katy's known history, of disruptiveness in classrooms, chaotic behaviors at home, was reviewed as proof of the argument. For a minute, I flashed back to my graduate school training experience, to instructors' musings about mirroring for wounded adults, rapport building with therapy-nubile teens, and considered that I had missed something; something important: the grey areas that were ever greying. "Slow down," said the team around me. I temporarily relented on my stance, for no other reason than to avoid unflattering comparisons with my peers: "other counselors let me…," clients often said, exploiting a perception of rivalry among staff. So I complied. Problem was I started observing Katy in different contexts. That previously noted dynamic worked both ways, and I often saw her in impromptu one-on-one meetings, as well as "stimulating" group activities, reclined slovenly on a couch, talking casually and at length, often seeming about as hyperkinetic as a damp log.

Something wasn't right with this picture. For weeks I pointed out this contrasting impression as part of an argument that standard limits for one-on-one counseling ought to be restored. In the service of rapport building, or this spurious claim of faulty self-regulation, nothing was happening in the therapy. Katy was hanging out, waiting for something to happen yet grinding to a halt in terms of her progress. The director, by now suspecting that Katy had sex contracts (never confirmed, actually) agreed with me. "I see it too," she said, adding serenely that the time had come to observe the discrepancies. I recall the beatific smile; the sense that she'd agreed with me all along but had a different feel for the timing of interventions. Katy was starting to sit still, the treatment team declared. I was sent out with a sort of give-it-a-try stamp with respect to limit-setting and confrontation. Actually, I re-introduced the boundaries gingerly, still unsure as to what would happen. Katy and I fought for several weeks. She bullied me for wasting the time of our meetings with trivial matters that she thought had long since been decided: the questions as to where we would meet, whether we might play pool during a session; whether she was expected to come to therapy with a topic.

The remainder of her program, at least with me, proceeded contentiously. Angrily, she asked to be assigned to another therapist, believing with some justification that I was jerking her around, altering the rules of treatment. Her request was rejected, but otherwise her grievous feelings about her one-on-therapy were subtly reinforced. My strictness competed with the seeming laxity of my peers, most of whom seemed content to achieve rapport with

Katy and thus avoid her periodic tantrums, which could be devastatingly abusive. I began to notice the boundary violations, would become frustrated at the lack of support from my colleagues. I'd start asking questions to a shift supervisor, inquiring why Katy was allowed to stay up past lights out having a one-on-one with a peer. I further asked why she was allowed to go on an outing when her then post-reassessment status (imposed after she'd stormed out of a confrontation group) should have warranted her exclusion. It was as if staff had taken in my position, yet decided to teach me a lesson by compensating for my strictness; they'd place indirect pressure on me and make what I thought was my job a lot more difficult. I was on the cusp of having my own tantrum until a shift supervisor pointed out that Katy had completed more bench time in her first six months of treatment than any other girl on the unit. I wasn't seeing everything—that was the point. I recall this supervisor pulling back the curtain of her office and directing my gaze out towards the benches flanking the girls' rooms. Right on cue, there was Katy, sitting more or less correctly on a bench, biting her tongue but raising her thumb; following the protocol—barely.

As I suggested, I did relent with respect to rules and limits of individual therapy sessions, though I was bewildered. If she could sit still on a bench for considerable stretches of time, what was the problem with sitting still and talking? Was I the problem? I didn't get a sensible answer to this question, either when sitting or walking. In fact, I gave up trying to get Katy to sit down and reflect soon thereafter. I wasn't proud of my retreat. I felt ashamed, and thereafter found it hard to share in the mood of celebration that accompanied her surge towards honorable discharge. Then, with about three weeks left, a surprise occurred. One day I was facilitating a drama therapy version of confrontation group. Katy had volunteered for an impromptu hot seat, and wanted to role play an exchange with her distant, yet largely amiable father. I was half-heartedly agreeable, but not especially impressed by Katy's eagerness.

The role-play kept being interrupted. As a director of the scene, I was meant to coach her acting partner, a young man selected for the role of passive fatherhood. Firstly, a nurse interrupted, looking to extract the young man playing Katy's father because he was due to take his afternoon meds. Then, a few minutes later, another shift supervisor anxiously looking to fill an understaffed shift, whispered in my ear, asking if I could come in early the following day. Katy noticed this second instance of distraction and stirred a long-incubating rage. However, Katy had not yet learned—had not yet been compelled to learn—how to express her feelings in a calming, mature, or even a fully truthful way. What I heard instead was a satellite from her repertoire: a partial truth, embedded in a provocation. Hearing the word "pervert" twice directed at the hapless kid now playing the father (looking bereft, this kid managed a thoughtful "uh…" before I intervened), I looked up from my whisperings with my colleague and said, "Wait, why are you calling him a pervert?" Katy stepped back and thrust her shoulders backwards, striking an affronted posture.

"Finally! I thought that might get your attention." The fall-out was a revelation in our subsequent one-on-one that her father had not molested her per se, but rather masturbated in front of her, repeatedly, even ritually, over the course of many years. She tearfully offered, in her last week sitting with me (and I mean sitting with me), that she could not sit still in a room with a man who was also sitting still. She had to get up, feel elastic, so that she might believe she could get away at any moment. That was a memorable session, and I was moved by Katy's share; even privileged by it. But I still believe an opportunity was lost. Had I proceeded with more conviction from the outset of her treatment, I might have perceived the instances of behavioral repetition, or rigorously confronted her denial and avoidance. Having done so, memories of abusive, perhaps older than the ones revealed, may have been forthcoming, along with the emotional outpouring. Collapse may have followed the breakdown, followed by grief. That was, I thought, the model of a Therapeutic Community. To provide safety, supportive comments might have stabilized Katy had she become overwhelmed—the cognitively-based suggestion that what had happened in the past was not happening in the present. More importantly, she might have discussed at greater length this and other troublesome memories, and then made links between these events and her latter day reactivity.

I put Katy's revelations in the category of insights that the troubled reveal at the eleventh hour, just as they are about to leave. In this respect, such revelations are a compromise of sorts: it is a relief to "get things of one's chest", but this act is more of an expulsion than anything close to a working through of issues. At Thunder Road, these abreactive moments of kids like Katy and Ray Joe were often left dangling, there for anyone to address, but easy to leave well alone. The unfolding of grief, as opposed to behavioral discharge, sat awkwardly upon a treatment plan, with platitudes outlining a vague therapeutic course to follow emotive outpourings. By this time in my life, I felt I'd traversed one or two significant losses in my life. I was poised to become a therapist. I was eager though not too eager to help others navigate protracted states of pain, sort through old wounds, vulnerabilities, just as someone had played that role with me. But it wasn't to be—not with enough kids, anyway, and with fewer and fewer of them as the years rolled on.

I am ever regretful that I didn't stick to my guns with Katy and insist on standard limits for one-on-one sessions. At the time, I found it doubly ironic that Thunder Road, which had taught me the value of limit setting, would undermine me on this matter. In retrospect, I believe I might have heard those revelations, those insights, making way for a deeper, unfolding process. Katy made it to the finish line; she completed the inpatient program and thereafter moved on to Continuing Care, and ultimately graduated from Thunder Road, clean and sober, seemingly happy, healthy and grounded. Others seemed to think it sufficient that she'd made it to the end of the program. In retrospect, this episode seems a glimpse into my later differences with my employers: a portent of a broader divide, one that pitted the philosophies of 12-step, behavior modification, the value of confrontation and limit setting versus the caveats of victim advocates. There were a kaleidoscope of competing ideas for which I had no names back in 1998.

Self disclosure and the wounded healer tradition

I wasn't prone, like many of my peers back in the nineties, to disclosing details of my drug history to kids, thus providing a cautionary tale as central to an intervention. This wasn't because I was ashamed of my drug use. If anything, I was mildly embarrassed that my drug use hadn't come close to matching the levels of most clients. This is an interesting facet of the drug subculture. While bemoaning the tradition of shaming addicts and alcoholics in so-called "normal" society, there is within the recovery community, and especially within the elite cliques of teenage drug culture, a clear disdain for the "squares" of the world; a sort of counter-shaming. The kids in treatment often bristled at the hypocrisy of parents who used drugs but warned others as to the "mistakes that they made". They begrudgingly accepted the lessons of those in the recovery community, who had paid their dues in jails and institutions, and who wore scores of tattoos as echoes of what is stylized as the "lifestyle". But they reserved their greatest prejudice towards either pretense, or the pedantic lessons of those who had never even participated in the drug using lifestyle. From my reticence, many kids inferred lack of experience with drugs, and therefore lack of identification with their lives.

I'd give some indication from time to time of my past proclivities, but I was for the most part generic. I rarely discussed specifics, such as frequency of use, or volume, or even what my "drug of choice" was. Occasionally, a reference to an alcoholic year or a methamphetamine-filled summer would pass my tongue if I felt on the spot; my boundaries more porous than usual. There were several reasons for my overall caution, the least important of which was my graduate school instructors' recommendations that therapists not disclose their personal details. First of all, there was the fact that I was drinking, albeit socially and minimally, during this period. So while I alluded to and even explicated 12-step principles—legitimately from my own experience of the fellowship—I refrained from presenting myself as an active member. I was careful not to share too much about depression; not at first, anyway. Still, kids occasionally asked, and so did parents: why are you doing this work?

I spoke of depression from time to time, and implied that the dulling of my own emotional life had been the most lasting mental health problem of mine. I reversed the prejudice of my peers: tending to share stories with kids who were more advanced in their programs, rather than those closer to admission. While stilled, if not bemused, by my shares, because they didn't entail jails, institutions, and death, or even relatively acceptable emotions like guilt, some listeners nodded reverently but were generally underwhelmed. More secretly, I think some were disdainful, and I think that most of these sharing moments were mistakes of mine; careless moments borne of old chestnuts like peer pressure, fear of separateness; the fear of not fitting in. The disdain of clients was real. Such was the general intolerance of depression, likely because of its association with weakness. For those forming (or trying to form) idealizing transferences with me, I was unwittingly deflating myself through my disclosures. Meanwhile, by implicating the effect of drugs upon the inner, emotional life, I was drawing attention to the least talked about consequences of addiction, by anyone. There are commercials about brain damage (thinly characterized), media onslaught about DUIs, the implication of alcohol in rates of physical and sexual assault. There are countless rat studies implying that human beings will steal from their grandmothers, let their teeth rot and give up eating, all for another hit from a crack pipe. The Thunder Road kids had either been there already, or thought they *wouldn't* go there, they insisted.

Many of the Thunder Road kids had already lived a different experience: they had seen their parents, or their parents' siblings or parents, use lots of drugs, and had seen all the teeth rotting, the slowed breathing, and the limbs prematurely fattened by poor circulation. They knew what was in store for the future—they knew it intellectually—but they didn't feel it. Again, youth didn't notice youth; or rather, they didn't notice it as something they might lose. Despite the gallons of alcohol imbibed, the unspeakable quantities of pills poured down their throats, or the toxic smoke filling up their lungs, these kids' potential energy and athleticism was, for the moment, something to behold. I knew because I'd watch them jealously. In the parking lot, on the basketball courts, during the one-hour recreation period that was scheduled each day, I'd watch these lithe, seemingly perfect physical specimens come alive. The wildest of them couldn't be contained, and couldn't resist the challenge of a mere eight foot wall separating the compound from the street beyond. Leaping over the wall like deer, bounding off the hood of a staff member's car as a parting insult, they could just disappear, AWOLing. I'd watch semi-admiringly as a herd of them would gleefully ignore mine and other adults' plaintive voices.

I might have talked to some of them about depression—their depression—such as the odd disaffected and insular kid that couldn't play basketball, and who would stand by the side of the court with arms folded, wishing he could have brought his guitar into treatment so he'd have something to do during recreation time. Some could look into the future and see themselves. Referencing an older brother or sister, a defeated uncle, or a mentally-ill parent, some kids had observed with languid interest the decline of some of their elders. Watching them burp, fart, and smell of old age, these kids would become inheritors of nihilistic values, waxing lyrical about Bob Marley and other supposedly pot-glorifying celebrities; hoping to die before they got old. Regarding tobacco, they might take for granted that cigarettes would bring forth cancer or emphysema, despite the resource-fueled denials of the tobacco industry. They had heard and read at length about the external consequences of a drug using lifestyle, the "stupid decisions" people—kids included—make when *on* drugs. But the consequences of tobacco (or marijuana) use to the young are a bit like student debt for psychotherapists, or the consequences of credit card debt to the middle-class: they are something to defer until a distant tomorrow.

Reticent about my own experience, I nonetheless responded to some clients' queries, with some attention given to the quieter side of the disease. I referred to effects that were pervasive, day-to-day, and chronic; the spiritual and mental effects, as well as the behavioral; the subtle as well as the obvious. Nothing about drug use was stupid, I wanted to say. Everything has a reason—drug use has its reasons. Violence has its reasons. The task was that of figuring out those reasons, truly understanding them so that the afflicted might never be caught off guard. This was the promise of treatment, of therapy: to understand oneself, as deeply and as spontaneously as possible, such that a list of so-called "triggers" might be known the way that riding a bike is proverbially known. This term, "trigger", is a common enough slang in rehab circles, encompassing ideas of feedback loops, self fulfilling prophecies; neurons firing and then wiring together. The words linked to these phenomena were scribbled down on pieces of paper by clients and then stuffed in a draw until needed to acquire approval from staff. Ideally, they might instead live upon the side of a recovering person's bed, there staring them in the face as they wake up each morning. The list, like that list of rules for confrontation group read out by that wooden-voiced boy named Raul, might become as ingrained as any value relating to secrets, any gang sign, any form of vernacular ever present in a kid's preconscious. These were the things I wanted to say. These were the principles that were being left unsaid, as though they were taboos.

I smoked, I sometimes conceded—at least until late 1997, the year I finally managed to quit that particular addiction—the most dangerous one of all, as it happens. What else could I say? They smelled it on me, the kids did. Paradoxically, they could see into others, their attending adults asserting *care*. As for what else was evident—alcohol use, past drug use, depression—who knows what was or wasn't assigned to me via the fantasies of my clients. I imagine they had a blind spot with respect to depression: that would require the empathy, or the ability to see into others what is denied in the self. Some of my peers might swear that their clients did possess this quality of empathy, though they might term it a "skill" instead. Empathy, I was once reminded, pertains to the ability to feel another's distress, not simply observe it and perhaps maneuver in order to make use of it. The world, I realize, is filled with successful narcissists, entrepreneurs of the unethical kind, who are geniuses when it comes to knowing others' hearts, reading their emotional states, just so they can sell them a product. I imagine that many of our greatest entrepreneurs are obsessive types, drug addicts; former clients of Therapeutic Communities, places like Thunder Road.

I had the advantage of knowing, with respect to depression at least, that few really wanted to talk about it. Meanwhile, I listened to my peers draw from their drug histories as a regular technique of intervention. I didn't begrudge anyone this style explicitly, except in so far as I thought it a bit pedestrian in technique. Most of my fellow case managers hadn't had the privilege to attend graduate school and learn techniques of therapeutic intervention. What my peers didn't know was that I hadn't learned that many techniques either. I mean, graduate school taught many things—theory, copious warnings as to what not to do—but not so much a rigorous training with respect to counseling technique. Psycho-education, for example, is not really a technique. It's more of an umbrella term for a body of knowledge, some of it research-based, some of it heuristic. Testimonials are not technique; they are cautionary tales. These were the standard interventions employed by case managers, girded by the credentials of a former addictive lifestyle that many wore upon their sleeves, or else injected underneath into their skins: *We've been there*, they were saying.

What all this self disclosure[14] reflected was the wounded healer tradition of the 12-step community. In the mid-nineties, when I began working at Thunder Road, it seemed as though at least three quarters of the staff identified as recovering addicts or alcoholics. Randy Snowden told me that he and his fellow group of founders aimed for a one-third contingent of recovery staff, supplemented by another third of staff who would be licensed clinicians. Regardless, the program was fully steeped in 12-step principles. The slogans adorned every hallway, the fronts of elevators and the beams across doorways; the arms and necks of several staff members, and sometimes the crevices of staircases. Though resistant to the application of its principles (especially that annoying 10th step, with its "promptly admitting we were wrong" principle), many kids seemed drawn to the essential "coolness" of the 12-step program. Some would even come to distinguish it from Thunder Road, as though using the larger fellowship as an ethereal other, outside the clutches of authority. The ephemera were often attractive to kids: especially the working class aura of tattoos, bikes and four wheel drive trucks with their familiar Narcotic's Anonymous stickers proudly displayed; the undercurrent of jail-energy, all vaguely suggestive of risk-taking and danger.

Among the indices of diversity that workplaces boast, class is usually not high on the list, but at Thunder Road class seemed quietly influential. White collars were prominent amongst the medical and teaching staff, but otherwise, blue collar hegemony prevailed, both across management and throughout the clinical staff. The most popular staff members with kids seemed to be men and women who were often a little salty in their language. They came from neighboring cities like Hayward, San Leandro, and Alameda, typically, and "called people out on their shit". Some were TC veterans of places like Walden House in San Francisco, or Daytop Village further down the peninsula, and they brought with them watered down versions of their hair raising counseling styles. They also told their picaresque drug histories with longwinded flourishes that often held the kids spellbound. I held a suspicious view of all this, partly because I wasn't from places like Alameda or Hayward, and partly because I had a different repertoire up my sleeve.

Apart from thinking it an unimaginative way to intervene, I thought that sharing personal stories enabled kids not to work on their own material. Listening to people speak at a 12-step meeting is an invaluable activity, but it can also be a passive activity, and if you were an average visitor to Thunder Road, poking your head through a window at such a meeting, looking in to see what's truly happening, you might see an example of what's wrong with the just-described scenario. The staff's doing most of the talking—most of the work, in effect. And the kids? A third of them are asleep. Of these, some are indifferent to appearances. Alternatively, they are attuned to appearances, and calculating that the existing activity won't significantly impact their record of compliance. Alternatively still, they are indeed sensitive to appearances, but driven by an impulse to oppose what they feel is being forced upon them. As to the rest, the seemingly attentive, I could speculate as to their inner processes, but ultimately speculations are just that, because actually, the inner worlds of others should never be cast in a definitive light. Point is, however, without words, or the outward demonstration of affect, there is little to show what is happening in those inner worlds to other MRI-less human beings.

Splitting

There is another, somewhat oblique objection I have to therapists' disclosures of personal histories. It's one I recently had the opportunity to share in a public forum, in a quite different context. At a conference in San Diego, I attended a lecture that was part of a three day event bringing together therapists that worked with individuals presenting problems of sexually compulsive behaviors—sex addiction, as a shorthand. A speaker was making an argument for the disclosure of therapists' personal histories (sexual histories) as a means of establishing therapeutic rapport. His proposition: making such disclosures models for the client the acceptance of such a history, thereby rendering it safe for the client to share his or her story. He asked for some among the one hundred-deep crowd to speak up and affirm his opinion.

Those who spoke up generally agreed, with both the first and latter statements. Sharing one's own history with a client does indeed make them feel comfortable, said many. One or two even declared this as a badge of honor, as if therapy were a kind of battlefield in which everyone—professional and layman alike—must present their wounds. The therapist models; that is, leads the client into their stories with intrepid shares of their own. They show the way, and demonstrate that what they are asking of the client, they are willing to do themselves. Sat in the front row, I was finding much of this discussion insufferable. I raised my hand. Then I waited patiently for my turn, and spent an anxious minute or two deciding whether I should amend my forthcoming comments. I'd planned to make a dissenting argument, but in doing so, I would also shift the discussion into abstract territory.

Finally the speaker's assistant, skipping his way through the audience passing a microphone from one person to the next, made his way to my side. When I spoke, I firstly acknowledged the point of view of the presenter, demonstrating that I could pay lip service also. Then I indicated that the speaker had rightly attributed some objections to therapist self-disclosure to the psychoanalytic tradition. However, the fuller arguments offered by psychoanalysis were not being represented. I began speaking of the defense of splitting. Splitting, a term originally used by Sigmund Freud, was later picked up and expanded upon by Melanie Klein and other exponents of the later Object Relations school. The concept of splitting holds that individuals, when in this primitive mode of defense, strain to hold simultaneously contrary truths. They struggle to hold concepts of "good" and "bad"; they struggle to see others (or self) as whole individuals; they struggle, as the language permits, to achieve whole object relations, instead splitting themselves and others along divisions: good versus bad; right versus wrong; self versus other.

The latter split is the one reinforced by a habit of self-disclosure, I offered. By pandering to clients' needs to identify—at best, a partial-identification and a crude form of empathy—clinicians stall the development of open mindedness, and perhaps even further the defense of splitting, by implicitly encouraging splitting. To cite a plainspoken example, people attending 12-step meetings, or therapy groups centered upon an identified presenting problem, often speak of these forums as "the only place where they can speak". That's nice that treatment and fellowship can provide this, but is this the goal of treatment? To provide a refuge from a presumably alien other, whether that other is an individual, a set of individuals, or a whole community? Are some treatment professionals or members of the 12-step community intending to suggest the impossibility of bonding with those outside the echo chamber? Besides the broader implications for a society divided over all kinds of differences, what does this position offer to those who long to connect with an estranged and misunderstanding loved one?

Self-disclosure of therapist personal histories, especially those which imply an exclusive understanding of client problems, furthers this manner of splitting. It's both a fallacy and a fantasy of like-mindedness. Close mindedness, they might say in 12-step circles, if truly reflecting on the matter. As I passed the microphone back to the breathless assistant, I heard some faint murmurings behind my back. "Hmm," a man next to me uttered in a clipped yet thoughtful voice. He might have been the only one, because the remainder of the discussion proceeded as though I'd not said anything; like I had been a curious blip in an otherwise agreeable chorus. Regarding a few blank, nonplussed stares behind me, I felt a collective *whatever* radiating through the room. Actually, the instance reminded me of my periodic experience when co-facilitating activities like confrontation group. Anyway, I was pleased with myself, thinking I'd said something out loud, before an audience of my peers, that I'd been percolating in my mind for over a decade.

When I speak to other therapists who work with adolescents, discussion often turns to the matter of therapist self-disclosure. With apologist tones, my peers often admit to sharing much about themselves with their younger clients. They know they're rebelling against their former training, and even think of this rebellion in terms of individuation[15]. For some, it seems like a quid pro quo, this self disclosure, and—quite plainly—a necessary rapport building tool, as if teens in general just wouldn't tolerate therapy any other way. They might be right, of course, but then again, they might not be, and as I've suggested, I've flexed my own thinking on this issue from time to time. I just can't seem to find a solid formula, much as my splitting mind would care to. For some, the tenets of psychoanalytically-derived therapies may seem archaic; an obsolescence. *Whatever*, I say. Putting aside for a moment the arguments for or against therapist self disclosure, I think what I object to is being told so definitively what *works* and what doesn't—what's effective and what isn't—by people who can't actually prove their stridently driven assumptions.

The word splitting was used daily at Thunder Road, but like most constructs with a psychoanalytic heritage, it was shorn of its original meaning in the behavior modification system. Actually, what's more precise is to assert that splitting was given an adapted meaning: one that emphasized the behavioral elements, not the unconscious underpinning. Black and White thinking—a staple phrase of 12-step circles, and a synonym for a Cognitive Behavioral Therapy term—"all or nothing" thinking—was routinely referenced to challenge a client's narrow mindedness; his or her blaming, devaluing reactions to feelings like disappointment and rejection. This, while not termed as such, is a conscious example of splitting, though one that emphasizes only the so-called "negative" elements. Idealization of others, to the extent that flaws are overlooked, is also an example of splitting, though all too often staff members failed to confront this as Black and White thinking, especially if they personally were the recipient of warm compliments.

An understanding of splitting was important for other reasons, some not derived from psychoanalysis, but rather from decades-old research into behavioral science. Skinner (1969) observed that if behavior is subject to an unpredictable partial reinforcement schedule—such as a pattern of inconsistent responses or consequences—then it is resistant to extinction[16]. Intermittent reinforcement, this is called. Addictive behaviors are in part fueled by intermittent reinforcement to the extent that the negative behaviors, so-called, entail risk: will using a certain drug achieve an optimal high? Will that behavior incur trouble? Beyond addictive behaviors, consider other behaviors that are anti-social, or just annoying: is fighting worth the risk of trouble? Is crying, clinging, arguing, nagging, or what Bowlby (1969, 1982) might have called "protesting" worth the trouble? Because the histories of insecurely attached children are littered with less than fully sensitive or responsive caregivers, these behaviors constitute gambles: they are sometimes effective in relieving stress, and sometimes not. The insecurely-attached are all gambling addicts in another sense, and because Therapeutic Communities contain multiple caregivers, the potential for inconsistent responses and therefore intermittent reinforcement of unhealthy or healthy behaviors is huge.

Most specifically, the word splitting was used at Thunder Road to reference clients' tendency to play off one staff against another. That complaint from Katy—the "other counselors don't…"—was an example of splitting staff. This was a feature explained in that orientation on my first day back in 96', and as Therapeutic Community concepts exist, it was as well grasped and articulated as any other. The etiology is as follows: kids drawn from broken homes, with inconsistent parenting—often parents with adversarial relationships—develop as an adaptive measure the practice of asking after their needs on multiple occasions, directing their appeals to whoever is available, therefore taking advantage of systemic disorder. This is not a moral failing or a stubborn refusal to take "no" for an answer. The practice of splitting at Thunder Road was a defense mechanism, not an act of defiance. This was the view of the program, with some variation from dissenting quarters who did think it an act of defiance. Engaging in splitting, as so defined, didn't break Cardinal rules per se. It was more of a secondary phenomenon, often drawn to a client's attention in a here and now fashion, a bit like rapping the knuckles of a kid habitually dipping fingers into a plate of food.

This is not to say that it didn't create arguments. But those arguments stemmed more from the confusion of the client as to the relevance of the behavior. Even if clients admitted they had gone from staff A to staff B on the matter of request X that had been denied by staff A, many a puzzled youth will have replied, "So what?" This was part of the problem of having a plethora of rules, the fuller legacy of which was understood by only a few people. Rules can speak to surface elements, but something else is needed to explain why the rules are there in the first place. Beyond that, a lengthier discussion is needed as to why such rules will have any relevance to the reasons clients are in treatment. Someone has to explain, for example, why defensiveness is a problem. If splitting, like violence, promiscuity, or even drug use, is employed in the service of feeling good, which is in the service of "getting by", or more dramatically put, of "surviving", then what's the problem? In other words, what's wrong with survival?

Well, survival is not happiness, and nor is it growth, or even resilience necessarily. Taking drugs is not resilience. Immersing oneself in a violent subculture, versus simply enduring it, is not resilience. At this point in this would-be exchange, some would bristle at my assertions. What does a middle class white guy know about resilience in the face of endemic drug abuse and violence? It's not so much that skeptics would disagree with my statements. There are countless parents, teachers, church and other community leaders who would agree that drug use and gang affiliation are not the healthiest ways to adapt to an at-risk living environment. The skepticism was and is about a wall between insiders and outsiders. They might doubt that I empathize. They might doubt that I *relate*.

It enables splitting to write defensively on these matters. Therefore, I will merely offer that as I was heading past my thirtieth birthday, happiness, growth, and resilience were becoming very important to me, both professionally and personally. That is not to say that everything that is important to me ought to be important to others, but as a budding therapist I thought personal growth was vital, a prerequisite value for continuing the work. How could I not impart the principle everyday I worked at Thunder Road? How could I not hold the possibility that a life without drugs, violence, sexual and emotional abuse was possible? After three years living and working amid this tension, I felt stretched, though not burnt out. I'd watched quite a turnover of peers in that time, mostly of those without a career stake in the field, but nonetheless people whose strength, wisdom and generally grounded presence I'd come to admire. I felt a part of something—a sense of belonging and mission—and was happy enough to foresee continuing to work with adolescents well into the future. At the same time, however, I was moderately concerned for the state of my workplace. I'd developed quite a stack of opinions about what needed to be done with kids' treatment plans, how the treatment program ought to be modified.

Everything at Thunder Road seemed just this side of equilibrium. I often felt as though I were riding a ship that was always teetering on the crest of a wave, yet capable of great things. One day we would touch hearts and minds, brings tears and joy: the prospect of real change. The next day we would be treading water, dabbling in quick sand and straining to understand what was happening. It seemed that at any moment the unspeakable might happen: a staff member would "lose it" and attack a client. Kids fraternizing with one another would eventually lead to someone getting pregnant, or more darkly, raped. Meds would go missing, and Thunder Road would someday become not so much a haven from drug use as a hotbed of drug using activity. A tool from maintenance might get stolen, and from that, kids would mount a late night jailbreak, emptying the hospital and filling the streets of North Oakland. Therapists would come to work the next day, learn of mass AWOLs—half the unit gone, hallucinating in the dark—and retreat to their offices to worry if their jobs might be eliminated as a result.

4

SHOOTING FROM THE HIP

Tools of a program

I'd had at least one memorable experience of the program's lurking chaos being thrown in my face, by a client. The story of Andre, a mixed race youth who spent a year at Thunder Road, featured an endless litany of the types of behaviors, attitudes, affects, defenses, of the type discussed so far in these pages. Towards the end of his program, I'd just about forgotten what his drug of choice originally had been. That's how far his program had strayed from those presumptive goals outlined at intake. Andre was a complex personality: manipulative, charming, handsome to the point of making female staff blush whenever he passed them. And he was destructive. Though not overtly violent, violence seemed ever present with Andre. He was ever seething, ever clenching his fists, and ever biting his lip with erotic ferocity, all about some manner of injustice within the program. Exuding righteousness, he stalked the hallways, thrusting out an ample chest, brooding over his mistreatment, and outraging management with the extent of sympathy he curried among the Therapeutic Community counselors. Brad Pitt with a pony tail and a darker tan, he was a menace to the female wing of the hospital; always eliciting distraction from the most vulnerable, a perpetual threat to their much embattled therapeutic goal: "focus on self".

It turned out that the girls on the unit were not Andre's ideal target, but rather the women. Two-thirds of the way into his program, it became known (through a very brave "snitch") that Andre was having a sexual relationship with his case manager, a woman more than twice his age. After a fall out that included some group process with the entire client population, Andre was assigned to my caseload for the remainder of his time at Thunder Road, roughly three months. I recall especially from this period the awkwardness of being a messenger of management denials: Andre's request for stage progression; Andre's request for a home pass; Andre's request to attend a funeral of a fallen friend; Andre's request for a series of grievances to be heard pertaining to his mistreatment from staff. Delivering rejections from above, with my tacit sanction attached, was a major part of my role with both him and his parents during the latter days of his program. I felt hapless, straining to make explanations, unable to coalesce all that I thought about him, about us—about the crazy system both within and outside of Andre's life. Regarding my dithering expression, Andre offered a cold summation about Thunder Road's process that I've never forgotten: "You guys are just shooting from the hip, aren't you?"

In the wake of that event, I began formulating ideas for what I'd change were I in charge, and I would never be in charge. Many of the changes would address the problem of assignments: a good, common sense place to start, I thought—one that reflected my academic predisposition—and an easier nut to crack than the style or size of group activities, for instance. To attend to this, I would have at least altered the way we presented assignments: to give shorter writing assignments, with more focused questions, with the understanding that any assignment must thereafter be the starting point for a conversation between clients and staff. A conversation: actual discussion, with time, and thoughtfulness. How does it get developed, this so-called reflective functioning? Good question. Observe the following examples:

"What were you feeling as you said that", as a question verbalized, rather than a statement extracted from a page of written instructions.

"What were you hoping for?" as a follow-up query in answer to staff's urgent request to know why client had made utterance X in the last therapy group.

"How do you imagine (or think) that made her feel?" in reference to another's experience.

Of course, any client—anyone—can answer "I don't know" to any of these leading questions, and questions aren't necessarily the best way to mentalize another. Exchanges between those in conflict, not just resistant clients and their wearied counselors, are littered with stone-walling responses such as "I don't know", or "I don't remember". But these responses are often dissociations, and are therefore defensive against a disturbed affect. Therapist inquiry as to feelings in such a moment may be an imposition, but that should not be presumed. Instead, a question so-timed might remind a struggling individual that feelings are indeed present, and that there is permission for their expression. Of course, some clients may still assert that they "do not know" what their feelings are. Helplessness is a commonly seized position of those who are hospitalized. Actually, from my observation, the most consistently defensive response of those resistant to mental health treatment is not one of defiance—it's one of helplessness.

Silence

The process of a therapeutic exchange entails not only patience, but determination, as well as a willingness to allow space, which is another way of referring to silence, and more importantly, to tolerate those awkward silences. That's easier, far easier, to say (or write) than enact. Silences can feel like eternities, and teens that are presumed to be more self-conscious than anyone else might look upon silences with derision: "Weird," they might say. "Can I go now?" the more opportunist or defiant might ask. They think their "I don't know" expressions end conversations—that silence marks the end of exploration rather than a beginning. In these moments, they aren't thinking of their therapist as a regulator of psychobiological states, as Schore (1994. 2005) would observe. Their complaint, "my last therapist just sat there staring at me" is one that many will take into adulthood, with a succession of therapists who are implicitly told to be more active: talk more, don't allow silence; don't generate the fatigue that stems from emptiness; don't stir reactions that come from long ago.

A jaded listener in a Therapeutic Community, or even a structured outpatient program might sigh in response to protracted silences, dismiss their clients from their offices, and then turn to workspace-sharing colleagues and bemoan the lack of recovery in the program. Someone determined but lacking patience might begin supplying a pressured series of menu questions: "Well, is it this, was it that? What do you mean, you don't know… " I have a memory of myself asking a client, "What do you think it could be?" with respect to an elusive, presumably disturbing memory. I wince slightly at the recollection, knowing I was sometimes too eager to pry insights from approval-seeking teens. I'd come off sounding like a desperate journalist in search of juicy secrets from a deep-throated informant. In behavioral terms, I was reinforcing helplessness. In psychodynamic[17] terms, I was colluding with the defensive structures, cajoling for secrets, looking for pat explanations and resonating in a fashion that does not support growth. Instead, what was called for was an abstract moment, one that is hard to document—one that might even be captured by a student in a graduate school training center with a recording device—and one that might result in not only a shift in behavior, but also an attendant shift in affect, one that is sustained such that change cannot be attributed to mere compliance.

What's called for with the passively resistant is a calm, insistent query that places responsibility with them, and is therefore not too eager to reach the finish line of insight: "What's keeping you from knowing?" Ostensibly, this kind of exchange has happened at Thunder Road. I know because I practiced them myself, and the clinical supervisor of my early years at Thunder Road encouraged silences as a therapeutic tool; thought them compatible, even logically so, with TC concepts such as the use of Monads, the meaning of the bench. Counselors and clients have had those staring contests marked by silence, in which one or both contestants might squirm, not knowing what to do, or how to be. They recall preverbal elements of communication—gaze, body posture—which generate the responses born of early caregiver-to-child relationships. But these exchanges are not in the manual. The conversations, the connections, the therapies that utilize silence, are not easily manualized. How does one manualize silence? Document or even track its efficacy? What is the value of silence?

That's the counter of those who problematize it. For many, silence represents abandonment, and therefore must be devalued. At least, that's the criticism that's often leveled at non-active therapists, ones that don't necessarily say anything in response to client disclosures, thereby leading to protracted gaps in speaking. Navel-gazing, some have pejoratively characterized this style.

What these critics overlook is the potential for deeper exploration of feelings; or else, they are defending through their opinions, against their own past experiences of silence. What is the value of silence? One might just as readily ask: what is the value of feelings? Well, no ever died from them, is one succinct answer, whereas many people have died from attempts to ward off feelings, and many more are stifled by shallow attempts to simplify or intellectualize feelings. This point of view inverts the standard criticism, offering that it is silence that allows for a deeper connection, and that words, especially words in the service of directing others, create distance. That old mentor of mine would have called the silent moments of therapy, even the silent moments (the "Monads") in the milieu, as "self" moments, which is an abstraction, but a critical one. Notice, for instance, that I do not refer to a "voice" moment, or a "solution" moment. A "self" moment is one in which the subject has reflected upon his or her own experience, as well as that of others, and does this in the company of another (ala the spirit of the fifth step of a recovery program). The aforementioned exchange offered no prescription, nor did it explore "options" as to what to do; rather, it offered what Schore and others might call a self organizing event, one in which a brain develops awareness and empathy because of its relationship to another brain. A *present* silence. The prescribed interventions of the treatment team tended to overlook these subtleties, and because many of the clients at Thunder Road did not understand their own experience, and certainly didn't understand the experiences of others, proposed "solutions" were all too often rehearsed, rote, or contrived to elicit approval. Often, they were simply unconvincing.

The manualizing of therapy is often attempted. Bullet-pointed seminars happen regularly, in classrooms, hospitals, sometimes in heavily chandeliered conference rooms in hotels, which purport to outline intervention strategies for mental health professionals. The previous conversation, if referenced in a presentation of such a seminar, might be covered under the *explore coping strategies* bullet point, and more or less described as an intervention that targets thoughts, non-weird feelings with a small *f*, and behavior—above all, behavior. At Thunder Road in the nineties, the psychodynamic, Kohutian-inspired thinking that emanated from graduate schools seemed to achieve a modest détente with adherents of the TC model, but one that seemed thinly understood. And so there was tension between those who conceived of treatment in terms that were hard to quantify. Some therapists thought the paraprofessional counselors were too shaming, heavyhanded, or concrete. Meanwhile, their counterparts, those directive-giving counselors often thought therapists were too soft-hearted, inattentive to realities, and generally not *with it*.

And yet there was a balance of sorts; a reasonable coexistence of professionals who fundamentally held similar ideas about the core client population. Counselors and therapists, managers and medical personnel: all seemed united in the belief that our clients were seriously at risk; suffering from embedded problems, internal and systemic, and soothing themselves with addictive habits. In time, each faction would take a hit from critics outside the program. One day, the repertoire of TC concepts would be dissembled. Armando Corpus, perhaps Thunder Road's longest serving employee (since 1989), points out that overseeing agencies such as Community Care Licensing and the department of Public Health have become increasingly instructive of programs' limit-setting tactics in recent years. Facing criticism about attempts to isolate youth (reassessment?), restrict movement and interaction (gender-splitting rules), and punitive measures (homework assignments, IT "chores"), he remarks that group homes and other residential programs are under increasing pressure to modify their former strategies.

Meanwhile, the practice of psychotherapy is also controlled. Over time, attempts to deepen beyond a surface level would be not so much prohibited as proscribed. The injunctions worked a bit like taxes do upon disreputable commodities. These days, it's not so much that it's forbidden to practice depth psychotherapy with clients in a residential setting; it's rather that there isn't time, because caseloads are too big, groups too big, time is too short and there are other important things to do, like documenting the therapy that is happening less. Silences take time. Feelings take time. A therapist can give it a shot, but life will be rendered very difficult in the process, and burn out will become likely because such a strategy is deemed expensive and time-consuming. Case managers who were rewarded in their positions with periodic accolades, who kept their jobs over time learned the more practical skill-sets, the less ambitious agendas. They developed heuristic strategies, some of which later flowered into "evidence-based" practices, and fashioned taut descriptions of their clients that could be easily presented in treatment planning meetings. Their interventions would adhere strictly to the conscious elements of an exchange, and emphasize a cooperative, pragmatic alliance with clients, in keeping with the egalitarian values that have scrubbed clean the thinking of those working with so-called "lower functioning" populations.

This egalitarianism—this *meet them where they're at* ethos—is probably why residents of the hospital are called clients and not patients, and this is several years before terms like "wellness", "partnership plans", "Strength-based approaches", and other such consumer models had even taken up residency. It's strange that few over the years have challenged this convention of calling Therapeutic Community residents "clients". Given the fact that Thunder Road is a licensed health facility, and that it describes its treatment planning approach as a medical model, you'd think this alone would merit use of the term "patient". Add to that the clearly hierarchical system that existed for over twenty years—a system that divided not only staff into levels of authority, but the kids also—and has used blatantly authoritative measures such as time-out devices and a system of assignments, removal of privileges—interventions invariably perceived as punishments—it becomes almost bizarre to think of Thunder Road kids as having earned the Rogerian status of client.

Perhaps client is a misunderstood term, but it seems to connate something collaborative, maybe even mutual, in relationship with a therapist, whereas the term patient implies more of an expert-to-subject relationship[18]. As suggested above, this connotation (of egalitarianism) has been present to a greater degree in recent years, but the practice of calling residents clients goes back as far as I can remember; certainly as far back as my early tenure beginning in 1996. I believe that Thunder Road clients (I guess I'll keep calling them that, as well as "kids") should bear responsibility for their treatment, which has very real implications for treatment. This is certainly not an original idea of mine, or even of Thunder Road. For years, this had been a rhetorical nicety thrown into the mix of a treatment planning meeting. Most would nod in agreement, especially if a gripping metaphor was attached. The differences among staff are indicated by how this "responsibility" should manifest. Some might think that "accountability" is a synonymous word; a client must receive consequences for negative behaviors, because if they don't, such behaviors will be reinforced, echoing Skinner and other behaviorists. I think my use of the word "responsibility" has a broader meaning than what most staff members at Thunder Road will have intended. What I thought was that clients shouldn't be spoon fed therapeutic answers; that staff should stake out positions of therapeutic neutrality. Regardless of academic aptitude, a client should understand that it is his or her job to understand themselves, articulate who they are. Staff's job is that of a listener, primarily; secondly, the job is to point out reality and to point out when the person is straying from reality, when they are breaking rules, and lying about doing so.

An unconscious core

Silence is an important technique: a tool in the metaphorical toolbelt. It gives room for a client's self experience in a way that a pedantic lecture or a 12-step testimonial never can. It marks the dividing line between therapy and counseling; between a process that is largely left-brained, and therefore linked in the mind with an academic exercise, and a process that is an exploratory, emotional experience, with the accent on *experience*. Those who utter "What else is there to say?" miss the point and soon flounder amid the silences. But it's not a therapist's job to save from floundering those who have forgotten how to express or experience feeling. And when they do experience themselves amongst witnesses, it's not the job of therapists to make reassuring noises, or give long-winded explanations that force clients to listen to SOMEONE ELSE while emoting. At these times it's the therapist's job to shut up and stay present. Monads. The client will live; perhaps thrive.

The spaces between exchanges, akin to what D.W. Winnicott (1971) called "potential space", leave room for an unconscious process; to a genuine development of an inner life, as opposed to a robotic, compliant, and climactically false product[19]. I will keep referring to phenomena that occurs unconsciously because—and this may seem absurd to have to assert this—the unconscious exists. That may seem like an obvious statement. It may seem as though people working in mental health accept the existence of an unconscious, rather like the religious accept *a priori* the existence of God. Even clients believe it exists—drugs addicts do, anyway. They are often claiming they don't why they do what they do, and that an underlying "healthy" motivation exists despite evidence to the contrary. But unconscious functioning is not easily manualized. The unconscious is not teleologically identified, empirically assessed, or attached with a numerical value. Therefore it is a problematic entity. And the reader may be surprised at how much it is ignored by many who hold positions of leadership within mental health services. They might argue that while the unconscious exists, its existence can't be demonstrated, and so its utility is limited, and so it is exiled from the treatment plan. Rightly or wrongly, working in this business—or indeed any business—professionals are called upon to demonstrate outcomes to bean counters; tangible outcomes, consciously examined. We attend to crises, the tangibly real behaviors that destroy individual lives, families, and communities.

A person dangling from a cliff needs to be told to grab the ledge that is nearest, not given "space" to contemplate what's being felt in the moment, or what is being felt by the person urgently pointing at the ledge. This figurative argument was often directed at either clients or their attending therapists, to which I sometimes flippantly replied, "what's a therapist doing standing near the edge of a cliff" (a wilderness program, maybe?). There isn't time, or space, it was often imputed, to attend to subtleties, the unconscious motivations. During my early days at Thunder Road, these were the TC counselors or managers calling the shots, as Armando Corpus put it, introducing me to the sketchy paradigm wars that would cycle back and forth over the next fifteen years:

about therapy versus counseling; attention to clients' behavior versus their internal processes; progress versus perfection; pragmatism versus whatever the antonym of that word is.

As the reader might imagine, it took quite some time for me to latch onto these debates, and they weary me I think, so my mind turns to escapist yet artful links. I am reminded of a comic scene in Stanley Kubrick's film, *A Clockwork Orange*. After Alex, the anti-hero, has been "conditioned" to respond to stimuli of sex and violence with revulsion, a priest caricature decries the behavioral technology, arguing that it deprives the subject of choice. A self-satisfied spokesman for the conditioning regimen and himself a caricature of political cynicism, arrogantly shouts the priest down, and points out with an empirical foresight that only fiction would allow, that "what we are concerned with is cutting down crime!" Well, I agree that those figuratively dangling from cliffs need to be informed of crises, but not necessarily told what to do as a result. First of all, if a client was truly hanging off a cliff, I'd call Thunder Road, ask for a maintenance worker, because they're not in denial about anything, and get them to come and rescue both the client and me from the cliff. Sometime thereafter, I'd have a chat with the client about how he or she got on the edge of the cliff in the first place. Amidst that conversation, wherein there *is* space, I'd ask after their feelings about the whole situation, or perhaps just leave a silent moment alone until the client starts speaking again.

Practical interventions provided containment, another term with a psychoanalytic pedigree appropriated by residential programs. Containment of negative behaviors: drug use, violence, and sexual behavior, principally, had to be stabilized before any other kind of therapeutic work could be done. I've no argument with that principle. Silences in therapy notwithstanding, most who worked in a clinical capacity at Thunder Road learned to be active long before they learned to not be intrusive. Meaning, they engaged verbally with clients about their behavior long before they settled in for reflective, silence-filled deepening. Basically, it's like this: How can individuals work on themselves, explore their feelings, if drug use and other avoidant behaviors block the access to those feelings?

Shavelson (2001) addresses this issue somewhat with respect to Bay Area rehabilitation programs working with "hardcore" addicts[20]. In such programs, the problem concerns those who come off the streets and participate in therapy groups while high. A conflict exists between those who suggest this is not useful, either to the "high" individual, or to the other participants in the program (those TC counselors that Armando Corpus spoke of). An opposing view suggests that programs shouldn't turn away individuals simply because they are manifesting the symptoms of their "disease". This is the view that informs so-called Harm Reduction programs, and seeks to make treatment more available to a wider range of people, regardless of capacity. Those who hold such views may scorn the opinions expressed in this narrative, arguing that abstinence-based drug programs as well as sophisticated or demanding courses of psychotherapy effectively gentrify the treatment culture.

But the point here is that residential programs are designed, literally and figuratively, to contain acting out behaviors and prevent drug use, thus making possible further therapeutic work. The word 'holding'—a D.W Winnicott idea—is often employed to highlight the residential program's initial task: retain the client, versus the outpatient program's mantra (borrowed from 12-step meetings), *keep them coming back*. To that end, staff at Thunder Road took controlling measures: When clients entered the program, staff took away their clothes, confiscated contraband, stuck them in a room with hospital scrubs, an NA book, and a tray of food delivered to them. This was called 1A, this stage of treatment: a holding pattern, sub-1A, as in "not yet in treatment". It was a compromise: room service combined with a literal stripping away of a lifestyle's ephemera. Loss: it seemed, and still seems, a prerequisite for change. Kids had to stay in their rooms for at least twenty four hours, during which staff would be directed to look in, introduce themselves, offer encouragement, "check in", and perhaps take them out of their rooms so that they might play pool or basketball and see that it wasn't all bad, this treatment thing. Other residential programs may take similar measures: providing living quarters that are comfortable, even luxurious, such that the prison-expecting admit might regard the treatment setting and say something like, "well, maybe I'll stay the night."

It is, as many tritely say, a balancing act, this question as to what properly engages the troubled individual entering services.

What is it that "holds" a disturbed youth who may or may not be motivated for treatment, and who may disappear from its back doors with the echo of a feeble alarm sounding out from behind. Stage 1A was where the rubber hit the road on each of these questions. Beyond that, where does the need for action and avoidance stop and the need to be still and contemplate begin? Not at the outset of treatment, it seemed, and so program design featured efforts to reduce client isolation as much as possible. The strategies initially employed recall Adler and Buie's (1982) construction of an outpatient therapeutic environment. In their model, therapists are encouraged to stray from a typical frame of treatment, wherein therapist and client/patient only have contact through a regularly-scheduled appointment in a therapist's office. Therapists from this model would call or receive calls in between sessions, exchange cards and such, with patients. The idea was to create a holding environment that allows for individuals to form stable introjects (internalized representations of caregivers), and therefore establish therapeutic alliances at the outset of treatment.

At times it seemed as though some kids could not be contained no matter what strategy was employed. I recall a 15 year old Vietnamese girl whose admission stirred anxiety amongst staff from day one. She wasn't assigned to me or my caseload, but I happened to witness an exchange between her and a colleague of mine on the afternoon she was removed from 1A status. The counselor, a male, was asking her background questions in keeping with one of the assessment tasks whose completion was required within the first seventy two hours of the program. The girl wasn't ready for the assessment, much less the treatment regimen that would follow. She didn't seem anxious to contact her family, or to be removed from treatment necessarily. She didn't seem interested in treatment, in the reasons she was referred to treatment. Other than being paranoid about what the other "bitches" on the unit were saying about her, she didn't seem concerned with others' opinions. She appeared to misunderstand most of the counselor's questions, instead asking after her personal belongings, the opportunities to have free time, or to "kick it" as she bluntly phrased that idea. Elsewhere, it was reported that she had been raped, molested several times in her life; that she had one child that was developmentally disabled, and another forthcoming. The father of the first child, it was darkly hinted (by admissions staff) was the girl's own father.

She was a feral child. I observed (as in listened, with my back turned for the most part) with semi-indecent interest to the surreal conversation between my colleague and this girl. Throughout the interview, she'd pause, turn silent, only to answer in non sequiturs regarding the questions asked. Obtaining an accurate drug history seemed unlikely let alone a reflection upon past or present traumas. I quietly shook my head and occasionally glanced over my shoulder to catch a glimpse of her. I wondered about her affect, her body language. The latter spoke volumes. Tugging at her loose fitting top, she appeared to be on the cusp of disrobing. Her bra was almost fully exposed; her naked midriff protruded with the early signs of pregnancy. The counselor fidgeted uncomfortably, and made odd, diffident requests for the girl to cover herself more. She'd look back at him with a blank expression, make a token movement towards the snakeskin fabric on her arm, but would soon let the clothing drift from her body. At this point I felt as though I ought to leave the room, either for mine or my colleague's sake or else to find a female counselor for the girl to speak to. I couldn't believe she'd been assigned to a male counselor given the level of dissociation and sexualizing present. In terms of that particular case, the issue became moot within another forty eight hours. Meaning, she AWOLed. We couldn't *hold* her.

It seemed as though Thunder Road was aiming for a similar model as that which Adler and Buie had proposed. Therapists and clients were meant to have "check-ins" in between one-on-ones, and also participate in several groups together. Also, because the rules called for case managers to oversee client belongings, monitor phone calls, act as liaison to collateral contacts, in addition to providing one-on-one therapy, the whole relationship appeared set-up as a kind of "holding" role. Though some care was taken to prevent staff from unduly falling into parental or even avuncular roles, this again seemed inevitable. In the residential unit, the roles might vary, with therapists not necessarily cast in the role of parents. As many kids were accustomed to extended family involvement—due, perhaps, to the collapse of the basic nuclear unit—the use of an oft-rotating support system of adults was for many kids a familiar and relatively comfortable set-up. So Mom and Dad were sometimes the directors, clinical and/or medical, with every other adult playing roles of uncle or auntie; perhaps a more aged staff would have a grandfatherly role, or a twenty-something Therapeutic Community Counselor might take on an elder sibling quality.

To what extent clients' real families noticed all of this was something of a mystery. Few ever commented on this phenomenon when I worked as a case manager, and I've not heard of too many reflections on this since becoming a supervisor either. I suspect it would be a source of shame for many family members—this quasi adoption by Thunder Road—a suggestion that their roles had been usurped. For some, this may have been a relief. As many kids were delivered to Thunder Road in the wake of parents' exhaustive efforts to intervene, there was a real sense of abandonment. Therein lay the danger of the Adler and Buie idea in my view. While adjusting to the Therapeutic Community, the young client, considering that he or she is unwanted by the parents, transfers their energies to the staff. While this may seem not only natural, but also necessary for the client's assimilation into the program, it may also prove an obstacle when time later arrives for reunion with the client's family.

Visiting time

I often thought this led to families' actively undermining the program. The reason: they didn't wish to be replaced by Thunder Road, as parents. This wouldn't be a literal replacement, of course—there would be no suggestion of Thunder Road actually adopting a resident (though it would approximate the act at times), even those whose treatment tenures were extended well beyond a year. It was instead the possibility that Thunder Road's success would reflect badly upon the parent. After all, if treatment succeeds where a parent hasn't, even if this is only perception, what does that say of the family's parenting style? It cannot be ignored that a prospectively successful treatment program for adolescents constitutes a potential humiliation for parents, one they might actively fight. These efforts to undermine the program have confused and frustrated many therapists, especially when subversive efforts occurred as clients appeared to be doing well in the program. I was confused by this phenomenon myself at first, though luckily I was attentive at a lecture in 1996, when a then graduate school instructor spoke eloquently of the problem of parents taking kids out of therapy.

For these reasons, Thunder Road made a laudable and tireless effort at engaging clients' families, with a checkered history of successful interventions, and scores of plainly inadequate forays into what systems theorists call "the family disease". Parents were reasonably enthusiastic about visiting days, which occurred on Saturdays. In the nineties, after I'd become a case manager, it was one of my secondary duties to act as shift supervisor on a Saturday day shift. That meant roughly that I was in charge of what happened in the building for an eight hour stretch. This was typically the end of my work week in this period, and family visiting would often be the last activity (if it could be called that) that I'd have to manage, along with a skeletal staff of six people. At two o'clock in the afternoon, parents and other families would arrive for a lecture on a topic related to addiction, and then be dismissed so as to visit with their sons and daughters. It was during these visiting periods that I'd observe the painful ruptures between parents and their kids.

By the pool room, a sullen teenage male client would sit with arms folded, watching his peers visit with their families. He'd look up at the clock over the nursing station and silently wonder whether his mom will make it that day. Meanwhile, staff, acting like guards at a detention facility would make a gingerly approach and ask "how're you doing", only to be met with a stiff shrugging of the shoulders; an implicit shunning of care. Another kid, seeing that his parent had arrived at the lobby, would be on the bench, sent there after picking a fight with a peer and then arguing with staff. Some kids liked the bench. It gave them a chance to zone out, with the back-drop of their acting out obscuring an underlying tension. Staff wandered in and out of connection, like babysitters or tentative parents. They sat with disconsolate kids, providing one-on-ones. They listened to embittered monologues, not sure whether to nod sympathetically, or else contest clients' negative thinking and urge spiritual solutions, a letting go of that which cannot be controlled.

On the other side of the unit, among the girls, a somewhat more demonstrative display might be happening. A girl whose parent had promised a visit earlier in the week might be missing, and ten minutes into the two-hour visiting time, the client's foot would be shaking in rage. The girl's case manager, attempting to hide in her office, finishing tasks twenty minutes ahead of her weekend, would hear yet another knock on her door. "Can we call her again?" the girl would demand, for about the sixth time that day. A sideways remark from another girl would query the drama. Her parents had unfailingly arrived twenty minutes prior to the lecture, and thereafter had been the first to enter the girls' living area. Ten minutes into visiting time this girl would be wishing that her parents would leave already. The reason: they had yet to gratify a single demand, and there had been several. Admittedly, she hadn't really expected her parents to remove her from the hospital. She'd known from prior experience in psyche hospitals that the expert's phrase, "against medical advice", would trump any of her wishes. However, she'd hoped for a certain percentage of requests to be met: surely, her parents would sympathize with her not getting along with the other girls; would see that she was not *like* them. Also, that case manager/therapist, so-called, had hardly met with her all week, wasn't nearly as attentive and caring as her outside therapist is.

Other damnations resulted from the failure to bring the right set of clothes, news of an impending school transfer following an undefined pattern of bullying, or the refusal to pass along a letter to someone's girlfriend or boyfriend—because the program had said not to do this. As I walked around the hallways on Saturdays, ostensibly checking to see that everything seemed stable enough, I'd observe awkward triads of parents and youth, mired in the silent aftermath of a disappointment. An angry father would be turning his face away, scanning the surroundings, though not so much in genuine interest as in the need to avoid his child's eyes. There would be hidden anger there, and pain, and the solution to this feeling was avoidance. An anxious mother, perhaps feeling more responsible for the maintaining of order, would appear to try harder. These mothers would be leaning forward on their seats, placing hands on their children's knees, touching them to the sides of their faces. The teens would hiss, turn away and ask if their parents would just leave them alone.

All these scenes appeared to mimic the states of childhood mourning, as described decades earlier by John Bowlby. The teens at Thunder Road played out the phases of separation: protest and wish for reunion, despair, and detachment. And yet, amid this visiting milieu, a celebratory gathering might be happening. Unveiling a large cake that—adhering to the house rules—would be shared with all clients and families, a staff member would announce that a birthday was happening, and everyone would be invited to have cake, congratulate the client in question, and generally contribute to the atmosphere of good cheer. That celebrating client and parent would seem cheerful; grateful for what Thunder Road represents: clean, drug-free goodwill. Even the unhappy parents would step into the mix and break a smile for the birthday client, if only to escape the sodden impasses that were the visits with their own children. As I completed my circuit of the unit, including a gratuitous descent into the downstairs area as a facility safety check (a "sweep" in facility parlance), I'd feel a touch on my arm. It would be somebody's parent who just can't get through to their child. They'd ask me a question: why? Why is their kid so unwilling to talk? Why are the kids so preoccupied with clothes, games, and material things in general? How can they learn to speak to them? How can they learn to relate?

5

A GROUND FLOOR OF FEELINGS

Multifamily Group

When I was interviewing for that original intern position, one of the activities I was told I'd be taking part in was a one-night per week activity called multi-family group. This was the watershed activity of the week, I was told. It was the chance to meet the clients' families, do some family therapy, educate them about drugs, chemical dependency, codependency[21], and coach them as to how they could support the process of treatment. Sounded great, I thought. Actually, I shouldn't imply that I was chomping at the bit. I knew this would be a stressful activity, this multi-family group. I gathered that many of the family members—like the kids—would be truculent in groups, if somewhat muted and less openly hostile in their opposition. I felt the tension and collective shame as parents assembled in the lobby of Thunder Road, waiting to be escorted to one of about five rooms that could accommodate groups that varied in size: from a total of five people on some nights, to a claustrophobic twenty to thirty people on others.

As an intern, and even later as a case manager, I'd be a co-facilitator of this activity. That is, I'd be one of two therapists, typically situated on opposite sides of the room so as to form a kind of watchdog system for the activity. The families and their kids/clients would be asked to sit opposite one another in the room so as to maximize the possibility of eye contact (quite unlike those contract breaking groups, where the intent was to create the opposite possibility). This unintentionally created another dynamic: that of adults sitting opposite kids, like forces about to do battle against one another. For a year, I was a supporting player in this group, uttering five or six sentences every night this not-quite two hour activity took place, while my then colleague and group leader, a robust woman with a matronly and gospel presence, drove the energy of the group.

Fifteen years later, I reflect upon my career thus far as a therapist. I've boasted at times that hardly a week has gone by in one and a half decades when I haven't been facilitating a group therapy session somewhere, and it's true. I've led countless groups of adolescents; men's groups; I've led parolee groups, groups of sex offenders; latterly, groups of interns processing their working lives. I once led a couples' group wherein the presenting problem was that one of the partners (typically the man) had been unfaithful in the marriage—that was a blast. Still, to this day, I'd say that the most difficult group to lead is a multi-family group at a facility like Thunder Road. And I'll go one step further: for those interested in the treatment of adolescents in drug treatment programs, inpatient or outpatient, there is no more important element than the family therapy component. As a result, there is no clinical position in the building more pivotal than that of the case manager/family therapist.

As the multi-family groups were always on a Tuesday, I'd start my bracing for this event on a Sunday afternoon. Not that I'd be planning a repertoire of strategies, necessarily: it was rather that my body—and specifically, my stomach, with its ominously skittish fluttering soon to be carried across vagal nerves—would start warning me of the tension. On the next day back to work I'd lead a preliminary group called pre-family dynamics, a sort of warm up activity. This is where kids would rehearse their topics or else process the strained visits of the weekend—not exactly a "here and now" strategy. The girls, in particular, made good use of this group, even if they subsequently got cold feet with their parents in the room. As an intern, I'd been more of a witness in multi-family group, as that leader, that redoubtable woman with little or no formal training, held her own with a blend of parenting experience and communal fervor. As an Oakland native, she could get away with this tact. Clearly as an outsider, I could not. For a while I sat back, watching the process, and feeling a bit like what I imagine a rodent feels like contemplating when to cross a freeway: *Uh, how do I get in here*.

The families' presentations were not monolithic, and not all of the families were difficult, oppositional, or even dominantly unconscious in their participation. Some parents came eagerly to the sessions, on the back of prolific reading at the recovery section of Barnes and Noble. Melody Beattie's *Codependent No More* was the signature book recommended to most parents, and some ate it up and came to group ready to prove what they'd learned; ready to show staff that whatever problems they'd had parenting their child in the past would be consigned to the past. On the other end of the spectrum, we had the parents who offered mostly contempt for this multi-family group thing. With gloomy expressions, a disgruntled parent might enter the group room, incuriously glance at the set up of adults sitting opposite clients, and take a seat next to their child. Seeing such parents join the group for the first time, I'd immediately go through my projections: they don't want to be here; this is interrupting their free time, or else causing them to miss work or their favorite TV shows; this shouldn't be a required activity for parents, they'd evince; this is not *their* program.

Filling the rooms with people, places, and things

"Welcome," I'd say earnestly at the outset of multi-family group, followed often by "we actually ask parents to sit opposite their children, if you don't mind." Upon becoming a case manager, it would be my task to begin the group, remind everyone of the rules, the norms; the purposes of each. Then the group would begin in a style that had never been manualized per se, but rather handed down in another example of the program's oral tradition. First there would be introductions, which, depending upon the size of the group, could last a half-hour in and of itself. They might also prove lengthy because of the individual characteristics of each member.

Some group members—often the kids—were ridiculously brief in their introductions and check-ins. A begrudging volunteering of names might be followed by a terse, "nothing", in response to a query about topics for group, or existing feeling states. Then the next person might introduce themselves, and begin an inventory of daily events, seemingly hour by hour, as a reporting of events substituting for feelings. Interrupting would happen after a few minutes. In redirecting a monopolist, I often used the tactic of scanning the room, in reference to the twenty or so who were yet to utter a word, hoping that the person checking in would take the hint. The contrary styles had counterintuitive effects. One might think that those who spoke more would receive more feedback. Actually, by the time monopolists had finished sharing, fellow group members might be so eager to move on that few if any questions would be asked. Unconsciously, it seemed as though monopolists may have intended this phenomenon—so anxious were they to not allow space for others' opinions. The reticent, meanwhile, likely hoped to be left alone through their brevity. More commonly, they elicited curiosity as to their process; concern as to their "isolating" tendencies. For those at the extremes of this spectrum, the lesson wasn't so much, *be careful what you ask for*. It was more like, *be careful what you display.*

The room I'd use was sometimes that so-called family room, which was more than capable of accommodating a sizable group. The other designated group rooms, none of which had been originally designed with group therapy in mind, did not. Often I was left with a group room that doubled as a library for the facility, of used books that nobody read. With a full group, the resulting circle would become not so much a circle as a square, with each chair wedged in as tightly as possible. Once I led a group with a disabled woman half-seated in the room, with her right leg, a bloody limb afflicted with phlebitis, dangling in the open doorway. The room needed a fan to stir the air and disperse the heat borne of human congestion. During those preliminary pre-family dynamics groups, a tentatively inspired youth might say something like, "I think I need to confront my Dad about his drinking," only to proclaim ignorance of the remark the following Tuesday night. Another client would offer his or her topic—"anger"—in a generic fashion, and begin describing, with almost rehearsed glibness, how said anger had been a problem in the past, but could now be subdued because of the need to get off probation and generally put life in order. The parent of this child might silently nod throughout this share, or else make comments echoing the central goal. Both might ignore that the client was on reassessment assignment (as signified by the wearing of a hospital scrub) following a weekend assault.

It was the therapist's job, in theory, to point out the so-called pink elephants in the room: the hospital scrubs signifying the breaking of a Cardinal rule; the lack of reference to that parent's drinking, which every other client in the room had heard during that previous pre-family dynamics activity. Essentially, the same counter rules existed in this mini-society as did in the milieu, in the clients' home, and by extension, in society as a whole: don't snitch, don't open a can of worms, protect the family, take the fall and be a team/family player. *Don't throw nobody under the bus*, and so on. Otherwise, move on, focus on the future and not the distant past of two days earlier; above all, don't talk. Gradually, the group would open up space for a more honest process, though the development of groups at Thunder Road was rarely as linear as treatment plans might suggest. Client turnover, staff turnover, not to mention client progress followed by client regression, resulted in an ever tenuous presence of truth.

Sometimes months would pass before a client would feel ready to acknowledge in the parents presence, the reality of drinking throughout a family tree. Sometimes clients would refuse entirely to address a parents' drinking, their parents' legacy of drinking, or a parents' abusive or other neglectful behavior: such was the toxic attachment some kids felt towards those flawed objects, the grim settling combined with a savant's knowledge of everything that adults think is well hidden. Listening was absent; empathy was misunderstood. The poor reflective capacities of parents and children often mirrored one another, which rendered the process of family therapy, much less family therapy in a large group setting, extremely difficult[22]. As a result, process tended to focus upon the generalized here and now of the program, with an externalized focus (i.e: "I don't like the rules of this program") and without reflective function. In a way, this was designed into the program. As suggested earlier, Thunder Road's system of treatment proceeded in stages, and there were three stages in all (not counting 1A). In theory, they were meant to last three months each, but in reality, a centripetal momentum occurred as time passed, with stages II and III pushing up against time, the call of deadlines from outside referral sources. In the first stage, the family program mirrored that of the milieu: clients and families were supposed to be oriented to the program, provided some baseline education as to a 12-step recovery program, the nature of the disease model of addiction, and the purpose and meaning of program rules. In keeping with this, it was understood that clients and families would use multi-family group to work through their adjustment to this new world called Thunder Road.

So, multi-family group would be a forum for lamenting the loss of one set of realities, while being a place for learning new perspectives (in intervention terms, this was what was meant by the term, "reframing")—if you like, new, previously unseen realities. Anyway, these were the platitudes that pleasantly described the wars that would follow. With one, sometimes two therapists operating in defense of the facility's aims, a group of twenty plus might start a feeding frenzy: about the unfairness of rules, the shaming nature of reassessment, or—if the entire community had been placed on restriction, which happened often—about the victimization of innocent clients by either an acting out few, or by an oppressive behavior modification system. Multi-family group was sort of advertised as a place where clients and families would "work on their issues". Invariably, that goal of "working on their issues" traversed a thick bog of defensiveness; a catalogue of externalizations that would be dumped on therapists every Tuesday. Thunder Road took the projections on the chin, with the therapists, like World War I soldiers stranded in no-man's land, serving as the first line of absorption. The conflicts reflected the back-stories: they reflected the porous boundaries of previous living environments; the habit of blame, the inference of abuse from attempts to restore order. The parents and kids were like allied siblings reflecting a symptomatic disorder: the breakdown in their original roles.

This wasn't how it was supposed to be. In treatment planning, when describing a group process dominated by venting, managers would advise redirecting the topic away from events in the milieu. We were supposed to instruct group members as to the purpose of multi-family group, remind them that everyone was assembled to address clients' family matters and not issues between staff and clients. Besides thinking this censorious, I found this a hard directive to follow. Somehow, telling kids and their families something to the effect of, *we're not going to talk about that here*, smacked of the kind of process that prevailed in alcoholic homes. Instead, I experimented. Indulging spells of venting, I'd eventually find ways to ask how disputes reflected similar conflicts in group members' homes. Hadn't an adult ever identified with the role of the allegedly strict or unfair authority? What happened when a household item went missing, and no one in the house appeared to take responsibility? Not everyone appreciated this re-direction. Some accused me of being slick: turning the tables, avoiding their rightful complaints about Thunder Road. Others, even some who were typically defiant, saw the parallels, and further saw the wisdom in stepping outside the existing contexts, examining the fluidity of roles.

You'd think I'd have gotten some training on these things. You might think that, alongside nearly fifteen years of experience leading or co-facilitating groups, that I'd have experienced prodigious training to supplement my experience. Actually, I had precious little, I'm sorry to say. And neither had most of my peers, at least not those working in places like Thunder Road at the level I was working at. At the time, during my first three years in the program, I didn't really notice the learning gap. Strange, but I was drawn into the prevailing disconnected feeling, like everyone else was. With a little distance it might have been different. In my free time, had anyone asked me whether the program trained its therapists in the practice of group therapy, the neglect might have struck me. After all, group therapy was what we did more than any other type of therapeutic activity. But as it was, I plugged away, learning the ropes, employing heuristic strategies as modeled by my predecessors with little or no sense of standard practices. Truth is: in my first three years, I cannot recall a single all-staff training session that devoted its agenda to the imparting of group therapy principles.

It may have been that management couldn't agree on what to train. I recall talking informally at times to medical directors, psychiatrists, and program directors about group therapy practices, and receiving disparate ideas on how to intervene in different group scenarios. For example, most staff members running groups appeared to have learned the norm wherein group members "check-in" sequentially, followed by processes that focused attention on one individual, or one family—a kind of serial family therapy with audience participation. When I spoke to certain members of management, including the most senior and experienced practitioners, it was apparent that this style was not deemed ideal. At times, the standard of group process would even resemble a TV show, with family dramas facilitated by someone like Dr. Phil. A select few within management spoke of the problem of focusing attention so singularly upon individuals, or single families; those sequences of what effectively were "hot seats" were not conducive to group cohesion and likely caused undue stress for some, amplifying the dread that they might already feel towards group therapy.

Parent resistance

The active, tangible undermining of the program by parents had to be identified, interpreted, or confronted. A parent who brought cigarettes to the unit, or who appeared intoxicated on a visiting day, would be confronted by staff, and asked to leave the facility (and sometimes, owing to staff's own parallel jadedness, they would be left alone and not confronted). A parent who attended multi-family group inconsistently, or who attended but disrespected its rules, would also be confronted, hopefully with some attention drawn to this pattern and previous patterns of neglect. Staff, whether case managers, shift supervisors, or directors, would also have to confront parents who broke facility rules: who smuggled cigarettes, cell phones, client belongings that were not allowed on the unit; who passed notes from clients to boyfriends or girlfriends; who—later in the program—looked the other way as their sons or daughters broke the structure of passes so as to visit an inappropriate peer. I thought it my role to add to these confrontations by observing the underlying anxieties that were concealed through a focus upon program inadequacies: the fear of inadequate parenting being exposed.

I remember a single mother who "broke contracts" on her daughter in multi-family group after the latter had broken a weekend pass structure by inviting her boyfriend to come over to the family home. The young couple had disappeared into the girl's room, in defiance of the mother's objections, though the girl had presumed that an old and tacit status quo would still be in effect.

This was a fascinating event all around. This was the first pass the girl had received after nearly ten months living at Thunder Road. She and her mother had spent weeks talking about this event: planning for it, negotiating its structure, going over each others' understandings as to its rules, its limits. Still, after all that, the girl—the Thunder Road client—believed that one old rule, one old standard, would never be breached: *don't snitch.* The mother broke the rule, as in the old rule between her and her daughter. Stirring with resentment for having been taken for granted, and hurt that a long-planned day together had turned into the hosting of a conjugal visit, the mother, after years of colluding with her daughter's defenses, and months of bucking Thunder Road's rules so as to deflect from the real problems at home, chose finally to break the cycle.

Usually, and particularly during the early stages of the program, active undermining was betrayed by the unfolding struggle to adhere to program structure. Those who weren't consciously helping their kids to break rules might be cajoled into breaking the structure in other ways. The ultimate breaking of structure was a discharge from the program. Kids desperate to leave would nag staff parents and beg for removal from the building. The kids' biggest complaints: that the program was too strict, or too "boring", weren't always featured in the appeals. Sometimes, kids put on their thinking caps, aimed at what adults wanted to hear, and spoke to the program's usefulness or corruptibility. I'd be impressed. I thought some ought to be granted audiences with public officials, and be used as expert witnesses on how to dupe mental health professionals. Kids that were mandated by legal authority had less leverage than supposedly voluntary clients in the shorter term track, but that didn't stop some. A kid might be on the phone daily with a gullible parent, giving instructions as to what must be passed on to a lawyer or a probation officer, so that the hitherto unknown inhumanity of Thunder Road could be revealed to the world. Or, if a probation officer were in the role (effectively) of being the decision-maker, they might be treated as a credulous outsider who must be convinced of the need for discharge.

Many kids, however, needed to stay in the program in order to satisfy a legal authority. Theirs was a modified acceptance.

These kids would not so much campaign for an instant discharge as much as an early one. It would start during admissions: "My P.O. says I only gotta be here 30 days," was the predictable interpretation of a client informed that the program was "at least" thirty days. These kids campaigned for early release, thinking treatment tantamount to a stretch in prison. After a few weeks, some argued that they would prefer incarceration, pointing out that in juvenile hall they were at least left alone so they could sleep whenever they felt like it, or else ponder their lives privately, without nosy counselors getting into their business. Otherwise restless and under-stimulated, some of these kids couldn't stand a lengthy day moving from one activity to the next, staying present while others lectured or testified. Having formed the habits of shutting down and moving through life on auto-pilot, many struggled to maintain aliveness. For them, the slogan, *One Day At A Time*, was a problem, because actually a day is just too long.

Then there were those who wanted to stay but fell afoul of the program. Their plaintive phone calls were calls for back up. Calling upon the last fibers of a parent's energy, they solicited defense in the wake of an unjust "dishonorable" discharge. This term, applying of course to those expelled from the program, usually for the violation of Cardinal rules, also meant a return to juvenile hall or some other detention camp. There were many occasions when I sat with a client, monitoring a phone call, listening to him or her trying to persuade a parent that the program was being unfair, that it was just too difficult; that it was harming or else victimizing them. If the parents argued, the kids would up the ante and become abusive—cite abandonment by the parent. Counselors often got to see or hear who was in charge on these occasions. Parents were on the spot, playing out a game that had long since gone wrong. They either stood up at these times and said or did the right thing, or else they withered in the face of tears or abuse, and resigned themselves to another defeat.

They'd absorb the complaints of their children. They'd heard before about the strictness of the program: its many rules, its ruthless punishments, pathologizing language, and abusive methods. Decision time: where did they stand as the past and future parents? Unfortunately, some were rigidified in their defenses through their interaction with Thunder Road. In plainer terms, they got worse. They observed the rules of our program, considered the team's pronouncements as to systemic problems, and reacted. They reacted badly in some cases, and withdrew from the scary prospect of changes they hadn't bargained for. Some made judgments as to how we intervened, and in defense of themselves, asserted vindication of their own past strategies, despite their past troubles. And they weren't the only ones to object. Some (outside observers, industry overseeing agencies) thought the strict regimen a "set-up" for a demoralizing experience, and thus thought the program fundamentally unjust and wrongheaded.

As I was becoming aware of this burgeoning opinion, mostly heard outside the program walls, I listened. I listened hard, but more often than not found the arguments naïve. To understand the distortions involved, imagine you go to a doctor[23], and though ambivalent about the proposed medical procedures, you are still seeking treatment for a distressing condition. Now imagine that as the doctor delineates symptoms, you not only reject that such symptoms exist, you also chide the doctor for asking after such concerns, thinking the questions intrusive, the concerns obscure. You then consider that prescriptive measures will not help the condition, and may possibly bring about the condition that you're not sure you have. So, you leave the doctor's office in disgust.

This is absurd. Likewise, the attitude of some regarding Therapeutic Communities is absurd. These communities, when appropriately run, set up a consistent, firm structure in order to provide an antidote to established patterns of loose structure, with all of its attendant neglect, abuse, and false promises of fun, freedom, and soothing function. They aren't abandoning those who struggle in treatment—who struggle to remain drug or violence free—when they discharge for cause. They are delivering a statement with a long-term therapeutic aim. They should not allow rampant drug use, violence, or sexual harassment to compromise not only the integrity, but more importantly, the safety of others in the milieu. The rigorous structure of treatment is meant to provide safety, contain out of control behaviors, and impart values such as interdependence and responsibility not only for self, but also towards others. The structure is meant to rival a much different world—not copy or compete with its rewards systems—and confront a catalog of harmful beliefs.

The program, for example, is meant to combat the false freedom of the drug using lifestyle, or to rebuke the false maturation of teens that seem to think that un-checked license is a birthright. I'm referring to able-bodied 14 year olds who celebrate their use of medical marijuana as though they are terminally ill or glaucoma-suffering patients and that marijuana is the moral equivalent of a polio vaccine. I'm referring to a 15 year old male who asserts that he is a man because he has sired a child; because he earns money for his diabetic mother and 11 year old brother through "slangin" (dealing drugs), and therefore deserves to party through the night without parental limits, the curfews that are *just for kids*. And I'm writing of a 13 year old girl who, as a result of her (sexualized) experience, feels she is ready to have a consensual sexual relationship, and is nothing less than idealizing of the person twice her age who is prepared to accommodate this arrangement.

It is understandable that kids who are not used to rules, much less appropriate and non-abusive punishments, would react negatively towards a system looking to restore order. Once they might have wretched as they were fed pills for medicinal purposes. For most of us, swallowing pills is a seminal task of childhood. It is meant to be a bitter, mildly unpleasant act; endured because it is good for the body, not because it feels good. The subculture that surrounds addiction turns this commonplace memory on its head, and generates pleasure from former drudgeries. Magic? Addiction, the apparently personified creature that it is, promises to transform the dull and painful experience into an exciting or pleasantly sedative act. Therefore recovery programs should stand in opposition with a harsher reality, but a reality nonetheless, against a subculture grounded in such lies. Meanwhile, it's understandable that parents of troubled teens would resist what is at least an implicit critique of their parenting habits. It's understandable that they would feel as though their own lifestyles, if not their entire personhoods, were under attack.

Discussions, negotiations, process: Whatever it was called at any one time, the conversation about rules was the battle-ground in which the deficits of both clients and their family members were laid out, fought over, confronted, and defended. The difference with parents was that many were slow to realize that their beliefs, behaviors, and affects were also on the table for discussion. For years, this unwritten mission statement bonded most who worked at Thunder Road, despite the otherwise diverse methods and ideas amongst staff and management. At times, however, I wondered what might happen if one day we lost our resolve as a program. What would happen if we lost sight of the basics? What would happen if we lost containment and became outnumbered by those who normalized drug use; those who were insecurely attached and avoidant of conflict, ever looking for ways to feel better instead of get better and re-positioning that paradigm as a standard for the program. What would happen if these people became not just numerous, but better positioned, because in a democratic world, the most popular opinions, right or wrong, are the ones that seize the bully pulpits. At some point, they might even be the ones in charge.

Parent resistance: whose kid is this anyway?

The following is an example—not a real example—more a composite of all the discussions that took place when parents came to participate in the program and then visit (as opposed to joining a therapy group). In this scenario, a disgruntled father has arrived 45 minutes late for a lecture on "the disease concept", which precedes a two-hour family visiting time, and which is required for family members wanting to visit children in the program. Reception and then staff has allowed his entry into the lecture without comment as to his lateness, and he doesn't comment either on this. This lecture has begun with the day's shift supervisor reminding all in attendance as to the basic rules of visiting, including the stipulation that any gifts for clients be presented at reception so that they might be cleared by staff, as well as a request that clients not be given, or loaned, any candy, cigarettes, or electronic devices. The disgruntled father has missed this opening, as well as most of the lecture. He later allows his son, a Thunder Road client, to borrow his cell-phone so that he can disappear into his bathroom and make a call to his girlfriend who is *on the outs*, as the kids say. Through the miracle of contract breaking, the borrowing of the phone comes to the attention of staff. Now cut to the following Tuesday, when the therapist of the client, and the case manager of his and the parents' caseload, must confront the parent:

Therapist: "I understand that you offered your cell phone for your son to use during visiting last Saturday"
Parent: "I didn't know that was a problem. He (his son) should have told me. I told you he was manipulative"

Comment: interesting that the parent doesn't deny the therapist's assertion, nor does he seem curious about how the information came to staff's attention. Also, note the readiness to scapegoat his son.

Therapist: "Well…ok…do you not recall this being discussed during the admissions process when you first arrived?
Parent: "They never said anything like that"

Comment: a common happening. The therapist implies responsibility on the part of the admissions department, who is supposed to have oriented the man to the Thunder Road structure by handing him documents and "going over" a few basics.

Therapist: "OK. Well, it's also indicated in the 'Welcome to Thunder Road' packet that I believe we provided you"
Parent: (impassively) "I never got that. Maybe his mom took the copy, I don't know"
Therapist: "Well, maybe we can get you another copy so you can be familiar with the house standards, including our policies about any electronic items"
Parent: (shrugs) "Alright"
Therapist: "Um, I'm curious if you recall the lecture on Saturday covering the topic?"
Parent: (under breath, concealing face with hand) "Man…"
Therapist: "I'm sorry. What's happening now?"
Parent: (looking away) "I thought we were gonna' talk about my son and his program"
Therapist: "I'm sorry. I thought that was what we were doing"

Comment: Note the therapist beginning two statements with apologies—likely an indicator of anxiety—but an indicator that will be noted (unconsciously, perhaps) by this parent. The therapist's initial avoidance of the conflict is also indicated by the reference to "get another copy" (of the rules packet) as if that would solve the problem. This is an example of counter-transference acting out, with the therapist acting to placate this parent. Note the parent's own avoidance strategy: looking away and speaking under his breath; conflicted about appearing angry. This recalls the insights of couples' therapist John Gottman (1999) who wrote of men who stonewall, suppress rage, incurring ongoing problems like high blood pressure, leading (speculatively) to heart disease. The dilemma is that of feeling the impulse within, but fearing where it will go.

Parent: "Nah, you're talking about some stuff to do with cell phones. I didn't come here on my day off to talk about this, and this is taking time away from me being with my son"
Therapist: "Well, I hear that. It's just that we need to talk about the need Thunder Road has to not have items like cell phones on the unit, even for small amounts of time. We've known this to be dangerous in the sense that clients might easily arrange pick-up for an AWOL with peers in the community."
Parent: (avoiding eye contact) "Alright. Well, we're clear now—can we move on?"
Therapist: "Well, we can, though I'm not clear on why this seems to be upsetting you"
Parent: (by now hissing audibly through his teeth) "Man, what is it with this place? I don't understand why you can't let this go. Why we gotta keep talking about it?"
Therapist: (a bit stiffly) "Well, I think we need to understand—"
Parent: (interrupting) "To what?"
Therapist: "—to understand what happened here. I mean, I think this is not just about reminding you about a rule. Maybe it's about what you feel about the rule—about Thunder Road—or maybe it's about your role in your son's program, his life"
Parent: (sounding angry and righteous) "My role is to support my son while he's here in this program"

Therapist: "And so is ours, but can we talk about where we might have disagreements, even though we have the same goal"

Comment: There are several points to highlight in this exchange. First of all, as suggested earlier, troubled parents, like their sons and daughters, exhibit projections in their complaints; note that it is Thunder Road that has kept the father away from his son, not the father's likely absenteeism over a protracted period. The avoidance continues, now with a cognitive addendum: *why can't we move on.* The parent is getting angrier, and more specifically, his container is unhinging, causing leaks. In a more private context, this parent would likely have become enraged by this point. The therapist of this scene more or less sticks to the task despite the countertransference fears, and asserts that the problem is deeper than the breaking of a single rule; it is interpersonal, and therefore threatens a working alliance. Most crucially, the therapist asserts that the problem *is* worth talking about.

The long, lost "I" statement

The issues are actually deeper than the interpersonal; they are deeply intrapsychic, which was why multi-family group so often seemed an ineffective activity. Exploring the interpersonal was essentially the point of multi-family group, with the premise being that if clients and their families would choose to be honest, communication would develop in a positive, healthy way. But it wasn't as simple as that. Encouraging group members to use the pedestrian technique of "I" statements, for example, seemed worthy enough, but more often than not, the strategy presumed that the spirit of the exercise was fully understood. Clients often did not know what they felt; nor did parents, at least not beyond a narrow range of feelings that primarily served defensiveness. The words that spoke to this thin layer, like "pissed", "disrespected", "frustrated", "mad", were invariably secondary, inclined towards the aggressive, focused upon the external: not the point of "I" statements.

For many, using "I" statements meant sticking the words "I feel" in front of a monologue that otherwise echoed older communication habits. For instance, someone might say something like, "I feel unsafe talking right now," and thus make appropriate use of the "I" statement protocol. Minutes later, the same individual might say, "I feel like you're being strict. There's no point in talking to you," (In other words, placing "I feel" in front of an opinion about another), oblivious as to the difference between one's own feelings and a projection. Many struggled to deepen beyond the layers of blame, and would become confused. These same individuals would rebel, soliciting support from other group members, and turn on a therapist who was *trippin'* with strange observations.

Another example: a client may share with a group about an assault upon another. The facilitator might ask after feelings relating to the incident, to which the client might simply reply, "disrespected", and think that the end of that particular exchange. The facilitator might ask, "and how does that feel—to be disrespected?" Clients grimace in confusion, and reply, "I don't know what you're getting at." The therapist presses, repeats (or perhaps paraphrases) the same question, implying that layers of feeling exist below what is constructed as "respect". The group fidgets, becoming uncomfortable. They squirm. No one else knows how to answer the question either, and restlessness follows. Those sympathetic to the program's cause become anxious, hoping the intervention's purpose becomes clearer such that the integrity of the group is preserved. Those less allied become contemptuous, and move to side with the exposed client. A cultural divide? Possibly. I noticed that for many the word "respect" was sort of totemic; a singular notion torn from the crypt of a family or cultural mythos. Ask someone to speak to the meaning of respect, they might repeat "respect" in an exasperated voice, as if the concept, much less the history or the weight of feelings beneath it, bore no further explanation. For many, a wall would be erected at this point, or more accurately, considering the metaphor of descent as opposed to upwards movement, a ground floor; a ground floor of feelings.

Clients and their families either consciously or unconsciously resisted the path that might follow, the prescription that John Bowlby had supplied for a generation of practitioners: the task of linking present or "here and now" feelings to past, early development experience. The client in the above scenario might have delved further into the meaning of "respect". The client might have explored the antecedent events, the explanations, not so much as to why respect is important, but why it is *so* important; why the need for respect merited aggression, and why it seemed important to risk life and limb, the potential rupture of relationships, in order to seek this supposedly vital interpersonal commodity. Those truly working on themselves in treatment sought to make links between their hot-button tendencies and the past deprivations—phenomena that had distorted their perception of needs. They didn't just apologize for bad behavior, or promise not to do it again; they had graduated "ah-hah" moments that they could speak to.

But the seemingly rote and banal manner in which multi-family group proceeded left little room for a full understanding of therapeutic tasks. The notion of using an "I" statement to fully explore that inner process was lost on many. This despite the relentless supply of slogans, admonitions, and daily encouragement to go inward: "focus on self", "look at yourself", "use 'I' statements", "take ownership", and on and on and on. The psycho-education on this concept was daily and repetitive, but all too often without the necessary *in vivo* attention. The messages were therefore lost, like invisible particles disappearing into the atmosphere. There were problems with structures, I thought: the internal structures of the clients and families; the external structure of a program designed to address their problems. I started to think that the capacity for a proper working through of issues simply wasn't there, inside the kids or their parents—not enough of them, anyway. Then at some point I reflected on Thunder Road—on its staff, leadership, even its legacy—as well as myself. I started to think the capacity wasn't in us.

Meanwhile, the business of that group would continue with an injunction against family dynamics that would thrust process back upon a default position: that routine assault upon reality testing, as in that of the kids in the separate pursuit of their dangerous lifestyles. I suspect, among other things, that it was too painful for many to address so called "family" dynamics. It seemed too painful for some to assert things like, "you're letting the family down", and such; or to just experience what was implied by others' behavior: *I don't care*. Addicts: they're good at demonstrating how little they care, whether that's true or not. So the discussions would recapitulate pre-treatment build-ups: the questions as to whether a clients' drug histories were indeed what they were reporting; whether the circumstances leading to admission had in fact been what was reported by collateral contacts; with that concurrent conversation about the existing solution—the Thunder Road structure—regardless of whether the nature of the problem was agreed upon in the first place.

There were many examples of kids and parents who failed to show their hearts behind their defenses. Some were conscious and deliberate in their resistance, but many kidded themselves, believing they had traversed their defenses, or at least they presented as though they had. These were self-congratulatory clients and families: the ones who spoke of "old me" versus "new me" as an advertisement of their change; who said things like, "I was never brought up to show my feelings", as if by making that declaration they were doing just that[24]. Caring others, including loved ones and counselors, were left guessing, "feeling into", as one supervisor put it, those individuals with hardened, self-centered, or seductive fronts. That dilemma, of how to empathize with a defense, seemed center stage for all to witness.

One of the more heartbreaking examples of family impasse concerned a young man named Philip who did seem to care. Like many kids in the program, Philip had entered with little understanding as to how the program would really proceed. He was somewhat motivated with respect to abstaining from drugs, and certainly motivated to cooperate with the terms of his probation and complete a year's course of treatment. Despite a flash temperament that regularly brought him trouble during his initial stage of treatment, he was well-liked by peers and staff, and soon managed to advance to the second stage of the program. In multi-family group, he was supported by his biological mother, who suffered from a variety of physical ailments, including an ill-defined heart condition, as well as a gruff, largely silent step-father who was unusually solicitous of his wife. Philip's father, described as a physically abusive absentee, had not been in contact for years, and thus took no part in the program.

As part of a stage II of treatment, clients were directed to reflect upon issues that were longstanding and/or critical with respect to family functioning. In keeping with 12-step assignments that directed clients to observe past resentments, many clients, with or without staff encouragement, turned attention to breakdowns in family functioning, with serendipitous and heartfelt interest. Protective or not of their families, they'd begin sharing with staff and peers, sometimes in groups, and sometimes in individual sessions. Like the pre-family dynamics groups, these one-on-ones were precursors to the big stage that was multi-family group. Philip decided to reflect upon the long-suppressed topic of the physical abuse he'd experienced at the hands of his now absent father. He was sure he had been negatively shaped by the once chronic pattern, and regardless of whatever else was asked of him, had come to believe that Thunder Road's family group program was his best opportunity for healing. Until that point he'd talked about his abuse history with me, other counselors, and several of his peers. But somehow it wasn't enough. More than anything, he explained, he needed his mother to hear the story, and validate his memory. Without that, he could never be sure that what happened was real. With my support, as well as that of his caseload, he prepared his mother for the topic on a Saturday visiting, and then delved further into the history on two consecutive Tuesday nights. The mother nodded, smiled gingerly and appeared to listen, but made only glib, forgettable comments in response to the initial disclosures.

On the Saturday following the latter multi-family group process, I was approached by the fidgety step-father and pulled aside for a quiet one-on-one. Sternly, he told me that as a result of Philip's insistence upon sharing his abuse history (or my coaching of him in this area) his wife was now suffering nightmares, resulting in panic attacks. She had also been a victim of the father's abuse, of course, and despite a tentative support of Philip's disclosures, was struggling to contain the feelings that were emerging for her. Her sensitivity to the subject had likely inhibited Philip for years; her ailments were likely a somatic syndrome warding off conscious acknowledgement of this unresolved stressor. The step-father, the latter-day protector of this woman, glared hotly at me and demanded that the discussion of past abuse in multi-family group cease immediately. I tried to be empathetic and pointed out that Philip's mother surely needed therapeutic attention of her own to address the problem of her trauma.

The man shook his head vigorously. He had his own ideas of coping: stop talking about it! Unsatisfied by my circumspect, if concerned response, he then bypassed me and took his demands directly to his step-son. Counting on Philip's temporarily sidelined need to protect his mother from pain, the man shamed Philip into censorship: bringing up the past was making everyone feel bad. *What was the use of that*? By the way, that question—the "what good would it do" argument—is my informal nomination for the prize of most employed rationale for secrecy. It is an almost unanswerable provocation. Philip and his step-father agreed to halt the historical review, and so the conversation about the shared abuse history was blocked. Solemnly, Philip informed me of this ahead of the next multi-family group, and despite my exhortation that he continue to explore his own dysfunctional past regardless of his mother's intentions, he was resolute. He didn't have an alternative plan for healing, however, and by the end of the following week he had AWOLed from Thunder Road. He never returned.

Socratic Method

Unless specifically steered elsewhere, multi-family groups often fell back upon a default purpose: the ongoing deliberation of recent events that brought kids into the program. It was a safer topic, basically. For some, playing the role of scapegoat, absorbing that burden, was preferable to challenging family homeostasis. This superficially positioned kids against adults, sometimes with senior clients as nominal allies of staff, conducting a cross-examination of an identified suspect. I think that one of the reasons that clients often came to associate Thunder Road therapists with lawyers is that both made prolific use of Socratic Method. It must have seemed familiar the way questions were asked, particularly in group sessions, with other group members/jurors present, and with therapists listening for inconsistencies, ever ready to pounce upon errors. Defense of one position—the assertion of a pattern of drug use and negative consequences—was pitted against the defense of another position—the client's assertion that drug use had either been exaggerated, or that the consequences have; and that the persons reporting the patterns were biased such that the consequences were not real.

Next, therapists would paraphrase the arguments, and solicit feedback from other group members. Those in alliance with the therapist, or at least looking to appear so, might pose a counter-argument to the group member of focus; challenge assumptions, question whether drug use had indeed been exaggerated by others. Group members, peers and adults, might argue with a client stating that the consequences of drug use were benign. The path the client was leading: it was an invariably destructive road, they typically warned. That particular assertion was rarely disputed, so the resistant client would back up, re-assert that the events leading to admission had been exaggerated instead. Alternatively, the client might take flight into health, and pour all energies into persuading anyone who would listen that drug use and other behaviors were simply behind them. For these kids, Tuesday multi-family groups were the forums wherein they would mount their campaigns, replete with promises, for the reclamation of a once untainted image.

Ironically, those clients who acknowledged their drug use and other negative behaviors, but were unrepentant about these habits, seemed easier to work with. At times, I felt refreshed by their honesty, even if it was defiant. I also respected their unwillingness to accept sole responsibility for systemic problems—that *it's down to me* attitude that others presented so as to protect their family members. Some of my colleagues empathized with my preference, while others didn't. Some of my peers seemed more comfortable in the authoritative position, with the straightforward roles of pedagogue and un-reluctant leadership. I was more sensitive (and more righteous) around pretense; I disliked lies and politics, the designation of sacrificial lambs: these vices stirred my countertransference; had me revisiting the belief that someone was trying to make a fool of me; the fear, ultimately, that I was a fool.

The more conscious parents: they were not refreshed by defiant honesty; they were frightened by it. They seemed, on the whole, more passive or burnt out. They'd little appetite for the fights that their kids still seemed willing to have with them. These parents spoke past the olive branch of this brand of honesty, and sought to make bargains instead. With a group's help, they might challenge the all-or-nothing thinking of such a client. Upon hearing a rationale like, "smoking weed is the only thing that makes me feel better," group feedback might pose a scenario that demands an exception, more than one "correct" answer. "Can you think of situations that would lead you to *not* use drugs?" a mother with a limited agenda might ask: she'd hope to hear her children promise that they'd not smoke around her, or desecrate her family home with ugly paraphernalia.

The externalization of consequences was habitual, and there was always someone to blame, even if this strategy absolved those attachment figures that the troubled are most wary of alienating. Meanwhile, it is relatively easy for an inveterate drug user, especially an adolescent, to attribute so-called negative consequences to perception, not fact. If only marijuana was legal, for instance, there would be no problem with its use. That's one argument. If only parents or school officials *understood* (whatever exactly they are to understand), then a leniency towards drug use—effectively a sanctioning of drug use—would prevail. Again, notions of problems and solutions were often conflated when it came to the subjects of drug use and violence. Drugs may lead to legal and academic problems, but they are often considered the most efficient solution for uncomfortable feeling states rather than a precipitant. Though acts of violence may be denounced in principle, few actions are as gratifyingly primal as that of revenge, and revenge against perceived slights was the usual pretext for violence. The possibilities of health consequences related to drug use, especially marijuana, were either unmoving (future bronchial difficulties), or felt remote (alleged links to Schizophrenia or reduced sperm counts). Their drugs of choice would not harm them, kids confidently declared. For those asserting this stance in a difficult family therapy activity, the implication was clear: drugs, not people and relationships, are the solution.

In multi-family group, as in any activity within the therapeutic milieu, cautionary tales of long-term, drug-induced hardship were the interventions of choice, especially when a root conflict was exposed, and no one, including myself, knew quite what to say. I knew that kids, much less drug-addicted kids, hadn't an ear or a right brain for discussions of that which was long-term. Still, I had a stock anecdote or two of my own, despite my misgivings about self-disclosure, or testimonials-as-interventions. My favorite was one that didn't concern me directly, but instead an anonymous sufferer. The memory stayed with me after I'd once visited a hospital and observed a man being wheeled via a gurney onto a freight elevator. I shared the elevator, and was squeezed into the side, next to the machine attached via a spider's web of wires, to the underside of the man's neck. Clearly he'd just undergone some horrendous procedure in which portions of his throat had been removed—a result of mouth or throat cancer I presumed. He was semi-conscious, stupefied from painkillers and gazing up at the bright elevator lights like he was looking for evidence of God. He was wheezing yet looked as if he wanted a cigarette. That was my take, anyway, as I was a smoker at the time and recognized the look. Feeling the distinct pinch of craving, I shared a dark moment of attunement with that old man. It was a disorienting feeling, competing with revulsion, which in those moments I was straining to link with our shared toxic habit. He wanted it, I thought. His brain wants it, the nicotine. Doesn't it care? I wondered, of his brain. And wouldn't mine? Doesn't it know? Well, his body cared: that was the point. His body was rebelling against his craving: it was setting limits finally; coldly and ruthlessly, without any deference to what was deemed just, unjust, understanding or not.

When the body delivers consequences choice and understanding are no longer relevant. This is not true of any other kind of consequence. The body speaks and cannot be argued with, basically. Drug users can blame legal systems, or broader social mores, for an extensive arrest record. Home-based consequences can be laid at the feet of an uptight or hypocritical parent for those ready to have *those* conversations. Overreactions can be imputed.

But who says to the body, "Come on now, aren't you being a little harsh? Can't you cut me some slack", as it delivers its verdicts and doesn't even bother with "I" statements. That's an interesting dynamic, between the body and the mind. The anecdote of the old man with the wires living in his neck was perhaps no more effective than many others that speak of future consequences, dire warnings of health hazards in middle age and beyond: Again, the youth nodded, or else they debated the inconclusive assertions of medical science with respect to drugs like marijuana. For the most part they absorbed the truest warnings while sparing everyone the deeper conversations that no one wanted to have.

Still, the educational lessons were useful filler following obvious stalls in the therapeutic process, and management seemed content to hear of cautionary tales as the ingredients of group therapy. Besides, the old man with the wires in his neck story was good filler. Otherwise, interventions with clients and families were a rough mix of psycho-educational pronouncements, chestnut suggestions like "use 'I' statements", cognitive reframes, such as attempts to persuade clients that interventions were intended as *support*. Purely cognitive measures seemed effective at times: it often moved clients who absorbed blame to consider how they might treat someone else with their circumstances. Miracle questions, designed to have clients imagine a reality without the existence of problems (internally or externally defined) were also used. Within the family component of the program, I eventually detected the influence of Strategic Family therapy; of the problem solving techniques associated with brief therapy models supervised at the famous Mental Research Institute in Palo Alto.

Unless group members wanted time to vent about the therapeutic milieu, many were content to endure the activity, and even preferred suffering the long-windedness of (typically) a self-involved client or parent to the deepening of so-called process. I have to admit that on many Tuesday nights I allowed this. Meaning, I couldn't really stop people talking about that which wasn't on the treatment plan—the off-the-topic stuff they weren't supposed to be talking about. 12-step testimonials sometimes formed the core of the activity, and tended to be rhetorical and dull. It's not that I object to them; it's that testimonials are not group therapy, and people get confused about the differences between therapy and 12-step meetings if the differences aren't explained. Otherwise, the processes were simply remedial. A monosyllabic client might utter his topic with eyes fixed to the ground. An overbearing parent, seated across the room, might reflect back what has been heard and attach a response, perfunctorily using an "I" statement. A reluctant, roughly two-second long "Well, I hear what he's saying" might be followed by a diatribe, half-directed at the client, one quarter targeted at the agency, and one quarter aimed at the group audience.

Monopoly and avoidance

For a variety of reasons, monopolists were welcome and implicitly encouraged in groups, especially multi-family group. The argument that others needed time to share was undercut by the faulty premise. Others may have needed time, but many didn't want it. Those that did surreptitiously looked to the therapist to step in and interrupt those who took up too much *space*, and some of those group members wanted time for a similar reason: to seize the bully pulpit themselves and orate instead of truly improving communication skills. At these times, the interpersonal, much less the intrapsychic value of the exercises was forsaken. Furtive glances in the facilitator's direction, at about the five minute mark of someone's share, were the most risk-taking these exercises would become. Few would make complaints about another's monopoly of time, especially if the person speaking was someone else's parent or even someone else's kid. In this respect, group members unquestioningly followed rules; society's rules; their rules.

In time, in the absence of rigorous training, I developed my own ideas about how group therapy was supposed to upset the rigid, unconsciously driven rules of a dysfunctional system. I knew that the half-supervised, anemic and rote interventions of the brief therapy models weren't speaking to the problems of clients and families. Modeling the strategies of one or two independently-thinking peers, I encouraged kids to direct questions and comments about the "parental" decisions of the adults, to the parents themselves. Parents were often encouraged to direct feedback not only to their own children, but those of others also. Many complied with this, though not without resistance. Parents preferred to direct advice at youth, as that seems to be how adults like to talk to young people. With ironic effect, parents would direct compliments at clients other than their own sons or daughters, or else direct those compliments to kids' parents instead. I was fascinated and amused by the perpetual advocacy and positioning that was happening: clients pleading their cases; parents pleading theirs; parents offering sympathy and encouragement to other families, seeking reciprocity. The aggression, the venting, when not projected at Thunder Road in the person of the therapist, was often subdued; conflict was avoided more often than not.

I know that some will disagree with the observation that clients and families avoided conflict in treatment. I think it's been a constant area of misunderstanding, actually, reflecting the assumption that because oppositional attitudes are apparent, conflict is being addressed openly and honestly. This point of view neglects the principle of "fight, flight, or freeze": three distinct methods of dissociation, and therefore avoidance. The conflicts to which I refer are those that lay beneath the noise and confusion of the program imbroglio—the endless disputes over rules, boundaries, fairness, respect, and so on. These conflicts masked the underlying issues, the subjects un-broached, the secrets untouched from which the noisy arguments deflected. I noticed when multi-family groups reached these kinds of stalemates. I'd speak to those moments, press the point with a client who suddenly can't remember his spontaneously declared core issue of the previous week; asked "why" with implied confrontation—why had something that seemed so important previously be forgotten once multi-family group begins. I'd stretch out the words for effect, looking to insinuate doubt, actually hoping someone might even call me on the insinuation, for at least then a discussion of process—what one client called "the conversation about the conversation"—might follow. Then I'd have my opportunity to address defenses, as well as secrets that might be peeled away.

I observed the silences being played out in those overstuffed rooms, with the dread of honest talk hanging thickly, and I'd do a lot of waiting and watching. Sometimes I'd play dumb, shrug my shoulders, and wonder aloud about who wanted to speak; who wanted to speak to the real issues—the ones clients and parents would spontaneously let slip—take some time and do some work. I'd feel righteous and bold, though I probably came off as arrogant, inspiring hate in some. Still, it was interesting to observe how the group's process would move; how some defied leadership while others not only tolerated my leadership, they depended upon it. I am reminded often of Bion's (1961) assumptions about group process. Groups evolve with certain dynamics, with some creating reliance upon a strong leader figure (my first group, when I was an intern, seemed like this). In these groups, spokesmen and women ask questions of group leaders, seeking advice, psychoeducational lessons that patronized an "expert" facilitator, while defending against an anxious independence. Other groups developed "us versus them" positions, such as when the multi-family group united like a grass roots protest movement against the Thunder Road and (by extension) legal establishment. Group members sought scapegoats, both within and outside the groups; people to "hot seat". Others still, especially the bigger groups, paired off in the way that Bion described, forming cliques, whispering in safe pockets instead of dealing with the group/community as a whole.

The commonplace groups of the day treatment program seemed especially like this. The more unruly the clients, and the less reflective they seemed, the more I began to perceive them like cattle being herded from one activity to the next, ever mooing in complaint. On the surface, a group process might proceed quietly, with clients seemingly in cooperation, giving one another feedback, usually with a focus upon the individual dynamics and not so much the group phenomena. Looking closely, there would be tensions present, sometimes ugly undercurrents. Clique-building, ostracism, and bullying often played out while the targeted shamefacedly turned away and insisted that nothing was wrong. This phenomenon was observed by Foster, Nathan, and Ferry (2010) in their study of that adolescent residence in Australia: groups could be used to demonstrate social power and ostracize; for staff, they observed that a delicate balance is required such that interpersonal process might occur without alienating vulnerable residents. The problem in nutshell, I suppose. As a facilitator of such groups, I had numerous opportunities to turn a spotlight on such moments, and at least speak to the tension, even if everyone in the room denied the problem and agreed that the counselor was *on* something. That *trippin'* accusation: it targets those therapists who see into false scenes and call out tacit messages. I'd feel the chill as kids alluded to conflicts between themselves, only to then try and assuage me: "Don't worry about it," a teen leader would say of himself and his self-governing peers: "We're taking care of it."

In reading this jaundiced account, the reader might wonder about a host of things: whether day-treatment groups or multi-family groups achieve anything of value; about why I continued to participate if these activities were so fundamentally ill-conceived; about whether I was a burn-out case, or simply incompetent to effect positive results. I suppose I think that all these perspectives are possible, though I would only agree with the one about burn-out. In fact, I did think at times that some good derived from groups. There were clients and families that were motivated to make the best of the opportunities provided; that were grateful for a forum to try and work through misunderstandings. They had relatively clear ideas about what they wanted to say to one another from the outset, but they'd always struggled to find the right words and context. They were clear about the goal of straightening out their lives, being abstinent from drugs, which many truly understood to be ruining their lives. Unlike other factions of clients and parents, these people didn't dispute the premise of treatment: they understood and accepted that negative consequences had befallen them because of drugs; that unhealthy attitudes had contributed to their problems. These people came to those groups with topics at the ready, with thumbs shooting from their hips, ready to talk; ready to *get real*.

For these people, the obstacles were not so much problems of tenuous motivation, or distrust in the helping system, or even an implicit pact of secrecy embedded within families and peer groups. The obstacle was that of not knowing how to make the necessary changes: how to communicate differently, relate differently. It was my introduction to a critical dialectic: knowing "what" versus knowing "how", as termed by Lyons-Ruth (2001). Motivation, narrowly defined as it commonly is, is simply not enough to create the change that is desired—the "what". I still think that motivation is the most important factor on a treatment plan, but it must be an informed motivation. My colleagues and I relied too heavily upon a simplified notion of motivation, and thereafter upon a predominantly behavioral focus, but without attention to an internal process. As a result, many exchanges between staff and clients, and between parents and clients, would grind to a near halt wherein understanding of the problems would trail off, to be replaced by pat exhortations for individuals to simply keep focus, not give up hope—everything except true and full understandings of their maladaptive patterns.

I found these to be the most frustrating experiences at Thunder Road: to watch clients and parents, people who were genuinely trying to get better, improve their relationships and make the most of the program, but nonetheless fail to achieve a true knowledge of one another, and then settle for shallow cheerleading efforts as a soothing consolation. In some cases it was heartbreaking to observe. I realize that some might bristle at the term "settle" and reject my attitude. *Progress not perfection*: that's the saying that's often called out from the bullpen of 12-stepisms to mollify feelings accompanying an unfinished treatment episode. The spirit of the phrase is (I think) meant to counter the addict's perceived tendency towards despair, and thereupon, self-destruction. Unfortunately, the phrase is also used as a crutch; to simultaneously excuse lack of progress, ignore frozen moments wherein feelings disappear, and then dismiss further expectations.

I hold that more elaborate goals are not simply a projection of mine. I'm referring to those clients and families who seemed to feel the missing pieces of their process, and actually hungered for more, despite having been mandated into treatment originally, and despite being impaired internally. On the one hand, these were serendipitous adventurers, similar in one sense to what Campbell (1949) finds in traditional mythology[25]. For them it was important to uncover what concrete secrets were being kept in the family history, just as it is important to know what concrete secrets are being held in the facility. These were parallel goals pursued by everyone concerned. But beyond the confessional layer, it was also important to understand how secrets were kept, what rules governed the expression of feelings; how people felt in relationship, about one another. What was the history of the dynamic, the secret-keeping narrative? Understood in these terms,

I'd find that many clients and families would warm to the process of family therapy, having gradually absorbed what it had to offer. They had stories—stories that they found themselves desperately wanting to tell. Despite the deficits that many presented, progress (and not perfection) on these layers was there for the taking. The time was there (a ninety minute group, once a week, for upwards of a year). The space, as in a "good enough" room, was there. Yet there were obstacles—external obstacles—even for the motivated and capable. Sadly, it was the structure that would so often let people down.

More often than not, groups, including multi-family groups, were simply too big. Twenty, sometimes thirty people would be squeezed into rooms, with little or no regard as to how group size might impact the process. While Yalom (1995) writes that this is not uncommon in clinical settings, he points out that such groups are devoted to the didactic imparting of psycho-education, not interactional group therapy. For this latter type of activity, between six and eight members is ideal and no more than ten is deemed acceptable[26]. But oversized groups and high turnover of group members was endemic at Thunder Road. If the program admitted three clients in a day, and assigned two of those to a caseload, adding a prospective four to five people to an already oversized multi-family group, it didn't matter. It certainly didn't matter what processes were currently happening in the group; processes that would merit a delay, or at least a staggering of others' participation. Consider that groups are the dominant format of psychotherapy in hospital settings. Consider also that group therapy offers an array of therapeutic factors including what Yalom (1985) terms universality, altruism, and instillation of hope. Fellowship, a virtue attached to group therapy yet borrowed from 12-step programs, is a quality that no other format of therapy can offer. The groups in the program were conducive to psycho-educational exercises, wherein group members could obtain insight about theirs and others thinking and behavior, but not process at a deeper level, despite the "core" issue agenda implied by the stage progression system.

So imagine that you are a member of a group in which you have participated for several months. After a lengthy period of delay you are finally ready to address a subject that has been on and off your tongue since the day you were admitted. Now consider that on the night you are ready and sufficiently trusting of the process in order to address your delicate subject, three new people are introduced to the group. Prior to check-ins of any kind, thorough introductions are necessary, of every member of the group, which is time-consuming. A prefacing orientation is called for, of another few minutes so that typical norms are understood by new members. Imagine that some of these norms and introductions will have to be repeated because halfway through the group three other new members—all parents that have either forgotten or not yet understood about the group's beginning and end times—grumpily arrive at the group room, muttering under their breaths about how no one told when the activity was happening. Now, after another few minutes of delay, in which extra chairs for the newcomers have to be retrieved from the school classrooms, everyone is more or less settled. The therapist then turns to you and invites the share that you've been preparing over the last week, and working towards for at least six months. I can bring to mind the glassy-eyed look of a frustrated kid that was once poised to share, only to proceed in a staccato fashion due to repeated interruptions; the sometimes farcical lack of cohesion.

The task during middle-to-late stages of a client's program was to attend to what was called "core" issues, and in the operations manual of Thunder Road, core issues were cast as a central goal of a Stage II of a client's program. At this stage, it would be expected that a client had assimilated the rules and structure of the program; that they had just about accepted the necessity of treatment, and had stopped insistent campaigning for an early discharge. Achieving stage II was important for clients because, among other things, it enabled certain privileges within the unit, or—as many alternatively suggest—it boosted wounded self esteems. It also contained expectations; specifically, it contained the expectation that clients entering stage II were ready to work upon these core issues. According to Pazaratz (2009), the stage progression system so common in residential programs is based upon Margaret Mahler's theoretical stages of child development; what is termed separation/individuation in the language of Object Relations Theory. Therefore, teens in such programs are meant to traverse the sequence of separateness: from a symbiotic beginning (assimilation to new reality), to practicing (of new models of being in relationship—one of the definitions of "core" issues), towards a climax of rapprochement and departure, wherein fantasies of grandiose omnipotence are brought into alignment with reality and then necessarily deflated.

In practical terms, the concept of core issues did not appear to be torn from the pages of Object Relations Theory. So what was a core issue? Well, at least in terms of pedigree, core issues were likely drawn from the work of Aaron Beck and Albert Ellis, as reference to a set of fundamental beliefs, many of which would be deemed *a priori* false from the point of view of treatment. Ostensibly, "core" referred to schemas such as self-image, ego capacities such as self esteem, or relationship templates, role models. Addressing core issues meant challenging one's self identity and re-negotiating the conditions by which relationships of all kinds would be entered into and maintained. For clients like Philip, as well as his mother, it would have meant addressing their shared abuse history: exploring how Philip reenacted the physical aggression of his father; for the mother, it may have compelled a painful reflection upon why she had for so long tolerated such treatment of herself and her son.

6

FAKE IT TIL YOU MAKE IT

Program stage progression: "core" issues and cognitive goals

The tasks of stage II, from a Cognitive Behavioral standpoint, would more or less resemble the approach of a Psychodynamic model. Upon a foundation of values such as honesty, open-mindedness, and willingness, core issues would be conveyed to clients and families in various ways, largely reflecting the language and biases of whatever therapist/case manager was assigned to a client and family. Shortcuts, supposedly a result of clients' limited capacities, were predictable. Since clients were meant to have a ready understanding of their core issues when in stage II, it was common for them to be referenced in shorthand: "Anger is my core issue," a client would say if asked; or, "My relationship with my Dad is my core issue" might be offered, without much emotional or relational context. The assignments, those ponderous essays or the ritual "one-on-ones" that were sometimes given as a supplement, were meant to draw out the conversation and expand upon the themes.

I'm sure it would not be possible to prevent the confusion that typically followed, as clients went from one staff member to another with an assignment to define their core issues, and likely receiving a disparate soup of replies from a diverse base of staff. An alternative, I suppose, would have been to allow for a more private, internal process, by directing the client to contemplate for themselves what might be meant by core issues. For those who think of teaching and therapy as professions cut from the same cloth, this might lead to a philosophical conundrum: how can we teach if we don't rely upon instruction? For others, there is the notion that lessons are imparted via modeling, by the curiosity transmitted by a thoughtful, querulous mentor; by who we are as helpers. Pitfalls exist. How can a young person develop his or her own thinking if they merely parrot what is presented to them? Eventually, a murky assessment is made, reflecting another dialectical issue: what is integrated from others versus what emerges from within a person's mind.

Above all, the notion of core issues attended to what was available to the conscious experience of the client, or perhaps the preconscious if it were a matter of memory. The assumptions of Aaron Beck or Albert Ellis, and in turn, of programs like Thunder Road trumpeting an essentially (conscious) cognitive approach, was that internal processes, feelings, relational "ways of being" are in the client's awareness, as well as their capacity to alter and adapt. The approach largely eschews an exploration of past events, reflecting the biases of its theorists. For example, Ellis (1999) renounced his psychoanalytic training, complaining that the theory taught many to obsess fruitlessly over their personal histories. But an experience of the past, understood or not, was nonetheless present for many clients at Thunder Road, and therefore presented obstacles at crucial stages of the program. This is where treatment hit a wall with so many because the underlying dynamics of those so-called core issues did not seem to be in most clients' awareness.

"We're not here to do Freud stuff," a Thunder Road manager once joked—and I mean joked—to clucks of amusement from her subordinates. It was as if she was speaking the obvious. Actually, it was only obvious that we wouldn't be treating clients as classically psychoanalytic patients: having them recline upon couches, recite dreams and generally free associate while stretched out on their backs. Admittedly, some might have become psychotic through this technique. They might, as self psychologists describe, fragment: that is, fall apart. Whether this is necessary, harmful, or salutary is possibly philosophical, and subject to debate. In the meantime, what was prominent in the program was an ongoing analysis of resistant behavior and attitudes, although psychodynamic interventions tend to steer beyond the identification of defenses, towards an analysis of the purposes beneath the defenses.

A CBT intervention states something like, "you're talking about what's cool about getting high so you can rationalize your next relapse." The other states, "I think you're feeling a lot of stress about your situation", and—if the person were able to absorb a more elaborate statement—"and struggling to cope with that feeling, so you're rationalizing your next relapse so as to push away that stress." The differences are subtle and meaningful, but still distinguished by plain language. Some think that Psychoanalytic therapists use big words when talking to clients. Not true, although they often use big words when talking about them. Anyway, I heard the flippant dismissal of psychoanalysis at places like Thunder Road on a number of occasions; a sufficient number for me to wonder as to the real sources of the hostility, especially as the program was so obviously, but unwittingly, influenced by this bedrock discipline of the industry.

That smug manager, for example, seemed unaware that several terms that were used routinely at Thunder Road are derived from psychoanalysis. I remember a staff member offering that Thunder Road provided for clients a "holding" experience. I replied that the term "holding", in a psychological context, was a Winnicottian concept, and therefore a part of the psychoanalytic lexicon. So, too, are terms like "splitting" (Melanie Klein), "containment" (Wilfred Bion); "failure to thrive" was originally a term coined by Rene Spitz. It was used at Thunder Road to describe clients that were superficially compliant but not progressing. Even the baseline notion that behavioral "acting out" constitutes an expression of unconscious wishes is originally a Freudian idea[27]. Last year, an intern and friend schooled me on the fact that the 12-step founders drew ideas from conversations with Carl Jung. Listening to exchanges within the wide constituency of post-modern disdain, I considered the oedipal underpinnings. Killing the fathers of the profession, I observed. Less fancifully, I considered more politicized roots to the negative attitudes: from within the schools of cultural diversity, and then even more insidiously, from the cavern of class hatred.

Psychoanalysis is undoubtedly linked in the imaginations of many with the traditions and culture of middle and northern Europe, masculine hierarchies, and with ruling classes, wealthy elites. Within the United States, psychoanalysis appeared to thrive in the post World War II years, with an American population ripe to explore debilitating neurosis that theoretically resulted from sexual repression—topics that were previously verboten. But the marginalized in the culture, including feminists, ethnic and sexual minorities, later balked at ideas that appeared to fault mothers for developmental deficits, assert masculine privilege, assign narcissistic drive to homosexuality, or else pathologize close family ties as being inhibitory of individual growth. Meanwhile, the structure and seeming exclusivity of psychoanalytic process, with its insistence upon multiple sessions per week, maybe costing hundreds of dollars per week[28], seemed available only to the wealthy few. A generation ago, community advocates complained about the waiting lists of psychoanalysts, the effective exclusion of many needing services. In the future, more providers trained in shorter term models of treatment would be needed to accommodate all that need to be fed.

As it happens, psychoanalysis wasn't the only orientation in subtle or not-so-subtle opposition to practices at Thunder Road. A commonplace assumption was that Cognitive Behavioral Therapy, with its focus upon homework, attention to maladaptive belief systems, assumptions, and so on, was in natural alliance with the goals and norms of treatment; at least, much more so than the obscure, elusive world of psychoanalysis. However, I think there were conflicts, especially with respect to assessing client motivation. Aaron Beck's constructs, for example, posit attributional bias to client's faulty schemas, not motivational bias. Cognitive therapists often assert that their clients mistakenly apprehend the situations that bring problems, therefore what is needed is a redirection of thinking onto a new perspective, and therefore a new appraisal of what is happening in any given situation, as if this was readily available to the disturbed individual. A drug addict feels compelled to act upon their impulses to drink or use drugs. Desire is cast as a need. Cognitively, choice can be inserted, with self-talk designed to remind the individual that negative consequences accompany using, and that healthy alternatives exist, such as the availability of trustworthy human beings, ready to offer emotional succor. "You think helpers are trying to harm, but that is a false belief?" the cognitive therapist challenges, in essence.

Unconscious motivation, such as the rejection of impingement upon self that may come with "help"—what in some quarters is termed the *help-rejecting position*—is sort of irrelevant to these exchanges in so far as the defensive postures are not explored. The therapeutic solution of the cognitive therapist ignores or speaks past the possibility that an individual may not want help, or that words may contradict feeling states. In this regard, I have found that Cognitive Behavioral therapists have often been at odds not only with Psychodynamic therapists, but also counselors from the 12-step community, who certainly believe in maintaining a skeptical attitude with respect to client motivation. 12-step counselors, by my observations, commonly assess and then challenge the motivation of clients, the seeming authenticity of client shares, and even posit to an extreme degree the preeminence of these factors in a client's treatment. It's embedded in the 12-step philosophy, whose admittedly circular logic speaks to the invariable power of the program: "Does she really want her recovery?" such a staff will ask?

Cognitive Behavioral therapists do address rationalizations, such as AVE, or abstinence violation effect, wherein a substance abuser justifies a binge as a result of failing to meet the desired goal of abstinence. The faulty logic of the drug user proceeds as follows: because the user's goals and thinking had not been flexible; because their beliefs had been maladaptive and narrowly defined (perfectionism?), the goal of maintaining a drug-free existence is recklessly abandoned in the wake of a slip. CBT offers that the perception of external reality—that defenses such as rationalization and minimization—are the abiding problems of the mentally afflicted. But CBT does not address the internal function of those defenses, and it does not seem to present a strategy for the confrontation of lying, or the so-called "character flaws" of step six of the 12-step program.

Most interventions at Thunder Road aimed at behavior and the attached cognition. At the outset of treatment, when orientation to treatment norms is imparted, and challenging notions were first presented to clients and families, this seemed natural, and therefore interventions were polemical. There was much to explain in the beginning of a treatment episode and misunderstandings were common, even for those with previous experience of counseling. For example, a client who struggled to understand the team approach would likely bristle at the broad and therefore loose parameters of confidentiality. They might insist that their counselors hold sacrosanct their disclosures, and feel offended should their "contracts" be made known to program directors or psychiatrists, much less probation officers or collateral social workers. They would soon resign themselves to this reality. But as a case manager, I had my share of discussions with kids who'd been informed of the confidentiality rules—the boundaries of who might say what to whom—only for these talks to hit seemingly unsurpassable walls of resistance. I'd work hard at these times to persuade the client as to the incorrectness of their point of view; the sheer reasonableness of mine. For some, this would work: therefore, the application of cognitive strategies. But for so many others, the cognitive approach simply did not dent resistance.

Treatment planning and the multi-disciplinary staff

The old school counselors, as they were patronizingly known, those attached to Behavior Modification, and Therapeutic Community Concepts, didn't doubt the value of Cognitive Behavioral therapy, or a Solution-Focused or even the latterly-termed Strength-based approaches initially. When it came to conversations about client motivation for a drug-free life style, or the pre or post-binge management of craving states and their attendant distorted thinking, the techniques associated with these approaches were readily accepted. What the staff working the floor objected to was the way in which all theoretical approaches repeatedly hit walls with a core constituency of clients, or else didn't attend to the negative events that were repeatedly happening in the building. I remember the way treatment planning meetings best displayed this oft-muted opinion. The meetings would begin with case managers (usually three or four) in casual conversation with a program director and perhaps a head of either the school or nursing department. The medical director, an oft-hurried psychiatrist, would come in and out of such meetings, and would immediately be granted the floor so that clients' medication regimens could be reviewed. The program directors would lead these discussions, occasionally offering their two cents from impressions made after prowling the facility hallways like mother hens. Each case manager would have about ten minutes to present a general statement as to how his or her kids were doing: in the "community" (meaning, on the floor of the milieu, in the various activities), in their family therapy; in terms of their stage work assignments; and finally, with respect to any issues pertaining to a projected discharge, such as passes or court appearances.

About two-thirds into these meetings, two things would typically happen: first of all, someone from the admissions department would poke their head in the door, and ask for time so they could excitably introduce three new clients who would be getting admitted later in the day. At this point, the faces of case managers would cloud over as each went inward, calculating the additional work—especially documentation—that would soon be heading their way. The admissions counselor would then deliver a quick preview of each kid, and of the difficult families with whom hours had already been spent, but whom the admissions counselor would not have to deal with again. Then another counselor would walk in. The turnover of participants in these activities seemed a microcosm of the entire system. This next person would be a shift supervisor, a member of kitchen staff, or another member of nursing perhaps. They'd walk in with a certain attitude; a knowing, *I-told-you-so* attitude. Skipping the strategic discussions about how to move Johnny from a precontemplative stage of change to a contemplative stage, or whether to give his rules-undermining family a "codependency" homework packet to complete, this staff member would wait a few minutes, and then raise his or her hand to deliver the news of what's really going on in the kid's program.

Johnny has been cheeking his meds; Johnny has been carrying on a relationship with Julie on the girl's side; Johnny's dad let him have a beer on a Sunday church pass; Johnny has been selling his own meds, and has a cash and porn stash in his room. Johnny hasn't really been working his program for months, and therefore his proposal for stage promotion ought to be summarily rebuffed. Oh, and one last thing: Johnny also brought a full pack of cigarettes onto the unit, when Eddie from continuing care showed up during recreation time in the parking lot last week and started passing out gifts to all of his friends still on the "inside". Through all of this divulging, the reporting staff would exude the qualities of a father confessor. The guilt-ridden client that is Johnny is cast as a Sisyphus-like figure, pushing the burden of his aggregating contracts up a long incline, perhaps knowing in his gut that his bubble of secrecy could (and should) burst at any time.

The meeting would stop. The strategic discussion of how to motivate Johnny or attend to his unique skill or deficit set would shift to a discussion of more incisive aims: soliciting honesty, breaking secrets; the importance of consequences for the purpose of teaching limits. Johnny would next be given a reassessment shirt, with an essay about how secrets will keep him sick, and a climactic confrontation group hot seat as to how long he'd been holding such secrets. Motivation? Motivation to lie, withhold, and manipulate until it kills him, many would say of this average client. Coming clean, in the spiritual sense, would save his life. Guilt and shame played their parts. Guilt inspired disclosures, sometimes to staff in peripheral roles, subordinate roles with which the kids more likely identified. Shame, and fear, of course, had played a role in the initial denials, and would re-emerge when time came for explanations and scrutiny: insights that might serve learning; a disclosure to a parent or a probation officer that might disappoint or deflate expectations; a disclosure that might compromise one of those parents by exposing their complicity.

The typical intervention strategies seemed to have few answers to these habitual sabotages. There were the obligatory "What were you thinking?" questions, asked with affected calmness by therapists, and with little disguise of frustration by everyone else. Kids would shake their heads, hang their heads, flutter their arms, sink into their chairs and wait out the predictable lectures. They were after all a replay of all the exchanges they'd been having as long as they could remember. Silences wouldn't last long. After a requisite thirty seconds of contemplation, adults would resume commentary, cast their warnings, repeat their slogans, and dispense assignments and punishments, ever reminding the youngsters that they were appreciated, cared for, *supported.* How can they move on from this? How could they learn? An essay would demonstrate this, maybe? A few public moments of humiliation, framed as healing, would be the reward for all of this disclosure. The essays would focus on solutions: how could the client prevent the negative behavior in the future? Who can the individual go to for support?

When therapeutic impasses seemed to persist, the treatment team would call in one other staple activity from its repertoire: the dreaded staffing. Staffings were the ultimate interventions; the presumed last stop for a client prior to a dishonorable discharge and a last ditch effort by staff to reach a young mind—"this is it" moments; the bottom line delivery. Staffings, as the term suggests, were activities wherein defiant and/or persistently acting out clients were called in for a meeting with five or more staff, to address problem behaviors known by everyone, ask after contracts as yet undisclosed, and generally review the treatment plan. They were interesting as far as what they implied about safety, structure, and that Bionian notion of containment. Staffings contained acting out of clients by the nature of their structure. What is it that truly contains acting out adolescents? Outnumbering them with adults is one simple answer. If the ratio was five adults to one client, or greater, there was little to worry about as far as impulsivity or low frustration tolerance was concerned—at least, not immediately. Clients in this context were typically docile, shamefaced and alexithymic ("I don't know", "I can't remember"). If anything, observing staff were concerned as to the re-traumatizing potential of such meetings. Some, those most frequently on the receiving end of clients' abuses, seemed to enjoy staffings. Schadenfreude.

Shame. These activities, staffings and other confrontation exercises, would rarely speak to the shame. Staff offered solutions. They provided reassurance, spoke to the clients' abilities, and provided support as a denouement following sometimes epic attacks upon clients' shortcomings. But the shame that attended these processes was rarely discussed, and therefore not metabolized. Shame is probably the hardest feeling to talk about; the hardest to sit with, both from the point of view of the recipient, as well as the catalyst of the feeling. And because it is the hardest feeling to integrate, it also seems the most difficult to soothe. It generates silence, awkwardness; everyone looks away, and because it is so difficult a feeling to speak to, it is therefore the most likely feeling to be acted upon in unhealthy ways: therefore manic defense, addictive behaviors; runaways and rage.

Staffings, the most pressured of therapeutic activities, delivered both shame and containment for clients. In later years, when expounding upon the unique value of a residential setting, I'd break it down for interns: if you want to observe containment of behavior, go to a staffing. Nothing contains behavior like disapproval in numbers. Next, look at confrontation group, or contract breaking, or the community "benchings" that occurred wherein clients en masse would be directed to line the walls, backsides pinned to pine, with a presiding audience of every available clinical staff in the building. If you want to see shame, look at the heads that are hanging; the bodies that slump, and the shoulders that shrug, sometimes in exhibition, sometimes imperceptibly. I'd suggest the following: as you collect the scrubs for your client's reassessment assignment, look as the kid turns away from your gaze. Try having those awkward conversations and try reassuring them that they have good hearts and minds when voices inside them are pointing to the irredeemable.

If you wanted to observe chaos and grandiosity, go to either side of the hospital—boys or girls side—to the area flanking a pool room on the boys' side, a documents closet on the girls' wing. Go on a Saturday night, when the ratio is five or six clients to every adult, if not more. Go when two or three staff members have called in sick; when the administrators have long since left for the day; after the HR and admissions staff members have giddily left around six o'clock. Observe how docile the clients seem at these times: how shamefaced, traumatized, guilt-ridden and adult-pleasing they seem. Try asking a question born of Cognitive Behavioral theory, Psychodynamic, or any kind of theory, in this context. Ask those Solution-Focused questions amid the din of throbbing music. Listen to the kid that earlier spoke in pious terms in front of his family about the joys of being clean and sober. Now he wears a grin from ear to ear and speaks in tongues, spitting tight rhymes laden with glorified drug references. The word "Chronic", thanks to the likes of Dr. Dre or Snoop Dog, now has a different meaning[29]. Shout affirmations and encouragement over clients' profane singing along with violent, misogynistic lyrics. Try liking them, empathizing with them, while they're like this. As a committed helper of troubled youth, try to not feel ashamed if you're not *feeling* it.

The staffings succeeded as containment exercises, at least temporarily. To those for whom it did not appear to work—who perhaps resumed their acting out immediately afterwards, if not during the meeting itself—I'd almost tip my hat. Almost. Here again, my comparative sympathy for the outwardly (versus hypocritically) delinquent or dissident betrays itself. I'd thought myself a failed refusenik in my adolescent years, so to some extent I was living vicariously through some of these brave miscreants. But the thing about heavy-handed methods such as staffings is this: not only do they not seem to bring about change, they might even rigidify defenses, by fossilizing resentment, despite the anxiety that is initially triggered. Furthermore, many amongst staff resented being enlisted into staffings, especially if they were to offer little more than a motivational harangue. They were basically authoritarian. Even the physicality of the exercise was autocratic: clients were directed to stand before staff, with their arms by their sides, as in confrontation groups. This began the staffing on an adversarial footing, as though the activity were a court-martial hearing rather than a meeting with a presumed therapeutic meaning. I'd watch as clients bodily relived the experience of "hot seats", only more so because there were no onlooking peers to intimidate with their heated glares. Frowning, vexed, they'd stare into speakers' eyes and strain to follow staff's wordy lessons. They'd struggle to "take in" the messages, and lapse unknowingly into shame.

The various staff members, representatives of the so-called multi-disciplinary team, would play out their roles, leading with their biases. The directors, compelled to set the tone, would ask, "Do you know why you're here?" followed by a familiar proclamation: "We're all here to support you". The seasoned veterans in the room, those manning the floor on those most difficult of shifts, would fire out the most damning charges: the insinuations of contracts held; or an imputation of pattern behavior, negative attitudes and destructive outbursts. The therapists, straddling a line between gunning for the team and holding on to a fragile alliance with their clients, would echo the general concerns, but flavor their comments with appeal. The message from the staff was always the same: *trust us*. The process was something else: *listen to us*. The clients would nod on cue, generally look back with blank expressions and hang on to some ambiguous notion of who they were. After twenty minutes, the client would be dismissed, and a debriefing, led by a director or psychiatrist, would ask, "Well…?"

The team approach seemed essential for the containment of dangerous behaviors and for the general imparting of reality. For an individual therapist, convinced that he or she is hearing a true and full reporting at any given moment from a client, a team's perspective of different points of view, reports of happenings not reported by clients, is a galvanizing wake-up call. I still believe this, especially in private practice settings where team approaches are less indigenous. However, beyond achieving the aims of containment and reality testing, the team approach often seemed to get in the way of progress at Thunder Road. In fact, it was the process of activities like staffings that first gave me pause about so-called team thinking. On paper, it seems uncontestable: It takes a village to keep Johnny off drugs. The more the merrier: let school, nursing, kitchen staff, visiting probation officers, and whoever else join in and have their say. And not only have a say, but report in upon that which is often missed in an isolated, individual therapy. Thunder Road is a family, a community designed to temporarily replace the dysfunctional families that destiny originally provided for its clients.

To be fair, some have whispered disagreement and pointed out the flaw in this argument. Too many cooks in the kitchen, was an oft-cited problem. Invisible two-sided mirrors started appearing in treatment planning meetings. Gratuitous comments came from staff members looking to have their voice heard: too many people in the room or too many people calling in with agendas. Those dissenting colleagues of mine always spoke in hushed tones, as though knowing they were speaking heresy. I agreed with them. I likened the process to some of those old Woody Allen movies—the ones that depict his humble beginnings in dense Semitic households, with everyone speaking at once. It's meant to be funny when his family in Brooklyn is cast as a cacophony of chatter, with everyone shouting over one another?

Actually, staffings didn't feature a lot of shouting. Despite what some seem to think about Therapeutic Communities, there isn't quite as much shouting as is often supposed. The reason is that the business simply doesn't (or can't) hire enough people who are able and willing to shout at people consistently. Such programs have to rely upon the few who are either constitutionally inclined, or else intrepid enough to give it a try. Regardless, the problem with staffings wasn't so much one of people speaking over one another, but rather past one another. A question from one staff would be undermined by a question from another. A response that begged interpretation would be met by another question from another staff member, or a confrontation that missed a significant element of a previous statement. Non sequiturs would follow; three topics would be introduced in a space of minutes, mirroring the worst of confrontation groups. Different agendas would vie for position, leaving the client, as well as the quieter staff members in the room feeling confused and disconnected. Those aforementioned silences, so often golden in a therapy session, seemed impossible to insert at times like these. Like a parent doing the heavy work of communication, the team would allow a few seconds to pass; then, in the absence of meaningful client response, someone else would speak up, try another question, as if the exercise was one of reciting a menu to one frozen in indecision.

Of course, there were exceptions. Sometimes, it took a moment of skill, even genius, to aim for the undergrowth and pry apart the defenses. Soft-spoken or not, a timely, truthful, and strong statement would occasionally grip the client by the heart, and shift them into an affective state they'd rarely let their peers witness. About one in five staffings, I'd say, produced this kind of magic, whether it led to a program turnaround or not. But more often than not, staffings, along with multi-family group, confrontation group, and contract-breaking, were frustrating exercises in missed opportunities: activities that skirted potential, approached truth and then ducked away.

Here I go again with this Gordian Knot. A Behavioral Modification system, be it a family, a drug treatment program, or a larger society, must focus first on controlling negative behavior. That's dogma of addictions work—perhaps the dogma of a reductionist society. Of course, a hospital or group home must attend to the safety of its patients (or "clients"); and again, you can't have meaningful conversations about deeper feelings while the patient is pervasively acting out upon those feelings. But what I'm addressing, perhaps circularly, in this narrative is the perpetual avoidance of this territory—the arrested development of the process—not the necessary grounding that takes place in the early stages of treatment. In my first tenure at Thunder Road, from 1996 to 1999, I'd often feel frustrated as a client reached a ten month mark of a program, apparently clean and sober, yet no more developed in their self capacities than they were on day one. Negative behaviors had reduced—on that score, there would be little doubt. No one could argue that a client who had stayed at Thunder Road for a year hadn't reduced their drug use, made fewer suicidal gestures, stolen from fewer people, assaulted less of the elderly, and dated-raped fewer peers. Less flippantly, perhaps, I could offer that many honorably discharging clients had indeed made meaningful advances in terms of impulse control, frustration tolerance, and reality testing.

Many of these kids had exhibited significant reductions, not only in terms of drug use, but also with respect to instances of verbal altercations, reports of fights with peers, instances of non-compliance with staff, and so on. These were kids that had learned to pause, perhaps take a seat on a bench; take a time-out. Twenty minutes later they'd be standing before a supportive peer or an impassioned adult, urging them to think through a check-list of dos and don'ts: contemplate fully whether they wanted to use, fight, AWOL, or whatever else their impulses were demanding. Consistently, these kids might have learned to make good use of what the staff and the more motivated clients had to offer. Consistently they absorbed a challenging question—"Is it worth it?"—and the clients that made it to the end of the program thus checked their gambling impulses. They answered the question, privately or not, with a resounding *no*.

Endgame battles

Endings. Lo and behold, it often turns out that human beings in a contained system want more; the illuminati in us wants to venture deeper, undo secrets; go *there*. The latent misgivings of staff would be expressed at the tail ends of tedious team meetings. Deep sighs would sound out, typically as staff contemplated a request from a senior client for stage III promotion: a final stage of the program, and a relatively quick furlong thereafter to the finish line of honorable discharge. At this point in the program, discharge dates would be suggested, then negotiated, or later pushed back because of a behavioral setback or some manner of parental collapse (Here, the program might learn of parents' relapses, or misgivings about resuming custodial responsibility). According to Thunder Road's 2003 manual, completion of Stage III (leading to "honorable" discharge) entailed some the following achievements, here relayed nearly verbatim: a sufficient time away from substance abuse to develop a fresh view of himself or herself; getting in touch with basic feelings about self, peers, and family; knowledge of the effects of drugs and alcohol on physical self and the ability to cope emotionally; awareness of the effects of nicotine; control of impulses to behave in dysfunctional ways; ability to express painful emotional experiences through talking to others (Shane, Cherry, Snowden, Gerstel, P. 46, 2003). In treatment planning, shifty looks would bounce about the room, with staff members asking tentative questions roughly based upon this criteria: "Do you think she's ready?", or "Does he really doesn't wanna give up his using friends?"

By the time a client had reached the cusp of stage III, he or she had learned the value of compliance. By learned, I mean integrated; that is, organized into their affect, their demeanor, through those reduced instances of negative destructive behavior. Becoming stage III really meant that a client had demonstrated consistent compliance. They had demonstrated leadership, which meant that they had made the right moves with respect to their peers at the correct times: they had broken notable contracts; they had been visibly confronting of acting out peers; they had perhaps been instrumental in the blocking of an AWOL or two. They had answered repeatedly, with modest permutations from time to time, all those tendentious questions of counselors who had been advised towards directive, attitude-confronting approaches; taking responsibility for the client's therapy in the manner that strategic therapists speak of. In theory, clients were responsible for changing; actually, what they were responsible for was compliance. In short, clients who navigated the stages of the program were those who had spoken up just enough, on a sufficient number of occasions, with the desired humility.

But this didn't mean there weren't more challenges to come. Problem and paradox: had that compliance of clients been a mere strategy? many asked. I frequently thought the question obtuse. "Of course it was", I wanted to say. Had it all been a ruse designed to hoodwink staff into thinking they were *ready*? Ready for change? Now staff started to wonder, and some would insist on pressing the issue. The 12-steppers among staff told their own cautionary tales in the team meetings: they, too, had gone through treatment and told counselors everything they wanted to hear, and behaved. Their personified addicts had fooled many people in the process of self-destruction. These pronouncements often came late in the game of a client's program, following a consistent streak of good feedback, perhaps months of positive affirmations about progress in behavior. The feedback would be relayed to parents, families; to probation officers and social workers. As stage III proposals arrived on case managers' desks, quick rubber stamps were anticipated.

Everyone reviewed reality at the ambiguous points in the endgame. An ending, internalized for many as abandonment, loomed. The problem of the compliant kid approaching discharge after nearly a year in treatment regularly caused team arguments. No recent reassessments? No breaking of Cardinal rules? A further question begged itself: what was the problem? As a delegated messenger/advocate, I couldn't really speak to the issue when these nodal points approached. I was lost, not understanding the unconscious process. I was tongue-tied. I couldn't really say to kids or parents that treatment team members were looking for some kind of internal change—signs of recovery, after months of "behavior" modification. This term, "recovery", which served as shorthand for all things internal and external, seemed especially inadequate at times like this. The word seemed too abstract, too unwieldy in its meaning. And yet, it was a formidable word, invoked by staff members who thought of themselves as guardians of a cause. They formed a wall at the climax of treatment like a football team's defensive unit lining up for a heroic goal-line stand.

The clients and parents, whose stage III proposals were dismissed or delayed amidst this process, frothed in protest. They also misunderstood and accused Thunder Road of being unfair, of changing its rules, of perhaps wanting people to fail. "It's like they're testing us," clients and parents would say as their long-subdued paranoid defenses made flamboyant returns. They'd either give up or come out fighting. These outbursts reinforced staff's misgivings, demonstrating unresolved tendencies towards poor impulse control, low frustration tolerance. They were a kind of rapprochement of those earlier protests at intake, or those early trial runs in multi-family group. So-called old behaviors would at this point be unleashed, leading to other kinds of abstinence violation effects. The effects were insidiously circular. Fulminating, clients would tear up their thoughtfully-composed stage III proposals, stride out of case managers' offices, slam doors, and then burst out into the Thunder Road parking lot, defying the alarms whose volume, it seemed, became weaker with each passing year. Now these clients would be in need of support. Now they would need patient AWOL blocking: an inspirational anecdote from an aged staff member; a hardened don't-let-it-get-to-you support from a peer. And treatment. *Obviously*, the client needed more treatment.

Out in the parking lots, these rejected clients, who'd spent months enduring confrontation groups, contract breaking, multi-family groups, benchings, ritual activities of different types, now paced and raged. They thought compliance had been what it was all about—what surviving the program, and by extension life, was all about. As far as the first three months or so of treatment was concerned, they were right. After that, a subtle shift occurred; a shift desultorily spelled out, but not organized into a coherent plan. It had been there all along, within us. But it had been proscribed, contained and denied. The Therapeutic Community, it finally seemed, really did want to see more than compliance; much more than what those in 12-step meetings call *fake it til' you make it*. To determine change, staff wanted clients to squirm, because they wanted was to see what was real.

The question of iatrogenic finales

What was *real* was beguiling at these climactic stages of treatment. The rejections, such as the refusal of stage progressions, of the setting of discharge dates, often led to clients' fragmenting into collapsed mental states: an iatrogenic[30] phenomenon some thought—a healthy shattering of denial, others argued. In sporting terms, the last ninety days of a long-term client's program was like the latter stages of marathon foot-race. Legs are cramping, the mind is weary; support from the sidelines starts to seem hallucinogenic, and delirium hovers. Wayward, some of these late-stage clients might have been seen wandering the unit halls while other residents sat within usual activities. With seniority came freedom, the space to "schuck"—that is, dodge—activities. "Where you supposed to be at?" a manager might call out, observing these youths idle through the last days of their programs. An irony lay in how treatment might resemble a mind-altering experience; an institutionally imposed mind-fuck.

And it was. Kids that reached this watershed stage of the program might well have asked whether they were supposed to attach or separate. Do both, everyone replied, mindful that context was the key, not an either-or proposition. As the limit-setting waned, some kids might have wondered: are the limits real? Who really cares about me? I think some kids sensed that they may want to be rescued, that they might need to collapse and accept that powerlessness feeling that everyone had been talking about for months. They might need to cry, abase themselves; maybe even talk about shame as they look up and notice something horrific: the rescue isn't forthcoming, and they're alone. At this stage, everyone seemed to be standing by, watching them fall down, with some thinking it cruel, and others not only thinking it necessary, but also healing, like the blood-letting of a root canal. There's only a little ways to go, those closest to the action said. But after every turn in the road, there would appear to be another stretch of pavement blocking the endgame.

Clients that were dug into their defenses, including those who thought they'd dropped their defenses, tended to think real anything that conveyed outrage, but not so much those softer expressions of vulnerability which therapists and recovery counselors (in occasional displays of unity) preferred to think of as real. What was real in the clients' world was an obdurate set of understandings about not only themselves, but their families, their neighborhoods, and their mini-cultures: anger was real; survival was real. The soothing effects of drug use were real. Survival in context meant accessing anger, at least in a controlled fashion, and thereafter displaying invulnerability. Survival had meant the acceptance of circumstances that individuals can't control. The reward for enduring obstacles had been the early introduction to adult privileges, love's consolation prizes: drugs, the soldierly feeling of gangs, and of course, sex. Once, treatment had nudged along a treatment plan, gauging compliance largely through an observation of outcomes, trackable changes in behavior. Wasn't that what adults wanted? What else could Thunder Road want?

In the nineties, I trusted the treatment planning process for the most part. I observed numerous instances wherein the stubborn call for change seemed to yield good results. Meaning, there were clients whose defenses seemed to break in such a way as to produce genuine change, not only in behavior, but in clients' general way of being. By the end of treatment, staff could see this in a kid's eyes: a certain change, because some kids were looking back, maintaining eye contact. In later years, upon becoming a clinical supervisor, I'd engage in good-natured debates about the limitations of some counselors' late stage interventions: the urgent management of a client's reunification with both family and community—the advice-giving and menu-style questions directed at clients. Solution-focused questions, I'd argue, were actually designed for a shorter-term treatment. But the adherents of briefer models were still jogging out the same questions in confrontation groups or staffings well into stage II, even well after some kids had passed the nine month mark of an intensive live-in program. Arrested in Stage I thinking, clients fielded the now tired, "what are your goals?" questions, along with its anxious cousins, the "what are you going to do about your using friends?" questions with airs of tedium. Staff members of this ilk seemed to be bashing their heads against walls, asking with dogmatic fervor, "What are you going to do?" when the broader question facing clients was something more like, Who are you?

I have one particular memory relating to this craziness. Once I was standing at the window of a treatment room, looking out towards the Thunder Road parking lot and watching one of my clients, Edgar, stride back and forth and spitting hateful noises in my direction. The reason: I'd just presented the news of his stage III proposal being rejected by the treatment team. He would not, as boys at war say, be going home for Christmas. I was warned not to go out to the parking lot and "support" his process. Instead, a team of four, including one teen, sort of shepherded Edgar across the lot, forming a rough circle around the troubled youth and moving like a pack of hunters around a wounded animal. I stood at the window, scratching my head as the client with whom I'd spent maybe fifty hours of one-on-one time became "real" on his own terms.

When he came back inside, he approached me aggressively, shooting me a glare that sought to dig through my eyes. With this episode, thoughts, feelings, ancient fantasies congealed, forming some kind of toxic, charging mass. Edgar's humiliation was externalized: I'd *disrespected* him. His fear, his long-contained fear, had been dissociated; had transformed into a boiling state. He felt inflated, and his mind was working feverishly, tabulating all the distortions I'd been imparting over the previous ten months. I'd been lying to him, he insisted; I'd treated him like a fool, and he was no fool. Now he wanted to fight. He was surrounded by others, peers and staff alike, all imploring him to calm down, rethink himself; not do what he was doing. *Think of the consequences! Think?* He continued to stare unblinkingly through the crowd. Those clients who had stood at the window by my side—who had moments earlier been giggling at the spectacle of their peer "losing it"—now looked sheepish and impassive. I kept a solemn expression—maybe a frown to convey concern, the dregs of evidence that I still cared about him.

I said nothing. Intuiting that words would escalate argument, I let my non-verbal foundations work, though I worried they might also be having a bad day at the office. What might I exude just from being present? Might I receive absolution from Edgar, for having *been there*, all along, throughout his treatment? It didn't seem so at the time. For those moments, I knew what it was to live as prey. "What's sup," Edgar asked provocatively. It was a versatile phrase, this quasi-greeting: sometimes a threat, otherwise an inert salutation. Edgar thrust out his chest, invited me to step forward: a threat. He wanted to see me angry, make me feel vulnerable. Around us there were peers of his, and of mine, and the reactions of others were telling. When clients had meltdowns like this, some counselors or managers liked to step in and shout down the drama, calling for peace. Some, like me, thought it best to wait out these tantrums, stay at least physically present, but not try and argue, much less point out things like projections. Some wouldn't deal with these situations at all. To my right, as I recall, I caught a glance of a staff member disappearing around a corner. Then, to my left, I saw a diminutive thirteen year old, a client who prior to this point had been the main focal point of the community's interventions—so chaotic had he been in his tantrums. Now this other kid sat quietly in the doorway of his room, working on one of those monotonous essays; indifferent to the fracas around him, and perhaps accustomed to such disruptions yet happy to not be the center of everyone's attention for a change.

In a quite unwelcome change, I was. Fitting in was one thing: being the center of attention is another. Notwithstanding the conceit of this book, attention has never been something I've coveted. I've never felt the need to draw converging focus the way that so many troubled youth have. I'd always settled for a compromised attention in tighter circles. For a few seconds I ruminated on the experience of that thirteen year old, for whom this scene would have felt commonplace had he been in either mine or Edgar's shoes. For another second or so, I considered that Edgar, by now escalating his demand for a physical resolution, had likewise been on both sides of this divide. I thought that for one of only a couple of times in my career, I'd be lunged at and assaulted. "Why not," Edgar snapped, in answer to a peer challenging the sanity of picking a fight with me. "He's a man, isn't he? He can handle his business."

Many years later, I supervised an intern who had experienced a similar episode as this. Some things don't change. Regarding the former incident, Edgar's remark took my breath away. I was astonished by the sheer disconnection. I probably dissociated (tellingly, I can't remember?). Who was I to him in those moments? Who was he? The ego boundaries, it seemed, had collapsed, and clearly something deeper than a faulty cognition was happening. How could he get support around this? What was he thinking? What was he feeling? In the days ahead he'd report, truthfully (I think) that he didn't know. He couldn't remember; likened the experience to an alcoholic blackout (had never heard the word fugue, I guess), and pointed out, with some kind of backwards purpose and logic, that he didn't need substances to seem crazy. It was crazy, he conceded, to think that we'd resolve our actual conflict with a physical conflict. He didn't understand why he needed to act like this. He affably shook his head, thinking that was the end of the matter.

And yet, there was something preferable in his response, at least relative to other defensive reactions that are less memorable, and therefore less reported by those who work with individuals mandated into treatment. I'm referring to those innumerable kids who, when learning of treatment team rejections, indulged their oppositional tendencies, but then later withdrew into subdued silences. They sulked, and then denied they were sulking. They co-opted the language of 12-step, saying they *accepted* their situations, and were ready to move on. They refused to emote; in this way, they refused to gratify their antagonists, the staff members and other adults who had cast judgments upon their program, stalling the headlong progress towards successful discharges. They sought to inoculate themselves from disappointment and run out the clock of treatment, calculating that acting out in explosive ways might prolong their programs (a reasonable suspicion). Because there were so many kids that fit this profile it seems arbitrary to even cite an example.

Edgar's disadvantage was a poor attachment history, of course, comprised of constantly failed mentalization efforts, as Fonagy and Bateman (2006) might observe. Compelled towards a pretend, teleological mode, Edgar had lost (or never developed) his capacity to conceive of mental states. As was my tendency, I probed further with Edgar, stretched out the discussions to see what truthful juice could be squeezed out of him. He indulged me, thinking no doubt that he had little program capital left to spend on disagreeable attitudes, but offered little insight. I wondered aloud as to how it was possible for him to think that I, his therapist, would possibly want a physical battle with him? I thought twice about a more sociological comment, was tempted to excoriate his sexist linking of responsibility, manhood, and violence. Intuitively, I knew it would have been a mistake to *educate* him. Edgar laughed off the episode, ultimately apologized and sought to shake my hand instead of "dwelling" upon that which was past. Was this a temporary failure, this lapse into psychic equivalence[31], or a chronic condition? I wasn't sure. Now I am. He touched his fist to mine, which was a good, minor example of how staff sometimes did the little things, like the gestures of subcultures, on clients' terms. Rapport building, I guess you'd call it.

That young man and I parted on good terms, largely because he had a good heart, despite his deficits, and he could just about see into the hearts of others. This wasn't always true of the clients I worked with at Thunder Road, though most endings both there and at the group home I managed in San Diego were gracious in spirit. On this, I often went back in my mind to that orientation back in 1996. The director had spoken of staff members' jobs, but also those of the clients. As clients finished their programs, they typically received a farewell ceremony in recognition of their achievements. Some were celebratory while others were nervous—knowing in their guts there was unfinished business. Others still were restrained, yet simply itching to leave. For these successful few, treatment had been a transformation; an ambiguous humiliation, yet a potential life saver. The most knowing of these kids thanked staff through gritted teeth. Really, would we expect any more from those whose seemingly life-saving defenses we'd tried to tear apart? For all of them it was as if a job assignment was coming to an end, and not just the job of their treatment, as it had been outlined and discussed at length, but rather a job of a parallel kind. Clients upon discharge sometimes held the aura of those who have survived an exhausting game, who wearily mope across the field of play, shaking hands, softly punching fists, giving hugs, and whispering tepid gratitude into former adversaries' ears. The previously unyielding let go their anger. They held back whatever parting shots they may have wanted to make, thinking that without the in-the-moment stimulus of opposition, there is no need: life as reaction. There were tacit no-hard-feelings expressions. Should I see them later in the community, I'd receive a cordial, unprovocative "what's sup", and a token nod. They had been doing their jobs, just as that former director had described, and I had been doing mine.

The treatment team wasn't wrong in its assessment of Edgar's progress, even if the last meetings about him hadn't emphasized such things as paranoid tendencies, or poor ego boundaries. His apology aside, the damage was done to his then stage aspirations, and his treatment was extended by a month. He perhaps knew that at the time of his explosion, and figured he'd go down fighting, but with "acceptance". With management's and other staff's seeming approval, he moved on from this incident, put it behind him, and focused on the future, the largely concrete tasks that still stood between him and a successful completion of treatment. There was an opportunity here to keep the focus on the problem; keep the discussion alive, and therefore attend to those mysterious concerns that lingered within the team's doubts. There was a chance to address some real feelings: dissociated, split-off feelings of anger, as in suppressed rage, followed by rage unleashed: impulses towards revenge, intolerance of criticism, rejection; of failure.

The team directed another two hot seats at Edgar, aiming to stir emotions not previously seen in him: tearfulness, fear instead of rage. He nearly broke. But he whined more so than cried, continued to act out with fits of rage, and ultimately the team called it a day. "Hot seat off," the director said morosely, hanging her head. A longstanding caveat of this business, *you can't make people do the work*, soothed a disappointed team. By that point, Thunder Road may have seemed to Edgar like an ogre playing a tantalizing game. In his resistant fantasy, he must have thought staff a sadistic child standing at the top of a well, with a rodent tied to a string—himself. In the fantasy, the child lowers the animal down the well, shouting cheers of encouragement as the rodent scratches its way down the side wall—the descent into depression. As the creature reaches the point of despair, where the aura of light from behind has disappeared and all that lies ahead is blackness, the string is yanked. It clambers back up the wall nine-tenths relieved, one tenth—an invisible tenth—disappointed to have been called back from the brink. My colleagues called it "letting go", or more plainly, "cutting some slack". They loosened the grip upon clients' fraying nerves, letting everyone off the hook. One might imagine that another drop would follow these respites, that clients would venture deeper into themselves. Perhaps they would, quietly and with at best fleeting attention, because what I think happens when people are rescued is a forgetting.

There had been something missing from Edgar's treatment plan: something that would take him where he didn't want to go, or couldn't go—who knows. Those plans were quite incomplete. At times, the program seemed so staggeringly incomplete. That wasn't the fault on any particular individual, of course. People tried; gifted people, I mean, really gave it their all. Treatment plans are like road-maps from which the machinery of mental health services isn't meant to stray. But plans do stray, and necessarily so, because sometimes human beings, the brave ones, travel off-script. The treatment process, intended to be all-encompassing in its reaches, often seemed chaotic at Thunder Road, and that was sometimes a positive event, sometimes not. It's hard to write creativity into a treatment plan—a fatuity to include spontaneity. Meanwhile, those plans were conveyed to kids like Edgar, to parents, through the lens of so many people: through the collective thinking of staff, which was itself derived from a range of historical influences; through collateral contacts and the governing systems they represent. And all this was transmitted to all of these people, across all of these boundaries, in such a way as to defy succinct or even coherent description. As a result, we often seemed, as that other client Andre had once said, as though we were all shooting from the hip.

Leaving for the first time

I managed to say a raw, fragmented version of all this to the hospital's administrator in the spring of 1999, just as I was leaving Thunder Road after my first tenure. I was relocating to San Diego, to live with my then girlfriend, and I'd accepted a job as part of a team of six staff that would run a six bed group home in nearby Oceanside. I was leaving Thunder Road on good terms, with the best wishes of my colleagues, even a week's worth of magnanimous celebrations that would enjoin the clients. It was fun to be the focus of that kind of attention. After three years, I'd felt I'd come to the end of a successful spell of a fledgling career. I was in the latter stages of my internship years. At that time, I'd amassed almost 2500 hours of practicum experience; much of which had been earned at Thunder Road. More importantly, I felt like I belonged in the workplace, like I was a respected member of the team; a strong voice, as one peer put it. The goodbyes were profuse and generous; there was play of the right kind along with a few tears. Privately, though I had some regrets, I was ready to leave. The job had been exhausting as well as stressful on several other levels, though I strained to express the nature of those levels to those not familiar with Thunder Road from the inside.

I also had nagging misgivings about the program. Alongside my doubts about the efficacy of written assignments, the sometimes heavy-handedness of staffings and confrontation groups, or the limited utility of the treatment plans, I was concerned for the continuity of care as impinged upon by an alarming turnover rate amongst staff. I commented on this to an administrator of that period, during an exit interview set up on my last day. He nodded sympathetically and seemed generally earnest on this issue. I told him I'd overheard a family speaking to him during the aftercare program's graduation ceremony the previous fall. The administrator, who was presiding over the event and moving among the throngs, spreading goodwill, was gently upbraided by this family for not fostering retention of staff. They'd had three case managers in their time in the residential component, they complained, nicely but insistently. The administrator looked on with a diplomatic air while his eye furtively searched past the shoulders of the family's spokesman father, looking for people who'd emphasize nice things, positive thoughts about how great Thunder Road was.

The administrator of this period typified the TC approach during the nineties and at least the first half of the next decade. As a leader, he fostered uneasy relationships; as a visible presence on the floor, he inspired something in between respect and terror. Once, during my early weeks as an intern, I witnessed him in one of the community rooms, wedged between a pair of clients, initially to observe the process of a house meeting with a discreet presence. In response to a client who had just finished reading post-reassessment commitments to his peers in a limp, apathetic manner, he shot up from his seat, rounded the pool table that was a centerpiece of the room, and started berating the youth about his negative attitude. At Thunder Road, there were at any one time about five or six members of staff who felt either comfortable with or gleeful at the prospect of engaging clients with intensity. I couldn't berate clients. I could occasionally mock them as a group. A few times I think I might have drawn out a kid in a way that to others might have deemed mean-spirited. But I wasn't one of the heavies in the building, not by a long shot. Compared to this administrator, certainly, I was a light-weight.

That said I'd hoped he'd spend more time doing whatever administrators do rather than take over the jobs of therapists or recovery counselors. Stupidly, I'd assumed when I came to Thunder Road that the task of intervening would be left to the clinical staff, and that therapeutic interventions would be informed by not only clients' backgrounds and individual treatment plans, but by an educated knowledge of either addiction or psychopathology. Shaking his head with bombastic certainty, this administrator would speak to me informally from time to time, asserting what he thought worked with kids, and what he was sure did not. He stood over kids with the folded arms and mustachioed smile of a recruiting sergeant. "I've been doing this stuff for twenty years," he once boasted, having just feted a diatribe he'd directed at one of the clients on my caseload. Twenty years? That's a long time to be doing something wrong, I thought privately. He must feel terrible. Deep down.

I gathered that this administrator didn't take to criticism very well. His opaque gaze in response to that disgruntled family at the graduation ceremony suggested his own dissociating tendency, one coupled with angry fits directed at hapless subordinates. Secondly, I was a diffident, largely politic and therefore hypocritical employee of Thunder Road during this era—as most people who wish to survive within systems are. My desire to preserve my image as a team player—a Thunder Road team player—took over and I resolved to keep my concerns generic and blame-free. Only later did I let myself realize, as I drove down the Five freeway heading to my new home, that I'd sat there with that man, discussing the need to retain qualified and dedicated staff, watching him nod in seeming agreement while knowing in my heart that something was wrong in the state of Denmark, and more importantly, that I'd failed to say anything about it. I was playing along, complying, saying farewell graciously like the kids in my caseload; not rocking the boat, not throwing anyone under the bus, and thinking that without the thrust of opposition in my face, there was no longer any need to assert matters. Life as reaction. I was attending to the conscious elements only, while ignoring what was real underneath: what I thought meant nothing.

PART TWO

7

PLANTING SEEDS, WATERING LIVES

A Sober living house

I knew I'd gone slightly nuts during my first tenure at Thunder Road. I'd tied myself in knots, was thinking in circles, and talking to myself. While that may have ensured decent conversation, I was hoping for fresh sea breeze and a change of pace, so I moved to San Diego, a big town will a small town feel to it, quite unlike Oakland. The community felt a bit sleepy to me, but if you lived downtown, as I did, within San Diego's poor man's equivalent of the Castro district, you kept your head low, sometimes cowering at the sight and sound of flights sluggishly floating past the skyline and then down into Lindberg field.

Forty five minutes north was the group home at which I'd be working, mostly on night shifts at first. The facility was one of nearly twenty headed by a CEO that I hadn't met during the hiring process, but whom I would meet and get to know quite well soon thereafter. It was versatile organization, offering an array of services directed at a diversity of populations. The company, named McAlister Institute, had a program—an outpatient program—that catered specifically to the hearing impaired, and also an inpatient program that served single mothers and their children. The CEO, a woman then in her sixties, ran the organization as a charismatic leader, inspiring almost fanatical popularity amongst staff. Her celebrity, local of course, was referenced at every turn. At first, I didn't understand her role. I was slow to realize that her consultation, on all major decisions concerning all programs, had to involve her directly.

I was actually hired in San Francisco, on the back of a meeting in a Castro Starbucks with the CEO's direct subordinate, a man who seemed enthusiastic to have someone on board who was experienced with Therapeutic Community Concepts. I'd be working at a group home in Oceanside that was one of four adolescent facilities within the organization, all containing six beds, modeled on sober living homes and situated at different ends of San Diego County. The house in Oceanside was the newest at that time, though a further group home was mooted to be opening near El Cajon, east of the city. I was to be the second in command, sort of, as I had a degree and also a three-year experience working in a residential setting. That placed me above most of the already established employees apparently. That setting wasn't anything like a hospital though; of that I was clear. It was a house, like any other—embedded in a quiet neighborhood, minutes from the sea. And the kids? They'd be much like the youth at Thunder Road, I was told, and they were pretty much, save for the fact that the program had no license for the treatment of dually-diagnosed youth. That didn't mean we didn't have dually-diagnosed youth. It meant that we didn't diagnose them as such. Regardless, these kids were invariably mandated into the program; were between the ages of 13 to 18. They had arrest records for incidences of drug possession, trafficking, or intoxication, but they were also as likely to be admitted in the wake of an assault charge or a burglary. At least two things were different: gender make-up and length of stay.

With only six beds (2 per a three bedroom house) on the property, a coed mingling was out of the question. Of the four different group homes owned by the company, only one was for girls; thereby matching the ratio overall that I'd known at Thunder Road. It was a lonely bachelor's life for those living at the group home where I worked. But the kids—the boys in the case of the Oceanside house—wouldn't have to stay long. Twenty eight days, the traditional duration of the Minnesota Model, was the average length of stay, give or take one or two days. I'd known going in that the dynamics would be quite different: that motivation would be even slighter given the fact that clients would need to do little in the program to effect progression. Simply endure the twenty eight days was the overriding cause of most admitted youth. My role, though apparently the same as the rest of a six-deep set of employees, was to come up with ideas that might enliven the program.

The manager that hired me was the driving figure in this plan. In staff meetings, he'd continuously reference me as a newcomer with ideas. On matters related to program structure, the engagement of client motivation, therapeutic principles, I was presented as a go-to guy, a man with education, experience, *expertise*. I found this quite embarrassing, actually, especially as I was making about eleven dollars an hour at the time. If I was an expert, shouldn't I be getting paid as one? I thought. I'm paid a little better these days, but I still reflect on the way managers of mental health professionals patronize employees in lieu of paying them competitive wages. Don't let anyone say that working with teens in residential settings is a thankless job. Actually, there are plenty of thanks to go around. It's the money that's missing; or rather, it's being shuffled elsewhere.

Anyway, during those staff meetings with my new peers, I'd note the reverent yet skeptical nods pointed in my direction. *Who was this guy*? I felt them thinking. It wasn't long before the full scope of the class divide made itself known. A more senior staff member, a woman ten years older than me, let it be known, albeit with sideways, passing remarks, that I'd usurped her position, passed her by as next in line for a manager's position, because of my degree and experience. She and the other employees were college graduates, but not aspiring to Master degrees, much less things like therapist licenses. Some will have been ambitious of obtaining credentials as substance abuse counselors, such as a CADAAC license, but within this organization, few of my colleagues seemed knowledgeable of the range opportunities in the field. These people were like some at Thunder Road: they were recovering addicts, veterans of 12-step.

As it turned out, my consultation duties were largely ignored. Rarely around for support, that flattering manager, the one who built me up and presented me as a new star, left me to my own devices, and so for the first three months I was interchangeable with anyone else working a shift. At meetings, he and the CEO paid lip service to my role as unofficial consultant, but few were moved by my ideas, especially those concerning assignments. The conceit of hyping new employees was part of a bigger front: an attempt by the institute to present itself as ambitious and open-minded. The existing curriculum for the program was negligible: rudiments of art therapy exercises, such as collage-like depictions of the progression of an addictive lifestyle, were the central tasks of the twenty-eight day period, and the only seeming requirements, in assignment terms, for completion of the program. One of my first projects was to scrutinize the different collages, most of which were left by indifferent clients upon discharge, and thereafter placed in storage, and see how they could be improved. The collages that I looked at tended to have little direction, though a lot of meaning. If intended to convey remorse over past misbehaviors, or suffering at the hands of a deepening addiction or the promise of a clean and sober future, most depictions fell well short.

Images of fast cars, supermodels, touchdowns being scored or basketballs being dunked—bottles of Hennessey or Vodka because that's what can be advertised in a magazine—tended to dominate a glorified anticipation of unabated freedom and license. As ever, I could admire the gleeful denial of defiant teens stuck in "stuck-like" circumstances. I know that if I had spent a month in a group home at age 16 during, especially during the middle of a school year, I would have thought my life had come to an end. Given an assignment about my future, I would have searched for that image of a screaming soul by Munch and stuck it in the center of my collage. Then I would have found images of homelessness, or starvation; black-hearted penury would have been the theme of my collage. I would have anticipated failure and humiliation, a future of living alone licking my wounds in self pity. Once again, as I regarded the works of kids who'd known abuse, the addiction of caregivers, not to mention all manner of neglect, I had to leave space for a begrudging admiration of their defensive fronts.

At Thunder Road, those fronts, as they were often termed, would have been relentlessly confronted amid the structure and philosophy of the Therapeutic Community. Not so at the group home in Oceanside. Confrontation groups didn't exist; neither did contract breaking. There were no benches at the group homes—no time-out devices—and mirrors on the wall, designed for contemplative reflection, would have been considered weird. I didn't bother proposing these tools, though when staff members bemoaned the lack of structural elements for the imposition of limits, I did point out—on cue from my manager—what options I knew to be available. Some looked at me and squinted in-comprehendingly. Some knew that similar techniques were employed at a Phoenix house program that was situated west of the city, out in the desert. This place may have held mythical significance for some, but it mystified others, and left them cold. The manager would translate my comments as if I were a foreign interloper speaking in tongues.

What we did have was an even greater approximation of that parent-to-child dynamic, such as I'd already experienced at Thunder Road. A lot of that had to do with the physical nature of the group home. Rather than waking up in what looked like a hospital ward that someone has painted several times with warmer hues, kids at the Oceanside group home woke up to a normal, suburban house, complete with average-looking kitchens, bedrooms with normal-looking closets; a room for a TV and a video-game set-up; even what looked like a bar, albeit one that had been locked up, its contents long removed, leaving cobwebs and dust mites behind. In this environment, an average teenager might expect to plod down in the middle of the night, expecting no particular resistance as he opens up a refrigerator laden with a week's worth of groceries. He might not think twice about flopping onto a couch in a TV room, putting his feet on the coffee table after searching through the sofas for a remote control.

It was a sober living house, basically. At any given time, there was at least one staff member on site monitoring the clients. This was deliberate. It met the minimum standards of the community licensing board, for the proper care and monitoring of minors living in a licensed group home: six to one was the required ratio. Clearly, as far as a meaningful treatment episode was concerned, it was inadequate, this ratio, for little beyond a competent act of babysitting was called for on these shifts that I worked. I was more or less capable, which meant roughly that no one was killed or seriously injured on my succession of watches. On an eight hour stint, I'd need to facilitate one check-in group, which usually meant keeping clients reasonably awake while speaking about principles of addiction, or else fielding complaints about the deficiencies of the house. This wasn't group therapy. This was more like an exercise in keeping kids interested or entertained. No small task, actually. It was like being a teacher, only with less authority. Kids acted out relentlessly in these groups: they slept, farted, or flicked rubber bands at one another. They teased my British accent, poked fun at my clothes, my red hair. They interrupted discussions with non sequiturs, asking after my love life, insinuating that I was gay if I didn't answer. Mostly I "rolled with it" as my then supervisor advised. Sometimes I broke out the latent teacher in me—the "stop it" voice that most adults have to use at some point with kids—and brought a semblance of order. Keeping clients engaged was the toughest challenge. That was the task that had me machinating on the way to work; preoccupied, even, on my days off. Pleasing kids: it's a real anxiety-inducer. In fact, ever since my early days at Thunder Road, the only times I've gotten nervous ahead of a group process were those times when a teen group activity approached and ideas for "fun" exercises seemed few.

Next, clients would attend to chores under my supervision. This meant standing nearby as clients looked at a list prepared by over-night (noc shift) staff, and then negotiated with or else bullied one another over the trading of assigned duties. Cleaning the refrigerator was one chore that was fundamentally misunderstood, and I derived much comic pleasure watching nonplussed youths stare at open refrigerators, looking past spills and stains, seemingly unaware that any reparative action might be needed. A more sophisticated kid might complain about the chores, especially the least dignified tasks of cleaning toilets or the bases of shower stalls. I heard many diatribes about slave labor during these shifts. The outside chores were the plum jobs. This piece of work, as interpreted by the average client, consisted of wandering about the front yard, kicking at twigs, occasionally breaking into a sprint should a squirrel trespass into the area. Despite the kids' continued appeals, there were no pets allowed at the group homes; no outlets for either compartmentalized nurturing instincts or sadistic impulses.

Beyond that, it was my job to escort kids to 12-steps meetings in the community, and make sure they returned to the group home safely and un-intoxicated. I'm not sure that I expected the group home to provide a significant therapeutic episode for these kids. I wasn't so naïve to think that a twenty eight day program for teens mandated via the juvenile justice system would present a client base consisting of young people eager for psychotherapy or 12 step recovery. Furthermore, as the program didn't provide any family therapy, besides a before-and-after meeting facilitated by the organization's one overworked social worker, I knew there would be little scope for addressing relational issues, or "core" issues as I'd previously understood them. Management trotted out the usual platitudes: "We're here to plant seeds," they'd say repeatedly. I nodded along during the meetings. Thing is I'm not that interested in planting seeds. I don't think mental health treatment ought to be about that; not really. It's really not an academic exercise, which is what the hackneyed aphorism intends, I think. Psychotherapy, as well as any sound mental health treatment, is much more than a planting of seeds. Treatment means watering those seeds, removing them from dark closeted spaces, placing them in sunlight and standing over them with care.

At the group home, by mid-99', I was already starting to feel a bit like a journeyman in the residential treatment business. I was biding my time until the next real opportunity came along. Fortunately, it wasn't the only iron I had in the fire. I still had a few hundred hours to accrue so that I might sit for licensing exams at some point, and since the organization didn't provide any clinical supervision, I went looking for an internship to supplement my day job. I found one after a couple of months, in Chula Vista, south of the city. That placement was a family services agency, an outpatient setting—the first I'd worked at in over three years—in which I'd receive training in play therapy, the multi-family systems approach of Murray Bowen, while co-facilitating an ongoing group comprised of convicted sex offenders. I started that position in July of 99', just as I learned that life at the group home was about to change.

The guy in charge

On a mid-afternoon in early summer, just as I was about to head out from my downtown apartment and drive up to Oceanside for my next shift, I received a call from the company CEO. I was surprised to hear from her, and thought for a moment that I'd won the organization-wide raffle that she'd announced during the last staff meeting. She was pleasant and deferential, wondering how my day was going, and whether I enjoyed working at the group home in Oceanside. Star-struck, like a plant worker looking up from his welding task only to see the company president standing over him with a smiling face, an outstretched hand and an overlooking entourage, I stuttered out a few obsequious words of content. Then she turned serious. She told me that her subordinate, the manager in charge of the group homes, and the manager who had hired me in San Francisco, had just quit his position, having lined up another job for himself. For a few minutes, I indulged a tirade from this CEO. With a sharp, bitter voice, she confided in me as though we'd known each other for years, and spoke acerbically of the shifty, treacherous little man who'd just vacated his position. Anyway, she said finally, a position was therefore available: not his overseeing position, as such—she was eliminating that—but rather the job of program administrator, or house manager, for a new boys' group in Spring Valley, minutes south of company headquarters in El Cajon. Was I interested? she asked.

I paused, thinking that such a job meant being at this woman's beckon call on a daily basis. I'm not sure exactly what I said, but I just about managed to thank her and that I was excited about the opportunity. However, I was concerned about the time requirements of the position, indicating that I'd just accepted an internship at a placement in Chula Vista. She didn't understand my language; she hadn't done since day one, it seemed to me. Briefly, I explained that internship didn't mean job, and that placements were necessary for the pursuit of my therapist license. She interrupted me during the second part. Like many executives, she had a well-tuned filter, one that screened out unnecessary verbiage, distilled the essential facts, and blended it with unabashed bluntness[32]. "That's fine, we'll work around that," she insisted. But was I interested? she again asked. Yes, I replied. The next day I was in her office going over details, including a significantly improved salary for me, and then a week later, a new staff was assembled and presented in a team meeting.

One or two of the other staff members were also Oceanside employees; people who had been campaigning for relocation for some time, and who seemed, to my mild surprise, sympathetic to my prospective leadership. Upon being presented as the group home administrator, those colleagues broke wide smiles, which felt great. In retrospect, I don't think I realized the extent to which I felt isolated and unhappy. I'd been working long hours, commuting to Oceanside, and otherwise driving around to different sites, looking for an internship. I felt distrusted in the workplace: tolerated by some, actively disliked by others, kids and colleagues alike. Despite the surface politeness from peers, I sensed tension, perhaps envy. Meanwhile, my then primary relationship was strained. My girlfriend and I, living together in close quarters, were squabbling daily, frustrated over poverty, the incompatibility of our schedules (sadly, despite moving to San Diego to live with her, our relationship didn't last the three years of my time there). Now I'd be adding a twenty-hour/week internship to a full-time position that threatened to ask for at least forty hours of my week, perhaps more. Despite the prospect of overwork and burn-out, having evidence of being welcome meant the world to me. All of a sudden, I was jazzed to be working in this organization, and I couldn't wait to get started at the new group home.

The next two and a half years were long and arduous. They taught me a lot about managing time, keeping boundaries with employers, clinical supervisors; clients of different levels of care, motivation levels and other levels of functioning. Love suffered; work, in terms of psychotherapy, did also, but my time in San Diego was nonetheless an education. The specter of Thunder Road lingered throughout my time there. At the new group home, which was at least closer to my home in the city, I was able to introduce certain elements of a behavioral modification program, albeit in a compromised form. The assignments were altered, with written work alternating with verbal one-on-ones, drawn from my time at Thunder Road. There were no benches, of course, but consequences in the form of expulsion of clients from privileged areas—like the TV room—were put in place, and enthusiastically supported by the staff.

Meanwhile, we were able to introduce a modest rewards system owing to the fact that the house contained no more than six kids at any one time and so the tracking of point systems, though still not perfect, was far less cumbersome. As for the rewards themselves, we didn't have a huge budget for snacks or other minor goodies, but they weren't so much in demand anyway. Surveying opinion of clients one day I found that one thing was coveted more than anything else: time, as in free time—time to do nothing. The McAlister kids, no less than their counterparts at Thunder Road, cited boredom as their biggest enemy, and in the absence of stimulating physical activities, clients requested down time, natural sedation; face-down in a pillow, literal unconsciousness. With tongue-in-cheek, I worked it into the system, and so kids that either finished their chores early on a consistent basis, or passed a certain threshold of hours or days without being obviously unpleasant, were afforded with extra time—half hour slots, typically—wherein they could disappear to their rooms and navel-gaze, sleep, or pleasure themselves[33]. Monads came naturally; the kids typically napped during these breaks. One or two staff objected, thinking the measures colluded with clients' bad habits, reinforced isolation. They weren't wrong, but they didn't have better ideas for rewards, and that was the buzz word at the time—rewards. Staff thought the rewards effective, and the kids in particular reacted as though we were acknowledging some core need of theirs.

As a manager of a group home and not so much a therapist, I noted that these kinds of compromises were easy to make, and that I was more likely to make them in my managerial/patriarchal role. They didn't necessarily feel good, the compromises. It never feels good to capitulate on matters of principle. It's like cheating on taxes, running red lights, or sneaking a look at the backside of a hot, scantily-clad woman. It's like a sell-out, and that's the problem with compromise. On the one hand it seems right to compromise, to *meet them where they're at*, to make concessions to feeling good versus feeling good about the self. At times, it also seems necessary and normal. But it also seems insidious, if not vaguely sinister. Taking advantage of boredom, the encoded depression of youth, we allowed kids to slump back to their rooms and disappear from company; isolate themselves in a way that failed to honor the basic messages of recovery. More importantly, we failed to challenge them. We might have rationalized that we were attending to the adolescent's stage-appropriate need for separation, but given the profile of these kids, these not-so-normal kids, I don't think this was true. It seemed deeper than that, this profile of withdrawal; more obviously pathological. These kids that wanted to find a warm rock during the day and sleep: they were like reptiles conserving energy, shutting down systems, engaging the parasympathetic system; hiding. Dissociating. As often as not, I think we were witnessing emptiness in action, and waving it passively to the cave.

I felt less conflicted about other new measures, especially those designed to reduce the isolation between clients and their families. I introduced family meetings to dovetail with visiting days. On these days, I'd sit with family members and the client residents, discussing plans for aftercare, the use of outpatient programs, or 12-step meetings in the community. Upon agreement as to the necessity of a client's abstinence, I'd address the question of parents' using, and confront an intransigent mother or father, urging them to see that what they modeled was far more powerful than what they preached. This wasn't intensive family therapy, of course, and did little to dent the insecure attachments, or paucity of reflective functioning that was no less apparent with these families than with those at Thunder Road. But at least I had the chance to engage parents on more than one occasion (on average, three meetings) and impress upon them the necessity of structure, a clean and sober living environment, and the notion, simply put, that responsibility for meaningful change shouldn't fall exclusively upon the shoulders of youth.

Those kids at house, delinquent if not actively sociopathic in some cases, tended to sit quietly as I gave these messages, seemingly in agreement. By this time, my chops had been practiced over a few years; my messages about how a system can help an afflicted individual, or how it might collude with dysfunction, was getting clearer, and more convincing. I experienced fewer and fewer instances of youth attempting to shout me down; to leave their parents alone, or else dissolve family meetings altogether. I experienced fewer parents dismissing my opinions, or else disinterestedly listening, or becoming lost in my wordy tangents. I was becoming succinct, forthright, if at times dogmatic. I felt listened to rather than indulged, or fought against. Instead of avoiding these meetings, or scoffing their way through them, most parents thanked me for taking time with them. Some might have observed that the seeming compliance was a function of my position. I was, after all, the guy in charge of the house. I was no longer an avuncular case manager, relaying ideas thought of by invisible others; nor was I looking on from afar as others stole the clinical spotlight in front of visiting cameras. I was the voice of authority; the figurative dad of the household.

But I wasn't really the patriarch. We had a matriarch instead. That was the CEO, and she was in charge of most decisions, actually. We had no psychiatrist on staff, save for a man whom she hired occasionally as an independent contractor to lead trainings. Appeals for some kids to get fuller psychiatric evaluations were unmet, unfortunately. There was little money, I was told. I could make a request with a client's probation officer if I so pleased, but that would likely not influence matters. A probation officer, or a court, would not order a fuller evaluation on the back of a recommendation from a therapist, much less a registered intern therapist, which is what I still was during this period. Secondly, I could do little about such things as clients' smoking, or even their vandalism of the property. The first issue often reminded me of that first week at Thunder Road back in 96', when then residents were facing the reality that their nicotine needs would no longer be enabled by supervising adults. The rules against smoking were steadfast at Thunder Road and taken seriously. To smoke there, a client had to actually work their skills of subterfuge; they had to develop, if not continue, aptitudes for smuggling, or the manipulation of adults.

Not so at the San Diego group homes of McAlister Institute. This was just a group home, I was often reminded; not a hospital or a place of Therapeutic Community concepts, despite what may have been implied by the man who hired me. This was a twenty eight day program, a place for youth of the county to go instead of juvenile hall. Unless someone was being actively violent, or else consistently—and by consistently, the CEO meant relentlessly non-compliant—those twenty eight days would transpire without interruption, much less expulsion. There would be no reassessments, nothing like staffings, or bottom-line meetings with so-called treatment teams. No one had time for that, especially not over the trivial matter of smoking. No power struggling, the CEO would decree. In principle, smoking was not allowed; in practice, not only was it allowed, it was encouraged, as if in keeping with the milieu of an average Narcotics Anonymous meeting. With respect to this issue, my support staff even abandoned me. They didn't want to bother with giving assignments to kids who had collected a school of cigarettes at a 12-step meeting. They didn't relish trying to obstruct the third or fourth trip to the bathroom during such an activity; the sequential disappearance of every kid amongst the group of six for the same purpose. Smoking was allowed, in effect. I countered that we were supporting negative behaviors, colluding with secretive habits, being codependent. "These are subtleties, padre", said the political minister character from *A Clockwork Orange*, to the earnest man of the cloth. I was conflicted again, and identifying with that marginalized and ridiculed figure from the movie.

The limits against vandalism were similarly toothless, though the CEO tended to become more interested if costly damage was involved. I remember one kid, a pleasant-natured youth, actually, who came to the house with a reputation for tagging (graffiti), and therefore with the standard warning that these and other gang-related behaviors must be suspended while living at the group home. No argument on that: taciturn agreement was the norm. That wasn't the point of dispute. The point of dispute, whenever the iconography appeared, was to simply deny responsibility, or else pin responsibility upon the latest kid to have left the house; therefore, the kid who could no longer be punished for the act of vandalism. Regardless, the punishments were hardly onerous. The solution, as laid down by my boss, was for me to go down to the hardware store and procure whatever cleaning materials were necessary so that the culprits, if identified, might wipe away their territorial symbols. That was fine, sort of, for the average miscreant, but ultimately the problem of tagging became epidemic. That one kid in particular somehow managed to write his name, as well as that of his clique, on every bed in the house, on the underside of every step of the household's one staircase, across the underside of a six-foot wide kitchen dining table, and finally, covering them in their entirety, across every back seat of the house Van.

"Have him come talk to me," said the CEO. This was the standard for the delivery of bottom lines; the analogy to Thunder

Road's staffings, or contract breaking groups. If a kid seemed irredeemably uncooperative, or had damaged property in a significant way, or had damaged another human being in a significant way, they were compelled to go meet with the CEO for a one-on-one. This intervention, referenced with knowing smiles by long-standing employees, was deemed the ultimate intervention and a presumably terrifying prospect for any client, youth or adult. A meeting with the CEO was like an audience with the great and powerful Oz. It was thought that she would unleash her ruthless judgments, her torrent of charisma, leaving people trembling with anxiety and then begging for mercy.

Actually, she was like this on occasion, but only with adults, and more specifically, with her employees. I know this because I was the recipient of her volatile outrages on more than one occasion (she'd later apologize, strangely rationalizing, "it's not you that's frustrating. It's the situation"). But with the kids, she was tame; a patient, motherly confessor. I know because I'd be the one bringing them to her headquarters, and watching from the wings through a transparency that separated her office from the wider floor of company operations. I'd see the troublesome kid, his arms folded and his head down, as though he was talking to a nun; as if he were purging his soul, seeking absolution. After a half hour meeting, the CEO would walk the chastened boy to her door, release him to my care, and later pronounce the job done, predicting that all should be quiet from then on.

Upon returning to the house, the kids who had experienced these summit meetings would begin boasting about how cool the CEO was—much cooler than any of the staff at the house, certainly—especially me. Their reflections suggested a meeting consisting of shared anecdotes; the standard repertoire of an experienced sponsor, rather than a dressing down by the ultimate heavy of the organization. In subsequent meetings with the CEO, I'd report with a touch of *I-told-you-so* that the behaviors that had merited the meeting in the first place had resumed. Usually, by this point, the client in question would have only a few days left in the program, so further intervention would be dismissed on the grounds that it would be moot. If I was truly concerned, the CEO suggested, I could discharge the client early, thus sparing everybody any more hassle. Wouldn't that reinforce the negative behaviors? I argued. What were we trying to teach, after all? That's about as far as I would take the matter before receiving a stiff glare and a swift rebuke. I was appreciated in so far as I did not commit the most egregious of sins as a manager or employee: I hardly ever called in sick; I didn't show up to work drunk or stupefied, and I didn't seem inclined to physical altercations with young people. Unfortunately, quite a few people working in this business fail to meet one or more of these standards. On the other hand, I was too strict, she said. Me, strict? I questioned. For other kids, even those who begrudging admitted that I sought to "teach things", I was boring. Paraphrasing my friends from my early twenties, she implied that I needed to lighten up, make less fuss over the little things, the matters over which recovery professionals have no control. I saw it coming.

The tautologies were neatly arrayed, poured out over my precious idealism with righteous fervor: *progress not perfection* made its appearance; *we are powerless over the addiction*, many would drone. *We are planting seeds*, etcetera. This all sounded familiar, of course. But what did I expect, right? It was a short term program, characterized more or less as a refuge for youth from the juvenile justice system of Southern California. Well, I missed Thunder Road, for one thing. I was having a hard time shedding its lens, even a year or so into my new life; the Therapeutic Community's insistence on standards, structure and community. Change: that was the word the previous clinical director of Thunder Road had invoked once upon a time—we all struggle with change.

Maintaining staff

Putting aside the moral or just clinical arguments, I sidelined my dismay and focused on the more practical aspects of being a house manager. Maintaining a staff was a huge problem. As the program was small, we only needed a staff of about half a dozen people at any one time. Any other employees, under ordinary circumstances, would have been superfluous to requirements. However, there were problems whenever someone called in sick, or else failed to show up for a shift, or—worst of all—had to be removed from the work roster because of a mandate from Community Care Licensing, the governing body of group homes and foster care facilities. Supposedly, we had back-up employees, so-called on-call staff. But these were people who otherwise had different full-time jobs or obligations; other lives. The concept of on-call seemed inherently flawed: who could commit to a shift that might happen? In theory, several did, but in practice, I'd be the one calling these stand-by workers. I'd leave a hopeful message on their answering machines, and then wait a couple of hours to see if I'd get a call back. Then, within a half hour of the shift I'd yet to fill, I'd take a deep breath, throw a brief tantrum, and then either call up some overworked soul to do a double-shift, or else do it myself.

The orders to remove someone from the work rosters were the most difficult, and sometimes the most painful decisions to implement. The reason this typically happened was due to the sluggish process of social services' background screening system. In my time in San Diego, a new hire could begin working shifts at the group home, but later be ordered away if the background screen revealed an arrest record that had been unresolved. At this point, no further shifts could be granted, and the employee in question would need to undergo an exemption process that could take months. As many of the employees were drawn to the work because of their own past experiences with drugs, an extensive history of legal entanglements was common. Therefore, I often had the problem of hiring people on a knife edge: sometimes, we'd catch a break, and a solid and reliable counselor, someone who might have committed multiple armed robberies in their past could get a job with us, and proceed with no problem, pursuing their redemptive occupation in peace. At other times, I'd get one of those calls from HR, informing me with casual disregard—as though they were calling to remind me to sign a payroll record—that the overnight staff on whom I absolutely rely cannot work at the house anymore.

I once had to remove myself from the group home roster. The reason: a disgruntled client complained to his parents, who later complained to Community Care Licensing, that I had fondled him during a closing prayer exercise at a 12-step meeting wherein hand holding is customary. I still recall the flat, humorless expression of the CEO as she relayed this news to me. I recall my own struggle to keep my face straight—such was the pressure to act as though the matter was serious. Actually, it was serious, though not for the reasons Community Care Licensing thought it was serious. The details were sketchy at first, but I was ordered away from work for four days before a representative from CCL visited the company offices for an interview with me. Talking to one of the most dull-witted and unctuous bureaucrats I've ever come across working in this field, I learned that I was accused of protruding my middle finger into the client's palm during the hand-holding ritual that closed the 12-step meeting in question. The CCL representative suggested that I had traumatized the young man and exploited the power difference between us. I nodded with affected shame and later commented to the CEO that the man may have a point. After all, I'd not trimmed my nails in some time, so it was possible I'd broken skin with my relentless stroking. After the fourth day, the client retracted his story, however, claiming he'd felt resentful about my strict treatment of him in the program. No shit, I thought. The CEO cited this confession, adding her own version of the *I-told-you-so*—far more caustic than my own—and thus got her revenge upon my supercilious attitude. She then made an executive decision. The client was transferred to another group home, forestalling any possibility of conflict resolution, and I was restored to my duties as house manager. Meanwhile, my reputation as a hand fetishist was short-lived.

I burned out a few of my most reliable staff members—people on whom I called in a time of crisis time and time again. They got used up, the same three or four people. Privately, my best employees confided in me that they'd come to dread the ringing of their phones. They were having nightmares of being assaulted at the house, of their own impulses to assault kids, or else assail them with profanity-laced tirades that they'd been storing up for months. One staff member, as mild tempered a man as I'd ever met in this business, once declined my appeal for help in filling a shift, claiming he was at the end of his rope. He begged me not to order him into work—an extra shift—declaring himself unfit for the job. Working six days in a row, with no support for the most part; one man in charge of six kids seemingly bent on turning the McAlister group home into some cliché of frat house debauchery. I was in a bind. The CEO, poised to shut us down owing to the fact that the program wasn't making much money, would have mustered thin sympathy for my plight, but for the fact that I'd be out of a job.

Some weeks thereafter I got a call in the middle of the night. It was five minutes after midnight. As I picked up the line, I expected to hear my evening shift worker worriedly complaining that the overnight (noc) shift hadn't shown up yet. Actually, the opposite was true. The noc shift staff was there, and was ready to go about his normal routine of hourly bed checks and night audits, with the background sound of late-night talk radio. The problem was that the house was empty. "What?" I said. "Uh…there's nobody here," my staff dully replied. It seemed that the evening staff member had taken the clients on an outing, likely to a 12-step meeting, which was standard practice, but not returned to the house. The noc shift staff was asking me what to do. Since there were no clients around, might he go home, he asked stupidly. I told him to continue manning his post, of course, and hung up in order to give this problem some thought. My future, immediate and distant, flashed before me as I contemplated the prospect of informing company headquarters, and the CEO, that the following morning's census was zero.

A call back arrived five minutes later. All six kids had returned, said the overnight staff, minus the evening staff. The clients had apparently been taken to a downtown 12-step meeting, only to be dropped off by the evening staff, who then told the clients that he would pursue an "errand" while they were at the meeting (we later learned that he'd gone on a cocaine run and passed out). That staff never returned, and sometime after the meeting, two of the kids managed to contact parents who lived nearby, so they could be escorted back to the group home. This happened, but not before each of the kids managed to become either intoxicated or assaulted. One or two of the kids were bloodied, but only mildly unsettled. Two others were reportedly giddy, hyperactive, and to my noc staff's dismay (or inconvenience), unable to settle down to sleep for the remainder of his shift. The parents? Well, they were not giddy. They were un-amused, and unsettled, and over the next several days, many at McAlister, including the CEO and myself, spent considerable time on the phone, talking to licensing, talking to parents, talking to probation officers; talking back lawsuits.

Unfortunately for McAlister Institute's adolescent group home program, there were several incidents like this in my time in San Diego. Unfortunately, there are many instances of abuse and neglect in group homes. The industry hires many gifted people—some formally trained and educated, many not—and places like Thunder Road have been lucky to have a core staff of what are sometimes called paraprofessionals. Many have good hearts and minds, strong voices, and a firm center: people whose gifts the kids would frequently intuit. "That's just who they are," kids say of those adults that win a grounded acceptance. But the business also hires misguided people; those all too eager to help others before they have received help themselves. Or else it hires the cynical: those simply looking for what may seem like an easy job, monitoring kids while paying lip service to their needs. Most sinisterly, the industry hires some who are mentally ill; who are in the active phase of an addiction, and in denial; it hires people with porous boundaries, non-existent ethical wavelengths—those as likely to fornicate with clients as help them with serious mental health issues.

Fun in recovery

I wasn't reprimanded for the above described incident, despite the fact that I had hired the offending employee. It was the way of things, the CEO suggested with a philosophical shrug. Actually, she was sympathetic to several different aspects of working in her group homes. Acknowledging the difficulty of working with unmotivated and uncontained teens, with a thinly trained and underpaid staff, she'd admit that the system attending to youth was flawed: skimming rocks over the surface of turbulent seas and kicking up spray from the surf, but lacking the tools with which to dive underneath. She'd attempt to assuage my frustration, pointing out that all the education in the world, all the training of different intervention strategies, ideas for proper care, money, couldn't change the basic truth that we were dealing with the mysteries of human existence, and not the mechanical tweaking of what she called "widgets".

Still, it didn't feel good to be among that disorder; that toxic chaos. I got depressed again. I felt myself getting sick, inside and out. I completed my internship, meanwhile, and was ready by late 2000 to start taking licensing exams. Though my relationship was breaking up around that time, I was feeling down about the present, but reasonably hopeful about the future, looking forward to a career in which I'd do much more. I wanted to be a part of something that offered more than the glorified babysitting of delinquents. I was still in contact with one or two people from Thunder Road during this period. Though I'd visited only once, on a holiday trip to the Bay Area to see my parents, I'd heard from friends that life was changing at the group home/hospital. Among other things, the facility had become gender segregated; males on the 40th street side of the unit, girls flanking the 41st side. Actually, this change was underway just as I was leaving in early 99', but it was via those friends that I learned about the ongoing effects.

Onc of them called in early 2001, when I going through a period at McAlister in which I thought I was about to lose it. By *it*, I mean my collective ego capacity: frustration tolerance, my impulse control, my reality testing—perhaps my reflective function also. One morning I came to work and found the house dormant. It was my routine to arrive around eight in the morning, take over monitoring/check-ins with the kids, and then, if I was lucky enough to have my mid-shift staff member show up, relinquish any counseling or monitoring duties so that I could attend to management tasks. By eight in the morning the kids were supposed to be eating breakfast having gotten up and showered an hour earlier. This time, everyone was in the house. No one, it seemed, was running the streets of San Diego looking for alcohol, cocaine, or a fight. The reason: they were all in bed, enjoying a nice sleep-in courtesy of the overnight staff, whom I also found asleep in a supplies closet, himself wrapped in makeshift bed with the house keys and a malfunctioning alarm positioned next to his head. I stepped into the walk-in closet, silently lifted the man's keys, and then stood at the doorway, silhouetted against the harsh light of the office fluorescents behind me. I jangled the keys loudly enough to arouse my subordinate. As his eyes flickered and his head gingerly arose, he seemed to just about make out the shape of me standing over him. "Shit," he managed to utter. I said nothing. I mean afterwards: I said nothing. I needed him to come back the following night.

The friend from Thunder Road told me that the long-term track was hiring for day treatment counselors. This position would entail most of the same duties I'd known in my jobs of 96' through 99', only with some differences pertaining to an altered daytime structure. Still, it was a counseling job in a residential setting, complete with weekend shifts, working holidays, unpredictable spells of overtime. Wrinkling my nose at the prospect, I demurred on the quasi offer, as my friend was in a position to influence but not hire. Had I applied, I would, in all likelihood have gotten the position, owing to the fact that management seemed to have fond memories of my first tenure at Thunder Road. For the moment, though, it wasn't to be. I remained in San Diego for an additional nine months. Living alone, I endured the loneliest year of my adult life, but worked ridiculous numbers of hours, both at the group home, and in a lingering capacity at my internship placement so as to obscure the pervasive feeling of ennui. I had a brief affectation with carefree bachelorhood in my few off hours: I lazed in coffee shops in Kensington, reading Nick Hornby's *High Fidelity* three times over. I sat in a not quite trendy bar in Hillcrest, flirting with a bartendress who was way out of my league but too nice to say so. Down the hill, near the naval yard, was a gentleman's club that I visited half a dozen times. There I befriended a tomboyish stripper who, when I later told that I was leaving the area, lamented and told me that I was the only real friend that she had. I got a free lap dance as a going away present.

It was mid-summer when that same friend called again to speak of another Thunder Road opportunity, this time in the program's Intensive Outpatient Program. Its present coordinator was leaving, and the vacancy would be pretty much mine if I'd just say the word. That day I went to work, escorted the gang of youth in the house to Ocean beach for their obligatory mid-day recreation activity because my mid-day staff had called in sick—again. I gave the matter of Thunder Road and its enticing non-residential job opportunity some thought. It was as I let my guard down that I realized a change was needed before it was too late. To the kids' surprise, I sanctioned a reckless walk along a man-made peninsular that served as a dam. It was an unseasonably gusty day and the waves along the beach were high. The boys' risk-taking tendencies had been starved living at the group home, so a natural high, jumping on rocks and running with the sea currents was rigorously called for. I gave permission, watched from a safe distance, and relaxing, contemplated my future.

As I envisioned a working life that featured four nights a week, facilitating peer and then family therapy groups, with weekends off, and nary a holiday shift in sight, I was distracted from the imminent troubles of my teenage flock. In the distance, the six of them stood in a row, seemingly in awe as a mini-tsunami crashed over the rocks before them, and then over their heads. I watched with fleeting horror as they were each engulfed by the wave; for a few seconds, they each disappeared, as though they'd dissolved into sand. Moments later, as my numbness was settling in for a long residency, erect, drenched bodies started to re-appear, one after another. As I inventoried each succeeding body emerging from the surf, my mind carried on a surreal negotiation with itself. I reasoned that if I only lost one or two kids to the murderous sea, then my life might not yet be over. I'd still have a career. That license, only a test away by that point, could still be obtained. I'd still get that Thunder Road job as an outpatient coordinator; its management, and some good woman would still love me.

All six of the group returned, and my blood pressure returned to normal by about half way through the next day. There was no seeming trauma amongst the boys—only the hilarity of having seen one another soaked by the mighty Pacific. They delighted in the humiliation; the deformity of fashion and hairstyles that huge quantities of water brings, and the subsequent discomfort of riding back to the house in the van, shivering with the wet cold. But above all, what I noticed were the smiles: the broad smiles that betrayed spontaneous, innocent joy; play done right, as it turned out. Fun in recovery. For many, it had been an unconvincing saying; the slogan upon which 12-step pinned its hopes as far as reaching the youth of America was concerned. That afternoon I decided to leave McAlister Institute and return to the Bay Area, and back to Thunder Road. I'd have another six weeks left managing affairs, grooming my unlucky successor, bearing the Narcissistic wounding of the CEO, who could scarcely believe that I was leaving. That day by the ocean, however, watching those otherwise anti-social kids having fun: that might as well have been—it should have been—my last day.

In fact, the CEO let me go nicely, "with love" she said. It took her a little while, I think, to absorb that I wasn't leaving her. I was leaving San Diego, six-bed group homes, tawdry downtown apartments, and loneliness. She knew it wasn't for me, this continued role as a house manager/program administrator. I wanted to be a therapist; was poised to be a therapist again, in a program that was structured to provide a comprehensive treatment experience. I'll never forget standing at the CEO's office, filled as it was with about seventy five staff members, representatives of the various programs within her network, helping her celebrate her latest birthday with a hastily arranged party. She saw me at the back. She knew I'd taken my first licensing test that morning; had even bothered to learn something of its significance. She saw me smile from thirty yards away. "You passed your test!" she cried out, pumping her fist with pleasure. Bless her, and bless her modest stab at adolescent residential treatment.

8

LOOKING IN FROM THE OUTSIDE

IOP Coordinator

When I returned to Thunder Road in the late summer of 2001, it seemed that little had changed, except for some personnel. Though I'd been away for almost three years, some of the staff members I'd previously known, at least amongst management, were still employed by the hospital. The program director, that silky-voiced, larger than life character that had always seemed to like me, was still there in the same capacity. On my first day back, she called out my name in a sing-song voice that carried down the hallway of the boys side—the one that ran adjacent to 40th street in Oakland. The moment took me back as I recalled that this had been her familiar, playful way of addressing me all along. It was as though I'd been away on a long vacation, though in an emotional sense it was like time and space had folded in that way that quantum physics teaches. The reunions were in passing, as I wouldn't be working in the residential unit this time. After a tour through all departments, reconnecting with people, some of whom I remembered, some who (to my embarrassment) I did not, I was led to my downstairs and underground office, where I would situate myself for the better part of the next decade. IOP, standing for Intensive Outpatient Program, would be the department I'd run for the next three years of my Thunder Road rollercoaster ride.

On my first day I learned that the program was hanging on by tethers. The woman seemingly in charge was one whom I'd known since the mid-nineties. She was someone who had previously worked in Thunder Road's other more long-standing outpatient component, the aftercare component called Continuing Care. At this point, she seemed at best a nominal Thunder Road employee. A manager overseeing IOP, she was three weeks away from a due date for her first child, and days away from a maternity leave. She was grateful for my relatively quick turnaround after relocating from Southern California, adding that another counselor, a would-be subordinate to me, would be joining the effort in a couple of weeks following a previously planned vacation. For about two weeks she'd been running the program as a substitute, after my predecessor and his partner therapist had left the program in mid-summer. There were welcome noises and goodwill all around, but it was clear from the outset that the department was in some state of disarray, and the curious, not to mention unexplained way in which the previous therapists had abandoned ship seemed ominous.

That day I sat in on the first group, observing as the manager awkwardly facilitated a peer group consisting of three youths—a quiet and moderately depressed trio who said little but otherwise didn't seem particularly resistant. The day was outlined as a four hour event: an initial group with the kids enrolled in the program, followed by a one to two hour group with kids and parents—rather like the multi-family group of the residential program. Though she presented as competent, authoritative, and all-knowing with respect to the program's procedures and policies, the manager's connection to the kids seemed superficial; she went through the motions capably enough, but was obviously marking time, and within fifteen minutes of that first group, she was already making peripheral glances in my direction to see if I might step in, perhaps take over for the later group so she could go home. I have to admit that for a week or so I wondered if I'd been recruited to field a dropped ball that no one else wanted to pick up. I felt like a civil servant being delivered by a preoccupied supervisor to a basement office; given keys and a badge, best wishes, a handshake, and told to get on with the job.

I should have been unnerved. Had Thunder Road really campaigned, via a friend and former mentor, for almost three months, to bring me back from Southern California, only to leave me in charge of this moribund program? I wasn't distressed at this point; in fact, had that manager run out of questions for the taciturn threesome that showed up that first day, I might indeed have taken over. By that time, as I have boasted before and since, hardly a week had passed in several years wherein I wasn't running a therapy group somewhere. I was a duck taking to water, though perfunctorily nervous, because I was being introduced to the kids as the new guy in charge when at least two of the kids had been in the program long enough to have known the now departed former therapists. But the kids that were in the group that day seemed workable and not especially perturbed by the turnaround of leadership. On my second day, the manager called to say she'd be late coming in and asked if I'd mind leading the first group by myself. I wasn't surprised. In other circumstances, I might have thought this a kind of test—throwing me in at the deep end. However, I interpreted that she was just itching to move on, and had been sufficiently satisfied by her first impressions of me to allow for this. In fact, I wouldn't have been too shocked if I'd never seen her again.

I learned more at the start of my second week, when on my fourth day I met with the hospital administrator, the same man with whom I'd conducted that unsatisfactory exit interview three years earlier. He was in a hearty mood, I recall—enthusiastic about the future of Thunder Road's fledgling IOP (it, like the gender-demarcation, had gotten under way in early 99'); and boastful about his successful acquisition of a city contract for IOP, known by the acronym OFCY. This was the first acronym to really dent my consciousness at Thunder Road. Though it had been five years since first walking through the doors of the facility, I had until this point been shielded from the arcane system of acronyms that filled the mouths of administrative staff, mostly because my previous role had been strictly clinical, and I'd had little cause to familiarize myself with the vocabulary of funding sources. OFCY stood for Oakland Fund for Children and Youth. The latter term seemed redundant but nobody cared: this was about business, not the aesthetics of language.

There was a slight problem said the administrator with a confident grin. However, he was sure that Thunder Road—that I—could fix it. It seemed that the OFCY grant allocated funds on a yearly basis, based upon projections of service provided by the program. Thunder Road was to meet a threshold of youth served by the end of the year, in return for a renewal of funds. The administrator outlined the goals: IOP was supposed to serve (that is, admit) ten new kids per month, starting in July, which was the beginning of the fiscal year, and reach a target of sixty kids served by the end of the calendar year. None of these kids had to finish the program necessarily. IOP was designed to last eight weeks, with kids attending four days a week, for the aforementioned four hours each day. My job was to run this program; that is, facilitate the groups, prepare treatment plans, provide individual counseling when necessary, oversee urinalysis tests, manage utilization review for those cases paid for by insurance, complete the necessary OFCY documents, and then spend any spare time in promoting the program to the local community via outreach efforts. That was the job as it had been sold to me in July while I was in San Diego, and it was the job that I'd looked forward to doing.

It was early September and not only had the program failed to match the ten kids per month threshold, it had only admitted three kids overall under the OFCY guidelines. As I was being briefed by the administrator, he informed me that we were six weeks away from a site visit from an OFCY official, during which we were to provide an update as to how we were meeting our goals. As it stood, we'd need to admit nearly sixty kids into the program over the next three months in order to qualify for a renewal of funds. Oh, and by the way: OFCY was likely the biggest anticipated referral source over the next year. For IOP to survive—in other words, for me to have a job as IOP coordinator—Thunder Road must retain the OFCY fund into 2002. I looked back at the man whose Barnum and Bailey spirit seemed to carry him through endless travails and regarded the long-familiar look of gloating delusion. I briefly considered that I'd been victimized by some kind of scheme. IOP had been a ruse; a carrot in the form of an outpatient program, dangled before me so that I'd return to the hospital and take up that day treatment counselor job in the residential program just as soon as IOP folded. I felt like someone who'd impulsively bought a fancy car only to discover that there was no engine under the hood.

How was this possible? I asked credulously. The administrator shrugged and maintained his buoyancy. There was no problem as far as he was concerned; he had a plan—a strategy—that would rely upon my ability to get around to the different high schools in the area, and promote Thunder Road, drug treatment for adolescents; the noble cause of getting kids off the streets during the crucial after-school hours. We'd get those sixty kids, his energy said. I have to say I was seduced by the man's indomitable spirit; his not quite irresistible blarney. I think most organizations—successful ones at least—have bluff figures like this, men or women who can't help drawing attention to themselves and getting others caught up in their dogmatic fervor. I guess that's leadership for you. But leadership has consequences, especially if no one speaks back to power, or else interrupts the chorus of the echo chamber. For the second time in three years, or thereabouts, I gave a tentative nod to this man and offered that I'd do my humble best.

Six months later: no surprise that Thunder Road's IOP didn't come close to matching the projections originally offered to OFCY, and thereafter required in order to sustain the funding. In the interim, that official from OFCY made a site visit, asked questions of myself and the administrator, and gave suggestions as to marketing and outreach. He rather imperviously endured the same bluster from the administrator that I'd absorbed over my first two months, and in response offered conciliatory remarks about the modest increase in census we'd demonstrated since the beginning of September. He noted that the program had undergone a change in leadership, and that a near vacuum in care had existed in the late summer weeks (by this time, the previous manager had long since departed for her maternity leave). The official nodded at all the right times and seemed generally sympathetic. He affirmed the value of the program and the need for after school substance abuse treatment for kids. He reminded me of a bank manager I once met. He had the look of one who sits patiently with customers but secretly knows that underwriters aren't going to approve their loan applications.

We received news via mail that our funding was to be cut. The administrator was undeterred. With his inimitable never-say-die attitude, he told me we'd have a chance to appeal the decision at a public hearing in the spring. He seemed excited, as if the opportunity to speak at a podium in front of a watching audience was worth all the trouble. For my part, I was unconcerned about the appeal process. By this time, I'd been assured that the program would continue regardless of the fate of the OFCY money. If the census dropped too low, I might have my hours cut, or else have the option of working a few shifts in the residential component, but IOP was a long-term project and I'd still have a job. On the day of the hearing, the administrator and I went together to a downtown assembly hall wherein a panel of adults and selected "youth leaders" presided over a meeting of under-functioning programs. Thunder Road was one of several organizations—some schools, others an assortment of non-profits, after school programs—that showed up ready to fight for their cause. As we looked around, we realized we'd made a mistake in not bringing any of our kids with us. Around us there were scores of youth, the faces of those other programs, huddled around their adult supervisors, looking eager for the city to preserve their basketball leagues and wilderness camps. The panel, we realized, might have prejudices informing their decisions: they may favor programs whose youthful participants appeared to actually want the services provided for them. Meanwhile, my administrator was rehearsing his presentation, modifying in his mind his argument; poised to emphasize concepts like need instead of want; intervention instead of fun.

Feeling bored, I people watched and ran my eyes over the room, the panel members. The panel's apparent chairperson was a girl of about sixteen years wearing a red sweater. At first, her attire didn't strike me one way or the other. Then I looked closer and saw that the familiar logo across her front was that of Sierra Nevada, the popular brand of beer. Ever on the lookout for a tasty piece of irony, my eyes locked on the girl and her alcohol-advertising sweater. Pleased with myself, I leaned over and shared what I thought was my astute observation with the administrator. He emitted a small sound; something in between a sniff and a smirk, and turned away, uninterested. Moments later he leaned back towards me and whispered conspiratorially into my ear: "Good spot. I'm gonna nail 'em on that." With regret over my small part in the play, I later stood next to the administrator at the podium, and listened haplessly as he upbraided the panel for not taking seriously the problem of drug abuse in teens. The various members of the panel wrinkled their brows, bemused at this pronouncement. As evidence of his assertion, the administrator pointed to the offending red sweater, suggesting it signified the lax attitude OFCY took toward our cause.

Quite understandably, the adult panel members at the head table took exception to this diatribe, and moved quickly to protect the girl from any further public dressing down—sorry—chastisement. "Talk about your program, please" growled a senior member of the committee. We did, but to no avail. Thunder Road would likely have lost the fund anyway, and knowing this, the administrator perhaps settled for the glory of going down with fighting words, rather like a late-stage group home kid throwing fits after a stage proposal is rejected. However, I wish I'd thought twice before supplying him with ammunition. I wish I'd paused to consider why I was doing what I was doing, what my true feelings were about this unholy daytrip with management into the world of municipal politics. I should have acted like a therapist: I should have practiced impulse control and reflective function.

For another two and a half years I continued to run Thunder Road's Intensive Outpatient Program: for another year with a part-time co-facilitator, then finally by myself as the numbers in the program gradually dwindled. The demographic of the kids changed somewhat, with more kids coming from different parts of the county of Alameda. Technically, though kids from all districts of Oakland were eligible for OFCY funds, clearly it was intended to target kids from lower income neighborhoods. Once we'd lost that fund, we spread our outreach plan, started calling people from neighboring counties, as well as high schools in the Oakland hills, where there is more money generally but less color amongst the student bodies.

Kids from the hills

The so-called acuity of the cases in IOP was less than those in the residential component, but I disagree with those who think this tantamount to more global comparisons: "The kids are more difficult," or "they are lower functioning," some say, contrasting not only clients of a residential component with those of the outpatient programs, but also clients of a former era of residential treatment, with their latter day counterparts. The conventional wisdom is that the kids in residence are more acute, and that they are becoming more so with each passing year. And with respect to the proverbial rap sheet of crimes and misdemeanors, this is undoubtedly true. Traumatic separations in early development were also becoming more numerously represented: kids drawn from the broader foster placement system. But the quality of human attachments are mysteriously elusive, and with regards to those deficits that are the focus of this book's concern—poor reality testing, low frustration tolerance, poor reflective function, and rigid defense mechanisms—the differences between clients of one era versus another, or between one department versus another, were less than what many suppose.

Again, much of what was assessed at the level of intake was teleological in nature: the degree of problems was largely inferred from the list of negative consequences, whether legal, academic, or health-related, and not so much a thorough developmental history. A kid referred to the outpatient program would likely have fewer instances of arrests or hospitalizations. In general, their behaviors will have been deemed less life-threatening, and they were also less likely to have had previous experience with group homes or drug courts, though many had prior experience of psychotherapy and psyche hospitals. They were less institutionalized, on the whole; less studied in their gamesmanship with professionals. Their expertise lay more in the home, in the space between the polarized preoccupations of separated parents, and in the increasing privileges, illusory though they may be, that are afforded teens in this culture. The kids of IOP came to the program after school or else with their parents if not in school. A good percentage were being home-schooled and exuded a contempt for anything structured; anything that thwarted the fundamental right to free movement, the unfettered imbibing, smoking, or injecting of substances.

One of the early interventions I made concerned boundaries of the program itself. During the first week, I noticed that kids arrived at different times for the first group, scheduled to begin each day at 5pm. Hearing that I'd four kids enrolled for the group, I'd start the activity looking at only two faces, and then have to stop the group in order to open the door for the pair of stragglers who, as a matter of norm, arrived at different points thereafter. The door in question was a back door to the facility—downstairs, next to that basement office of mine. To this day, I bring to mind the familiar clunking sound of the heavy partition with its squeaking, warped metal being opened, or else being thumped upon by a latecomer. By the second week, I'd fashioned a rule that at first was met with no protest: no being late to group—that was the rule. If late, clients must wait outside until the end of the first group, be admitted for the second activity, but later—that is, on another day—make up that first group. Again, nobody protested as this policy was first announced. The kids stared back at me and seemed unimpressed. The reason: they either weren't listening, or they didn't believe me. More importantly, it was a rule that had not yet been tested.

The tests came in the following weeks. As a few kids sat in the group, they'd begin looking at one another, sniggering, and then looking at me, to see if I'd "let in" whoever was banging on the back door, obviously arriving late for group. They looked at me with blank stares, as if my rule about not being late had not registered. Upon being reminded, one or two shrugged, as if to say "so what" with respect to the previous announcement. My rule was stupid, they simply replied, undeterred. Minutes later, the youth hitherto knocking at the back door would appear at the door to the group room with an upstairs residential staff as an escort. The youths in question simply assessed other ways to enter the building, and likewise imagined that having arrived at the program, admission to the room would happen without fuss. Blocked at the back door, kids simply walked up to reception, casually informed staff that they were IOP clients, and were soon shepherded downstairs. In response, I'd coolly refuse entry to the group, eliciting incredulous responses—mostly ridiculing laughter—even bewildered expressions from the inconvenienced staff members from upstairs. What struck me most about the response of the kids to this kind of limit were not so much their objections to the rules, or their distinctive mocking of my application, but rather the general stolidity. Amongst the IOP kids, in particular, there was an air of taking freedoms for granted; of the meaninglessness of adult pronouncements, and of the sheer irrelevance of discussion.

It was during this period—late 2001 and early 2002—that I was revisiting the writings of James Masterson, whose books on self disorders I'd first read during my graduate school days. Masterson had not been on the required reading list, I recall. In the broad area of psychoanalytically-derived therapies, he'd seemed a bronze medalist in a triumvirate of contemporary thinkers, behind the likes of Heinz Kohut and Otto Kernberg. However, after becoming licensed in the spring of 2002, I started reading theoretical text for the purposes of professional development for the first time in months. I re-read *Treatment of the Borderline Adolescent*, Masterson's seminal work of the early-seventies, and was doing double takes after reading every other page, realizing that his description of stage progressions at the Paine Whitney hospital for adolescents affiliated with Cornell University bore a distinct resemblance to the structure and norms of Thunder Road. Written a good decade prior to the establishment of the Oakland program, Masterson's depiction of life on the Paine Whitney adolescent unit, though undoubtedly a more sophisticated program in downtown New York City, had surely influenced someone in the design of Thunder Road's program. If not, then there have been some interesting coincidences in area of adolescent residential treatment.

Though writing specifically about a residential treatment structure, Masterson's description of an initial "testing" phase of treatment resonated broadly with my experience running the IOP, as well as making fuller sense of the stage I tasks of the residential component, such as had been so bluntly translated for me by that program director back in 1996. It occurred to me that I had been reading Masterson's work around about that time also, but it had taken another five years and a random decision to return to his material for some ideas to digest. Reading with a fresh set of eyes, I logged some familiar ideas: that "patients" extol the benefits of acting out and manipulations; that they test therapists to see if they "care", and generally substitute them as parents; that it was the "job" of an adolescent to exploit the loopholes of parents; that the task of the therapist was to set limits and convert patients from actors and non-feelers to feelers and talkers (Masterson, 72, P. 114-115). In Masterson's case examples, patients became depressed upon the containment of their acting out, and sought to elicit therapist guilt: "Everybody expects me to fail". Therapists or physicians who relented at these stages, who diverted attention from depression, enabled regressions. Angry, disappointed, even hopeless, patients resumed acting out, sometimes even more so than they had originally. Masterson argues that important moments must be seized in the therapy of acting out teens: that once acting out is stabilized patients ought to be encouraged to delve further into their conflicts with the understanding that feeling bad is the path towards getting better (Masterson, 1972).

I knew that I'd have to endure a rigorous testing period again, this time with the kids in IOP: a testing period that would take on a unique flavor, with all the nuances that came with the fact that I was no longer providing therapy in the setting wherein clients lived. At the same time, Masterson's description of a later stage of treatment, called "working through" and drawn from earlier psychoanalysts' writings, struck me as being more abstract, akin to a spiritual awakening as suggested by the latter steps of a 12-step program. At first glance, I thought it might correspond to what Thunder Road called the "core" issues of stage II, but then it seemed that Masterson was referring to a deeper and more painful transformation, one that was internal and not interpersonal, or "systemic", as some might interpret. Strategically, "working through" is a stage wherein negative (or "acting out") behavior is contained, the client/patient is feeling and is encouraged to deepen their process, link acting out behaviors to feelings, having integrated a belief that this will be beneficial. In re-reading Masterson, I recalled old controversies that related to his pronouncements. I knew that some Thunder Road kids had achieved a "working through" as he'd described it, but not many. Perhaps few wanted this kind of growth experience, and even they would face obstacles beyond their control. As I contemplated whether I had "worked through" enduring conflicts, I hid myself in my downstairs corner office. I set aside old preoccupations about life upstairs in the residential unit. I had no idea the world would turn upside down over the next decade.

In IOP, for the time being, the oppositions that were enacted by kids suggested a greater sense of power, of freedom and entitlement that still had room to maneuver. The testing continued: kids brought their homes, their lives, into the therapy room; they turned out their pockets and flaunted their lighters, unmoved by the likelihood of my disapproval; unknowing and uninterested in concepts like contract breaking, reassessment, or Cardinal rules. They spoke of sexual acting out, truancy, violence—everything except drug use (the one behavior they presumed I'd report to their parents)—with impunity. On the steps leading down into the facility one kid would regularly ride his skateboard and continue his run inside the building, across the polished tile of the hospital floor. At the lip of the group room, he'd skillfully flip the board into his hands and greet me with a smirk. As group process began, the room, one that would be used the next day for schooling the residential kids, would reek of tobacco. Sitting with these kids, I'd hear less maneuvering; less of the politics of youth learning the art of parole-seeking. In some respects, I heard of more licentious behavior than I'd ever heard listening to kids in a residential program. It was an experience that was at once refreshing and disturbing.

The essentials of testing, however—the dynamics—were more or less the same, save for that initial lack of response that reflected the IOP client's relative complacency; the absence of jolting consequences from the disease of addiction. A more significant area of power struggle was around urinalysis testing. I'd hardly monitored any urinalysis tests during my first three years at Thunder Road, but I did regularly monitor such tests when working with McAlister Institute in San Diego. On the one hand, this can be an awkward task, this watching-over exercise. For most who are subjected to UA testing, what's required of a monitoring staff is a simple, manful stoicism, with as little said during the process as possible. A discreet distance is kept behind the urinal; maybe a glance over the upper arm to see evidence of a stream is called for—not much more. Then a hygienic care is needed: taking the plastic cup with either a glove on hand, or at least a piece of tissue, but not so much insulation that one can't determine whether the warmth of the cup approximates that of body temperature. The client offers a thin smile and a shrug—the dignity of the subject and the monitor is just about preserved—and life goes on. That's the standard scenario.

In IOP, as in other outpatient programs, the gamesmanship played out over the unwillingness to provide samples, and the later disputes over their positive results. The "I can't go right now," protestations, or the lesser problematic "I can't pee in front of someone" statements were common. The latter complaints were fairly easy to handle: these clients simply had to deal with it, as gruff sportsmen like to say, because the tests were required, simply put. The other form of obstinacy—the "I can't go right now"—was more intriguing, because it tended to reflect clients' history of exhausting adults into submission. The experience, and thus the presumption, went something like this: *If I wait long enough, you'll soon get tired, or inconvenienced, and therefore frustrated, and you'll eventually relinquish control over the restriction you can't sustain.* Therefore, clients assumed that if they just held out long enough, through the first group at 5pm, and past the second group that ended at 8pm, then sometime thereafter I would want to go home, and as a result would release them from the program, essentially forgiving their failure to provide a urine sample.

That hardly ever happened. Self-satisfied, I'd instead prepare some paperwork after the end of the second group, inform the client that my record as far as staying late at the program was 9:30pm (total apocrypha, actually); that I was fully prepared to break that record, and finally, of course, that a sample was required before they left. Annoyed, kids usually complied, and this tactic generally succeeded in curtailing an enactment that was performed by thousands of parents and teens across the country because of home tests that could be bought at drug stores or online. One of the more fascinating episodes was one in which a kid turned away from my rule-setting and instead started arguing with his mother, who was far more perturbed than I at the prospect of waiting beyond 8pm to supply a cup of urine. Observing that I seemed dispassionate but steadfast, the youth simply transferred his energy to the person responsible for his admission in the first place. That night, he and his mother had barely said a word in either of the activities structured into the program. After hours, tensions mounted and patience frayed. Having been on their best behavior in front of the doctor/therapist, symptoms leaked: the kid made unconvincing promises, and futilely decried the necessity of urine tests. The mother rebutted with unsustainable threats, invoked the specter of out-of-state boarding schools.

All this occurred long before I became aware of things like Whizzinators, which are fake penis devices peddled to drug users so they can evade positive results on urinalysis testing. Whizzinators gained notoriety halfway through the last decade following some high profile cases of celebrities who were said to have used the devices. I became aware of them through a weekly group I ran for a year, from 2004 to 2005. This was a moonlighting gig for me. I was supplementing income the first year of my marriage, leading a group of parolees as part of an outpatient program in San Francisco that shall remain nameless. One night one of the group members, a disgruntled African American man, was bemoaning his purchase of a so-called Whizzinator, complaining that it "didn't work for him". Too bad, I thought, initially thinking the device was simply defective. I didn't suppose such items came with money back guarantees. Anyway, it turned out that the device worked well enough, but it was the wrong color—white. The man hadn't done due diligence with his purchase, as Whizzinators are apparently sold in many colors, reflecting the diversity of the customer base. The group (and I) found this quite amusing. The customer didn't.

At Thunder Road, when a positive UA test returned from a lab, another kind of chess match played out. Clients invested in disputing the results fashioned typical defenses. Regarding marijuana use, the most familiar argument was that of being present while others "hot-boxed". This term referred to being in a confined environment—like a car—wherein someone is smoking, and others not directly ingesting smoke (i.e.: smoking) would benefit from a so-called contact high. Protesting innocence, IOP clients would often attribute positive test results to this practice, as if not responsible for the subsequent presence of THC in their systems. While the argument often led to a wholly separate discussion as to the wisdom of socializing with still-using friends, it failed to win amnesty from previously negotiated consequences. My other nomination for the positive-UA-result-excuse-greatest hits list is the poppy seed story. With *aw-shucks* delivery, clients cited this one to explain away positive tests for morphine or codeine. Claiming that poppy-seeded bagels or buns eaten hours prior to tests were simulating opiates, a positive result would be protested. I tried common sense. Especially if a client had a history of opiate use I tended to disagree, and so did then Thunder Road doctors with whom I consulted, though sometime later I became aware that many medical researchers were in fact corroborating this once urban legend. Oops.

The outpatient dynamic

Despite this, the dynamic between client and me was different than it had been when I was a case manager within the residential component, or a program administrator at the McAlister group home. A fundamental difference concerned the relative lack of parental transference. This is the nature of the outpatient setting versus the residence. Parents are more active in their role, presumed to be present and able to fulfill that role, and are bringing into the program problems as they are concurrently happening outside of the facility. Instead of coming to Thunder Road to hear of staff's strengths or shortcomings as quasi-parents, parents came to IOP with their nerves ever on high alert, or else fixed into a detached aura of burn out. The tendency of IOP parents was to be more engaged, more anxious, more demanding of care, and more present as opposed to retrospective, with respect to conflicts with their sons and daughters. They'd brought their problems in, but rather than dumping them on our doorstep, they were still riding their troubles, and looked to me as an expert to guide them in their ever pressing decisions.

The kids tended to be more reticent, to which I attributed issues of property and power. Taking part in a multi-family group upstairs and then returning to your room is different than sitting in IOP's corresponding activity and then driving home with the parents afterwards. Over the years, I've imagined all the post-therapy conversations that happen between couples, between family members, as they travel away from my office. It's an ongoing fantasy of mine; one that will never be realized, of course, because of the boundaries of the process. For kids in particular, I've imagined, and interpreted, a latent inhibition resulting from the arrangement. The kids upstairs, once having traversed the early stages of the program; once having tested the staff rigorously to see if the place really would contain theirs and their families acting out, might ultimately make bold use of the weekly Tuesday night forum. In IOP, the kids were more careful, and more wary of the conversations that might happen on the ride home; the "why did you bring that up?" questions coming from the proverbial driver's seat. The IOP kids seemed politically savvy in different ways. They seemed more focused upon the dynamics of family communication, and were largely indifferent (that issue with the back door notwithstanding) to matters that were peer-related, at least within the IOP group itself.

The program was split in structural and psychological terms, into a late afternoon and an evening component. The 5pm group was one in which kids talked with me and their peers about the things they felt they couldn't talk about with their parents. It truly was, as OFCY had intended, an after school program, with kids using the forum to speak to that which was censored at home;

in this respect, my role was that of a facilitator of the kind of discussion group that might happen at any American high school. In general, the kids got along with each other; they neither seemed cagey, or jostling for popularity. During the later group, which mirrored the structure of the residential multi-family group, kids would transition into their family roles, and enter into negotiations of home rules, or discussions about existing and future expectations, with an urgency borne of the fact that it was all happening closer to real time.

Thankfully, my groups in IOP rarely reached the overspilling size of their residential counterparts. Likewise, frictions within the groups, or containment of cliques or acting out conspiracies weren't anywhere near as commonplace. Partly, this was attributable to diversity: the census was made up of kids from all over the county, so it wasn't often that kids knew one another outside of the program. This enabled a lessened self consciousness, and with it, a kind of liberation that many appeared to appreciate. With a softened impetus toward attachment, the bonding was relatively lukewarm, but as a result, the potential for drama was also blunted. Also, the average census of IOP was kept to a modest size, making group facilitation a more manageable task. For the three years I ran IOP, I felt able to direct the therapy in a manner that I thought was most effective, and the containment of group size was a major factor in that experience.

While this was happenstance as far as administration was concerned, it didn't happen entirely without others' influence. During the second and third year of my IOP leadership, I was lucky enough to be supervised by a woman who supported me in my role, and appeared to trust my judgment as far as structural decisions were concerned. One third cheerleader, two thirds a typical manager, this woman oozed calm when reckless egos ran rampant; she brought gaiety to despondent rooms, knowing when to celebrate and when not to. Though often pulled in different directions, she knew how to move amid flying shrapnel, and be elusive when necessary. She acted the way Hollywood talent agents are characterized: ubiquitous, yet ever proclaiming a need to be somewhere else. At some point she'd appear and respond just in time to soothe those who clutched at her shirtsleeves. She'd be patient and attentive addressing others' needs, and had a knack of making frazzled subordinates or parents feel like their questions had been answered when clearly they hadn't. Above all, she protected the people around her, including me. While she didn't officially set a cap on the number of IOP participants at any one time, she'd consult with me in a collegial manner and strategize around timing of discharges and subsequent admissions. Clients weren't plugged in simply because an opening existed and a seat needed to be filled; actual care was taken, and thoughtfulness was applied.

On the other hand, census in IOP did fluctuate at times, and friendly managers couldn't buffer me entirely from the tyranny of numbers. On nights when I'd sit with only one kid in the program, the future viability of the program seemed suspect. Those nights were a bit like lonely office days in private practice, when the restless eagerness to practice therapy is thwarted by a plethora of no shows, or a downturn in referrals. Fortunately, in IOP I didn't have to contend with the obstacle of gender segregation, such as it was during the residential component at that time. Over the years, I've gone back and forth on this particular issue: at times, I've thought that a separation of genders was essential for appropriate care. Otherwise, I've felt more flexible about it. On balance, I come down on the side of segregation. In the residential component, sexual liaisons were happening so often that a real concern emerged as to whether the hospital might be shut down. Sooner or later, it was said, someone was going to get raped, or become pregnant. Well, no one got pregnant while living at Thunder Road; not as far as I know. As for rape? That probably happened, and if it did, it was likely a same-gender event.

Boys and Girls in treatment together

My misgivings about the mixing of genders in treatment concerned the therapeutic process itself. In the nineties, when I was a case manager on the residential unit, mixed caseloads had been the norm. A "brothers and sisters" recovery ethos, derived from Synanon programs, was promoted, and at times genuinely practiced. Clients could, and would provide for one another a whole experience, giving feedback from the perspective of the opposite sex, and in so doing, give what seemed a naturally rounded experience. To separate seemed artificial, a false attempt at a narrow, half-object forum of relatedness. On the other hand, I was aware of the contaminations in mixing the activities. Girls, in particular, appeared to subjugate themselves into passivity in mixed-gender environments, or else struggled with the pathologizing attention to the addict's self-centeredness, which is an observation that has been made by others such as Kasl (1992). Boys showed off, became more aggressive, yet both boys and girls seemed to alter their affect in order to manipulate one another's sympathies. The problem, as I saw it, was one of authenticity: can you really talk openly and honestly about all that is potentially shameful if you prioritize looking your best to someone else in the room?

Management was primarily concerned with safety and with the containment of sexualized behavior that might threaten the integrity of the program. More importantly, management was legitimately concerned with the safety of individuals. Quite secondarily, it seemed, they were concerned with program dynamics, the broader questions as to whether the sexes could truly help each other in recovery, or else be an impediment. By the midway point of the new decade, the separation of the genders' treatment experience was a given, and few even recalled the era wherein Thunder Road will at times have resembled a high school. For a few years, that gender segregation seemed to be the only major change in the program from the period of the nineties. Otherwise, the clients, at casual glance, seemed more or less the same. From my office, I could hear the chants of confrontation group, or feel the tension as a line of youths were marched on Monads towards a contract breaking session. The cultural diversity may have shifted slightly, with a disproportionate representation of African American kids being apparent. But the group home track's structure was largely unchanged: a year-long treatment, roughly, in three stages. There was, just as there had been all along, a short-term residential program, called "hospital" track, wherein clients stayed anywhere from a week to six weeks, depending upon the insurance provider, and for whom treatment was largely a triage of the most salient clinical and/or medical problems. The benches were still the totemic time-out devices of before. The wall-length mirrors, lesser used perhaps, were still fixtures along the corridors.

The day treatment groups, with kids languishing on couches or staring longingly out the windows, looking uninterested or angry, still looked and sounded the same. From 2001 to 2004, as I occasionally walked the halls of the residential unit, I did so with detachment and mild curiosity about the changes that seemed minor and few. I was nostalgic yet vaguely amused by the general sameness.

Alison

That detachment was broken for a spell when management noted the drop in IOP census and, owing to a concurrent influx of clients in the residential component, recruited me to manage a caseload of short-term clients for what was projected to be a ninety day period. I reluctantly agreed, thinking I'd have my hours cut in half if I didn't cooperate with a smile. Actually, I was more nervous than resistant. By that time, it had been about five years since I'd directed anyone to a bench or raised my voice in fervent TC style, so I was wary of taking on an old role. My first client, however, had me forgetting all of my reservations. Her name was Alison, and from the first moment I met her, I was spurred by the challenge she presented. It's hard to explain but there is something about the limp handshake of a truculent teen, the sullen, passing eye contact, and a terse, whispered greeting that I find irresistible. Alison had the long, flowing hair of a beautiful girl, but the mannish jaw and general bulk of a boxer. As we were introduced, she was sat quietly in her 1A room wearing hospital scrubs, and stewing over the treachery of parents who had just told her an hour earlier that she'd be staying at Thunder Road for three months.

Alison was among the first of a new type of client at Thunder Road: not long-term or group home clients, as they were known, but also not short-term, as in fourteen to 28-day residents. Her program length was an unprecedented median, and I was to devise an unorthodox treatment plan that would straddle brief and longer term goals. Her peers weren't very helpful at first, to her or me. They pointed out that I wasn't a regular floor counselor, and that I was the only male counselor working on the girls' side. If Alison complained long enough, she might get assigned to someone else; someone who would know what they were doing, her peers implied. Alison, when she did come out of her room, seemed not so interested in replacing me as she did in employing me—as a servant. Could I get her clothes? Could I call her parents? Could I get her diary from the personals closet? she asked, glaring at me with disdainful, Garfield (the cat) eyes. She was an aspiring writer, she declared ardently, and would need her writing tools the way others needed air. Could she bring her pet dog from home? Could I get her proper stationary on which to write a letter to her boyfriend? Could she change her room because the fluorescents outside in the hallway were too bright, making it hard for her to sleep? Lastly, if she did her program right, could she go home in thirty days instead of ninety?

We got off on the right foot in so far as I could say "yes" to the first two questions, and later to the one about the diary. Everything else received a negative response, and things deteriorated soon thereafter between us. Alison demanded; Alison whined; Alison barked, and Alison cried. Alison's face went into contortions—she wore looks of pained confusion, of despair, that were so expressive it was as though she'd never have to use words to convey feeling. Over the next three months, she'd act out a pantomime, a cartoon of teen angst and frustration. She made turning her back on people an art form. With precise timing, she'd leave a peer, a staff member, a nurse, psychiatrist, or me, floundering in mid-sentence with our mouths hanging open. It wasn't just that she was rude, or that she didn't want to hear what others had to say. It was more that she ingeniously assessed the wanting of each speaker and then exacted a kind of global revenge. She could tell when someone before her had reached a pitch of righteousness, ready to launch into a statement and set her straight. That's when she'd turn, knowing she'd draw a slavish following.

Alison's drug using history was somewhat unremarkable, surprisingly enough. Alcohol and marijuana were the intoxicants of choice, but they'd played at best a supporting role in the events that had led to her admission. Those events, including three suicide attempts and a few other episodes broadly described as *misadventures*, had been frightening, inexplicable incidents. So far she'd explained nothing of her reasons. Alison managed to stay in 1A longer than most. She wore the hospital scrubs staff supplied in place of regular clothing longer than most. The reason: with casual defiance, she stated she had no interest in coming out of her room after her first day. "Nah, that's ok," she said, as though she were a guest in a hotel brushing off maid service. When informed that participation in activities was required, she scowled at the floor supervisor of the day, and turned her back. That supervisor noted the attitude but turned away also, thinking that reluctant cooperation would soon follow. Instead, Alison quietly locked herself in her bathroom and refused to come out for over an hour. She went silent, ignoring the successive appeals of counselors, fretting management, and nurses who stood at her door reenacting the roles of anxious parents. When she did come out it seemed for the sake of an affable maintenance man who'd been summoned from his office in order to dislodge the door with a hammer. Before he lifted a finger in anger, she stepped out, smiled flirtatiously at the man and waded through the small gathering of onlookers. She pulled off her hospital shirt, plucked a shirt of her own from her newly assigned drawer, and declared herself ready to start the program, on her terms. She'd drawn a crowd, and thus seemed satisfied.

She had Bipolar Disorder, the head psychiatrist explained in treatment planning as he told the story of and behind this scene. She was used to hospitalization; used to staying in bed. She was used to Lithium, abusing nurses, and locking herself in bathrooms and sulking until she got her way. Problem was she sometimes came out of bathrooms with cuts on her wrists and thin streams of blood disfiguring her. Seven ER admissions in a year was the succinct back-story. Her parents, a solemn, but shaken couple in their late fifties, wore perpetually dark circles under their eyes and were desperate not to take her home and ride the Alison rollercoaster once again. They'd pleaded for Thunder Road to take her in, despite her volatility, and against its better judgment, Thunder Road obliged. The room strikes were semi-regular happenings. I wasn't around for these displays, typically. This fact annoyed Alison, who imagined that as her therapist and case manager, I should always be in spitting distance. From the moment she learned of my role, she did her best to keep me within arms length at all times: I'd be paged to the girls' side from my office to attend to one of her questions; extracted from meetings to hear some remonstration of hers about program restrictions. Alison resented my having free time, my days off. Why, she asked with self assured entitlement, should those restraining her freedoms enjoy freedoms of their own?

I'd be simultaneously devalued and clung to, and cast as a jailer or confessor in separate moments that were only minutes apart. In one-on-ones, she sometimes dominated with stories about the pets she doted upon, about her older sister, whom she admired enormously; about her parents, for whom she felt alternating rage and guilt. When finishing her talks, she'd ask for quiet time so she might jot down ideas that had emerged from our conversations. At these times, she seemed insatiably curious about herself, about recovery or psychology, and seemed determined to use any means possible for the expression of her turbulent mind. The next day, I'd visit her either in her room, or else within the lounge area that was set aside for the girls, and ask after her writing. She'd appear sullen and defeated, and sometimes just shake her head as though talking had suddenly become an anathema to her. Off to her side, a female peer would signal to me that it was best not to ask any more questions, and gesture sideways towards Alison's room wherein the discarded and torn up remnants of her once precious diary now sat within a trashcan.

Alison would be like this throughout her time at Thunder Road: vibrant, intelligent, and engaging one day; flat and misanthropic the next. More than anything, she was a vicious self-critic, hence the mutilation. Neither side of her seemed to know the other, or even reflect upon the other. In some respects, she seemed undefended. Meaning, she lacked the usual artifices, the smooth cant that solicits nodding validation, refers to "new me" versus "old me" in order to curry favor, privileges, and stage progression. Alison was blunt and honest; needy and insistent of others' energies and spirit. A spoiled brat to some, she demanded the time of others, the indulgence of others, and even within the fantasy of those conditions, I couldn't help but feel sympathy for her; even admiration. In some ways, I often wish I could have been as brave or brazen as Alison, and as vulnerable. That's how I imagined her experience as she sat or lay wasted by a setback: someone's failure to understand or be interested; someone's abandonment of her; someone's imperfection.

But there was no cause to romanticize Alison's difficulties. Her estrangement from family and peers was real, and her efforts at closeness were mostly damaged by petulant withdrawals that caused pain for loved ones and ultimately led her to despise herself. Having decided early on that I couldn't control this girl, and because managers were simply asking me to shepherd her as best I could through her program (a rather vague directive that strangely afforded me some freedom to maneuver), I was at times able to relax with Alison: I listened to her lengthy monologues, and engaged in banter with her when she was in a jovial mood. At other times, I was short with her, and authoritative. I pointed out that she was responsible for how she acted, and she didn't like that. Privately, I found her grimaces endearing, but I kept my poker face as she caviled at me for not indulging her every demand. At the point of splitting—"you never do anything I want!"—she'd start giving me what I wanted: namely, her story.

It was around about the two month mark when she stopped talking about her boyfriend and her pets. That's when she started talking about her sister. Gretchen, her older sister of nearly ten years, had once been a competitive swimmer of collegiate standards, whose athletic career was interrupted by the onset of niggling physical problems, such as numbness, tingling, and balance difficulties that were later diagnosed as symptoms of Multiple Sclerosis. Now it was some five years later and Gretchen's Olympic ambitions were history: a casualty of a debilitating illness that left her barely able to walk by herself, let alone swim as a top athlete. Gretchen bore her burden, the cruel twist of fate that had befallen her, with dignity and courage, said everyone. She didn't have tantrums. She didn't withdraw into herself, or compel others' pity. She hadn't done drugs, and she certainly hadn't made any attempts to harm herself. She went the other way entirely, and modeled a stoicism that reflected the proud traditions of the family, but also marginalized what would surely have been a reasonable protest against the pathos of life. That was left to Alison, it seemed. She lived the message that not only was life short, so was youth. She was the child that cried and raged, or else indulged all kinds of liberties in defiance of the perceived family way. She didn't do this for herself, she more or less explained. She wasn't even doing it for her sister. She did it because someone in her world had to express themselves to the fullest, no matter what the cost.

Alison's quasi hospital track program, traversed under mine and others' stewardship, paved the way for a fuller road to recovery that continued for several months thereafter. Among other things, I convinced Alison's parents that they must invest in therapy for their daughter, and continue their participation with Thunder Road through its own aftercare program, the largely unheralded Continuing Care department in which some clients and families participated for as long as a year, and sometimes even longer. I felt strongly that while her drug use and manipulative behaviors had been contained, she held the potential for a proper working through of her chronic underlying depression. Thankfully, Alison and parents followed my recommendations. Over the next several months, after I had returned to my more comfortable role as IOP coordinator, I continued to hear about Alison's progress. Every week I saw the department's one therapist/group facilitator in passing, and every time she'd offer a brief update to dispel my ongoing fears. "She's still coming," the staff member would say with a tough smile. I'd always expected to hear of another calamity, like a runaway or another hospitalization. Sometimes I'd see Alison out near the lip of the parking lot, smoking a cigarette with a Continuing Care peer, usually a boy. She'd nod and smile as she saw me, and keep staring until I nodded back, acknowledging the fact that she was there; *still coming*.

She kept coming back as they say in 12-step meetings. She re-entered therapy, which she perhaps used as a springboard for her participation in the Continuing Care department's version of multi-family group. Apparently, she and her parents used that forum to speak about the years of distress that surrounded Gretchen's illness. Clean, focused, and contained, not to mention compliant with medication regimens, Alison shared with her parents how she'd felt compelled to act out during that difficult period of their lives; how she'd felt so keenly the pain of her sister's illness, the sheer unfairness of it all. Above all, she reflected how she'd always felt restricted by the emotional climate of the family: how she'd always felt as though she had to hide her own talents or ambitions; how everyone seemed to chastise pretension and understate dreams. Alison reviewed all this with me on a day in which I'd stepped outside to pull her up about smoking on the premises. She smiled, flicked the offending butt away, but insisted I talk to her in exchange for her compliance. She explained the process she was having with her family in her own terms. She told me a little of what she was learning about her family, and about herself: "stuff that made sense of everything," she summarized. "By the way, that's my last one," she said, gesturing towards the cigarette.

"Really?" I answered skeptically.

Three months later she was telling me she was still clean, sober, and nicotine free. She also seemed stable in other ways: confident, engaged at school, making friends, pursuing her writing and staying out of hospitals. She seemed contained and alive; the product, at least in part, of just over a year's worth of daily or several days per week treatment. I could tell she was proud of herself, and now proud of her whole family, not just her brave, legacy-fronting sister. I was proud of her also, and accepted an invitation to attend Alison's full (residential plus Continuing Care completion) graduation, which was to happen shortly thereafter. I think Alison represented, as much as anyone, the potential of the program: the possibilities for containment of destructive behaviors; the opportunity for a working through of underlying pain. It seemed a rare occurrence. As for the closure ceremony from Continuing Care, it was always a little strange attending these particular events, partly because I had never been an active member of that department; also because graduates tended to reflect upon more recent events, the Continuing Care experience, as if the residential stage were a distant and relatively insignificant memory. Not Alison. She remembered it all; wrote eloquent journals—readable essays—describing in vivid detail, her life at Thunder Road: everything, from ignoring the itch in her ass while sitting on a bench (which she compared to observing a craving), to the drudgery of cleaning pots in the kitchen, to the "drama" of living day in and day out with girls, women; ultimately learning to bond with them versus seeking a fix amid male company. Speaking at graduation, she offered these reflections, and mirrored back to the attending staff what she had once absorbed but not registered. I reflect that Alison was one of only three clients of mine to reach this particular end to the Thunder Road process.

9

CUT OFF AT THE NECK

The organizing of mental health workers

As it happens, there were quite a few changes happening around this time, and many more to come over the next several years. By 2004 I'd known many people to have come and gone at Thunder Road. Some, like me, had come, gone, and come again, but only a handful fit into that category. More commonly, staff emerged, were central, if not seemingly indispensable for a discreet period, only to fall out of favor with management for various reasons, and then get cut from the Thunder Road squad and soon forgotten. Because the program leadership didn't consider that it was providing psychotherapy in the traditional sense, departures of clinical staff, like those of any hospital employee, were handled shoddily, with case managers and other counselors appearing to disappear in the night in some cases. Termination, as in a stage of a psychotherapeutic episode, seemed a trivial concern. A case in point was an episode in mid-2002, in which two counselors who were prominent within the group home track were suddenly and unceremoniously absented from the treatment team. Reportedly, they had vehemently disputed the dishonorable discharge of two of their clients—a position that supposedly rendered their employment untenable.

This may have been the case, but I cannot help wonder, especially as fragile attachments to other insecurely attached clients were often at stake, why such an abrupt separation was necessary in so many cases. Talking to one esteemed yet jaded co-worker a year later, I was made aware of a meeting that was happening across town, with a representative of a local chapter of SEIU, the workers' union, at their local offices. I accepted an invitation to attend, and later took part in a meeting that featured another half dozen or so Thunder Road employees, each looking disgruntled and weary, yet committed to affecting the conditions in which they worked. As a coordinator of outpatient services, I felt remote from most of my peers' complaints, many of which concerned matters from the residential unit: unreasonable work schedules and unsatisfactory conflict resolution policies. The staff that was present wanted more options in the workplace: expansion of benefits, genuine avenues for appeal of disciplinary measures; advocates in times of dispute with management. I was sympathetic, but my concerns were broader, less bound in the present circumstances. For the most part, I was comfortable in my position at that time, yet I wanted to support the bigger cause of staff retention, which would also entail things like professional development, wage distributions commensurate with levels of training and education. These matters, I believed—and still believe—were crucial for an improved continuity of care.

The meetings, of which there were three, were secretive, sobering, and anti-climactic. At first, everyone seemed enthusiastic, and basked in the conspiratorial spirit of the gathering. Underwhelmed by the turnout, the SEIU representative was sour and pedantic. She lectured us about the complications of the process; told us we'd need to gather signatures, about five or six times as many as that suggested by our numbers at the meeting. Plus, we'd need to be patient, very patient. The process could take months just to cast an initial vote, a preliminary petition for union formulation. At some point, Alta Bates, the parent hospital of Thunder Road, would become aware of the movement, and mobilize resistant measures. While not casting specific warnings about whether individuals would lose their jobs, the woman commented generally that the hospital had deep pockets, was experienced at what she termed "union-busting", and would go to great lengths to prevent the organizing of Thunder Road's workforce. By the second meeting, the attendance had already dropped by two or three people. This was a screening process, I realized; this representative's job was to wean out the un-serious by being as frank and discouraging as possible. Reality testing. That initial good feeling soon transformed into glum defeatism, though few of us admitted as much at the time. We knew the turnover at Thunder Road. We knew we'd have a hard time getting as many signatures as we needed, and we knew that a good percentage of those signatures would be those of ex-employees within six months time.

Amidst this talk, my mind flashed back to that exit interview of 1999, to that perfunctory meeting with that nodding, then-indulgent administrator. I'd spoken naively to him of staff retention that day, of its importance with respect to continuity of client care. I came to believe, calling to mind his glazed, opaque stare, that neither he nor the hospital had a real interest in retaining staff. A durable body of staff is one that might organize, and labor organization was something that might disrupt the system: its wage structures, hierarchies; perhaps the existence of the system itself. Besides, employees were disposable. Demand for services was high and ever expanding. Scores of new people were entering the mental health profession each year, as therapists, social workers, counselors, child care workers, and so on. Plenty of people wanted to do this kind of work, and plenty more wanted to work at the levels that made this work possible, in public services administration. With society suffering business was thriving, so there was much money to be made off the back of mental health workers, and yet more to be made educating this army of would-be healers. Either new credentials were being invented to create jobs for people with lesser education and training, or existing licensees would be offered new certifications (at a cost, of course) that enhanced their competitive edge.

Within three months, the labor action was all but forgotten, and the jaded and esteemed friend who'd initiated the contact with SEIU moved on soon thereafter. He was going to work at a wilderness camp, he said forlornly. As he left, he surreptitiously passed me the thick binder that was comprised of SEIU policies and procedures. He offered a wry smile, wished me luck, thinking I might carry the torch of this cause. He didn't exactly fill me with inspiration. Instead, he wordlessly conveyed his belief that nothing would come of the need to organize mental health professionals, and that life at Thunder Road would surely deteriorate for staff, and ultimately, for clients.

Funding sources have their say

Another major change, around 2003 or 2004, was the introduction of Medi-Cal as the dominant funding source for the long-term group home track. Ostensibly, this was heralded as a boon for the future of the program, and specifically the group home track, which was at the time in modest decline in terms of its census. However, the stipulations of the contract sent shock waves throughout the staff. As a requirement for reimbursement of all day treatment services, documentation pertaining to those services had to be prepared and signed by license eligible staff—that is, those who had earned a Master's degree and were registered with the Board of Behavioral Sciences (once BBSE, now BSE) in Sacramento, or at least those currently enrolled in a Master's program. This in turn meant that those assigned case manager duties had to meet these qualifications. Almost overnight, some people, including one or two with considerable experience as case managers and counselors, lost their jobs, or at least lost these particular positions, and had to be assigned elsewhere if continuing as employees of the hospital.

On the one hand, this was a positive development in so far as it would likely foster reduced turnover of staff in these positions. If those attaining case manager status were career oriented, they would likely endure longer stretches of poor reimbursement in exchange for the currency of practicum hours, as well as the work experience and resume eye candy that the Thunder Road name might someday provide. In my experience, it had been those who were not career-oriented in the field who would, of their own accord, turn their heads to other more lucrative work options. Still, I bemoaned the impact on some who were committed to Thunder Road over time, who were veterans of the 12-step community, skilled counselors, and who through no fault of their own were victimized by this shift. Additionally, as existing registered interns or graduate school trainees were recruited to fill the case manager positions, resentment no doubt stirred in those compelled to make way, surely creating a tense and divisive work environment for all concerned.

Once again, I was separate yet attentive to these developments, but until the spring went about my business running

IOP four late afternoons and evenings per week. Then one day I was sharing an office space with a colleague that worked at an off-site satellite program known as Camp Sweeney. In walked an intern from the residential component, looking anxious and hurried. Her clinical supervisor had left the program suddenly, she'd just been told. At that time, there was no one else qualified who was available to provide clinical supervision, so this strange and unexplained absconding by the supervisor was a disaster for her internship: who would sign off on her hours? With whom would she consult regarding her cases? Catching my eye, she spoke impulsively. "Wait. Graeme, you're licensed. Maybe you can—no, you're doing IOP. Never mind." She flailed her arms, looked away, and sped out of the office and down the hallway to seek out someone else to hear her complaints.

I could barely keep my concentration the rest of the day. By that time, the spring of 04', I was actually a month away from my two-year mark of licensure, having finally navigated that landmark in the midst of the OFCY drama. I knew that two years was the minimum period of licensure required in order to provide clinical supervision to training therapists. While content in my role with IOP, I was dimly aware of wanting another challenge. Secondly, I'd not had a raise in the two and a half years in the IOP position (my licensure elicited congratulations, but no material reward); lastly, I was eager to cut my hours somewhat so as to expand my interests in the realm of private practice. The role of clinical supervisor, that of a consultant to each of the license eligible staff, a liaison to the graduate schools in the area, yet a peripheral figure as far as clinical management was concerned, was a fifteen-to-twenty hours per week position—ideal, I thought, as far as my future goals were concerned.

A new clinical supervisor

That same week I approached management and offered myself for the vacancy. I emphasized not so much how the change would be ideal for me as it would be for them. I reminded them that I had been an intern myself; that I had worked as a full-time case manager/therapist in the group home track, and even for a spell (about six months in total) in the shorter hospital track; that I had been IOP coordinator for three years, and a licensed therapist for nearly two. Exploiting self disclosure and identification to the max for the first time at Thunder Road, I boasted that I'd know what it was like to walk in my supervisee's shoes, and that I'd be uniquely positioned to offer guidance. Furthermore, I argued that rather than hire an outsider, or else overburden an existing manager to absorb the clinical supervisor's duties, Thunder Road, should hire me to take over the job for which I was not only a natural fit, but a convenient one. They agreed, but there were delays, largely due a needlessly long grinding of hospital machinery. In fact, I didn't begin the position until much later in the year, long after I'd passed the two-year threshold, months after completing the necessary continuing education credits, and—incidentally—a month or so after getting married in late summer to a one-time receptionist at Thunder Road.

When I did start the job, I found myself in charge of a group that was as despondent and lackluster as that motley collection of employees who'd attended the ill-fated union meetings a year or so earlier. A transitional figure in the early weeks was a manager within the long-term program who had been the interim supervisor for several months. For a week, at least, I was to shadow him, learn the basics of my new role, and then take over, leaving him, he quickly implied, to get on with his own job. It seemed to me that his job might not last too long. He seemed irritable; was short with interns, and half-attentive to me. Privately, he confided that he was disgruntled with administration, as well as the passivity of his peers in management. I sat in with him on one supervision group, a two-hour activity required of all those seeking to use Thunder Road to accrue hours towards professional licensure. This was a consultation meeting of six to eight members, typically—a standard format for the training of new therapists in a group context[34]. That single meeting with the interim figure was quiet and tense, with lengthy spells of uncomfortable silence. While not averse to periods of such stillness, I thought this felt toxic. In response to one intern's disclosure of countertransference feelings towards her clients, the supervisor curtly responded, "Is this about you?" There was a harsh, impatient air, and a generally inhibited quality to the discussion. So, as usual, I thought, I'd be starting a new position thinking about all the changes I'd make; how I'd make it all *better*.

The problem with moustaches

Oddly enough, my own relationship with the overbearing administrator was fairly benign. On the whole, he seemed to appreciate my long-standing commitment to the program, my reputation as one who made little fuss, got on well with others, and seemed *down* for the Thunder Road cause. In meetings to discuss IOP census, or later, the status of the intern/trainee program (with which he seemed genuinely interested), he treated me collegially, even fraternally at times, albeit with the distracted presence of one who is constantly looking over others' shoulders to see if there are more important people to engage in discussion. He seemed to like me. He'd ask after my wife, his former receptionist, and tease me about having kept the "contract" of our dating for well over a year. I was wary of him, having known countless peers who had crossed his path and drawn a sword, only to feel the cold, cutting slice of his. None of them were around anymore, so it was vital to be moderate with any dissent I had to offer. From 2001 to 2006, roughly, I was as close to management as I'd ever be without actually becoming a member of the clinical management team. The administrator had encouraged me to pursue this course only once, during the post-OFCY debacle, when I was receiving mixed messages about the sustainability of IOP, and when it had seemed to some as though the department's demise was a foregone conclusion. I politely deferred on a return to management, though, offering that I was but a humble therapist, a mere servant of the process.

It was during the mid-portion of the decade, however, that I had one or two testy conversations with him. Superficially, this was in defense of my intern supervisees, one of whom had been plainly bullied into taking a leave by the administrator following a supposed instance of insubordination. The fallout actually led to the administrator making the apologies, but from the vantage point of the intern, the damage had been done. An already fragile confidence fragmented, and the intern left soon afterwards. But in the midst of that episode, a broader conversation was mooted about the role of therapists in the program, with the administrator seeming to take a strange and hostile position.

"We're not here to do therapy!" he commanded with philistine arrogance. It was in those meetings wherein terms like "support", "recovery", and "therapy" were used, abused, repeated or defeated, but never defined. Initially, he'd seem sympathetic, even passionate about clinical matters. Invoke someone like Terry Gorski, a noted author on the topics of addiction and relapse prevention, he'd say something like, "Oh yeah, Terry's the best," with pally familiarity. Reference Irvin Yalom's ideas about group therapy in a hospital setting, he might bobble his head and boast, "Ya know, I had lunch with Irvin a month or so ago. I gotta say, I don't think he gets it about kids and substance abuse." The man's favorite word was *tools*, as in tools for recovery. "We are the tools of recovery," he'd say to staff, paraphrasing someone. I keyed on the word "tool", often suspecting devaluation. We were tools, as in someone's tools, his tools. On this and other subjects he was a demagogue filling the air with his filibusters. For the most part, I tolerated his oratories, as any hamstrung employee would. I nodded, and before speaking, waited patiently for the ten second gap that opened up about once every three minutes. However, with respect to the "therapy" comment, I gingerly, yet quickly responded with, "then why do you hire us?" He averted his gaze, appeared to zone out upon some space upon his desk, and went silent for several moments before changing the subject. He had no answer for me, and as likely over the last year of his tenure, he'd have fewer compliments also.

Though a lay person with respect to mental health, his remark about therapy may have been prescient, and also a function of some considerable homework. He might, for example, have been thrown by the subtle changes that had affected Masters' level therapists since the mid-nineties. When he came on board in 1996, many interns and some full-time case managers were seeking a credential then-designated as MFCC, or Marriage, Family, and Child Counselor. Counselor! It was around this time that the Board of Behavioral Sciences authorized a change in the title, to the broader-sounding Marriage and Family Therapist, or MFT. Therapist! This change caused consternation for some, or merely inconvenience, while many others welcomed the change, thinking it afforded the credential with greater prestige. Was it possible, or even likely, that management had never wanted "therapists" per se, but rather counselors: directive, thick-skinned, rapport-generating, psycho-educational, support-providing counselors?

Finally, mid-way through the decade, that administrator left Thunder Road suddenly, without fanfare or ceremony, and without an honorable discharge. One day I was in a consultation with the medical director who matter-of-factly informed the team that the administrator was being replaced. For a year or so, the position seemed an invisible sinecure, for the woman who inhabited his role for that spell appeared to make no incursions whatsoever into the clinical realm. For me, in my position as clinical supervisor, that meant I'd have little or no sense of her influence, distanced as I was from purely administrative matters. Regarding the departed patriarch, there was a muted feeling of relief, it seemed; though this was perhaps my projection. The chronology eludes me now, but I have a vague recollection that the Iraq War was at its peak during this transition, and that the former Iraqi leader, Saddam Hussein, had been captured, tried, and executed around about this time. For a year or so, there seemed to be peace and synchronicity in this world.

Staffings and hospital track

Meanwhile, I was enjoying my new role as clinical supervisor. After an initial period working that fifteen-to-twenty hours per week schedule, my duties expanded somewhat, owing to the departure of one of the psychiatrists. Soon I'd be providing psycho-social assessments of clients admitted to the short-term track, as well as providing periodic trainings to the entire staff, on topics like mandated reporting of child abuse and adolescent development. As clinical supervisor, it was my tacit role to be the go-to guy with respect to legal and ethical questions for all clinical staff—not that others in the building weren't qualified or capable—but again because I was better positioned, and had less pressing duties with respect to client care or the oversight of ever-expanding documentation requirements. I also attended different treatment team meetings during this period, presenting impressions from my assessments, offering my two cents as a consultation upon interventions, and sometimes taking part in specialized therapeutic activities such as staffings.

For about a year, I managed to effect a minor, though significant change in the way in which staffings were conducted, at least within the confines of the hospital track's treatment planning meetings. Previously, staffings proceeded as they had always done, with obstinate clients brought to the meeting as though summoned for a court appearance, told to wait outside on a bench, and then admitted for the requisite Q & A while standing to attention. Asserting that these measures, which had militaristic overtones, were unnecessary, I convinced a newer team of counselors and manager that a more collaborative engagement was called for, especially with clients who were projected to be in the program for just a matter of weeks, and therefore had much less time to be assimilated into Thunder Road's idiosyncratic mini-culture. To my mild and pleasant surprise, the counselors were enthusiastic about altering the spirit of staffings (the manager, I think, was quietly truculent, but agreeable). Therefore, for a brief, long forgotten minute, the previously adversarial norms of Thunder Road staffings were transformed into sit-down conversations between clients prepared in advance for meetings, and a team of staff members more thoughtfully prepared for purposeful and informed discussions.

Uncoordinated interventions still occurred; in fact, it was an unspoken tradition throughout my years at Thunder Road that team decisions, approaches, and team treatment plans could and would be undermined from all directions at any given time. I would find it quite frustrating to discuss the fragile ego strength of a client one day, and therefore strategize appropriately focused yet non-bombarding interventions with seemingly agreeable team members, only to hear of "hot seats" and other weighty interventions that were spontaneously orchestrated by those not even present for the treatment team meetings. What was the point of the meeting? I'd complain as the presumed positive outcomes of hot seats and staffings were reported. A counselor would summarily offer something like, "He had a hot seat, and staff and peers really let him have it for his attitude. It was good." Everyone would chuckle triumphantly, having forgotten the previous week's plan. I'd strike the discordant note: in what way was that intervention informed by the treatment plan, or by the client's attending team? The staff members relaying the information were often thrown by my reactions. Few seemed to register the problem of treatment planning being disjointed from the activities of the milieu. At times alone in my opinion, I thought the so-called team approach resembled a low-functioning dissociative disorder, with the brain and body severed from each other at the neck.

The short-term, or hospital track, enjoyed a positive transformation around the mid-point of the last decade. Thereabouts, Thunder Road began receiving more referrals from outpatient programs like Kaiser, or from other local funding sources specifically aimed at substance-abusing populations. More clients like Alison. What came with these admissions was the prospect of longer treatment durations—not the near year of residential treatment common within the group home track—but a relatively healthy two or sometimes three months of care. This perhaps reflected contemporaneous studies, published by the Substance Abuse and Mental Health Services Administration (SAMSHA) as well as others, in which findings asserted that at least three months of treatment services were required for any sustainable outcome, such as a meaningful stretch of abstinence from substances. These recommendations didn't necessarily posit the level of care (inpatient or outpatient) required for attainment of positive outcomes. Nonetheless, the shift gradually enabled a departure from the 14-day detox model previously in place.

Prior to 2006, I'd attended hospital track meetings about once a month, mostly to stay abreast of happenings that would affect the interns assigned to that department. I actually didn't approve of interns being involved in the short-term track, largely because it was just that—a short-term track. I thought that the experience of an intern working with kids and families present only for a matter of weeks wouldn't be so valuable for them. As head of the intern department, I naturally wished to advocate for an optimal learning experience and an experience, more specifically, that was consistent with the schooling of most therapists. I wasn't disparaging of this department, and certainly not of its staff, but others gave it a black eye, and the kids admitted to this track were clearly the step-children of the group home. "McTreatment", many called the hospital short-term track: fast food therapy.

Still, as I took over the position, there were at least two interns concurrently ensconced within the hospital track department, so there was little I could do about it at first. Of course, I was already familiar with the track's routine, both from my brief experience, to the hearsay accounts I'd known all along. The head of the department, a charismatic psychiatrist who carried with him an obsessive acrimony towards managed care systems, ran the hospital treatment team meetings with a furious attention to task management. In these discussions, clinical reflections were fleeting; directives were fast-paced. The team of counselors would listen intently to the psychiatrist, and to his seemingly subordinate track coordinator, with pens ever at the ready, taking notes. A review of medications was delivered; the psychiatrist's sometimes whimsical impressions as to clients' deficits were shared with good-humored yet head-shaking solemnity. There were few opportunities and little room, it was smilingly offered, for anything ambitious.

If you wanted a crash course in case management in a hospital setting, this was it. But interns training to be therapists versus, say, social workers, were in the way of this process. The counselor/case managers, those in the full time positions versus the part time position that I had once inhabited, had little time or space to accommodate the off-the-pace contributions of their part-time helpers. The case managers had phone calls to make, discharge plans to consolidate; aftercare arrangements, with follow-up care providers, to attend to. Meanwhile, a short-term client's family had to be urgently addressed about central problems, obstacles that existed, whether understood or not. A drinking parent needed to be referred to both AA and to Thunder Road's sister adult program for an assessment, regardless of whether he or she was oblivious to the problem of said drinking pattern. Quick decisions had to be made about reunification plans; which of two separated parents were to be the physical custodian of a client upon discharge, and what did the client want with respect to this issue?

As I took over a modified version of the psychiatrist's role after he left in 2006, we were able to relax the pace somewhat because of those extended treatment durations. By 2009, admissions referred by third party payers who negotiated treatment day to day were down to single digits in any fiscal quarter, and the number of clients over the course of the year whose authorizations for residential care were restricted to days instead of weeks could be counted on two hands, perhaps one. In both departments of the residential component of treatment, it seemed as though we had the opportunity to impart a cohesive set of standards for care, as well as provide a fuller guideline to clinical staff for the appropriate execution of their roles.

Staff boundaries: an introduction

For instance, I started challenging staff members to adhere to boundaries with clients and families that were closer to the standards taught to those preparing to work in private practice or outpatient settings. Boundaries were an important issue to tackle first. When I was a case manager, it had been routine for me to stay late after a shift, girded by the mixed messages of management ("you need to take care of yourself"), in order to accommodate a family that hadn't shown up on time, or even close to on time, for a previously scheduled family therapy session. It had also been common for counselors to stay at work long after group therapy sessions had ended, to field the supposedly urgent questions of parents who, it seemed, had little intention of making full use of the group format, but rather wanted private audience with their therapists after those noisome activities were over. Again, management, despite the rhetoric that was poured out in all-staff trainings pertaining to staff self-care, reinforced counselors over-working with rewards: the "employee of the month" placards that followed in curious proximity to stretches of overlong shifts. Staff members that over-functioned were treated as heroes by management, and were still being feted in their absence, months after the onset of their medically-induced leaves.

To be fair, in that previous era of the nineties, managers were appropriately responsive if counselors asserted a need, either on their own behalf or that of a client, to have clear and consistent boundaries. The lesson that I learned both then and even more so at McAlister Institute was that I couldn't take such things for granted. I couldn't expect that I wouldn't have to ask for certain things, like boundaries, repeatedly. I couldn't expect that I wouldn't be asked to perform duties that might unduly tax my resources. I had to stand up for myself; in order to thrive I had to set limits with my employer, not just my clients. I don't think as many of my forebears in the positions of case management have either felt or seized this kind of parallel prerogative—at least not in recent years. Times change, people say, with respect to a wide range of phenomena.

I recall an instance wherein a counselor from the hospital track, pleased to have the opportunity, at my soliciting, to speak of countertransference, discussed her resentful feelings towards a client's family—a family she described as not having any boundaries; a family that seemed entitled to her time. Upon asking for details, I discovered that it had been the counselor who had not been keeping good boundaries: privately arranged meetings started egregiously late, and were being continued long after a previously appointed time and therefore long after the end of the counselor's shift. Group therapy sessions were starting late and finishing late. If a family arrived late for the group, the counselor would have the entire group wait so that the meeting could begin with everyone present. Wouldn't that generate resentment amongst the other clients and families? I challenged. The counselor didn't think so, and made a comment about good manners, as though the therapeutic activity were akin to a family dinner gathering. Finally, she admitted that she had originally offered what she termed "flexibility" to her families, and didn't mind staying late because she "had nothing especially important to do after work". She referenced another's supervisor's credo—"go with the flow" (apparently intended to support this boundary mindset)—as her own guiding principle. I countered that the "flow" was like that of a ball eluding the grasp of a baseball mitt, and thereafter tumbling erringly to the ground. I further pointed out two other things: firstly, that she was contradicting her initial feelings of resentment, as directed at her clients (she was being defensive, having felt criticized by me, no doubt); secondly, that her rationales seemed to not even touch on the fact that she was modeling poor boundaries for her clients.

Training group facilitation: Joshua

I agitated for, and was subsequently encouraged to devise a staff training class on the subject of group facilitation. Soon I'd have a regular time-slot in those quarterly new-staff orientations, on the same topic. In the training, I focused on two areas. Firstly, I emphasized the importance of structure: consistent beginning and end times, norms of participation between members, and the importance of group members remaining in the process for the duration of activities. The absurdity lay in the fact that staff members tended to walk in and out of these trainings as a matter of routine. These meetings felt a bit like 12-step gatherings wherein members step outside for a smoke after finishing their shares. Another parallel problem was transmitted to the clients by this in-and-out tendency. Clients would be pulled from groups, or else introduced to a group, with little consideration as to the disruptive potential. If group therapy coincided with a 2pm meds call, then a client needed to step out of the room, regardless of the process, in order to take the required medication. If a client's probation officer had arrived for a visit, either with an appointment or not, then that client would be extracted from group with few questions asked. I don't recall this happening as much in the nineties when I worked in the group home track, but it was happening more frequently in the next decade. I openly challenged these norms (though I didn't pick on probation officers or nurses, necessarily).

A second area of concern was the process of group therapy itself. This thing about the group format: it seemed for so long my personal bone to pick, and mostly because the subject was ignored. Despite the fact that most therapeutic activities happened in groups, or the fact that multiple staff meetings existed during the week—each with a presumably distinct purpose—few seemed to speak of the ways in which people were communicating with one another in group-like circumstances. By this point, I'd been in the field for just over a decade, and had witnessed this inattention to groupspeak not only at Thunder Road, but also within the McAlister Institute also. I couldn't understand it. Group process and its parallel, the staff meeting, were the symbolic microcosms of community. Residential programs are mini-communities, even families, depending on who is being asked. How was it that the ways of group process; the techniques of group facilitation, or the decoding of metacommunications in crowds still hadn't made it onto the agendas of any staff trainings?

At Thunder Road, the word "process" was used with at least two different meanings, sometimes three or four. Process, from a management or administrative point of view, simply referred to procedures, mechanistic, sequential, and largely hierarchical. For many within the clinical team, the word process referred to the techniques, exchanges that were involved with contract breaking, or the revealing of previously withheld thoughts and feelings about some distressing event within the milieu, such as an AWOL, or the dishonorable discharge of an established and popular peer. For many therapists, especially the multi-colored shawl-wearing new age types that usually came from either Berkeley or Marin County, processing referred to a body-centered movement of unresolved emotions through organ systems and things like chakras. They used their hands to illustrate the psycho-spiritual actions, usually rotating them in a counterclockwise fashion at chest level as they spoke. The term process, as I spoke of it, either to interns or else to the broader staff within these trainings had a more specific meaning relating to the practice of group therapy.

Bringing worksheets to these discussions, I presented scenarios of actual dialogue between clients and group facilitators, or snatches of talk between group members, adult or youth. Underlying the content were the meanings of the exchanges, in terms of how the individuals were relating to one another—what from disparate models of care might be termed metacognition, or mentalization. I pointed out that identifying the process between group members was the actual job of a group facilitator. It's the task that distinguishes a group therapist (or a couples' therapist, for that matter), from other kinds of mediators—negotiators, or advocates; even educators. The therapist in a group, charged with the job of helping to teach communication skills, must first identify what patterns of communication exist in the first place, and what feelings underlie those communications. The therapist models for those in the room the capacity to reflect different points of view, and hold those perspectives in abeyance, suspending judgment. If a parent in multi-family group, for example, insisted that his daughter not get a tattoo, or be more careful in the selection of boyfriends that "respected women", it was at best secondarily important for a group therapist to either agree or disagree with these assertions. More important was to question why the parent and daughter seemed at odds on these issues—what unspoken divide formed the premise of the standoff. Curiosity ahead of reaction.

Staff members of various disciplines attended my trainings. Quick to catch on, they entered the spirit of the exercises, and made eager interpretations of messages that lay within the content. By the end of the trainings, few seemed to dispute that the task of a group or family counselor was not so much arguing for tattoo removal or not, but rather addressing the assumptions that existed within that particular dispute, the ability to consider another's mind at work. Staff gave voice to the competing ideas: the parent's assertion of authority, of greater life experience, versus the youth's drive towards separation and autonomy. Staff nodded agreeably, took an active part in the role plays that I devised. They took the different scenarios provided, made their interpretations of content in dialogue, and practiced transforming would-be didactic responses into comments that neutrally spoke to what was happening in the exchanges. I referenced the "here and now" ethos that many others, across orientations use, and coached that focusing upon the "here and now" was the goal of the group facilitator. "I get it. It's not about tattoos," reflected a satisfied member of my audience. His arms bulged with inky symbols.

He did get it. It wasn't about tattoos. Except maybe on one occasion. A year or so earlier, while I was still in charge of IOP, I worked with a kid named Joshua who entered the program on the back of a relatively benign set of problems: his grades were dropping, allegedly due to a marijuana habit, and above all, this disappointed his father, on whose approval seemed to hinge his entire self-worth. Josh was a good kid and I liked him. He was quiet, yet thoughtful; articulate and troubled, yet sensitive, cut from Holden Caulfield cloth. At the time he was in the program, the census was threadbare, and on some days, he was the only member of my group, not that I minded much. Josh was the kind of kid I would have welcomed into my then fledgling part-time practice, and the type of client that occasionally found a way into the group home at Thunder Road. They were of a type that mingled well enough with their peers, but kept invisible a secret longing to bond with adults, have *adult* conversations. Anyway, I was ok with meeting one-on-one with Joshua, despite the languishing census of my department. During the later process, I met the father, a dignified, late middle-aged gentleman who was a retired teacher. He seemed likeable, not especially authoritarian, but not obviously heroic, either. Josh spoke of his father in generic terms, and thus belied an otherwise candid and attentive nature. Quietly I wondered what it was that he idealized so much.

One night I was asked by my supervisor if I could lead the Continuing Care department's concurrently running multi-family group. Initially, I begged off, citing my IOP commitment, but then I considered that Josh might be the only client attending, and perhaps for just one night I could enjoin he plus his mother and father into the larger group, while also helping out the treatment team. Acting as substitute, I later facilitated a group that was apparently embroiled in an ongoing dispute that divided the room in half: youth versus adults over the question of tattoos. A thirty person deep discussion weighed the pros and cons of one kid's wish to get a tattoo, set against the hygiene and aesthetic concerns of his obdurate mother. Everyone had an opinion, it seemed. Everyone, that is, except Josh and his dad. Josh had his head down, which was unusual. Ordinarily, he was engaged in group discussions, even if he didn't relate directly to the issue at hand. He politely offered his views and could speak reasonably to both sides of an argument; he could reflect. At first, I thought I'd made a mistake. Perhaps he and his parents had something personal to work on that night, and despite an agreeable cooperation when first telling them of the plan, were now regretting sitting amidst this fairly trivial discussion.

Another group member, a client, had a creative idea. Can everyone who has a tattoo in the room show it off, and then tell the story of how it got on their bodies and what went into the original decision? Heads started to nod, with the kids in particular thinking this a great idea. The parents nodded more uncertainly, but once one or two of them broke the ice and gave testimonial, the process started to move. I think I might have blocked this activity had it been my usual group, but this group seemed to run itself, and was likely taking advantage of the usual facilitator's absence by changing the norms. I watched indulgently as several adults, mostly with substance abuse histories of their own, told rueful stories punctuated with guffaws, about body art applied under a hazy alcoholic buzz. The kids seemed to enjoy the recollections, and as the process plodded its way around the circle towards Josh and his father, still seated with gnomic, disinterested looks, I was battling with boredom as much as anything. The man seated to the left of Josh's father finished his relatively undistinguished tale. Everyone glanced at Josh's dad and owing to his previous silence, appeared ready for him to pass. I briefly met his eye and offered an apologetic smile—little did I know. Then something dawned on me: a fleeting link. Recalling his and Josh's minimally explored Judaism, I guessed at the man's age and realized in an instant what was coming.

Josh's father unbuttoned his cuffs and rolled up his sleeve. Twisting his bare arm slightly, he leaned forward and exposed to the room a row of numbers tattooed just below his elbow. Patiently, and in a low voice, he explained that he didn't recall the precise moment wherein he was branded with the code. He dryly added that he was sober at the time, and that he likely didn't choose the tattoo. Nor did he imagine that his parents would have approved, even though they also received tattoos around about the same time. The year was 1944, he said in a grave tone, and the place, for anyone who hadn't by now guessed it, was East Germany. The room went silent. I mean nothing. I looked around the circle and saw the frozen expressions of kids who'd been known to smirk through some pretty grisly stories. Now they were stilled by reverence; some of their heads dropped, as did those of many adults in the room. Collective guilt. Collective shame. Inexplicable grief. Josh looked up and locked eyes, first with his softly weeping, diffident mother, and then with his father. I said some words—process comments, I think. I don't remember what else I said, except that it was about tattoos.

Group facilitation: the fallout

Latterly, on the fairly trivial matter of group process, the focus of my coaching was on cognitive exchanges, by which I mean conscious, or preconscious material (that is, accessible to memory). There was nothing in these meetings that was incompatible with CBT, but rather, perhaps, an approach proffered by strategic psychotherapy, or so-called solution-focused approaches, which tended to insist upon problems being solved rather than the more vague task of learning about the mind. More subtly, perhaps, I was urging a less directive approach in general, to a staff that was habitually directive. Nonetheless, the online staff as well as the interns in my supervision groups seemed to appreciate, albeit briefly, the attention towards strategies that enabled neutrality. For some, it was a welcome change from the oppressive Eldridge Cleaver-like processes that otherwise reigned[35] . After all, everyone understood that to be an effective counselor (or therapist) in an environment wherein relationships of all kinds were volatile, an ability to speak to the process of communication without alienating either side of a divided exchange was vital.

That groups within a Therapeutic Community tend not to practice these principles is partly a matter of philosophical disagreement, but more commonly, I think, just a matter of habit, expediency, and institutional carelessness. Though some misunderstood and thought that I was coaching attention to something obscure, most struggled to sustain attention to group process because of the inertia created by other demands—the weight of pressure presented by those oblivious to the therapeutic technique I was encouraging, and more insistent upon a psycho-educational or interrogatory method: old chestnuts. Managers, for example, seemed to want problem-solving—content-driven, practical problem-solving—as well as the imparting of principles, 12-step slogans and *tools*, such as the use of "I" statements, or the solicitation of recovery-minded testimonials from adults deemed to be positive influences. While management supportively provided me a forum to present my trainings, it basically ignored the messages I gave.

I gleaned some conscious intent with respect to group process. Through the nineties and into the new century, management's position was that clinical staff members were not intended to stake out "neutral" positions with Thunder Road clients. There were at least two areas where staff was anything but neutral. Firstly, resembling a Structural Family Therapist, Thunder

Road was implicitly in support of parental authority, owing to its own system of rules and behavior modification. Secondly, we were an abstinence-based program; that is, a program in which abstinence from substances was an understood treatment goal. Beyond these two areas, there was room for neutrality with clients and their family, in theory. In practice, staff members tended towards advocacy on a whole range of issues not directly related to substance abuse. A client who denied that drug use was a problem would be confronted until that denial was lessened. The group facilitator, managers asserted, shouldn't be a neutral in this discussion, but rather a leader of an assault upon *stinkin'* thinking. Questions that were obviously tendentious needed to be asked and the role of the group leader was that of an advocate: for Thunder Road, for the "disease concept" of addiction, and the presumption, steadfast until proven otherwise (and it hardly ever was), that the kids in the program were addicts whose lives were at stake. And this was the position that prevailed at Thunder Road throughout most of my fifteen years, only to abate towards the end of the last decade.

As it happened, I tended to agree that most of the kids were indeed addicted to substances, as well as disordered in other ways, but I bristled against the norms of didacticism, crude identification, and interrogatory procedures that lingered as group practices. Consulting afterwards, and hearing of exchanges from these activities, I'd feel an increasing dismay at not hearing of a single process comment being made. And if that wasn't frustrating enough, the disregard of group boundaries pushed me further into despondency. Well into 2006 I was hearing of practices that took me further by surprise: kids admitted to the unit on a Tuesday afternoon were being immediately thrust into hospital track's version of multi-family group, with little or no preparation for that activity. Meanwhile, due to a lack of staffing, multi-family groups in the long-term track were getting spontaneously combined on certain nights, leaving fledgling therapists figuring out how to facilitate a meaningful discussion with as many as thirty people in the room. Why not split the groups? I asked, knowing it wasn't a matter of unavailable staff. A manager would point out that intern facilitators, known for being quiet in groups, were not sufficiently experienced to "handle" the intensity of multi-family group. In other words, a bland lecture offered by an experienced pedagogue was preferable to a smaller activity wherein group members might actually interact and process, if perhaps act out in their process.

Managers seemed to want order and calm above all else. For years, I gave this bias the benefit of the doubt: that is, I trusted that a group that prioritized safety was one in which meaningful work might eventually get done. But the notion that a group of thirty people constituted group therapy seemed absurd to me; so did the idea that such a group would necessarily be more orderly (or safe) than a group a half or a third of the size, simply because it had more experienced staff members facilitating the exercises. Those facilitators were not more experienced with (meaning trained in) group therapy, I asserted. Doing something for a long time doesn't equate to superior practice. These counselors had rather become like teachers of overstuffed classrooms: loyal, soldierly, doing as they were told. I was never convinced that Thunder Road's twenty to thirty-person deep group sessions were less volatile, or more contained. Though some might cite occasions as moving as that group of Josh and his father, I think that most of these larger activities were and are deadened exercises that short-change kids and families of a real therapeutic opportunity.

In the late fall of 2006 I traveled to Los Angeles, to the Evolution of Psychotherapy conference being held in Anaheim. This was a huge, all-star gathering of mental health professions, with thousands of therapists in attendance, and several celebrity theorists and/or researchers lined up as key speakers. Among the list of presenters was Irvin Yalom, author of the near-Bible of group psychotherapy text, *The Theory And Practice Of Group Psychotherapy* (1995). I had group therapy on my mind. At that time, Yalom was something of a hero of mine. His books, especially his novels, dominated my shelves, and I was constantly referencing his oft-promulgated ideas of group process to interns. He was due to speak at the convention center on the last night, and I was eager to hear him in person for the first time. Though equally famous for his interest in existentialism, I knew that his address would cover the topic of group therapy, if for no other reason than to promote his then novel, *The Schopenhauer Cure* (2005), which dramatizes a group therapy episode. While the group dynamic of that particular story is a universe apart from the group program practiced at places like Thunder Road, I knew that Yalom also had something to say of group therapy in hospital settings, with significantly disturbed, if not necessarily adolescent populations. His earlier book, *Inpatient Group Psychotherapy* (1983), had actively criticized the practice of group therapy in hospitals, and had specifically called attention to the neglect of group therapy programs by hospital psychiatric leadership. His presentation at the Anaheim conference reflected upon the state of group therapy in hospitals after nearly thirty years of research. His comments on this topic seemed resigned, retrospective, and lamenting. Addressing the lack of orientation of hospital admits to the processes of group therapy, he offered that the practice of group therapy in hospitals across the nation was treading a line just this side of malpractice. There were about two or three thousand people in the audience, few of whom seemed to react one way or another to this astonishing statement.

Except myself. I returned to Thunder Road feeling oddly ashamed because I knew I'd developed my skills on the practice of group therapy in a hospital-like setting, at Thunder Road. While I knew that the standard of practice was less than ideal, I asked myself: had I really been guilty, along with countless others, of malpractice for all those years? For months I ruminated on this matter, not knowing what if anything I could do about it. Then, after several months I became energized, as employers like to say. Some time later, after a few nights of thinking and pacing, I approached my supervisor with a different idea than that of teaching group process two or three times a year in the weekly all-staff meeting. By this time, I'd long since moved on from promoting the types of group practices such as what was taught back in my grad school days. So I focused on the most salient of Yalom's criticisms in Anaheim: the lack of orientation given to newcomers to the unique format of group therapy. And Yalom wasn't alone: others have argued that pre-group preparation plays a vital role in the subsequent cohesion of a therapy group (Rutan & Stone, 2001; Burlingame et al., 2002; Yalom & Leszcz, 2005). I offered a plan to provide an orientation for all new clients and families entering the program: an orientation specific to the process of group therapy, and in particular, multi-family group therapy. I had an outline, a series of bullet-points for a powerpoint display, a video slide show with my narrative voice-over, and a goal of making sense of the process such that no one need come to Thunder Road on a Tuesday afternoon or evening without knowing what to expect.

The clinical director (they started being called this instead of program director around 2005) of that period was indulgent, if half-interested. She was modestly encouraging, but made it clear that she'd do little to accommodate the changes herself. She laughingly expressed surprise that Irvin Yalom was even still alive (a telling prejudice, or ignorance), but conceded that a client and family orientation to group therapy, still the dominant format of counseling in the entire program, might be called for. Therefore, if alterations to either the afternoon or evening schedules were necessary, then it was incumbent on me to consult with the appropriate people in the admissions department, or in either residential track. Patiently, I went about the task of speaking to leaders of those different departments, obtaining support along the way. Many were enthusiastic, and were certainly pleased that I would take on the duty rather than assign it to one of them, but the process of persuasion was not without complications. Like legislators looking to attach pet concerns to a bill of someone else's creation, one or two managers sought for the curriculum of this project to include extraneous issues, caveats to parents about house rules, for example, or an attached lecture on codependency.

The project bogged down for a while as my agenda competed with that of people who could give or take the cause of group therapy. Change, any kind of change in a system as rooted in its ways as Thunder Road is, doesn't happen overnight, and I'd been present for one or two of the notable ones at Thunder Road—the smoke-free shift of 96', the gender split of early 99'—both of which had been treated like the fall of the Berlin Wall. However, I was dogged enough, committed enough, to proselytize the virtues my orientation activity, and ultimately, because I'd put more thought and work into the project than anyone else, I more or less got my way. Anyway, wouldn't staff welcome reform such that the unnecessary disruptions of uninitiated families might be significantly diminished? One would think so. Furthermore, since the idea didn't require too much effort on anyone else's part, and because it didn't stretch even my own schedule unduly, my arguments eventually won the day, though in retrospect, the project wasn't so ambitious, and it surely should not have taken the nearly two years (from conception to first presentation) it did take for the orientations to get underway.

For about two years I led this exercise, which served as a precursor to multi-family group participation for all clients entering the short-term track. The reason I didn't present it to families of the long-term or group home track was because I had an ongoing schedule conflict—the result of my increasing immersion into private practice group work away from Thunder Road. Regardless, my failure to recruit an interested party from the group home track to at least present the diligently produced video version of this talk proved to be the downfall of the idea. After this period of presenting material to clients and families, I realized that it was simply not reaching enough people. Among other things, there seemed to be various pretexts for excluding new clients or their families, even from the shorter term hospital track. The handful of clients admitted for a month or less of treatment were exempted from the orientation, on the basis that only a couple—perhaps three—groups were likely to be experienced anyway, so orientation was deemed a waste of everyone's time. Then there was the problem—the age old problem—of families simply not showing for the session. My routine was to introduce myself first to the new client, and alert them to the fact that their first Tuesday would be an introduction to the process, and not the plunging into drug histories and other disclosures, which hitherto had been the norm within both tracks. Around mid afternoon, when the hospital track's version of multi-family group was due to start, I'd head to the lobby, and like any other case manager, I'd collect and escort those families scheduled for orientation to the designated room.

Parents that didn't show on the first day of multi-family group, or else showed up late on those first days, tended to repeat the habit of absence in other areas. They'd be escorted to the room wherein my presentation was taking place, just as I was getting to the piece about the importance of structure, and the specific importance of being on time. Some parents, typically the least functional, would not show at all, and would later offer the usual excuses: they hadn't been told; they couldn't get off work; they thought the groups were on Saturday, and so on. I began to notice that those who were present, the over-functioning grandmothers, parents of the using parent of the now resident clients, were not the ones most in need of my orientation. The people who most needed to be schooled, such as the potentially disruptive, overbearing and drunken father who might storm into a multi-family group and monopolize process, would be absent for my high-minded introduction. There I was, speaking of the contrast between group therapy and the procedures of a 12-step meeting; offering empathy for the fact that drug treatment's most prescribed format of care asked people to share personal information in rooms filled with strangers, and realizing that I was, for the most part, preaching to the converted.

With considerable disappointment, I went about my business, but eventually discontinued the orientation class in the spring of 2011, and quietly retired the disks that captured my lesson on group therapy. This was a watershed moment for me, one that forced me to acknowledge the thrust of expediency in the program, and the sheer expendability of clinical virtues. It is several years now since I heard Yalom decry the practice of group therapy in hospital settings, and I feel sure that his words continue to fall on deaf ears. Something here got lost—an idea, fleetingly galvanizing—fell into dark water and got submerged. Yet the project was a success, relatively speaking. The demise of my Yalom-inspired orientation class may have gone unnoticed, but unlike my idea for introducing level groups, it had at least gotten some traction such that it had lasted for a year or so. In contrast, ideas for level groups didn't even get off the ground.

The idea for groups that separated clients into different activities based upon levels of functioning was not in and of itself brand new to Thunder Road. Something like this idea had existed in the nineties, when some groups separated clients based upon stage progression. My idea, raised intermittently between 2005 and 2010, roughly, wasn't an exact replica of this model. For one thing, the stage progression system was largely one in which progress was determined on the basis of behavior, with stabilization of negative behaviors being the principal criteria for advancement. I was keen to establish a group process that skirted this issue to some extent, such that different capacities amongst the kids might be accommodated, but not so much behavioral compliance. I understood, for example, that many clients couldn't tolerate the stimulation of a process activity as I had described it. Some couldn't contain affect if cravings were being discussed, or fantasies pertaining to drugs, sex, or even violence, were being shared. But some clients could contend with the feelings raised by these topics; in fact, it seemed necessary that they did have the opportunity to give voice to such process, in case their obsessions split-off into destructive behaviors. Additionally, the stuffed processes, such as fantasies of sex, violence, and drug use, were for many part of a broader isolationist tendency, which kept these clients locked in feelings of alienation, or frozen in shame. For these kids, the opportunity to share thoughts and feelings otherwise concealed was not just about relapse prevention. It was an opportunity to take another kind of therapeutic risk: to expose their inner worlds to others, and in so doing, begin cultivating real relationships, based upon honesty and not a mere strategy that echoed disordered attachment patterns.

Not interested, some among staff implied, by simply not responding to e-mails or phone messages requesting a meeting on the subject of level groups. I did get to speak on the matter with some supervisors, but they typically demurred, thinking the idea of level groups was potentially divisive; they (level groups) suggested that some clients were "better" than others. Perhaps, I replied, though I added that this argument seemed false. I argued that level groups would attend to the reality that different clients had different needs; that some were more motivated than others, or higher functioning. Besides, we were already suggesting competition via the stage progression system, not to mention the "client of the week" awards that we regularly passed out. The arguments for keeping clients within larger, heterogeneous groups weren't unique. Indeed, they were recycled ideas.

They also seemed like microcosms of disputes that were happening at levels of public policy. Do programs compromise the cohesion of sober communities by accommodating the most "hardcore" of addicts? Those who call for this integration disdain programs that exile the most difficult; the low functioning. They accuse practitioners of not meeting the needs of those whose drug use costs society the most. They argue that providers should give such people a chance. Some insinuate that programs reject admissions of "hardcore addicts", the seemingly unmotivated, or the seriously mentally ill because they don't wish to disaffect completion rates. From my meek corner of the business, I wasn't calling for anyone's discharge and subsequent exile to either the streets or the criminal justice system; just a segregation of activities that would have served everyone in the milieu: process groups for those who can regulate affect and reflect; basic skills groups for those who can't by staff's estimation. However, it would have been cumbersome and therefore inexpedient, I suspect, to break up groups into smaller units, especially given the paucity of staff members skilled in group facilitation. As a result, my rebuttals were rejected, and groups aiming for a common denominator of skills and functioning prevailed instead.

If it isn't documented, it didn't happen

Staff during this era was more hurried than ever, attending to countless distractions, details, pulls from management and collateral systems that torqued therapists' interests, compelled them to attend to documentation, phone calls, the management of a client's program rather than the provision of therapy. For several years, it was my job to be a clinical supervisor to both full and part time therapists at Thunder Road. I modeled the styles of my own former supervisors, with a slight lean towards one who was a bit sterner than others. Clinical supervisors often mirror with their supervisees the positions they take with their clients: some are supportive, dominantly sympathetic in style, and think of therapy as a palliative exercise. At the other extreme are those who seem determined to turn certain cultural idioms upside down: if they can't say anything critical, they won't say anything at all. I've had both types, and I've supervised individuals who think of me as the first type and others who would swear that I've emulated the latter. The truth, I suppose, is somewhere in between. In general terms, it seemed as though I was doing what I was supposed to be doing: orienting new staff as to the culture of Thunder Road; offering directives as to legal and ethical questions; offering a theoretical context for the practice of therapy (especially group therapy) in a residential setting, casting its methods as compatible with either CBT or psychodynamic approaches; brainstorming interventions, both for individuals and families, in group, individual, and family session contexts; being an ear for the sometimes paralyzing countertransference feelings of inexperienced therapists.

In the last year or so, it seemed as though I was listening to a gradual dissembling of the therapist's role—a dissembling that would ultimately render my position absurd, and leave me feeling like a dinosaur. The culture was changing. Therapists would speak of sessions that would last all of ten minutes, because that's all they had time for, they insisted. My supervisor, the clinical director, wouldn't refute this growing trend. She would simply shrug and shift the conversation onto the subject of an ever-stalled average census. The pressures were undoubtedly real. While drug treatment for adolescents had grown considerably during the nineties, census levels across programs were in steady decline since 2002. Furthermore, there seemed to be more competition for the troubled adolescent's business, and not just from the like-sized programs in Napa, San Mateo, and Marin, such as Our Family, Our Common Ground (formerly Daytop Village), or Center Point. Wilderness camps, out-of-state boarding schools were the choice of exhausted parents willing to take out extra mortgages and separate from their kids for months at a time. Thunder Road increasingly focused on home territories, securing contracts that localized its services. Kids from Alameda, nearby Contra Costa, and even San Francisco, had replaced the once factions of youth from the northern counties. Referrals from cities like Santa Rosa or Sacramento still poured in, but these tended to be short-term cases, kids who had bombed out of Kaiser outpatient programs, having gotten lost in the shuffle of their similarly overstuffed psychoeducation groups.

During the latter half of the decade, that charismatic program director of a prior era had moved on, to be replaced by a succession of journeywomen social workers with more reserved bossy streaks. Whatever clinical interests these women had once held were now submerged under spreadsheets, documentation requirements, personnel issues, and hardly a single meeting occurred with these people without being interrupted by a page from the front desk. More than ever, it seemed, no one had time to sit still and listen to an involved discussion about the quality of treatment. At times, I'd wander past the pool room on the boys' side, frustrated that I couldn't find the latest client whose psychosocial assessment I'd yet to complete, only to witness a desultory exchange between a client and a staff member who'd likely been employed for maybe a week or so, but who had time to sit and listen to a client because he didn't have a quarterly report that was imminently due to be faxed to a court official. The documentation demands appeared to be growing, not diminishing, despite the automation system that was meant to make everyone's life easier. The opposite occurred: back in the nineties, case managers like me walked around with client charts, carrying them from one meeting to the next, writing notes in treatment planning meetings, catching up on a treatment plan while listening to the administrator's state of the hospital addresses. The former program director coached staff to bring client charts to a caseload group therapy session. In the event that clients were behaving incorrigibly, group could be suspended; everyone would be directed to the bench, and staff could silently preside over the ensuing quiet time while getting some paperwork done.

With the movement away from the handwritten documentation of progress notes and treatment plans, this was no longer possible. As a result of this, as well as the increasing diversity of paperwork, as required by different funding sources, or similar sources but from different counties, therapists appeared to be spending an increasing amount of time behind closed doors, engrossed in reports whose completion was crucial for program reimbursement. Attention to documentation, therapists were implicitly and then explicitly told, was the top priority. *Avatar* was the name of one documentation system[36]. That word means "God on Earth". "Huh?" I said bemusedly. Documentation was God—that was the explanation provided by one jaded case manager of this period. Second priority was communication with collateral contacts, the probation officers, social workers, lawyers, and court officials whom, to various degrees, played a peripheral role in clients' programs. By the time I'd become a clinical supervisor to intern therapists, the concept of treatment team at Thunder Road was stretching. A glance through an admissions packet, or a HIPAA[37] declarations form, would reveal a small army of people who might conceivably have access to client records. Supposedly, clients were meant to have informed consent for treatment, like anyone else provided with medical or mental health treatment. However, once I took time to look through the records of clients concurrently living in the program, and found that nearly three quarters of them had not even signed the forms that served to outline the ever widening parameters of confidentiality.

I urgently brought this to the attention of my supervisor, who, to her credit, promised quick attention, though once again I felt like I was checking fire extinguishers. The administrator of this period dismissively commented that Thunder Road's legal requirement was covered by having the clients' custodians—which in many cases were the probation officers—sign the documents in question. The legal requirement: that's all that mattered, apparently. In assessments, I'd speak with clients about informed consent, confidentiality—bedrock principles in medical care, as well as psychotherapy. Apathetic, half-attentive youths would nod unconvincingly as I sketched out the system within which their disclosures might be shared. They knew something I didn't; by now the kids knew that the scope of the team was an open field, and that information from their so-called treatment might be shared with scores of people before all was said and done. Even those who had once railed against this porous system of disclosures seemed resigned to the reality. Amidst all of this, I was finding it hard to guide new therapists educated in conscientious academic environments—settings wherein client confidentiality and informed consent are sacred concepts, not flimsy philosophical relics given lip service.

Fringes of the team approach

Meanwhile, interns in numbers appeared to be struggling with another dilemma, also pertaining to confidentiality, but also returning to the embattled issue of therapeutic alliance. Alliances: therapists wanted alliances with their clients, but all too often failed to recognize that the insecurely attached force loyalties, call for splitting, and insist that therapists behave as lawyers. On this issue of confidentiality between individual therapists and clients, I was consistently on the side of management, who insisted upon transparency of therapist-to-client process, because otherwise a problem would arise: that of therapists holding clients' contracts, therefore keeping secrets from the team. The extent of the problem took me by surprise because I thought I had the issue covered, having walked this path myself in years past. From the outset of a supervisee's internship, I'd speak of the challenges posed by the treatment team approach. As a therapist, you'd never be alone, I'd say—there's always support and consultation. Comforting on one level, many found it oppressive.

With respect to client contracts, I'd offer a three-fold rule of thumb: first, there were the disclosures (of information) from clients that had to be shared with the treatment team as soon as possible, as well as a back and forth communication. These included rule infractions, especially infractions of cardinal rules, as well as clients' responses to the limits set. Remember the example of the mother at the playground with the kid that didn't get why he needed to stay near the handlebars: if that's an online staff doing the chore of the limit-setting, then the therapist needs a working dialogue with that person, so that such episodes can be processed in the therapy. A therapist couldn't afford to be isolated on these issues; firstly, in case their clients were doing something risky to themselves or others, but also because the nuggets of information from the online staff were essential.

Secondly, there were disclosures that should also be shared with the treatment team, or at least a co-facilitator of groups, that perhaps needn't be shared immediately. These disclosures included items of family of origin information, such as the revelation that a client's father was still drinking, despite a previous assertion to the contrary. This was an example of a revelation that clients might work towards, over days, however—not weeks or months. The same was generally true of suppressed conflicts that clients would reveal, with other staff members or else with peers. Here again, the job was to explore the resistance to open communication, and encourage clients towards directness with others. A therapist needn't "out" a client on this issue; in fact, to do so would be counterproductive. Lastly, there were some disclosures that needn't be shared, especially the offhand remarks and diatribes directed at authority that typically filled a therapy session at Thunder Road.

In general, I'd describe the role of therapist in a Therapeutic Community as being a bit like a quarterback who is answerable to a dozen or so men and women with headsets, all standing on the sidelines calling in plays. Behind them, somewhere up in the stands, is another set of officials, the offensive coordinators and player agents (analogous to probation officers or social workers), who are also calling in plays while looking out at the broader field of play. There's trust being tested on both sides, and trust wounds. No one in the process is all-conscious in their interactions, and everyone's attachment style is thrown into the scrimmage. But what the coaches on the sidelines and the advisors up in the press boxes all seem to expect—and perhaps take for granted—is that the quarterback will talk back to the sidelines, and not keep private what's being said in the huddle.

Interns started confiding in me about the contracts they thought their clients were keeping, or knew they were keeping; contracts they didn't want to share with the treatment team, much less outside officials. In some cases, they weren't even sure they should be telling me. It seems ironic that as the team approach was being exalted, and boundaries around sharing client information became increasingly porous, therapists were passively rebelling. Once a melting pot of rowdy discussion, treatment planning was becoming a reticent activity, with a false deferential air concealing underlying conflicts. The managers of this period were less domineering than those of the nineties: phrases like "let's talk about this off-line", continuing psychology's tradition of borrowing terms from computer science, betrayed the increasing bias against dissenting process. Disagreements were tolerated, but contained; embarrassing stand-offs were interrupted, split-off into later discussions, kept behind closed doors. The concepts of conflict resolution and impassioned dispute were becoming conflated, and everyone seemed quieter, more genteel. A former psychiatrist, known for inviting arguments with a good-natured provocation—"let's make hate"—was occasionally remembered, but with only thin fondness, and more as a laughable eccentric rather than a capable or sophisticated clinician.

When I was a case manager, I'd experienced a more animated atmosphere in treatment planning—at times an intimidating atmosphere—but nonetheless one that taught me to stand up for myself and my ideas. It took time for me to discover the nooks wherein I could insinuate dissent. For example, I dreaded the slick use of the word "support" in treatment planning meetings. Regarding a decision as to the status of one of my clients, the program director of that earlier period would punctuate a fifteen-minute exchange with a question that would cut to the chase: "Can you support this decision?" I learned to hate that phrase, because I knew its meaning. The discussion was ending; all sides had been heard. At the end of those meetings, the former director struck her gavel, and delivered decisions. "Support" was an abstraction, but in this context it referred to the actions of the public face. Could I demonstrate my support of the decisions—the decisions about discharges, passes, stage regressions, and the like—regardless of my personal feelings, through the words I'd direct at clients or their families; through my non-verbal presentation? Could I affect agreement, and compromise my precious neutrality to that extent? The director would stare at me and smile, having *taken in* my sometimes ardent protests. If I flexed my elbows just enough on these occasions, space might open up, and I'd leverage some capital for the next dispute, for the next treatment planning.

More and more, in my role of clinical supervisor, I was hearing from interns, full and part-time employees, who didn't feel this heated freedom that I had once felt. Instead, I felt the dull apathy of those who navigate systems with survival at the forefront of their thinking; with fear that should they dissent too rigorously about the problems of the program, they would be either fired, or else coolly marginalized to the point wherein continued employment would become untenable. They would simply leave. One or two case managers, popular in both cases, were dismissed during this later period, reinforcing the prevailing caution. In my role, I was becoming the tiresome supervisor, ever challenging therapists as to why they chose to say certain things, and not say others: "What kept you from speaking to that concern?" or "What was your thinking as you asked that?" were the types of questions I'd ask, looking to promote reflection. Holding parallel contracts, I didn't break "contracts" on interns that held contracts; instead, I pressured and pressured—criticized and interpreted—to the extent that those interns thought me a broken record, a shaming record.

For some, my questions and comments were plainly tantamount to devaluation. Some merely felt misunderstood. For these interns, I was resonating with their defensive procedures, re-enacting the role of a disapproving, uncomprehending father. This was unfortunate, but not deterring. After all, I was there to be a supervisor to the interns, not a cheerleader (or even a therapist), and I was clear, for the most part, that internal obstacles to hearing criticism, or even implied criticism in the form of challenging questions, needed to be worked through if these people were to be career mental health professionals. That was the premise of my position as far as I was concerned, but not everyone saw it that way. Therefore, this was a difficult period for me to provide clinical supervision, for as I have previously suggested, I'd entered the position on the back of a fairly basic argument: that I'd been an intern, a case manager, a therapist at Thunder Road myself; that I'd walked the road my forebears were treading, and that I knew what it was like to do their jobs. It served me right. I mean, so much for identification, I thought again.

Interns increasingly looked upon me as a kind of relic from the nineties. How did I know? Some of them told me so, because if nothing else, I'd cultivated enough trust with my supervisees such that they could argue with me with relative impunity. Meaning, I didn't "fire" anyone in my time as clinical supervisor, though on two occasions I facilitated an intern's early departure through mutual consent. Impasses occurred with a few therapists, and some remained unresolved, if openly discussed, to the point wherein those therapists left with disgruntled baggage trailing behind them. I continued to indicate defensive obstacles in interns when I perceived them, though I also apologized from time to time if deciding I'd been too abrupt or (more likely) flippant and therefore disrespectful in giving feedback. While many commented upon, and in some cases, celebrated my droll observations, others were unmoved by my sense of humor. Some I'd wounded, even. What was most difficult, however, was pointing out what I thought were instances of countertransference acting out: the unconscious material obstructing therapists' work.

Some therapists appeared too reticent, too afraid to confront treatment team decisions, or too cowed by clients' anger, or the narcissistic rage of authority. A common obstacle was their over-investment in clients' lives, manifest as rescue fantasies. Too many therapists at Thunder Road, especially during the years 2006 thru 2011, lost their objectivity; they became advocates, quasi-lawyers standing up for some ill-defined position that allied themselves and their clients. Unsure of themselves, they'd offer halting arguments for the progress of their caseloads, but struggle to substantiate with clear arguments. Challenging therapists was difficult as the details were so often elusive. The lack of transcripts or direct observation curtailed true analysis. I was left guessing, operating on a gut level in deciding whether an intern was managing a case properly: seeing a case clearly, realistically, or else caught up in a denial system. I aimed for unconscious process, pointed out habits lurking beneath awareness. For some, this might have seemed like the raison d'etre of a clinical supervisor's position, but it was also the most difficult aspect of the role, this sketchy process. Everyone has an ego, and sound ego strength is essential for performance in any line of work. But a conscious life is what a psychotherapist aspires to—the territory we often smugly claim at the expense of common folk—and telling a therapist that he or she is acting unconsciously is a bit like telling a porn star that he's looking flaccid.

In the supervision group that I led every Thursday morning, there was parallel process with respect to "contracts", divisions with management, and sometimes feelings of hopelessness. The therapists would act out, a bit like those alternately guffawing and hand-wringing colleagues I'd supported in the nineties, with their own kinds of war stories: they giggled, teased, "related" to one another's indulgent fantasies of leaving Thunder Road, and dripped sarcasm as they offered mimicked versions of management's suggested interventions. As the energy settled, a more involved, heartfelt, and often difficult process would sometimes transpire: they queried one another's countertransference, careful not to confront, or "call out" one another. They sometimes compared projections, usually in a manner that obeyed hierarchies. Trainees, the part-timers that were still students, tended to receive more critiques, and they rarely hit back. They were, after all, at Thunder Road for "a learning experience". The full-time case managers, typically registered interns with the BSE, were the idealized therapists of the group—the most burdened, and the most dug-in to their own styles of working. I was the leader of these groups, but a detached figure: I was envied, idealized, resented, teased, sometimes mocked as ineffectual, and sometimes deemed benign. My interpretations and provocations were sometimes absorbed quietly, as so-inclined interns or trainees went inward. Sometimes tears flowed, and frustrated appeals for my support hit me square on the chin.

I'd offer my feedback in the form of interpretations, and sometimes with concrete suggestions, but I could do little to change the underlying disorder in the building. I could do little to stir any change in the system, or hope or inspiration amongst my supervisees. Case presentations, or the demise of them, were symptomatic of a wearied, *getting by* ambience. On several occasions, I'd ask interns or full-time therapists to prepare a full presentation, following standard guidelines of a client's background and course of treatment. With apologies, the therapists would produce half-hearted efforts, impromptu, disorganized sketches of the lives of kids they knew intimately, but could barely describe in a comprehensive, clinical fashion. Overwork was the issue, and so therapists were effectively excused from a rigorous training effort. Process discussions were likewise limited, reflecting a half-hearted commitment to growth. Occasionally, brave interns would share unflattering truths about themselves, or else be receptive to a deepening query from myself or one of their peers. But for the most part, face-saving conservatism prevailed. Weary case manager/therapists, feeling drained and used by an unwieldy system, called for "support" from these supervision gatherings; an oasis from the mechanical, boorish directives of the treatment planning treadmill. Despite lip service to the contrary, few wanted to really look at themselves.

I felt ineffective during this period, lacking any meaningful leverage with which to compel a greater dedication. Again, it was parallel process. The limitations of my supervision group mirrored the limitations of the Therapeutic Community. Once I shamed a supervision group for not taking itself seriously, though the context was not the passive refusal to read my attachment theory handouts, or give professional presentations, or even "call out" one another's imperfections, but rather their inability to even attend supervision group on time. The process felt remedial, like a limit-setting exercise. Then again, it was about structure, or what some call "frame", and from structure proceeds safety. These were the basics, I asserted. My group pushed back. The criticisms went back and forth, and skirted civility, but otherwise pushed the envelope of what was expected. It was one of the periodic *real* discussions, and if nothing else, thoroughly censored tongues were loosened for two hours that particular Thursday morning. One intern called *me* out, albeit in a manner that projected shame onto me: Did I really like my job? she challenged.

I liked it for a while. My authority was at best ambiguous, though ultimately, negligible. The word "supervisor" was, in many ways, a misnomer. I had no direct authority over treatment plans, whether clients were or were not discharged; or even the discharge plans of those who did complete the program. I had no direct authority with respect to the clients, and only thinly so with respect to interns. For a few years, I'd inject myself into clinical situations if I thought it necessary. I'd pull the "you're operating under my license also" card a few times, pointing out that I was liable for training therapists' actions. While this was technically true, I was rarely asked to answer for therapists' specific interventions, or a therapist's overall managing of a case. I was certainly buffered from any civil action. From my sinecure-like position, I could influence therapists to apply all kinds of intervention ideas, some cognitively-based, some others more psychodynamically-influenced. Any of these directions might be undermined. Managers simply directed interventions from their own vantage points; sometimes on the fly, oblivious, or perhaps just indifferent to what I was advising. But for me, it wasn't about being in control of things, much less being responsible. It was about teaching, and training, and being available for the conversations that are difficult to have with an employer: necessary conversations about feelings of overwhelm, of inadequacy, for example—things which people don't share with bosses, generally. The freedom I had in this position cut both ways: I was left alone to exert influence upon my supervisees. I was left alone.

10

LET'S MAKE HATE

Mean Psychodynamic white male

As I noted the changes in the program—one after another as each year passed—I had to concede that I was an onlooker to a gradually changing culture of treatment, one that didn't seem friendly to the aspiring psychotherapist, despite the greater shift towards Medical Model versus Social Models; modified TC's, and so on. Change: all change is difficult, it is soberly declared, yet even within the molasses-like world of Thunder Road, changes happened. Some interns and full-time therapists had to be reminded of this, for it seemed to them that changes—at least the changes they thought ought to happen—were simply not happening, while the Thunder Road of my past experience seemed to them a kind of ghost. Their concerns often diverged from mine, but I was largely sympathetic. The problems they shared tended to concern breakdowns in consistency, that once staple virtue of the program. On-line staff members were not sufficiently trained, it was said. "Some don't even know what they're doing," a frustrated therapist laughingly shared. The turnover of staff at the level case manager might have stabilized, but the comings and goings of staff working the milieu was as volatile as ever. As a result, treatment planning decisions were being routinely undermined by staff members left to their own devices, or else running their own agendas. Egregious boundary violations continued to happen, in greater numbers, and clients seemed to be living in a community that was not so much an antidote to previously neglectful homes, but rather a recreation of them.

Add to this the fact that philosophical changes were ever so gradually, yet surely, infiltrating the treatment environment, creating new schisms within the staff. New voices, some from within, but more commonly from outside the hospital, such as the department of health, or Community Care Licensing officials, observed that some practices of Thunder Road were too harsh or restrictive. Amid this onlooking influence, it seems it's not enough to exude calm and compassion while imposing limits. Now the limits themselves are decried as that which furthers feedback loops. While this was and is gleaned from hearsay and not direct exchanges with licensing officials—called analysts by the department of Social Services—the changes that followed were real enough. In researching for this book, I made several attempts to interview officials at the Community Care Licensing Board, in order to discuss things like confrontation groups, homework assignments given to clients, the use of time-out devices such as mirrors and benches, the background qualifications of visiting analysts, or the segregation of treatment facilities by gender. After being referred between departments over a matter of months, officials eventually declined to speak to me, instead directing my attention to its evaluator manuals which are made available for public viewing online. So I read through the manuals: the various sections that read like civil codes, but with largely in-specific rhetoric.

Many items seemed pertinent to my questions: in reading about the requirement that group homes provide money for and access to payphones, I noted the anachronism of some documents, and recalled from the nineties that use of payphones at Thunder Road was once a stage-earned privilege. But there was nothing about the use of cell phones. Through an item within a section entitled “Reference Material and Evaluation tools”, licensing regulations indicated that children of opposite sex should not share a room—a common sense idea, one would think. But I could find nothing that stipulated that boys and girls in group homes or other child care centers should or should not engage in program activities together. Among the obvious requirements for provision of food, shelter, and medical services, there were lists of clients’ personal rights: that clients should be provided a “dignified” experience, free of ridicule, physical, mental, emotional abuse, or use of restraints unless prescribed by a medical authority. Drawing from the California Penal Code, the documents further decreed that clients should not be punished with isolation, locked in rooms, subject to coercion, or given corporal punishments; that clients’ personal belongings should be safeguarded. While certainly relevant to activities like confrontation groups or contract breaking, the statements seemed largely subject to interpretation, which would surely place much responsibility of the heads of designated licensing analysts. How, for example, did analysts assess “coercion” in programs wherein participation was mandated by a legal authority?

And these questions begged a further set of questions: what were the qualifications of the analysts? Were they mental health professionals? Social Workers? Medical professionals? Did they have doctoral degrees, bachelor’s degrees? What was their expertise about child development, mental illness, or chemical dependency? In the online manual I could find nothing except vague references to “training and experience” followed by lengthy descriptions of analysts’ roles as evaluators of programs, such as detailed instructions as to how to conduct interviews with plaintive residents. Then, with considerably more specificity, I noted a section that described what was required in order to become an administrator of a group home or child care center. Why this contrast, I wondered, and why was it so hard to find information about who was standing in judgment of places like Thunder Road?

In time, significant changes were made, reportedly in adherence to this overseeing body: marathon process groups would be reduced, reassessment assignments renamed to sound less threatening; confrontation group was renamed as “CORE”; ultimately, even the bench, an icon of TC concepts, was retired ignominiously. Meanwhile, terms like "strength-based", "evidence-based", "wellness and recovery" were entering the lexicon and changing the rules. Somewhere along the line, someone, or a set of someones over time, were determining that the protocols hitherto of adolescent treatment and Therapeutic Communities were too rigid in their formulation; too much of an ill-considered echo of adult programs. Pathologizing terms, such as the word "addict" were becoming unfashionable, to be replaced by a sensibility that was more encouraging of the positive; more presumptively inclusive of marginalized populations (women, sexual and ethnic minorities; the acutely dual-diagnosed, the unmotivated) that were not sufficiently represented by a treatment philosophy that characterized clients strictly in terms of their problems. SNAP, an acronym referring to strengths, needs, abilities, and the dubiously termed "preferences", were added to all preliminary treatment plans, and thereafter referenced as an ongoing guideline.

The Humanism-derived Strength-based movement was one that I'd been familiar with for some time, though I'd associated it more with schools and social work than with psychotherapy or substance abuse treatment. I remember reading in the early part of the decade articles that referred to service plans, "wrap around" social services that integrated multi-disciplinary teams, provided "social rehabilitation", and sought to educate consumers about public resources. I thought Thunder Road was achieving this, or was set up to achieve this structure, through its multi-disciplinary treatment planning: through its absorption of educational, medical, and psychotherapeutic viewpoints into treatment plans; through the latter stages of its treatment plans, in which clients were intended to transition back to families and communities, making use of public resources along the way. Client "strengths" were observed in their capacities for creative expression, the exercise of hobbies; in the opportunities for leadership and communal cooperation (the client-driven "behavior modification" system); the spontaneous (versus impulsive) joy found in play; in humor, even dark and sadistic humor. Delpit (1996) cites students' reflections upon Strength-based teachers, using phrases like, "they hold views for us that we could not imagine for ourselves". Originally, I noted the tonal similarity with psychoanalytically-oriented concepts like "real self" or Winnicott's "true self"; Masterson's ideas of "capacities of the self", and thought a compatible ethos was being expressed.

But actually, the treatment focus is markedly different from Psychodynamic, or even Cognitive-Behavioral models, which are cast as deficit-based, and which focus more intently upon destructive behaviors, as well as cognitive or intrapsychic defenses. Researchers like Epstein (2003) observe that Strength-based models, with their emphasis upon marshalling the "unique skills" and resources of youth and families, are more attractive to those who don't ordinarily seek out services. Currently the zeitgeist of models relating to youth, Strength-based approaches are hailed as those which engage mandated youth and families into a treatment process. This seems likely, if not obvious. Those unmotivated for treatment are more likely to be engaged if their abilities are highlighted versus their deficits. No kidding, I'm tempted to reply. Returning to the study of Foster, Nathan, and Ferry (2010), the reader might again consider what truly engages adolescents in programs versus what simply enables their navigation through program hurdles. But the authors of the Australian study also caution that while it may be important to note what participants like or dislike, such factors may not reflect what is effective in addressing problems like drug dependency.

Those touting the Strength-Based approaches assert that they don't ignore problems; that they recognize the difficulties caused by episodic or chronic trauma, for instance. But their focus is upon the resilience of those afflicted, not upon the catalogue of deficits that accompany disturbance. They charge that pathology-based models harangue their clients with their shortcomings. Well, I wonder. It often seemed to me that problems were ignored by those who espoused the Strength-based lens. The adherents of these models, those that I have listened to before, during, and since my time at Thunder Road, seem to turn the tables of treatment: they speak of training staff about the need to work with the unmotivated, about the need to open treatment to all potential comers, including society's most marginalized, if dangerous citizens. Staff members at Thunder Road who believed ardently in the 12-step model, who talked up the virtues of TC concepts, or the necessary standard of abstinence, were starting to feel like wardens of an outdated apartheid system—such was the thread and tendentiousness of management's new rhetoric. All too often, in meetings, and sometimes in front of clients, latter day managers were acting like advocates pleading clemency for ill-treated youth, or else they struck secret bargains with kids and families; pardoning them of negative behaviors, overlooking their resistance to change.

Initially, the rhetoric surrounding the changes was welcomed enthusiastically. Most people are drawn to positive language, not just the intended recipients of care. But implementation of the paradigm shift caused some havoc, with consistency, now assuredly a hobgoblin of smaller minds, being sacrificed to the cause of change and of so-called individualized treatment plans. There was increasing confusion in the ranks. Treatment plans representing clients called for variations in how clients were to be treated; what consequences would be assigned in response to rule infractions; what rewards[38] might be given in the wake of progress. In theory, it sounded great: treating people as individuals speaks to the values of an individualistic society. At the same time, ours is a society whose inhabitants are constantly making comparisons of one another, ever scrutinizing who has what, and who doesn't. Add insecure attachment, as well as a host of other ego deficits—things that actually exist—to the mix, and what you have is a set-up for those feeling unjustly treated to cry foul, to utilize their oppositional tendencies (sorry, their strong, resilient voices) and speak up in protest at what managers sanguinely characterize as "individualized treatment plans."

The splits began to take on a surreal quality: a client known to have assaulted a peer, or relapsed, or humiliated a staff with verbal abuse would, in the same week, be awarded with a title "client of the week" and given a modest prize, presumably because the client's unique skills and strengths needed to be recognized, or because the significance of their behaviors had not been properly understood in the context of PTSD syndromes and other mental health conditions that increasingly held consequence-mitigating currency. A client refusing to take any further part in multi-family group and thus bursting out of its doors would no longer be directed to a bench, or else to wait upon an assignment packet or a removal of privileges, but would rather be told they could lay down in the recreation room, such that they might calm themselves (or more likely, dissociate) watching TV or playing video games with violent themes. An assignment packet would be reduced by half by a vetoing manager; an off-unit pass denied as a result of persistent defiance would be unilaterally re-instated. Clients refusing to come out of their rooms to attend therapy were being excused without meaningful consequences. That insidious phrase, "meet them where they're at" was being used more often, and quickly becoming code for a situation wherein clients were becoming less and less responsible for their treatment. These incidents at Thunder Road weren't unique to the post 2004 era; my episode with Katy, for example, had featured similar breaks in program structure. But those earlier experiences of mine had seemed aberrant—attributable to the quirks of individual personalities and their clashes with particular clients. Now the splits seemed more common; institutionalized, even.

Many staff members, those of the so-called old school variety, plus their allies within psychodynamic circles, objected to the changes, pointing out that these trends reflected professional codependency. This term, more commonly used in TC models to indicate excessive leniency in the face of acting out, rather than, say, an angry, rigid imposition of punishments, was commonly directed at the new practices. Also, the new directives seemed to violate important principles of treatment from a Psychodynamic point of view. While the TC approach was hardly one of therapeutic neutrality, the Strength-based approach seemed to call for a polar opposite bias, one that positioned counselors as apologists for kids. "He's only… (insert age)", staff would often hear, or "You have to remember that…(insert bad historical event justifying suspension of limit-setting)". It continued to be understood in theory that clients were suffering from chronic trauma, impaired selves, defended against by a host of behaviors and unconscious strategies that subverted growth. But you wouldn't know it from the language being used, both about and towards them.

The program now rewarded helplessness, or colluded with inflated self-images. Or else it decided (or someone did) that kids could no longer do what had long been asked of them: the arduous, setback-enduring journey through a three-to-five-tiered stage progression system. Steered away from their traditional roles, staff members were instead being trained to observe the positive and eschew focus on pathology. Shamed from outside into relinquishing containers, Thunder Road started rewarding behavioral regression, opening the doors to contaminating agendas, a vague yet broad need to deny the weight of problems; avoid conflict, that which is "negative" (because it's frightening) and please. Shame on shaming, a Strength-based bumper sticker might have read. With respect to TC haircuts (devaluing language, voice-raising), or the rote use of rhetorically-driven lectures aimed at impassive youth, I was sympathetic. But I also thought there was danger with the so-called positive approach. I think focusing on the positive protects, like denial, from the enormity and scale of difficulties. Of course, that interpretation can't be proven. That isn't evidence-based. What is? Well, studies in peer-reviewed professional journals are, and therefore a basic question is called for: were studies asserting that Strength-based programs produce better outcomes than so-called deficit-based programs?

Not necessarily, though they are undoubtedly becoming more popular. Actually, literature pertaining to efficacy of Strength-based models is inconclusive, while adherents of the model point out that the movement is in its infancy, evolving. Better outcomes? This might mean completion of programs, such as honorable discharges, from programs like Thunder Road, drug courts, and other foster-care-like placements. Or, outcome studies might refer to academic succession: rates of transition to higher grades within the school system. But if such improvement simply means that programs and school programs are becoming more lenient in their approaches, overlooking negative behaviors, drug relapses or violent episodes, then surely the value of these conclusions ought to be questioned. The pedigree of Strength-based programs lies within social services and the educational system, as a set of ideas originally designed for a wide spectrum of youth. It is a model aimed primarily at social workers and teachers, not therapists or substance abuse counselors in residential settings. Judges in drug courts, for example, can wave off relapses of program participants, believing that they are helping suffering, otherwise untreatable addicts whose behaviors are presumptively non-violent, and therefore not an egregious risk to a community[39].

They can wag their fingers at an industry that appears to neglect those hardest hit by drug addiction, those who are the hardest to treat.

But as I have earlier written, leaders of residential settings don't have the luxury of this perspective, and so must take a more stringent position in my opinion. Like parents of an incorrigible child, residential principals cannot simply dismiss struggling participants following an inspired lecture and tell them to come back in a week's time. As a result, I think the application of the Strength-based model to Thunder Road and places like it is an awkward fit; one that has caused a seismic jolt in previously cohesive treatment strategies. Paradoxically, the more lenient, "positive" approach inadvertently creates a more dangerous milieu, by allowing for a less contained, boundary-less, and therefore less safe environment: greater likelihood of substances on the unit; more violence and sexual acting out between peers. The Strength-based movement has led program designers away from traditional therapeutic models, Therapeutic Community Concepts models, in which the single-minded emphasis upon reality testing, limit-setting and containment of destructive behaviors dominates. In essence, the movement inclines adolescent residential programs towards the Harm Reduction philosophy that is meant to accommodate the most difficult of would-be clients.

When you tip a glass to let in water from outside, you might also spill what is inside. As I commented to the clinical director of this period, we could admit clients with less motivation, or lower levels of functioning—more "acute" cases, as it was often put—and we could flex standards such that we'd discharge fewer kids for non-compliance. But we'd see more AWOLs due to the lack of safety, and generate higher burn-out of staff, especially at the levels of front-line staff. Outsiders might bristle at this latter point, and argue that it is the job of anyone poised to work in a place like Thunder Road to gut-check and realize what it takes to work with difficult clients—in succinct terms, *deal with it*. However, stubborn old-school counselors and therapists with thin skins and low wages aren't the only one disaffected by the influx of difficult and destructive clients. So, too, are clients that have long-since experienced the comings and goings of drugs, sexual and violence in their homes and neighborhoods, and until they came to places like Thunder Road (they might have thought), there was nothing they could do about it. These kids deserve to believe that places like Thunder Road will be safe: free of drugs, violence, sexual harassment. They deserve to have a drug and violence free environment to go to in order to get better.

Not all staff members were shaken by the new approaches. Some among staff will have foreseen the difficulties posed by philosophical shifts but put their heads down and got on with their jobs. Determined to keep their jobs, and realistic about the influence of their opinions, some staff members, even some veterans, will have censured a few of their observations. I think some of my colleagues may have rolled with the changes, convincing themselves that times change—all things change—and that 12-step mantras like "focus on self" would carry them through disturbing upheavals. Nonetheless, in my view, a core of staff was feeling disempowered by the undermining not only of their authority, but also of their baseline beliefs. The new changes were sporadically applied, under the new "individualized treatment" heading, which theoretically meant that while some clients might be considered "addicts", others were not. "Individualized treatment" became shorthand for different rules for different clients (but not different treatment groups, apparently). It meant different treatment plans, with different assumptions underlying those plans; it meant lowered expectations for program completion, and as a result caused no little disillusionment for those with long memories. The sporadic infiltration of new Strength-based approaches was necessary for political reasons. Change was gradual. The changes traveled over the tundra of TC concepts like a massive army taking one stretch of field at a time. The managers driving these approaches were patient, politic in nature, and methodical. They took out one policy at a time, one dissenter at a time, and one day at a time, as they'd say in 12-step circles.

A focus on strengths, not deficits

A different view: One program, Our Common Ground in Redwood City, may have experienced a cleaner split between the TC concepts approaches and latter day, Strength-based strategies. Separating from the nationwide program known as Daytop Village in 2005, OCG is situated along a stretch of busy road, sandwiched between commercial properties, strip malls and fast food restaurants. Its entrance looks like the façade of a one-bedroom home that is destined to be squeezed out by corporate development. Inside, what looks like a living room has been converted into a lobby; master bedrooms into meeting spaces and offices. Out back, there's a grassy area, a basketball court, a warehouse for a day school, and a guest house that allows for a segregation of girls versus boys' activities. Further units, which include cafeterias and dorm-style rooms, more closely resemble the milieu of Thunder Road, though its capacity is about a third less, and the 12-step influence of TC models is diminished.

"The kids aren't that into it," explained Dr. Danielle Van Deventer, OCG's Mental Health Director. So whatever slogans, symbols, and steps used to adorn the hallways in the Daytop era, they were fewer now, and modified. Language deemed above the heads of youth has been teenified, rendered less portentous, though NA meetings still occur on site at least once a week. As Dr. Van Deventer gave me a tour of the facility, she reviewed the history of the program, from its establishment as a Daytop facility in 1988 (after having been a retirement home and an AIDS hospice prior to that), to the switch in 2005 to Our Common Ground. She described shifts in staff make-up, sharing that OCG began hiring increasing numbers of license-eligible staff around the same time that Thunder Road was consolidating case management with therapists versus paraprofessional counselors. She discussed the history of Therapeutic Communities, and described the transition from the older, TC concepts approach to the Strength-based model, a "modified" TC, she called it. "I refused to raise my voice at kids," she recalled of her early days at the program, over ten years ago. Describing gratuitously heavy-handed tactics of counselors, she struck a familiar chord with respect to Therapeutic Communities. Like many others, she had found many of the older approaches punitive, even humiliating of clients. Kids, she observed, were being given mindless chores as treatment assignments, instead of more thoughtful interventions, one-on-one or group processes. Some of the TC concepts measures were not only ineffective, she suggested; they were anachronistic. "The kids are changing," she asserted. She noted the ever lowering average age for onset of use;

the seemingly increased proportion of parents with not only active addictions, but also histories of shared use with their sons and daughters. The capacities for reflection, especially upon non-directive, open-ended questions, were severely limited.

As a result, OCG developed strategies of speaking to the positive. "We think of what they're doing right," said Van Deventer. Beyond that, therapists are trained to explain, in plainer, concrete terms, why a negative behavior is inappropriate, perhaps by way of modeling softer emotions, but also drawing attention to relational consequences: "I was sad to hear that you'd gotten in a fight with a peer," might be said to a client, for example. Therapist self-disclosure, of feelings versus personal stories, seemed to be encouraged, and staff members are trained to be authoritative, but not authoritarian. Not all TC concepts tools were expunged, however. The hierarchical system of self-governance, alongside a treatment milieu that emphasized accountability, has been retained at OCG. But Dr. Van Deventer compared talking to many of their clients to exchanges with small children. Such was the speculative arrest of so many of their residents. And that's the irony of the approach. It's not so much that client deficits are ignored; it's that the problems are so painfully apparent, so numerous, and so overwhelming. They are like elephants in the rooms—undislodgable.

And the thing is this: there are reasons why people both in and out of their professional roles refrain from naming the elephants. It feels bad; it can squash hope. At Thunder Road, I rarely thought we were squashing hope with our attention to problems. Though some may have used crude, overbearing methods, the naming of problems, explicitly or implicitly via the imposition of limits or the withholding of privileges, had always seemed salutary to me. I came to accept this somewhere between 1996 and 1998, and was still accepting it as late as 2011. In fact, I think my opinions solidified. I don't think the essentials changed. That "kids are changing" declaration: I'd heard that from Randy Snowden also, and he was reflecting on changes between the mid-eighties to the mid-nineties, not from the last decade. Other colleagues of mine have made similar pronouncements as their tenures matured. Commenting on the social trends seemed to be the prerogative of those working in this field, and with respect to drugs, adolescents, mental health problems, or family dysfunction, I came across few who would assert that things were getting better, regardless of the era in which they worked.

Changes in the rules

From where I was positioned, program cohesion was getting worse, not better. Disconnections between warring philosophies seemed to manifest in increasing inconsistencies in how rules were being applied. The rhetoric of one approach could be invoked to veto the rationales of another, and matters of reassessment, bench time, off-site passes, and stage progression became muddier, and what seemed like client progress to one staff might seem like regression to another. Who won the argument? Whoever was in charge at any given time. Staff A could invoke terms like "accountability" or "limit setting", or "boundaries" to justify an intervention that may be deemed too punitive in other quarters. Staff B, with authority or positioning (a sort of "who is available when" principle), might undermine those interventions, and break out their own lexicon of rationales: "supporting growth", "positive reinforcement", "boosting self-esteem".

Across the gender divide, inconsistencies became so glaring that it became difficult to think of the kids as living under the same roof—not that they should be, necessarily. Staff members unfortunate enough to be assigned shifts on either side of the facility, on alternate nights, often felt themselves trapped in the crossfire of this broken mirror, looking to negotiate rules that appeared to have different interpretations in separate quarters of the building. Examples of this centered about phone calls that clients were allowed to make to people outside of the program, and recreation time that was afforded boys versus girls. Girls, it seemed, were consistently being given more phone calls during the week than boys. Why? No one seemed to have a definitive answer, and the director of the period merely shrugged and re-iterated the basic rule that all clients should receive the same number of telephone coupons per week. That was the solution: re-state the policy and then disengage, leaving staff to attend to the rest. It may have been policy, but it wasn't the reality. Meanwhile, boys seemed to enjoy advantages related to recreation time, whether that was a preferential allocation of weight room time, or the tendency to use the parking lot/basketball court as an impromptu scene for an intervention.

More fire extinguisher moments: I pestered my supervisor, that director, with questions on these matters, wondering if there was an actual policy in place. She was preoccupied with precarious census counts, overdue documentation, or the potential emergencies confronting the hospital and not these petty matters about clients and their phone calls or recreation time. In the vacuum of insight, I offered my own: girls were simply more insistent about their need for verbal succor from peers and family, and were willing to go to greater lengths (even abase themselves) to obtain telephone privileges[40]. Boys, meanwhile, were more insistent about use of the weight room, the outdoor basketball court, or the latest video-game playing machine. Therefore, online staff would get bullied into providing phone coupons (the means of tracking # of calls outgoing), or else shamed by a collective audience manipulatively pointing out that "support" seeking was central to the program's message. Those plaintive female clients, at times reduced to tears, should be allowed to speak to those they loved, it was said. Boys were more likely to converge on staff and argue that exercise of limbs and fingers (video games) was critical, an unparalleled coping tool at times of stress. If you were a single staff member working on the girls' side on a Friday night, confronted with argument by a chorus of teenage girls shrieking, you might bend a rule to avoid being cast as an uncaring staff. If you were a female staff looking for a one-on-one with a male client, you might be sulked at and given the intrusive mom treatment for not giving permission to go out and play. Male staff members were often cowed by feminine tantrums, tearful outpourings. Boys were at least easier to disappoint on the matter of phone calls or recreation time. Boys, who tended to respond with tantrums of a restricted emotional range, therefore eliciting more indignation than sympathy, were easier to dismiss with curt refusals.

Few would admit this, but many among staff seemed to prefer working with the boys than with the girls. Some attribute this to the traditionally masculinized approach to treatment, as observed by authors such as Kasl (1992). Boys could be treated in the traditional manner more readily, with less of a stigma attached to the supposedly stigmatizing labels of "addict", "dope fiend", "tweaker", and other epithets that were semi-lovingly thrown about the unit, at least prior to the hegemony of Strength-based interventions. Boys could be confronted, pathologized, and contained with words like "accountability" and "ownership", coupled with the vernacular; these were words (and a manner of speaking) that spoke to a manly psychology: *handle your business*. On the girls' side, words like "empowerment", designed to push back against victim pathology, was prominent: gender politics inflected the language of staff. Talk about preferences, or what's attractive to kids. Note the ready assimilation of responsibility themes, the ubiquitous "nah, this is on me", or "it's (meaning treatment) down to me" proclamations of males; the "I need to stand up for myself", affirmations coached in girls. In either case, the gentleman—and the ladies, for that matter—doth protest an implied aspiration: independence.

Or sanctuary. Conscious of the striking rates of physical and sexual abuse to which the girls in the program had been subjected, staff members, particularly male staff members, tended to shy away from a presence on the girl's side, which often left those assigned to that territory feeling alone and vulnerable. In fact, with rare exception, male therapists were assigned exclusively to male clients, while it was very common for female therapists to be assigned to work with boys. This, some might argue, was simply a matter of demographics: many more boys than girls come to the attention of the juvenile justice system; meanwhile, the professions of psychotherapy and social work, at least at the practitioner level, are heavily weighted in favor of women. The reader may do the math. With respect, I think the feminist observers have it backwards, and the residential milieu reflects societal norms: the group home, with emphasis upon *home*, ultimately reflects the dominion of women (despite the macho air), leaving girls straining for absent masculine attention, and boys prying themselves from the care of women[41]. Layers of anxiety exist: a semi-conscious fear of placing girls in the care of men, while the converse scenario reflects the single-parent reality of a generation of young males.

In working with the girls in particular, staff members were at least as conscious of trauma as they were of addiction, and actual accounts or just speculations of trauma both informed and confounded treatment plans, again undermining the confrontation of acting out behaviors (they needed "space", the ambiguously-termed "support", not confrontation). The structure of treatment, with its benches and other limit-setting devices, was set up for group participation, confrontational approaches, and punishments meted out for all kinds of infractions. This was becoming increasingly problematic for staff both influenced by victim advocates, and contending with those who suffered from PTSD symptoms. Klein (1989) explains that techniques such as confrontation are contraindicated for those presenting with early development patterns of abuse, or serial separations from caregivers. Confrontation runs the risk of re-traumatizing clients, as the manner and context of the technique invariably triggers associations with past abuses[42]. Early caretakers had been confrontational; that is, critical of their children's behavior. Klein appears to echo Kohut & Wolf (1978), who similarly cautioned against the overstimulation of what they termed the *overburdened self*, although Kohut and Wolf seem more concerned with insight than confrontation. Pointing out that many patients lack self-soothing capacities, they warned that pouring too much insight into such individuals, especially all at once, poses these patients with an excessive task. Short (2005), writing about the importance of the therapist's continuing empathic presence, offers a nuanced tact, arguing for the mentalizing of patients' projections, simple reflections of that which elicits dissociation, such as the following "I" statement: "when I said that, I think it confused you, hurt you." Note the absence of criticism: the potential distortion of the patient—the "hurt you"—is cited as a passive event, with the neutral therapist neither accepting nor dispelling the role of perpetrator. I think that Short is suggesting that at times of strong affective arousal (such as a client/patient's melt-down within a milieu?) therapists are best advised to not call attention to the projective aspects of the patient's experience.

Confronting confrontation

The assimilation of concern for victims culminated in a directive from yet another Thunder Road clinical director around 2008. Confrontation, she fervently announced, was to be replaced by the word "challenge", and given a meaning that once again emphasized a client's strengths, their inner resources rather than their deficits. This meant that interventions were to be prefaced not only with encouragements, but also compliments, delivered in soothing tones. In hearing examples of these proposed interventions, many felt as though we were stepping into a fantasy, with *Alice In Wonderland* connotations. Or, if not *AIW*, then maybe *Goldilocks*: "this method has too much confrontation and pathology", to which someone might reply, "this method has too little." Anyway, in the new atmosphere, attention to problems was being replaced by placatory efforts, which often seemed insincere to me. As much as I was able to insinuate myself into the discussions, I questioned whether something was being missed amid the battling rhetoric. I felt sure that existing models for intervention were being misrepresented, and that ultimately, language from different approaches could be reconciled; that in the end of the day, we were saying the same things.

But we weren't saying the same things. Not quite, anyway. The problem, I asserted, was not with the word "confrontation", but rather with people's projections onto that concept. It seemed that many confused the idea of confrontation with intensity, with those hair-raising interventions of an earlier era, many of which had indeed seemed heavy-handed and unnecessary. However, the baseline purpose of confrontation had remained the same: attention drawn to reality; to the negative consequences of self-destructive behaviors, previously outlined and understood as the bedrock of an original therapeutic alliance, and most importantly, girded by an implied belief in the individual's capacity to grow. Confrontation is not about voice raising or the use of devaluing language. That confrontation should be flavored with compassion ought to be a given. Secondly, confrontation isn't simply an aspect of psychoeducation: many confrontations don't so much introduce dissonant information as much as they remind individuals of previously stated goals, and ways in which up-to-date behaviors compromise progress towards those goals: "You say you want to get clean and manage your anger better, yet you continue to use (drugs) and justify abusive outbursts in the community". Confrontation can draw attention to ambivalence, but this is not just about drug use or the decision to AWOL. On a deeper level, confrontation is an intervention that proceeds from a bond between therapist and client; it represents an understanding of who the client is amid the defensive swirl; it exhibits a determination to not let a person flounder[43].

Confrontation itself, I argued, was being pathologized, and misrepresented as a tool that merely upbraided the resistant thinking of those who didn't want to quit drugs, while retraumatizing those with fragile coping skills. Lumped together with notions of TC haircuts, confrontation was imbued with an umbrella meaning, and was being looked down upon as a crude and didactic tool—the obsolete choice of insensitive TC dinosaurs. The people extending this view were stereotyping, basically, and I found the ignorance that accompanied these discussions appalling. For one thing, the narrowed contexts of substance use and trauma that many drew upon was a major obstacle: opponents of confrontation often fail to address the many subtle and sometimes not-so-subtle ways in which individuals defend themselves, blame others, assert helplessness, or otherwise withdraw into defensive compliance. Furthermore, many overlook the tendency of the traumatized to act not only as victims, but also as victimizers. Anyone who has sat with a self-proclaimed trauma victim will have experienced the abusive manner in which such patients can draw attention to their own victimization. For some, the identification is so strong that the possibility of hurting another seems (to them) inconceivable.

Those opposing me at Thunder Road blinked as though straining to take in opposition. It was like being back in those overcrowded multi-family Groups, staring down stubborn fathers who looked back at me with sullen complaints expressed through their eyes: this guy is *trippin'*. Confrontation was being decried in the literature, my colleagues insisted: that was the word; that was the decree. But there had been no deconstruction of confrontation's true meaning, I replied. No one had transcripts. No one was citing examples. That fuller, nuanced conversation was getting blocked in favor of a strictly rhetorical, less time-consuming exchange. The evidence-based sound-bites my colleagues cited hadn't bothered with important questions: that when assessing the emotional state of patient/client, it was surely necessary to distinguish between a traumatized re-experiencing versus an instance of acting out born of some other disorder. Those making pronouncements at a distance from the clinical scenarios didn't see the blurring of roles: the projections that spun chaotically in therapeutic exchanges; ways in which victims become victimizers, crying foul, crying out in pain as they stand upon adversaries' necks. One thing was agreed upon: empathy. Everyone agreed that all interventions, involving confrontation or not, must contain empathy.

However, empathy is not the same thing as encouragement, even though encouragement may be helpful at times. I became pedantic: the task with the traumatized, with the impulsive and the dissociated, was to have them feel contained and understood, not merely gratified, or else falsely reassured. The kids to whom staff were referring in these strategic meetings had experienced many false reassurances in their lives, alternating with hurtful put-downs—usually from frustrated adults who wanted their children to simply calm down, as much for their own peace of mind as that of their children. Kids who report that they were repeatedly abused earlier in childhood, and further suggest that they merited such treatment because they are *bad*, are often told by social workers or counselors something like, "It's not your fault. You didn't create the problem." I don't have an objection per se to this kind of intervention, especially if something like this statement is aimed at pre-teens who have never considered that idea, or those who can't seem to mentalize. But with teenagers, especially, I'm biased towards a response that respects the emergent and not irrevocably destroyed abilities of the individual: a modestly confrontational, "was it your fault?" interruption which shapes the possibility that distantly past and recent events can be re-evaluated, but doesn't simply give the *right* answer.

The argument against confrontation also made the assumption that behaviors being confronted were *a priori* negative or destructive, such as relapse, violence, or program rule infractions. This was another narrow point of view, another misunderstanding view, for it seemed that no one had a problem confronting the beliefs of a kid who protected abusive parents, or who said things like, "I feel dumb. I'm never gonna be good at anything." In response to this defeatist talk, the average counselor would leap into confrontation and say something like, "Now, why do you beat up on yourself like that. Don't you see that you have many positive qualities," challenging the presumably faulty thinking, largely because the content—self-denigration—was meant to be confronted in the name of boosting clients' ego strength. Few at Thunder Road, particularly during the latter day Strength-based period, would rebuke this kind of intervention, managers or floor counselors.

And yet there is potential for regression in the above exchange. The problem in this scenario is that of a defensive (that is, potentially manipulative) function in the client's "I'm no good at anything" statement, or an unconsciously defensive maneuver wherein staff members feel drawn into clients' projection of a soothing, protective figure. A client that has suffered a set-back (even a relapse), and is prone to negative self talk may benefit from confrontation, but one that poses the question back to client, such that they might do their own reflecting. Who are we to say this is not possible? I suggest that a client who is engaging in argument to deflect responsibility and elicit caretaking is not helped by a therapist who is simply looking to counter such negative self-statements, especially if that same therapist is unwittingly soothing their own anxieties in the process.

I share modest sympathy with writers like Durrant (1993) and Maran (2003) who have argued that because programs have weighed too heavily the pathology of clients—the problemitizing of their lives—clients and families are left defending themselves against a demoralizing onslaught of criticism, and therefore struggle to engage with some providers. I can imagine that countless numbers of parents who have participated in drug rehab programs have felt the tacit sting of a counseling team's disapproval. From my point of view, perspectives of clients and families bore out the observations of attachment researchers, who track dismissive, preoccupied, and unresolved states of mind with respect to attachment; pathological bonding, the "identifications" with aggressors or abandoning figures that mark so many kids' insecure bonds. These were the realities that I saw in the program; the problems that needed to be assessed, and then named. There has to be a way to draw attention to problems in a respectful way, one that is attuned to the real needs of individuals, without simply replacing confrontation with forced attempts to placate and reassure.

In time, this matter would be rendered moot by the fact that reality asserted itself, and clients continued to act out in all the usual ways. It was therefore ever necessary to stop normal activities from time to time, call for a contract breaking session, and root out the wrongdoing and wrongdoers, regardless of whether we called it confrontation, or "challenging", or some other euphemism. This must have been frustrating for those searching for "what they're doing right" opportunities. Anyway, sometimes it is important to say to addicts, the well and even not-so-well defended, some version of *I don't believe you*, when they are acting out and then denying that behavior. I continued to assert (as did many others) that effective confrontation relied upon the solidity of the bond between staff member and client, a bond that begins with a sound introduction of behavioral limits; upon the timing of an intervention, and its attunement to the stated goals of the individual being addressed. I tended to argue that confrontations ought to start with empathetic statements and I'd sometimes correct therapists who thought they understood me, but habitually led with statements of problem-solving, reassurance or encouragement, thinking these qualities alone constituted an understanding approach.

Timing

The quality of timing is often referenced by teachers of psychotherapy as a key ingredient of a therapeutic relationship; the sine qua non of the skilled interventionist. But everyone has different ideas it seems about what constitutes a good intervention at supposedly ripe moments of therapy. Some assert that a good intervention is one timed to provide a useful reframe—a shift in perspective—for one locked in a maladaptive thought pattern, such that they might experience an "ah-hah" moment in close proximity to maladaptive thoughts. Others might observe that moments of emotional or environmental triggers, so-called, ought to be isolated, understood, and tackled with coping strategies that steer the vulnerable person from a slippery path, or feeling states that may overwhelm. Others still, speak of letting clients proceed unabated in their process, more or less free associating, perhaps even flooding with emotion, without intrusion upon affect-laden disclosures.

Schiller (2010) has produced experiments suggesting that timing, regardless of the style, is of paramount importance in the success of an intervention. In her study, human subjects took part in what may seem to have been an old-fashioned behavioral experiment: individuals were shown colored squares (CS) paired with electric shocks to the wrists, while physiological reactions were measured via skin conductance response technology (SCR). On the day following this trial, the group of subjects was to undergo an extinction exercise wherein the (CS) would be paired with no shock. The experiment called for a control group to be given a (CS) "reminder"—a CS paired with a shock—ten minutes prior to the extinction exercise. The ten minute period was dubbed a reconsolidation window. Then, on the day after that, another trial experiment was conducted, with subjects exposed to the CS, again without the accompanying shock. However, the control group subjects consistently exhibited no SCR, in contrast to their counterparts who had not received the CS reminder. Yet another trial, conducted a year later, repeated these same results, leading to some interesting interpretations. Gorman and Roose (2011), for example, point to the study as an indicator that timing of interventions (from their standpoint, interpretations) must exist in proximity to reactivation of trauma material in order to block consolidation of maladaptive response, and to allow for a re-writing of a traumatic narrative through a therapeutic discourse.

I'm inclined to think of these studies as affirmations of the "here and now" or proximity principle. The "here and now" idea calls for a therapist to be alert to cues, to verbal and non-verbal content, to recall past memories of a client, and to bring those elements into the moment, so that learning, perhaps of unconscious material, can be achieved. Upon the back of a solid bond and a consistent practice of concerned curiosity, a therapist can even confront or interpret material that may seem threatening to a client, and either "hold" or sustain the feeling of anxiety, without having to model flight through avoidance, or "fight" through an indignant, heavy-handed approach. Furthermore, the idea of a "window" allows for some flexibility; space for misunderstanding prior to figuring out—the reality that before emotionally charged material makes sense, a spell of being lost might be necessarily traversed. In this window, there is room for a time-out (perhaps even a few minutes sat on a bench) before a reconsolidation can occur. What is important is that the age-old habits of addictive families, traumatized and disordered systems, are not allowed to fossilize their distortions over time: over weeks, months, years, even generations.

As to the controversy around confrontation, that supervisor promoting a shift in vocabulary heard me and didn't hear me in quick succession. In truth, neither she nor anyone else seemed to have the time or inclination for a nuanced discussion of the matter. Therefore, staff brainstormed these matters in a maddeningly tangential fashion, with principals of opposing views ever speaking past one another. I stopped short of insinuating codependency on this director's part, but it got worse when she ventured past the issue of confrontation and began using terms like customer service. The word customer, at first, appeared to refer to collateral contacts—the funding sources with whom we seemed to be cultivating an obsequious relationship. Among other things, they seemed to be directing our admissions policy, or near enough. Increasingly, I'd hear of probation departments and social services all but insisting we accept placements into the program, regardless of the appropriateness of any given individual. I could just about accept the director's use of the term customer when referencing these referring parties, for it seemed they were just that—customers. But when she started using this term in reference to clients and their parents, I just about lost my cool. In the spirit of customer service, rules once maintained with consistency started falling like dominoes—rules for clients as well as their family members, as if they, too, were running the program.

Off-site passes were a particular bone of contention. Determining that clients had rights to leave the program for various reasons, management began granting passes simply because they were being demanded, with little consideration for the risks involved. A decade earlier, clients had been denied attendance at family funerals because of the risk of runaways and relapses (also, violent altercations often occurred at these funerals). Seemingly hardline decisions had been made in the service of client safety. Now clients who were obviously irreligious were heading off-site with family members, supposedly to attend church. Girls were excused to be bridesmaids at family weddings; to sign up for classes ahead of an upcoming school semester. So, what's wrong with that? you might ask. Many did, but without considering that these were typical of the kinds of obligations that had been sacrificed in the furtherance of a drug-using lifestyle. What lesson did it provide to excuse a client from not only the consequences of their progressively worsening behavior, but also from even a contemplation of those past decisions? My point: rewards kill reflection. Deepening, remorse, and acceptance happen in the wake of loss, not gratification. That's an old school axiom of treatment perhaps, akin to Masterson's assertion that rewards enable regressions. Besides, widening the criteria for allowing passes increased the likelihood of contraband being brought to the unit, as searches of clients' bodies and belongings were largely un-rigorous due to lack of training of an ever volatile turnover of staff.

Therapists were now directed to make multiple calls per week to clients' parents, no matter how intrusive they may have been, such that parental anxiety might be assuaged, and to negotiate the details over the aforementioned passes, the transition of clothes and other belongings, so that everyone—clients, parents, Thunder Road—could avoid the upset caused by problems. Avoidance: that was becoming the treatment strategy. Staff members were becoming afraid of client anger, wary of customer complaints; the potential threat of violence or maybe law suits. Perhaps refunds following relapses were being mooted. Attending to the various client demands on a constant basis altered the basic relationship between client and therapist, in my view. The changes contaminated the treatment, turned therapists into messengers, mediators of trivial disputes, or mere brokers of gatherings. Therapy appointments could be made with families, but not met, with impunity for the individuals involved. "Flexibility" was becoming a disingenuous by-word with a parent late or absent for any appointment, not boundaries.

The whole ethos of treatment shifted: customer service means saying things along the lines of "I'm sorry for your inconvenience, let's see if we can fix that for you." The therapeutic intervention is more like, "I see that you're angry, let's see if we can figure out what that reaction is about and also see if we can solve this problem." The differences are crucial and multi-layered, and I don't think non-clinicians (in many cases, policy makers) understand the differences. Therefore, managers were habitually striking impromptu bargains with family members, overruling clinical staff that had diligently counseled families about the importance of their participation. Invoking the flexibility mantra, a Saturday floor manager would grant full visiting to a parent that had missed required activities, and who had cited work or other supposedly unforeseeable conflicts. The activities stopped being required, in effect. Meanwhile, the only conflicts in these scenarios were the ones being habitually avoided. These parents that maneuvered their way around program structure: they had impassively heard the rules and structure outlined upon admission; they knew from experience how to maneuver within systems. They'd been doing it for years with schools, social services, employers and drug courts. They promised compliance up front but reserved their resistance for later times, when loop holes in the system had been cunningly assessed.

Claiming that which had been promised by case managers, who were often not around during visiting times, the splitting ruses started working and as a result, patterns of manipulation were reinforced. Flexibility indeed. The team approach was fostering increased instances of splitting, team fragmentation. The solution to this problem was to ignore it, and before long the term splitting seemed to become archaic; shuffled off to a TC concepts museum alongside benches, dusty hospital scrub shirts, image breakers and old man Bobby's suspenders. If nearby the case managers might have intervened with the visiting day arguments, but increasingly they weren't available for these kinds of situations. The availability of case managers, to collateral contacts, to the electronic pull of computer screens, and not the kids in the program was of supreme importance, meaning therapists were sometimes even missing group therapy sessions in order to complete documents, or to meet with collateral contacts who sometimes visited the facility without bothering to make appointments. I'd never been asked to compromise my direct duties to clients—certainly not spontaneously—when I was a case manager. Some kids, meanwhile, complained that they were hardly getting to speak to their therapists. Were they customers? Clients? Consumers? Patients? Kids? I wasn't sure what to call them any more.

In a meeting facilitated by another manager, I finally told my supervisor, the clinical director, that she was acting like a hotel manager, not a director; that she seemed concerned with actions akin to comping rooms and supplying free bottles of champagne to guests. The woman looked bewildered, as though my complaints had been spoken in Latin. The mediating manager looked on stoically, seemingly fascinated by the kind of fractured dispute that he perhaps saw happening throughout the program. I later apologized for the insult, but not for my position. Meanwhile, my diatribe was a flea biting at a dog's ass, and the march towards a customer service approach continued relentlessly onwards. I think, in retrospect, this director felt like she was between a rock and a hard place: secretively sympathetic to clinical argument, but answerable to a newer, more business-like authority. I felt frozen out, obsolete. I thought wistfully of that imperious former administrator. All of a sudden I wanted him to return, straighten us out, sit us all on a bench and tell us what's what. A fantasy? A dinosaur? The few that remained who recalled the approaches of yesteryear were similarly struck dumb by the changes; they tuned out, and were stilled into submission like a manufacturer of slide-rules that hadn't noted the arrival of digital technology. The issues, it has to be said, were complicated: they involved economics, shifting notions of how to treat chemical dependency in conjunction with co-occurring psychiatric disorders; of how to treat adolescents, girls versus boys; the mandated versus the seemingly self-motivated; diffuse ideas around cultural diversity; the naïve principle that expanding treatment teams necessarily improves care; the even more insipid notion that volumes of rote progress notes will enable effective public oversight.

Motivational Interviewing and Dialectical Behavior Therapy

Enter the treatment orientations of Motivational Interviewing (MI) and Dialectical Behavior Therapy (DBT). Motivational Interviewing, a term coined in the eighties, had been developed by the early nineties as a technique directed not only at substance users, but more generally at those who were resistant to the problematizing of supposedly negative behavior; people, like most of Thunder Road's clientele, who were mandated into treatment. At first glance, I thought the approach might resemble a Rogerian tact, with therapist/interviewers striking a genial, neutral position, asking a pattern of questions designed to instill (perhaps unconsciously) what are called "discrepancies", or thoughts that do not align with a resistant stance. MI practitioners lead with empathy, patiently encircle an interviewee's defensive position; they "roll" with a subject's externalizations, the cast of others who are to blame for even the suggestion of problems. MI teaches that practitioners not confront these likely distortions, but rather steer with their questions, a focus upon the individual's point of view, his or her feelings on the matters in question. Therefore, the technique is sort of semi-directive, unlike the otherwise similar Rogerian strategy, and designed for many who are at an early, so-called precontemplative stage of change.

I'd first become aware of Motivational Interviewing while I was coordinator of IOP. First described by William Miller and Stephen Rollnick in the early 80's, it has since become a widely heralded technique in chemical dependency circles[44]. After a succession of trainings at various locations, I was largely impressed with the technique, and thought its application to my then role with unmotivated teens was particularly apt. Utilizing the method allowed me to be my naturally inquisitive self: I could make circuitous, interested queries, presenting as neutral—concerned but not an advocate—as to whether my clients were addicts, or alcoholics. I could "roll" with the resistances, except for the UA refusals and the not-coming-on-time thing, be reflective in my thinking, empathetic in my approach; ride the path wherein clients invariably posited whatever problems existed outside of themselves, at the feet of parents, teachers, and probation officers. Then I'd ask my favorite questions, sometimes with my own spin upon the method, such as "what do you think ought to happen (with respect to, say, drinking)" and further inquire as to what clients noticed as to the effects of their drug use and other behaviors that seemed to draw attention. Other questions in the approach seemed similar to those that call for individuals' mentalizing capacities, as characterized by Fonagy: "What do you think they were noticing?" or "how do you think that impacted others?" in the sense of how others' felt, or what they thought. In IOP, since I was addressing behavior that almost exclusively happened outside of the program walls, the approach seemed appropriate. Furthermore, the duration of the program, eight weeks, seemed conducive to a process largely focused around questions and answers.

As a clinical supervisor to those working in the residential component, I was more skeptical. Though appreciative of MI, I thought it an awkward fit with a behavior modification approach, and from 2004 to 2008, roughly, I'd not yet any reason to believe that this treatment approach were under threat, from outside or within. The behavior modification system hardly offered a neutral position as to what was negative behavior. The quasi-religious term, Cardinal rules, had once made that clear enough. Furthermore, the prevailing bias of staff was that clients were indeed drug addicts and/or alcoholics, and the 12-step literature assigned to clients repeatedly addressed the problem of denial, which further implied staff's position. Against this backdrop, it would have been difficult for any staff member working within the larger treatment team, to present as neutral, or merely querulous with respect to substance use. Thirdly, the processes of confrontation group, contract breaking, and such measures as room searches, put paid to any suggestion of neutrality with respect to drug use, violence, or sexual acting out. How could a therapist exude neutrality on these matters a day after having ploughed through a client's room with latex gloves, looking for contraband?

Motivational Interviewing spoke most directly to the *meet them where they're at* principle, and in this respect seemed compatible with the “unique skills” focus of Strength based models. MI adherents neither presumed a comprehensive motivation for treatment nor a pathological defiance of it. From the point of view of this philosophy, practitioners adjust to a reality wherein commitment levels of admits are tenuous at best. They don’t assert that drugs, violence, or risky sexual behaviors are threatening individuals’ lives; they ask clients what *they* think the consequences are, and build up from there. Other treatment approaches, such as Cognitive Behavior Therapy, and especially Psychodynamic practices, may require a therapeutic alliance born of strong motivation on the part of the client; a conviction of belief within the institutions that support treatment. Even 12-step principles, the stalwart ideas that formed the foundation of chemical dependency treatment, assert the need for the afflicted to be truly motivated for change. *Attraction not promotion*, reads the tradition. However, despite this principle, the truth is that thousands of people across the nation are ordered by courts into substance abuse treatment every year, with little or no interest in the 12-step notion of sobriety, much less any particular model of psychotherapy. This, say the practitioners of Motivational Interviewing, is a huge problem facing providers and the principle reason that abstinence-based programs or so-called confrontational approaches are ineffective.

Still, MI, no more or less than Strength-based treatment strategies, doesn’t’ have answers for those impasses that are endemic to a residential setting designed to separate drug users from their lifestyles and therefore contain escalation of problems. What are the suggested interventions for the here and now disputes as to whether a forbidden behavior has even occurred; where the premises of the everyday therapist-to-client exchanges are even challenged? Meaning: clients in residential settings typically deny problematic behaviors long before they are willing to discuss their meanings; therefore contract breaking and confrontation groups. Such conflicts at Thunder Road mirrored the more natural battle lines that were being drawn across America on a nightly basis. Somewhere a parent is staying up late, anxious to confront their acting out teen that has violated curfew by several hours. The parent will confront the teen as they sneak in, demand to know if drinking or drugging has occurred, and insist that *contracts* as to who they were with be revealed. The defensive teen might blow mint-refreshed breath onto the parent's face, grimace in an inimitably teen fashion, and then wave their parent away. At the other end of the spectrum, there are teens who stroll through their homes' front doors with little resistance because they know their parent is oblivious, asleep on a couch in front of a blaring television with a smelly bong by their side. In these instances, as in so many confrontations between drug users, addicts and their codependent others, the denial is not so much of the extent or meaning of drug use, but of the very existence of it. These are watershed *gotcha* moments wherein shame reigns, and denial saves faces.

Maybe some of those parents ought to have rolled with resistance, asked reservedly at two in the morning whether keeping such hours was consistent with academic goals, or the preference for not being date raped, assaulted, or killed by drunk drivers. In recent years, I have taught supervisees my informal three-tiered system (one I'd devised at the McAlister group home, actually) of client denial, based upon the weight of staff/parental evidence: 1.) simple, or flat, denial: deny what is said to have happened ("No way, staff is trippin' "); 2.) blame: attribute behavior to harshness of program/society rules; impute that others ought not inspire rebellion through such restrictive measures ("This place is making me wanna use drugs!"), and 3.) minimize: a variation on #2, dispute the importance of the problem in the first place ("So what, marijuana should be legal anyway"). MI techniques could address the latter two tiers; it could "roll with" the resistances of blame or minimization, and stir a worthy therapeutic conversation in the spirit of therapeutic neutrality. But its techniques could do little with the problem of flat denial, or the past-denying defense of a flight into health, or help work through the underlying dynamic of shame. For many, the straightforward insertion of secrets and lies was a pervasive strategy; one that so many clients kept as a default position.

The government two cents

Shavelson (2001) cites a February 2000 report by the U.S. Department of Health Services that alerted drug rehabilitation programs across the nation to the need for dealing with the deeper psychological agonies that make it difficult for addicted individuals to maintain a clean and sober lifestyle[45]. The reference proceeds from the writer's experience following an early recovering addict who repeatedly relapses, leading to program failures, criminal behaviors, and incarceration. The relapses are characterized as inexplicable save for speculation around unresolved childhood abuse issues that were not addressed as part of the individual's treatment plan. This episode in Shavelson's book, and the Department of Health's report, highlight the need for drug counselors and psychotherapists to work together to contend with the underlying disorders that afflict substance abusers, but they don't necessarily further the discussion of how psychotherapy might integrate with drug rehabilitation services. For example, it's not clear from the findings whether clinical attention to childhood abuse should happen concurrently with early relapse prevention techniques, or whether such a focus should proceed from a threshold period of sobriety. Secondly, they don't solve the problem of how to maintain a clean and safe environment in a residential program if residents are relapsing on drugs.

In my own reading of the federal department's report, I note its recognition of limited resources preventing many from accessing treatment—a limitation the report places at the door of managed care systems that typically limit number of patient visits. It states that for many who need care, "mental problems" are not addressed adequately, if at all. Here, the term "mental problems" seems inadequate, as though psychological disorders of all kinds were being coalesced under a careless umbrella term.[46] Furthermore, by attending to trauma, it's not clear whether this call to action refers to a strictly teleological assessment. Are practitioners meant to offer palliative measures to those suffering from symptoms such as panic attacks or nightmares, as those symptoms are delineated in the DSM IV, or diagnostic standards manual, as produced by the American Psychiatric Association? Or, are programs meant to rigorously train counselors and therapists to recognize more subtle indicators of dissociation in clients, such as what the World Health Organization describes as "the failure to integrate past and present memories" (Schore, 2005), and manage their own feelings of distress in such situations such that traumatic re-enactments can be appropriately addressed? I wonder if programs will have known what to do with the report's findings, or any research for that matter. The study resonates with my own belief that programs like Thunder Road and others cast a skeptical eye upon psychotherapists; that administrators and program directors seem ever unsure of how to make use of their skills.

Again, over the last decade management at Thunder Road seemed increasingly resistant to perceiving clients as shame-based, face-saving, or beset with deep-rooted problems—at least not problems that treatment would address in a comprehensive, truly individualized fashion. It seemed to absolve the treatment teams of a broad responsibility in these areas, in favor of a more pedestrian, not to mention utilitarian, symptom-driven approach; a kind of treatment populism, designed to please the consumer, steer clear of the difficult and literally ignore some problems, like behaviorists looking to extinguish bad behavior. Have the customer keep coming back. According to Pazaratz (2009), the high demand for services, or the attempt to meet too many or too diverse service needs, has led to a reduction of clinical parameters, and a reductionist approach. And they keep coming back, the customers. Why would they return? Because when change isn't internalized, symptoms return, basically. Maybe not in three months; maybe not even before one of those six or twelve month follow-up surveys that track outcomes and inform evidence-based pronouncements. But symptoms return.

Responsive to outside influences, especially Community Care Licensing, Public Health departments and third party payers, the management team maintained a steady campaign, ever lacing their directives with reminders about clients' positive attributes, the changes that would be observable, not so much over time, but simply during the course of treatment, and perhaps shortly thereafter. Their rhetoric continued to bristle against the imputing of denial to anyone resistant to a therapeutic process; it decried pathologizing as well as allegedly demeaning language, called for services to be rendered more accessible to adolescents as if they were a newly elected victim group. With a sympathy born of years of perspective, Armando Corpus reflected upon the roles of outsiders, the industry overseeing officials. On the one hand, he seemed to acknowledge on their behalf an impossible job: the task of collating the collective wisdom of professionals across disciplines, not to mention generations and cultural divides. On the other hand, he seemingly attributed to all involved a kind of acting out upon the dilemmas of treatment: "If we are going to play a losing game, then so are you."

12-step language would either be dumbed down or else stripped of its weighty implications. Powerlessness? Kids apparently winced at this term, according to some. *Unmanageability*? They didn't know what it meant. They thought the language of 12-step, of psychotherapy, was uncool, and by the way, who knows what that word means? Whether Strength-based approaches would prove more effective or not, everyone agreed they were less offensive to the customer. And that was increasingly the goal: don't upset the customer, whether change is generated or not. This shift in sensibility was tailor made for a growing breed of counselors who saw themselves more as child advocates than therapists: theirs was the cause of the marginalized, for whom the negative consequences society (if not biology) had to offer substance users had already been imposed. These onlookers typically negotiated down the consequences leveled within the declining behavior modification system; they appealed for clemency, so no wonder so many kids thought of them as lawyers. Their stances wouldn't change over the months of treatment. As a result, rather than *meet them where their at*, the principle became more like, *linger throughout treatment where they're at.*

Amid this atmosphere, the principles of Dialectical Behavior Therapy (DBT) were intermittently thrown into the mix. This was an interesting addition to the treatment elixir given that the model of DBT emerged from the treatment of Borderline Personality Disorder, which is one of the more pathologizing labels in the entire mental health repertoire. Founded by Marsha Linehan, a one-time post doctorate student working under psychoanalyst Otto Kernberg, DBT combines cognitive and behavioral techniques, and is aimed at those who are repetitively suicidal; it posits a biological root to the problem of emotional regulation for the borderline individual, and speculates that because emotional reactivity is not recognized by the individual's caretakers, perpetual invalidation of emotional states results, leading to cycles of intense escalation of emotion, which is then further misunderstood by others, leading then to feelings of abandonment. The dialectic of DBT involves, on the one hand, a correction of one part of the problem—a validation of the emotional distress of the individual without trying to change the feeling—while helping the person develop skills of emotional tolerance and regulation.

I welcomed the introduction of DBT to the Thunder Road stable of tools, even if it was dominantly focused upon behavior and surface layers of cognition. I suppose I thought it inevitable that programs would scramble to use methods that didn't squash economic paradigms. But as a long-time facilitator of family sessions wherein person A says "I'm sad and frustrated" and person B reflexively answers "Well, there's no reason to get upset", I thought that DBT contained important ideas, ones that articulated the dysfunctional dynamic of an insecurely attached system. Furthermore, its techniques, couched in borrowed Zen Buddhist terms like *mindfulness* or *radical acceptance*, seemed to restore empathy to the forefront of intervention. Although, the model's emphasis upon acceptance of uncomfortable feeling states seemed to resemble what relapse prevention researchers like Alan Marlatt (1995) were already saying with respect to managing addictive impulses: namely, to not think so rigidly about drug use such that impulses must be denied, that self-denial must be exercised, or that relapse absolutely must *not* happen.

In addition, DBT seemed compatible with more durable traditions of TC concepts, such as interventions that directed clients to recognize the roles they had played in the emergence of their situations. An old-school reply to a client externalizing his or her problems would sound something like, "and what part did you play in that?" DBT practitioners, though they might query the timing of such an intervention, appeared to support this kind of stance through its emphasis upon radical acceptance. McKay, Wood, and Brantley (2007) discuss this intervention that follows upon the implementation of distress tolerance skills. According to the DBT strategy, afflicted individuals first look to distract, relax, and cope with distressing emotions through a variety of options. Then, once cooled off, a person can use radical acceptance to explore some of the following questions: what events led to the problem? What role did the person play in the situation, and what role(s) did others play? What control over a situation does the person have? What was the impact of the responses previously chosen in distressing situations?

The sequence of exploratory questions is meant to create space for choice[47], while attempting to broaden an individual's view of their own pain, versus the interpersonal conflict initially presented. This language appears to echo aspects of Short (2006) who indicates a "continuing empathic presence" with dissociated patients as a preferred therapeutic stance. The empathic presence doesn't contain cognitive or behavioral elements, necessarily (not unless all orientations can lay claim to the notion of leading with empathy), nor do her opinions suggest a menu of "coping" or self-soothing skills. Among other things, therapists such as Barbara Short argue that explicit attempts to comfort or reassure patients who are re-experiencing trauma may inadvertently send the message that such an experience cannot be tolerated by therapists, thus exacerbating a once abandoning experience that is brought into the present by the re-enactment.

DBT interventions seemed to be used sporadically at Thunder Road. Within the milieu, staff that referenced these tools utilized interventions that explored distress tolerance strategies, and perhaps later examined destructive behavior and negative consequences of that behavior[48]. However, the interpersonal aspects (actually, the underlying intrapsychic phenomenon) were more or less left well alone—perpetually. Client projections would be left unchallenged, in deference to a strategy that prioritized emotional regulation. As for cooling off: many observed that it didn't necessarily open the doors to reflection, and therefore assumptions about others went unchecked, absorbed into an ever vague understanding of feelings. Feelings were properly validated, but for pervasively disordered individuals, feelings and projections are often conflated, reflecting the psychic equivalence of their attachment disorders, and leading to those distorted "I" statements, expressions of *feelings*, that were lynchpins of the MFG process: "I feel like you're an asshole," and so on. Through emotional regulation strategies, destructive clients might learn to calm themselves down; they might agree that cutting their wrists is not a great idea. But they'd still come out of the therapeutic process thinking that others were the source of their problems, and therefore struggle to take any responsibility for their conflicts.

So, confused yet? What are providers—that "multidisciplinary" collective—supposed to be doing? Are they meant to confront, or merely ask tendentious questions? Do they lead with empathy, or else rely on reassurances, hoping to simply calm down those in distress? Do we look to help the suffering feel better, and suspend for the moment the values of insight or accountability? Do we give the afflicted "space" to reflect upon themselves; or, considered through yet another lens, until such a time as they are ready to hear something meaningful? And will they be sufficiently aroused, emotionally, to attach meaning to their experiences once their discomfort has been assuaged? Concerned onlookers might have a range of feelings, from disdain to alarm, knowing that providers don't really know the answers to these questions. On the other hand, they might feel comforted to know that some insiders are as confused as they are, therefore avoiding the arrogance and rigidity of dogmatism. Above all, insiders of all disciplines seem to not know whether consumers of services are sufficiently motivated to address problems; beyond that even, whether they have the capacity.

Time and time again I have revisited this concept, both internally and in conversation with colleagues, supervisees, even supervisors of mine. It seems to me a respectful position to assert *you can*, implicitly through the consistent administering of expectations—again, through confrontation—rather than to assert *you can't* through the consistent surrendering of standards in the name of de-escalation or "positive thinking". Fundamentally, it seems there exists a battle within treatment circles over what engenders containment, with some voices using terms like structure and confrontation on one side, while opposing voices use terms like encouragement and flexibility, echoing (or perhaps merely co-opting) the caveats of practitioners like Klein (1989), Short (2005), and Orcutt (2006, 2012). It seemed this issue of what clients are capable of versus what they are not was thrust into the line of scrimmage at Thunder Road, and then like abused pigskins kicked around and disputed, again and again, year after year. It must have been a dilemma for attentive members of management, for while influences outside the program called for more positive, depathologizing outlooks towards clients, the program itself was seeking to admit clients with an ever increasing acuity of problems—a trend management acknowledged. A paradox: the more acute the client, the less we might address them with our actual concerns? Pink elephants. Those touting emphasis upon unique skills and strengths didn't so much respect those capacities of clients as much as they doubted their capacity to contain affect; to tolerate techniques like confrontation; to do the hard work of recovery and depth psychotherapy. At the same time, I wonder if some may have sniffed in disapproval at the premise of methods like DBT: namely, the identification of Borderline Personality Disorder as the baseline condition.

Borderline and Narcissistic Personality Disorders

Despite the fact that theorists like Kohut, Masterson, Donald Rinsley, and Otto Kernberg had been studying BPD in adolescent cases as far back as the sixties, the diagnosis of personality disorder seems generally frowned upon with respect to youth, with little or no basis in research. In the treatment plans of Thunder Road, it was placed ever tentatively upon diagnosis pages. The term would appear as a "rule out" on Axis II; referenced as "provisional" or indicated as an afterthought: borderline "features". But as a friend and colleague of mine recently put it, the diagnosis is not an eighteenth birthday gift. The DSM allows for the diagnosis of personality disorder in adolescents, with the attached condition that its symptoms be present for at least a year. Given that many of Thunder Road's clients would be in residence for a year (if not longer), or had been at previous placements wherein similar problems had manifested and been reported, the diagnosis seemed appropriate, at least at an intermediate stage of treatment wherein updates of treatment plans were required.

At Thunder Road, Borderline Personality Disorder was one of two types of self disorder that were of at least peripheral concern to the staff; the other being Narcissistic Personality Disorder. The list of symptoms (as indicated by the DSM) for BPD are hardly esoteric: pattern of volatile or unstable relationships; impulsivity in at least two areas that are self-damaging; recurrent suicidal behaviors; chronic feelings of emptiness; frantic efforts to avoid real or imagined abandonment, severe dissociative symptoms, chronic feelings of emptiness, unstable sense of self.

Many who have worked in Therapeutic Communities would recognize this description and call it the typical client of the milieu. These kids presented with huge dependency needs. They exhausted staff with their demands, their expectations of being taken care of, of being led into recovery. These were the people (because this included many parents) who confused powerlessness with helplessness; they referenced tools of recovery as though constantly looking for tips on how to cope with all matters such that they'd need do little for themselves. They somaticized their helplessness and were often seen laying in bed having convinced staff that they were too ill to participate in activities. They often presented as though sobriety or self-soothing (as opposed to self-medication) were impossible goals to attain, and when relapsing, they'd distort the meaning of 12-step slogans in defense of themselves: "Isn't relapse a part of recovery", they'd say, seeking exemption from consequences; or they'd skillfully co-opt the pop jargon of psychotherapy in order to ward off confrontation: "boundaries! I need space."

Narcissistic clients were likewise sensitive to criticism, but unlike Borderlines, they thrived upon expectation, and defended against helplessness, not with it. Ironic, since Narcissistic personalities were in some ways even more vulnerable than Borderline personalities in the treatment setting. The reasons? Firstly, those with Narcissistic tendencies have been a traditional target of the 12-step community, and especially Therapeutic Communities. While the language of the 12-step literature draws repeated attention to the self-centeredness of the addict, his or her sense of entitlement, or needs for others' admiration, counselors in Therapeutic Communities are trained to perceive the so-called "special addict", the clients who think themselves different, better than, and therefore aloof from the rest of the community. The antennas of staff were rigorously tuned to those who sought separateness in this way, or who, in more sinister fashion, sought to exploit others' vulnerability to their own advantage. In some ways, the profile of the Narcissist is similar to that of the Borderline, with at least one significant distinction being that Borderlines tend to underestimate their abilities, while Narcissists tend to inflate theirs. This presents a dilemma for Narcissists, because while they are as likely as anyone to cast themselves as victims, they must simultaneously resist giving the appearance of weakness. As suggested earlier, Borderline personality types tend to be more openly clinging in their relationships, and seeking of care. The volume of their needs is turned up, as some say. Unlike Narcissistic personalities, who must deny/dissociate their vulnerability at all costs, Borderline personalities are relatively unashamed of showing feelings of distress, or exhibiting helplessness, as long as they achieve bonding as a result.

As much as anything, attention to the Narcissistic personality type had long justified (for many) the use of Therapeutic Community's more controversial interventions, such as confrontation groups, and contract breaking groups; even the use of intensity within the confines of these activities. TCs turned the volume up on feelings, and so it seemed that with Narcissists TC counselors were in their element. For years, I observed groups, especially groups of young males, being passionately berated by counselors, often female counselors transmitting grief from their own life experiences, for the disease of rampant anti-social behaviors: not only the drug use, but also the violence, gang-related or else plainly interpersonal, and in particular, the pervasive devaluation of women. Revenge? The young men would stand with hardened yet docile expressions, straining to maintain cool, concealing the turmoil inside that perhaps only tools like an MRI could detect. They shamefacedly took it all on the chin, and they would compliantly nod. But they would rarely cry. In essence, the 12-step community seemed to regard the term Narcissist as a synonym for addict, and figured, much like the culture at large, that the therapeutic task was to call these people out as publicly as possible, and challenge them to be nicer, more sensitive people.

Alternatively, staff might be squeamish about addressing clients' Narcissistic tendencies, thinking it unnecessary to address such qualities in terms of pathology. Here the focus upon SNAPs, drawn from Strength-based approaches (or maybe a return to a Kohutian idea of "healthy" Narcissism), afforded a more accepting stance towards Narcissistic presentations, especially when exhibited in ways that appeared benign. Good examples of this were the instances wherein clients would make personalized gifts to staff members, such as a card, a letter, or some creation that had seemed to entail significant effort. And this happened a lot: clients would present these gifts, and rather than explore the significance of the gifts, staff would commonly accept the items, and perhaps gush disingenuously, not wanting to hurt clients' feelings. Therapists, typically, wouldn't explain it this way. Wary of appearing less than clinical, therapists were more likely to jargonize these moments, often attributing the incurious acceptance of gifts to dubious arguments about cultural diversity; the idle speculation that exchanging gifts with doctors, teachers, and counselors was normal in the context of a client's upbringing. Once again, the problem wasn't so much in the acceptance or non-acceptance of gifts (such a behavioral focus utterly misses the point), but rather in the gingerly reticence: the lack of reflection; the fear of talking about it. Beyond this, staff members often made one other significant mistake with Narcissistic clients: they tended to assume that their needs for mirroring, like the needs of an addict, were satiable. If only they were nice enough, attentive enough, giving enough, good enough, then such clients would like them for who *they* are, and therefore accept the gifts of recovery in exchange for giving up their defenses. Problem is I don't think it works that way.

These days, Narcissistic Personality Disorder is an embattled diagnostic category, and its inclusion within the next Diagnostic Standards Manual is being challenged by some within the mental health industry (Ronningstam, 2011). Personally, I wonder if there are too many self-conscious Narcissists in charge of the research. Also, it's an inconvenient term to have lying around when a system is trying to reconcile mental health concerns with concepts like customer service, which is mostly about gratifying people, Narcissistic or not. However, working with substance abusers, or anyone within a residential milieu such as Thunder Road, it's hard to deny clinical significance of Narcissism, much less its existence, and personally, I have witnessed too many colleagues who burnt out and left their jobs largely because they couldn't attend to all the demands of their cust—excuse me, clients.

Perhaps the existence of personality disorders among Thunder Road clients has seemed a given due to the common phenomena: the seeming rigidity of many clients' defensive patterns; their seeming imperviousness to persistent reframes or directives. For these clients, there seemed to be a ceiling effect intruding upon their programs, or a ground floor below which their affects would not deepen. Among staff, there seemed a divide with respect to those personality disordered underpinnings of addiction; a divide that was three fold: 1.) a faction that more or less recognized Narcissistic tendencies, yet sort of appealed to them in a backhand way. Meaning, counselors of this ilk addressed negative consequences (jails, institutions, death) that affected these individuals, as if they affected *only* these individuals (forsaking the relational, *other* element). That's working *with* the disorder. Focus on self indeed. 2.) Another school of thought aimed at what was underneath the defensive, self-centered front; aimed at connecting with vulnerability—those emotive climaxes in confrontation groups, sometimes staffings. 3.) That other faction that sought to de-pathologize Narcissism entirely, ignore it as long as it is possible, if not celebrate its lesser destructive elements, as if to assert that Narcissism were a normal part of adolescence. However, impasses due to pervasive problems would grind treatment plans to a halt, and clinical teams would be left feeling exhausted of options while the more 12-step-influenced members of staff prescribed spiritual solutions: prayer and fellowship, letting go. Between Thunder Road and these wounded, disordered personalities, there were competing lines of expectation and willfulness. Between these kids and all the players in their lives, there seemed to be impenetrable barriers; everyone appeared to wait upon the other, ever expecting change to come from some outside event.

Ultimately, the ubiquity of personality disordered individuals within the program was not so much in dispute. Program leadership, attending to funding sources looking for observable outcomes from symptom-based disorders, simply opted for an alternative, less abstract menu of lenses through which client problems might be understood. Therefore, some may prefer to think in terms of insecure attachment styles versus personality disorders, and while these conditions may be correlated with one another, they are not necessarily synonymous. Meanwhile, through the perspective drawn from a co-occurring diagnosis, overseers prefer a focus on DSM Axis I behavioral conditions, such as ADHD, oppositional defiant disorder, or anxiety disorders such as complex PTSD—conditions that could be medicated, or tracked in terms of observable behaviors rather than interpretations of an internal process.

Through the alternative lenses, it may have seemed unreasonable to expect a fidgety, disruptive youth to stay focused in a classroom inhabited by twenty plus kids. From the culturally relativistic point of view of a disadvantaged youth, it may seem harsh to cast his or her persecutory anxiety as a selfish disregard of others' feelings, or to cast pathologizing language upon the sexually promiscuous, trading on good looks in the absence of society's other privileges. Through the eyes of a trauma model, it likely seemed devastating, the exchanges wherein staff confronted the negative behaviors of a client, thus risking either a re-enactment of abusive relationships, or a precipitate and therefore dangerous breakdown (as opposed to a breakthrough) of psychological defenses. Medical model, cultural diversity models, Strength-based models, trauma models: they all seemed to gang up on the pathologizing principles of Object Relations Theory, the practices of Behavior Modification, the Therapeutic Community Concepts Model. In adolescent treatment, they were all sent to the bench for a time-out. Then the bench itself got exiled, and so the time-out became indefinite.

Trauma issues: what versus how

Solutions? It's all about solutions, some say. Returning to the sententious ethos of Lyons-Ruth (2001), I think it's not so much a question of "what" as "how". The question wasn't so much whether we explored a client's distressing events, but rather how we did it: whether or not we maintained neutrality, conveyed concern but not "love"; how we set expectations with an underpinning of respect, not devaluing anger; whether we led with empathy, and sought to witness both the real experiences of our clients, and the true potential that lay beyond their deficits. That some may require more concrete direction, encouragement, or supportive coaching than others was not really in dispute—not even by me. What's disputed is the notion that supportive techniques might also be iatrogenic, just as techniques of confrontation have been characterized that way. Gratifying self centeredness is dangerous, some argue. It's necessary and healing, counter others. Providing direction, encouragement, reassurance, and the modeling of appropriate emotional responses, is vital for a core faction of youth entering residential treatment. That's the position of many, especially third party payers (funding parties), and institutional referral sources—those borrowing a Strength-based model way of thinking. From remoter positions, many other psychotherapists, especially those with psychodynamic training, warn that such approaches lead to a defensive resonance with internalized objects, and therefore limit personal growth rather than stimulate it. From what I observe, many program overseers, payers and referral sources either ignore this point of view, or else they just don't understand it; they think it obscure, academic, and not grounded in modern realities. They insist upon the teleological, what funding sources cast as specific, or "quantifiable" treatment goals, which were generally superficial[49]. How do I know? I don't? I have no idea what some of these people think or feel about my opinions because they've tended to speak past them. Ironically, I've tracked that behavior—informally; that is, not quantifiably.

As for that goal of aiming for what lies underneath, there are those who, again, question whether it can be done; a related objection which points to the resistance of the consumer; a third objection rendering the first two moot: *who would pay for such (elective?) treatment?* Among my colleagues everyone could cite a client who seemed able to link drug use or violence to a host of tangible consequences, but couldn't seem to delve further inwards to fully understand their inner turmoil. Everyone knew clients that were nonplussed by open-ended versus targeted questions, or left abandoned or disoriented by unexplained silences. There seemed to be many clients whom staff thought couldn't *do* therapy as many had been encouraged (though not necessarily trained) to provide it. *So why hire us*? many wondered. Some, myself included, paused from time to time to consider whether feeling good versus feeling better about oneself really was the best some could hope for. Still fewer experienced a dark empathy for families mired in cross-generational addiction and mental illness, for they already knew what it was like to simply live with and survive disorder. Working at Thunder Road, they were living that parallel process. I pined for clients and families that would prove wrong our prejudices, and sometimes the exceptions emerged, like Alison. Miracles: that's what this is called in religious or 12-step circles. But it's not magic. It's hard work transcending expectations, and while everyone acknowledges common denominators, can't everyone point to occasions, several clients or families, whom they had underestimated, if not in terms of motivation, then in terms of capacity?

The job, as far as I am concerned, is to orient clients towards reality, whatever that reality is, yet hold for them the possibility that inner change is possible; to hold the bar high enough such they might jump instead of laying still, waiting for a crash; to render self-destructive behaviors and attitudes ego-dystonic and ungratifying. The job is, as Bowlby had put it, to fully understand our clients' presenting difficulties, and link them to historical issues. Modeling this sensibility was central to my role as clinical supervisor, or so I strained to convey to the clinical director of that period. She, like the administrators over her, seemed to have wider, yet scattered concerns, distributed over several departments, disciplines, and therefore perspectives. They had fifty beds to fill, and in recent years, they were struggling to fill two thirds of that capacity. To achieve the potential of the facility was to accept admits from a diverse array of sources, and to somehow cater to them all. Someone was running the numbers, checking out the demographics of the community client-base: what profile of client was being placed where. My role was strictly clinical, it was suggested; my point of view limited (as was theirs, of course). Managers performed some reality testing with me; they broke down the essentials, schooled me about the forthcoming trend of cases, said to be more acute than those of previous eras.

Higher acuity youth

To explain what clinical directors in hospital facilities mean by the term "acute" requires a brief explanation of what are called Rate Classification Levels (RCLs). The group home rate-setting system, established in 1989 through California law, created for all group homes, whether they were foster care facilities or residential hospital programs, a point system designed to reflect the level of care and services they provide. The RCL system measures each program's staff-to-child ratio, weighted by the experience, training, education, and professional qualifications of the child care and social work staff. All group homes in the same RCL are paid the same standard rate, but higher rates of reimbursement were available should a program be designated higher up the 14-point rating scale.[50]

Now for years, Thunder Road had been designated as a level 7 facility, with clients screened out and referred elsewhere if presenting with either psychotic symptoms or prolific instances of assaultive behavior[51]. RCLs reflect the number and qualifications of staff in programs like Thunder Road, and while the point system was not specifically designed to classify group programs for placement purposes, it naturally followed that county placing agencies, as well as other referral sources, would attempt to place youth with higher or more intensive emotional and behavioral problems (sometimes called "Severely Emotionally Disturbed", or SED), in programs with higher RCLs. As previously indicated, in the latter half of the decade, Thunder Road was starting to notice the benefits of retaining staff with higher levels of education and training, at least at the level of case manager/therapist. While the former trio of psychiatrists had been reduced to one, the number of licensed MFTs in 2009 stood at four (including myself), while the number of license-eligible staff within the treatment teams (including part-time interns) was, on average, about a half dozen. The opportunity was there for the hospital to take advantage of the staff make-up of the time, obtain a higher RCL, and thus accrue a higher rate of reimbursement for each placement of a client.

This would, in effect, lead to more admissions of clients with more extensive histories of violent and other anti-social behaviors, extensive abuse histories, and more cases of individuals with at least discreet episodes of psychotic disorders. As part of my duty in providing psychosocial assessments, I was meant to work closely with the psychiatrist, coordinating with him as to what cases may require fuller assessment, while otherwise taking responsibility for those other clients who would be admitted to the facility, but, as the saying went, "be monitored closely". I was not rigorously trained for this duty; rather, I was sort of oriented, invited to "sit in" with my predecessor's assessments, and then cut loose to do them myself. I took the job seriously, though: did some review of literature pertaining to mental status exams; made an effort to assess a variety of presenting factors, including affect, physical appearance and demeanor, mood states, thought organization. Some aspects of functioning I could only assess superficially. I knew what perseveration was, for example, or so-called ideas of reference; but in truth, a thorough assessment of psychosis or cognitive disturbance was beyond my level of training. There was no question that anyone at Thunder Road would address this gap in training. I was supportively encouraged to do the best I could, and if in doubt, defer to medical authority. And I did my best, though when my hours were cut by a third in 2010, a thorough attempt at assessing each admit became challenging. Scarcely possibly, actually.

I rarely tried to block an admission, as I was advised that newer admits were ever necessary, and only in cases of serious doubt would a potential admission be denied, and even then I'd be delicately told that serious diplomacy would be required with the referral source. This admissions department: it was a tense, hectic epicenter when kids were being brought in; a breezy lounge of chatter once that task was over. I'd wander in and out of this changeable ambience, sometimes getting briefed prior to making an assessment; sometimes consulting over diagnoses if the medical director wasn't around. There were funny episodes. Once I sat with a young man who did little else but mouth the words "Got thizz" (in reference to the drug ecstasy), in staccato bursts, while he glared wide-eyed around the assessment room. The psychiatrist, who visited with him the following day, said that Schizoaffective disorder was a possible diagnosis, owing to the illogical language and disconnected presence. He actually thought the young man was gamey; as in, faking it so as to avoid admission. I offered my interpretations, suggesting the young man's phrase was a play upon a then popular TV commercial: "Got Milk," I said, marking the joke. Milk and drugs: equated as salutary influences. I thought it witty, and was quoting the line in personal circles for weeks. I cooperated as best I could with the ambiguous directives given to me, though I was more concerned with prospective violence than I was psychotic processes, the sometimes religious delusions of clients (addiction as demonic possession was an occasional story), or the complications of opiate withdrawal. Above all, I was uncomfortable with the number of kids admitted who presented with increasingly anti-social profiles.

On the other hand, I had always thought this the case with the group home track, and while there may have been in recent years more cases of clients with longer rap sheets, or kids with more numerous placements, or more documented histories of abuse, and earlier onsets of drug use, this didn't mean necessarily that they were more difficult to work with over time, or even that those documented histories told the full stories with respect to attachment histories (no AAIs were ever conducted at Thunder Road, for example) Again, this attitude, that clients of recent years have been "more difficult" reflected a teleological bias: a perspective reflecting the mindset of behavioral management, not that of psychotherapists, or even recovery counselors (though it may represent the view of psychiatrists). Externally, the hospital may indeed be more chaotic, and some these days may prefer to think of Thunder Road more as a psychiatric facility than a recovery program, but to attribute that change solely to a change in client profile is to risk confusing the cart for the horse. Have the clients changed? Maybe. The higher functioning kids, the ones with prodigious drug histories but more secure attachments, and more affluent families may be funneled to other programs: to wilderness camps, boarding schools, the lesser intensive commitments involved with hospital outpatient programs.

These options may be the preference of parents and probation officers from the supposedly safer, more affluent neighborhoods. But perhaps Thunder Road and other programs changed first; perhaps it sought those higher reimbursement rates, and so gradually, over the years, got what it bargained for. Meanwhile, how does a ship with a crowded and motley blend of sailors stay afloat? Uncertainty transmits across boundaries, and safety becomes brittle as a result. Psychosis and criminal tendencies aside, between the clients of recent times versus those of yesteryear, the levels of motivation, of insight, reflective function; the firmness of ego boundaries, and even the levels of sociopathy, may not be as different as many assume. The essential work of a therapist is blocked if clients—any clients—are not attuned to their inner worlds and willing to try something different. To argue differently is to say that Bernie Madoff is more workable than say, Casey Anthony or John Wayne Gacy, simply because his was a pattern of white collar crime that didn't ordinarily frighten people. I write as someone who has sat with gangsters with long arrest records and negligible early caretaking, as well as so-called white collar professionals with superficially secure upbringings. One or two of those gangster-types did as much therapeutic work as anyone else, in my opinion. They emoted in sessions, linked present behaviors to historical trends, and not only so as to justify an ongoing defensive habit, or to appease an onlooking authority. Those supposedly lower functioning people: some of them take as much responsibility for themselves as any of their supposedly higher functioning counterparts.

This is not to say that some people's concerns (including my own) about clients' volatility weren't well-founded, or that threats to physical safety aren't a real obstacle for those living and working in residential treatment facilities. One of the luxuries I'd felt working at Thunder Road in the nineties (though less so at the McAlister group home) was that of feeling more or less safe in the building. I'd sometimes go to work dreading a verbal bashing from a client, or set of clients, or a parent, or else I'd brace myself for a horror story connected with a client's admission, and sometimes an incident reported to have occurred in the milieu on one of the overnight shifts. Once I was witness to a staff being assaulted, and on two occasions someone vandalized my car, but for the most part I'd been spared from Thunder Road's darkest side. From about 2008 onwards, interns were commenting openly on their dislike for their clients, or more specifically—on their fear of their clients, and their sometimes relief if those clients ran away. At first I thought this a problem of selection: I had perhaps chosen a few people with unrealistic expectations, sanguine views about youth, and with too much belief in the influence of their own world-changing ideas. Then I noticed that others, staff whom I hadn't hired, were manifesting the same attitudes, the same demoralization. It seemed to cut across departments, this malaise. Some left quietly, traumatized perhaps, or disillusioned, while others soldiered on, increasingly with the belief that the grass was hardly greener elsewhere.

11

COCKROACHES IN NUCLEAR WINTER

Employee satisfaction in a residential setting

I wanted to do what I could to make the grass at Thunder Road greener. At this point, I if was to have any influence, it would have been with the lot of clinical staff, and not so much the clients themselves. Mindful of practicing in an area congested with both licensed and pre-licensed therapists, I nonetheless thought the program and its hospital overseers should be doing more to bring job satisfaction to its clinical staff. Despondent over the relentless criticisms aimed at the TC concepts model, I still held out hope that Thunder Road could be a workplace that supported the growth of psychotherapists. Sitting in on one of the administrator's state of Thunder Road addresses, I listened to an overview of results from a recent employee survey, a quite windy and self-congratulatory presentation. This had been a required survey, completed anonymously by every staff member, published a few months later in a bound report, and now passed out as a kind of review of our collective feedback. While the administrator drew attention to his favorite items, such as those that reflected well upon Thunder Road as well as its parent, Alta Bates Summit, I took note of one or two areas of concern: areas in which Thunder Road was reaching out to its workforce. One of these areas was that of professional development, growth opportunities, or words to that effect. I left the meeting (after its completion), put on my thinking cap, and later booked a few minutes' of time with that administrator.

In three years I don't think I ever spoke to this man for more than ten minutes in any one sitting. Despite a seemingly welcome attitude—even a hearty greeting to start things on the right foot—he seemed ever restless in talking to me; ever looking, like his predecessor, over my shoulder for someone more important to speak to. As a result, I was always conscious of speaking quickly to this man, as though he were an executive film producer and I was a brash scriptwriter desperate to make a fast pitch. On the question of staff dissatisfaction, I entered his office aware of a confluence of dichotomies: the increasing acuity of client problems versus the philosophical swerve towards positive or non-pathologizing lines of assessment; the seeming importance of credentialed staff with respect to the points system versus the seeming diminishment of their status, not to mention the obvious decline in staff morale.

I was careful in my language, and *positive* in my approach. That is, I respectfully noted the areas of concern as addressed in the survey—the areas of professional development and growth opportunities—and proposed a solution. Alluding to my years with the hospital, I pointed out that for the first time in my memory, the staff contained as many as six licensed professionals, and owing to the hours-accruing incentives of the intern program, the hospital promised to have another one, perhaps two, licensed clinicians over the next year or so. Given the visibility of Thunder Road in the community, its ready familiarity with professionals at all levels within local mental health and social services, the potential existed for Thunder Road to become a provider of Continuing Education units for professionals who were required to obtain a minimum annual number of such units by the BSE. Having written up an outline of this plan, including a breakdown of the likely topics on which Thunder Road could present, I argued that it was time to begin opening our all-staff presentations to outside professionals.

I proposed that we could devise three-to-four workshops per year, on topics such as adolescent development, substance abuse in teens, insecurely-attached youth, even Therapeutic Community Concepts. Maybe this was our chance to debunk myths about our program, by speaking directly to the service providers in the community, especially those from Alameda and Contra Costa Counties where we were best known. And we'd not just present to therapists: we could invite collateral contacts, probation officers, placement officers from social services, officials from Community Care Licensing or departments of public health. More than anything, it was necessary to educate these people about addiction, attachment research and its implications for the core of our clientele; about splitting, the purpose and tradition of behavioral modification. In addition to this, the payoff would be two-fold: we'd easily pay for any marketing or preparation expense by charging eighty dollars per head—a standard rate at that time for a two-to-three hour workshop by a licensed, Master's level professional. Finally, and surely as importantly, we'd redress that perceived lack of professional development or growth opportunities for staff, especially as presentations could dovetail contributions of both licensed and on-line staff.

He listened disinterestedly for a few minutes while gazing back and forth between me and his computer, a bit like Linus from Charlie Brown looking to his shoulder to keep tabs on his blanket. Because I'd used up my allocation of minutes with my pitch, I was dismissed and told that the matter would be given some thought. "Come back next week," he said with a perturbed twitch of his lip. At the second meeting, he did most of the talking: the idea wasn't possible, he was afraid. Despite my assertion that advertising of upcoming workshops could be made through a combination of Thunder Road's website and my own advertising through the local association of Marriage and Family Therapists (through whose e-mail networking system messages could be sent to hundreds of east bay therapists in an instant), he dismissed the idea; said it would be too expensive to prepare, and a diversion from staff's more pressing duties. "So, you're telling me to forget it?" I asked finally. He nodded, and added somewhat gratuitously that, after all, we're not creating an institute at Thunder Road. I narrowed my eyes and asked what he meant by the comment. He seemed to swallow heavily, and motioned his eyes to the door—the end of our conversation—before trailing off with more words about Thunder Road not being a place for the training or educating of therapists.

I walked away feeling as though I'd been slapped in the face. I slinked off down to my office, but not before walking by a kid standing next to a genial yet no-nonsense maintenance man. The two of them were patching up a hole the kid had placed in the wall next to his room; they were cooperating but not talking, repairing damage to the wall and perhaps something else. Who knows what happens amid silence? Downstairs, I walked past the kitchen department and its increasing numbers of cooks in its midst. More and more, the staff in this department resembled chefs, and many of the kids seemed to not only tolerate, but even enjoy working in the kitchens alongside the staff. The head chef would often walk around with a pair of clients diligently cooperating; sometimes following him around in a manner that might fascinate ethologists[52]. Well, we might not be an institute for mental health professionals, but we might well become a culinary institute; aspiring Delancey Street, maybe? Indeed, the catering side of Thunder Road was thriving, having been green-lighted by management some years earlier. Not that I begrudged this, necessarily. After all, I had enjoyed many a free meal while working at Thunder Road, and the food had become nearly epicurean by the end of the decade. But is this what Thunder Road was advertising? Is this the development that enabled the higher RCL rating, or the message it was sending to the community about what it centrally had to offer? Some of the kids, especially the males, wouldn't complain. Their ever stolid expressions cast the votes: Let us make cake, they might say, paraphrasing Marie Antoinette; give us a tub of spackle, or a mop and a bucket any day over an hour with a therapist and the empty black hole of our inner lives.

Some time later I was invited back to the administrator's office, though hardly for a re-think of the CEU proposal. Instead, he wanted to know more about the intern program's relationship with graduate schools in the Bay Area: what were the parameters of their responsibility for the performance of students placed at Thunder Road, but drawn from their student bodies. I informed him that agreement forms between schools and agencies specifically indemnified the schools from any liabilities, and that malpractice potential borne of students' performance were covered under Thunder Road's insurance policies, as well as my own, since I was the identified clinical supervisor. The administrator sought proof of this, so I was dispatched to collect documents pertaining to my insurance policy, and also the agreement forms between schools and Thunder Road. Meanwhile, another idea had come to him: that of hiring for the part-time positions only those therapists who were still within graduate school programs, instead of registered interns, who had completed Master's degree programs and registered with the BSE. The reason for this change was the apparent discovery that trainees (the designation for those still within an academic program) could be paid a stipend for educational expenses instead of an hourly wage. The costs associated with the program would be cut by almost two-thirds, the administrator enthused.

I objected strenuously, arguing that such a move would narrow the hiring pool by at least half, limiting my options; it meant that attractive candidates would be screened out not because they lacked a degree, but rather because they had one. It meant that future part-time employees would be producing documentation crucial for program reimbursement while earning a negligible wage, which seemed a set-up for poor performance in this area. I pointed out that trainees, unlike registered interns, weren't even eligible to accrue hours towards licensure in the category of administrative reports and progress notes (this rule was changed, actually, in January 2010, as the BSE either observed or anticipated the trend). For three months I did my own research, scrutinized the California Business and Professions Code to see if the language pertaining to trainees versus interns spoke to who could earn a stipend and who could not. I could find no definitive statements, and CAMFT lawyers with whom I consulted were promisingly equivocal, though more than one warned me that trainees who reported two thousand dollars—the estimated stipend total—of educational expenses pertaining to duties performed at Thunder Road might find themselves the subject of a BSE audit.

I chose not to fight the issue of the stipend. That was an economic decision and was going to happen no matter what I thought. We were heading back to the nineties, back to the era when I started accruing hours, when it was common for therapists to work for free, under the licenses of others so they could gain early experience in the field. Though I could do nothing about it, I've always objected to this practice on moral grounds. Some might point to market forces, supply and demand; the scarcity of positions, etcetera. If stipends or minimum wages constitute the going rate for novice therapists, then so be it. But it shouldn't be: novice therapists are being hired for some of the most challenging of therapeutic environments, to work with some of the most difficult of patients, with prodigious demands placed upon them, and with relatively little training or supervision of their day-to-day clinical interventions. To treat these would-be professionals as indentured servants, given the responsibilities they are asked to meet on a daily basis, is plainly wrong.

Anyway, no one within Thunder Road's management seemed to care about this, so instead I was left with the lesser-charged issue of whether I could still hire registered interns. Lengthy e-mails from me to Thunder Road's HR consultant, with whom I'd previously discussed this issue long before the administrator's brainchild came to the fore, argued for the retention of RIs. She'd respond diplomatically, copy the e-mail to the administrator, who made one or two terse but irrelevant rebuttals, and deferred to Alta Bates' own team (or army) of lawyers, also purportedly researching the issue. Without engaging me as to the specific language of the California code, I was later informed of risk management's deliberations: the decision to use only trainees would stand, as that was the recommendation of the legal team. My supervisor, the clinical director, added another piece. She politely delivered a gag order to me, relayed from the administrator, and I was to write no more of those argumentative e-mails to Alta Bates' human resources.

Advocacy

By the end of the decade, I felt as though I was running out of things to advocate for, and I hadn't even started the position thinking this my job, necessarily. It had been a serendipitous adventure of sorts, this pattern of finding issues to confront. I looked around and knew some people who had been at Thunder Road as long as I had, if not longer. Some had gotten closer than me to the front lines of battle, and were still around, protecting their niches of the program with quiet efficiency. Meanwhile, the big personalities were gone: the charismatic or eccentric psychiatrists, the previously bombastic administrator; the firebrand program director, and the many tireless floor supervisors with hard faces and fearless voices—most of these people had moved on, burnt out or gotten ill, or retired, or died. In the fall of 2010, another clinical director arrived, and cursorily briefed me as my next supervisor. This director was another Thunder Road re-tread, like myself. In this and one other meeting, I looked for indications of the new director's thinking: I wondered what treatment philosophy might result from her leadership, as I had been the coordinator of IOP during the period of her previous tenure, and was therefore unfamiliar with her biases. Was she enamored of DBT, of Motivational Interviewing? Would she drone on about Strength-based approaches, and speak past others' insights with reminders about attending to SNAPs, as her predecessor had done. Was she old-school? Meaning, did she believe in restoring the 12-step message to the core of the program? And would she support the preservation of TC totems, the bench, and confrontation group?

On these and other principles, she seemed unconvincingly non-committal. The bench, by that time, was already a goner, though she didn't seem to mourn its loss particularly. Above all, she seemed deferential, offering that she needed time to fit in, observe the system as it currently was, and then see what might happen. Some changes were already on the horizon, she and others were saying. Rumors stirred for a month or two, and were later realized: Community Care Licensing analysts were denouncing, after over a decade of apparently unwitting approval, the segregation of treatment services at Thunder Road by gender. Within months, a period of integration would begin, with select groups and activities becoming coed for the first time since 1999. There were other changes heralded, but this was the major one; this was the tsunami no one amongst staff wanted to build dams for. Regardless, at this stage it wasn't the change that would most affect yours truly.

At the end of 2010 I attended a workshop in the community that served as required educational units for the retention of my clinical supervisor's credential. At the training there was a Thunder Road colleague, and a former supervisee of mine, now qualified to become a supervisor in her own right having just passed the two year mark of her post-licensed experience. The woman was a full-time employee of the hospital, and as far as I could tell had no working life outside of Thunder Road. The reason she was there was obvious: she'd been directed to obtain her credential ahead of replacing my position at some point in the future. The observation stung but I said nothing about it, either to her or my supervisor, the newly appointed clinical director. For the time being, I put my head down, engaged in some of the current discussions about the future of the program, and continued to assert my "voice" wherever I could squeeze it in. Dead man walking: a clinical supervisor in denial. I dutifully went about my job, but gradually became more detached, jaded. In absenting myself, I may have reinforced for some my image as a cold, supercilious intellect, lacking true feeling for the clients. While I never bothered to combat this insinuation directly, I regularly weighed in with my support of an older treatment philosophy—that our task was nothing less than to promote altered terms for the kids' relatedness to peers, adults, and the community. Meanwhile, I echoed the medical director's amorphous description of current program philosophy: we were practicing Cognitive Behavioral Therapy, with a Psychodynamic underpinning, he'd say, speaking offhandedly.

In retrospect, as I look back at the various schools of therapeutic thought, supposedly all jostling with one another for pole position at Thunder Road, it's hard to see a clear winner. Maybe Strength-based approaches have their noses in front for the time being, but who knows. As I sometimes said to interns (and trainees) who bemoaned the imposition of styles or philosophies that seemed to not fit them: "they (meaning managers or oversight agencies) aren't in the room with you". There were no two-way mirrors at Thunder Road. Managers rarely sat in with therapists during their one-on-one sessions with clients. They rarely attended the multi-family groups, either on Tuesday afternoons or Tuesday evenings. Of course, I rarely did these things either, but I had one hour meetings each week, and two-hour groups with the interns wherein we could role-play anticipated exchanges, or pore over the details of previous ones, even if I couldn't get anyone to produce a thorough case history. But I could listen for nuances within cases the supervision group would come to know over time, and hear reflections upon affect, emotion. With interns, I could brainstorm interventions, not just direct them. I could listen for the inner processes of the clients, and speculate with the interns about theirs.

It may not be saying much, but I think I was best positioned to impart a model of psychotherapeutic treatment, for group, individual, or dyadic (such as family therapy) format, both in terms of philosophy and a detailed application of interventions. Was my approach ever cognitively-focused? Of course: when I was a case manager I waded through clients' thinking, looking for distortions, assumptions, values that might be articulated by observers and thus dissected and understood. When I was a supervisor I encouraged the same. At the outset of treatment, psycho-education is at its most important, and the crafting of our words, for those who cut across as many divides as possible—age, race, gender, language, even religion—is to be ever honed. Was I Psychodynamic in bias? Absolutely. I asserted vociferously that clients were governed by unconscious forces; that therapists and systems, including Thunder Road itself, routinely operated at an unconscious level, but it was the job of conscientious individuals to live consciously, to look beyond the surface and remain curious about undiscovered experience: transference in clients, countertransference in professionals. This tacit belief in the unconscious formed the basis of our best assumptions: the assumption, one the one hand, that the young want for themselves a healthy, wholesome, emotionally available life, despite the relentless assertion of entitlement and the testing of adult society's fortitude; the assumption, on the other hand, that the young carry alongside their needs for adult approval, a deep sea of libidinal energy that pokes constantly at society's need to assign innocence to them.

The supposed divide between Cognitive-Behavioral psychotherapists and those of a Psychodynamic background is overstated in my opinion. I've known Psychodynamic therapists who are or were very cognitive in their approach, and I've known CBT-biased therapists who retain some clients for years, and are as capable of a deepening process as anyone. That word "cognition" refers to knowledge, and many have either implied or stated explicitly that cognition might be unconscious as well as conscious knowledge. In my fantasy, I imagine myself as a facilitator of a process group that brings together providers from supposedly different schools of thought. On one side of the room there will be a pocket of Ellis and Beck acolytes, flanked by allies, DBT practitioners, Motivational Interviewing specialists. On the opposite side, sulking like family scapegoats, the adherents of Klein, Lacan, Fonagy and others will sit, readying for a meaty debate, and insisting that the work of neuroscientists, Schore, Siegel et al, affirms their work. I'd be in the middle, catching the nervous eyes of a transpersonal therapist, and fancifully saying "relax, there's room for everyone."

A place for depth therapy

In theory, there was room at Thunder Road for all kinds of orientations, or even modalities such as art, drama, or play therapy, that haven't been the focus of this treatment, but which nonetheless have found their niches within the hospital setting from time to time. Only those who led with transpersonal biases were consistently *not* hired by my observation—ironic, perhaps, given the spiritual underpinnings of the 12-step movement and the ubiquity of ritual: the Thunder Road mythology. But I saw little evidence in my fifteen years of a comprehensive theory, rigorously trained and taught, being integrated by a wide crossection of staff. For years, a common understanding of 12-step philosophy and TC concepts came closest to achieving this level of cohesion. In time, I might have fashioned a manual for my plans, and patiently sought to have others read it. Manuals are popular tools in our profession. No therapy office is complete without a therapeutic workbook, and a quick glance at the bookshelf of an average therapist would reveal an eclectic search for the best (or most fashionable) approaches to treatment of mental health problems. Looking at the spines, one could get a good introduction to an inventory of three and four letter terms: CBT, DBT, MET (synonymous with Motivational Interviewing), EFT, EMDR, and so on.

It's often assumed that Psychodynamic theories have missed the boat when it comes to the manualization of therapy, and thus suffered the most in recent years from the Balkanization of mental health treatment. This is almost, but not quite true, for codified approaches have been devised and disseminated in manual formats: the Mentalization-Based treatment approach (MBT), as devised by Fonagy, Bateman, and Target, for example, or the Transference-Focused approach (TFB), as designed by Otto Kernberg and his colleagues. It's true that such approaches aren't typically cited by those speaking of "evidence-based approaches". But even researchers from Psychodynamic models are promoting their books and articles, utilizing this buzz term of the health industry. Speakers in agency-based training commonly tout evidence-based approaches, such as CBT and Motivational Interviewing. "Evidence-based" is presented as being synonymous with greater effectiveness, while Psychodynamic models are often cast as unmeasurable. This is not true, and both the teams of Fonagy, Bateman, and Target, as well as Kernberg and company, as well as others can cite research supporting the efficacy of their treatment models[53].

Fonagy and Bateman (2006), writing about treatment of severe personality disorders, warn that a treatment focused solely on cognition (defined in conscious terms) or the environment does not satisfy the patient who feels uniquely vulnerable in intimate inter-personal relationships. They offer the sobering view that some patients are unable to make therapeutic use of cognitive insight, or consider their own experience alongside the re-representations of others—such is the impoverishment of thought that they are so vulnerable to powerful emotional storms. They are unable to compare the coherent and perhaps correct view of mental function, as provided by another, with the self-generated model of self which is all too often accepted uncritically. They are impervious to cognitive reframing, it seems, which, if true, leaves providers with the dilemma of how to treat the disturbances. Fonagy and Bateman conclude that therapy which attempts to enhance mentalization can be effective as long as serious side-effects such as behavioral disturbance can be averted. To this end, the MBT therapist attempts to define accurately what the patient is feeling and doing in the here and now, and to identify what in the interpersonal environment the person is responding to. For example, they assert that a definitive "You are angry with me" mirroring statement to a patient is not helpful, even if accurate. Rather, they recommend that a non expert-like focus on the therapist's mind models mentalizing, instead of merely flouting the principle—therefore, "The way you are frowning makes me think you may be angry", would be the prescribed intervention. In this way, treatment can avoid iatrogenic effects, while lending credence to a perennial client/patient complaint: *Stop telling me how I feel.*

The model of Kernberg and his colleagues, Yoemans and Clarkin, meanwhile, seeks to offer a fuller interpretation of transference, observing the ways in which client/patients relate to the therapists. While acknowledging that some may benefit from a strictly supportive approach in which encouragement and advice-giving are notable techniques, they suggest practitioners examine their countertransference when poised to use these methods. In other words: use a critical lens upon what may seem common sense, or supportive, as it may not foster growth. Their approach emphasizes affect-laden themes, but without explicit direction onto past experiences. Meanwhile, there is attention to containment, in the form of contract-setting (agreements about destructive behavior), and through the use of confrontation. TFB contrasts with supportive models of treatment, which put forward the idea that a warm, giving human relationship permits the growth of individuals, and instead argues that an analysis of transference is what gradually permits an individual to accept a new relationship on different terms. Like a DBT practitioner, they initially validate a distortion, but then move to confront the distortions, and by extension, the intrapsychic formulations: "If I'm an uncaring and harsh person, as you suggest, it would make sense that you'd no longer want to talk with me. However, if your perception is not accurate, then it would make sense to look at where the sense of danger is coming from."[54] Disputing the commonsense assumption that one has to build up a good relationship with a patient, TFB suggests that a therapeutic alliance is a consequence of good treatment, not a prerequisite.

Outcomes upon outcomes

At Thunder Road, it seemed that the institutional preference for so-called cognitive, or even straightforwardly supportive or educational approaches had little to do with efficacy or the findings of evidence-based research, even though managers tended to cite this oft-promulgated argument. Bettman and Jasperson (2009) point out that operationalizing treatment efficacy is essential in the field of drug rehabilitation and mental health services, with measurable outcomes that define success. Is it? Their review of the research relating to adolescents in residential and outpatient programs reveals a plethora of confounding factors in such research: they cite critics who argue that treatment cost, rather than clinical need, unduly influences many programs' decisions towards residential treatment (Schmidt, 2000); that most studies of treatment outcomes provide only short-term follow up and limited clinical measures. (Mock et al., 2001) asserts that generalizations are difficult due to research methodological problems: small sample sizes, lack of randomization, and high dropout rates. Researchers further point out that different assessment tools are used across studies (cited in Tripodi, 2009). Meanwhile, others argue, with respect to the question of treatment orientation, that studies often present idealized descriptions of orientations, but fail to demonstrate that elements of those orientations were actually implemented (no transcripts or tapes?). In one study, Weir (2005) conducted a review of 242 adolescents in various residential programs, and concluded that adolescents who completed their programs generally exhibited a reduction in symptoms. But findings like these seem to have thin meanings. Research into the efficacy of rehabilitation programs lacks uniform definitions of "treatment"; a general failure of studies to provide sufficient detail about the programs whose efficacy was being assessed and later pronounced (Butler and McPherson, 2007).

Writing in *American Psychologist* in March 2010, Dr. Jonathan Shedler has drawn much attention for his article, "The Efficacy of Psychodynamic Psychotherapy", in which he reviews academic and institutional prejudices against psychoanalytically-derived therapies, and then purports, through a review of research literature, that Psychodynamic psychotherapy is indeed "evidence-based"; that it is grounded in science, despite what its detractors either assert or imply. Firstly, in researching studies that compared technique and process of manualized psychodynamic therapy with that of manualized cognitive behavioral therapy, he outlines several features that distinguish a Psychodynamic approach: a focus on expression of emotion; exploration of attempts to avoid distressing feelings; identification of recurrent themes; discussion of past experiences; focus upon the therapy relationship (Transference phenomena); and exploration of inner fantasy life. While the goals of such a process may include symptom reduction, Shedler points out that effective therapy also fosters broader psychological capacities, such as the ability to have more fulfilling relationships, or make greater use of one's talents.

In tracking efficacy, Shedler cites meta-analysis research, which is the method for summarizing synthesizing the findings of independent studies; indicates effect size as the metric that aggregates findings, revealing the difference between treatment and control groups. An effect size of 1.0 indicates a standard deviation on a normal distribution, and an effect size of .8 is considered a large effect in psychological and medical research. With this established, Shedler reports numerous rigorous studies which demonstrate positive outcomes for treatments utilizing a Psychodynamic approach, while also referencing meta-analysis research upon antidepressant medications approved by the FDA between 1987 and 2004 that yielded a mean effect size of .31; a somewhat meager outcome by comparison. The problem of determining what actually happens in a session is addressed through the use of a tool known as the Psychotherapy Process Q-sort. This instrument consists of 100 variables that assess therapist technique based on specific actions. Blind raters score the 100 PQS variables from session transcripts for therapy hours from outcome studies of both Psychodynamic therapy and Cognitive Behavior Therapy (CBT).

One meta-analysis included 17 controlled trials of short-term (avg.: 21 sessions) psychodynamic therapy with an effect size of 1.17; increasing to 1.57 at long-term follow-up—13 months (Liechsenring, Rabung, & Liebing, 2004; cited in Shedler, 2010). Another meta-analysis: 14 studies of Psychodynamic therapies set against 11 of CBT for personality disorders. With a mean follow-up period of 1.5 years, the pretreatment to posttreatment effect size was 1.46 for Psychodynamic therapy; 1.0 for CBT. A more recent study examines efficacy of long-term psychodynamic therapy (defined as longer than a year, or more than 50 sessions) that yielded an effect size of 1.8 for overall outcome (Liechsenring & Rabung, 2008). Also, in a separate study: for patients with severe personality pathology, the pretreatment to posttreatment effect was .78 for general symptom improvement, which increased to .94 at long-term follow-up, an average of 3.2 years posttreatment (de Maat, de Jonghe, Shoevers, & Dekker, 2009; cited in Shedler, 2010). In all, Shedler tracks 8 different meta-analyses of Psychodynamic treatments, covering over 70 studies, with nearly all yielding positive effect size outcomes.

But let's say (just for fun?) that the phrase "evidence-based" is bogus with respect to mental health treatment, outpatient or residential; it is, as Sheldon, my favorite character from TV's *Big Bang Theory* would say, "hokum". As a therapist and non-scientist, I am pleased by research that pushes back against recently institutionalized echo chambers, but with respect to one area, at least, I'll remain an amateur skeptic: Let's acknowledge that no one—not researchers, policy makers, public health officials, journalists, or care managers of insurance companies—knows what's really happening in a room between a therapist and a client. No telephone follow up assessment, whether it is made within forty eight hours of a program completion, or forty eight months, can attribute changes to the words said, or the words unsaid, in those sessions. No confrontation group can be properly assessed by an outcome study. Who knows how many future relapses were averted by contract breaking sessions, or by an AWOL blocking performed by an unsung staff member working an on-call shift on a weekend? No treatment report, plan, or discharge summary can capture the interventions that make the difference between an authentic therapeutic alliance and an empathic failure. And BTW: no matter how many movies are made lampooning my profession, or HBO series that aim to be flies on the walls of our offices, the media will never understand what therapy is unless its members pick up phones, give us a call, and say something like, "I think I need to work on my issues."

On the matter of specific treatment approaches, I think that CBT and/or so-called supportive therapies are taught or promoted more readily because they are understood more readily; because they are generally easier to manualize, and therefore teach to therapists, especially lesser experienced therapists whom management is not obliged to pay very much. It fits the paradigm familiar to lay persons to ask therapists to act more or less as teachers or parents. Similarly, because Cognitive Behavioral therapy, or Solution-Focused therapy, and other supportive therapies are associated with briefer tenures of treatment, they are generally presumed to be more cost effective and less emotionally demanding, either of clients or therapists. Less mature therapists, it is quietly believed, are not seasoned enough to lead broken individuals into the depths of their disturbances. Because the preferred treatment approaches are compatible with psycho-educational models of treatment they are more conducive to a superficial understanding of each particular case, which again, contrary to the lip service often given, is the desired scenario.

A fuller understanding of Psychodynamic approaches requires a willingness to think of the process as an emotional experience, not an educational or merely practical one. It calls for an appreciation of the evolution of Psychoanalysis, which requires learning something about Object Relations Theory, which entails a complex set of ideas, admittedly written about with sometimes convoluted or esoteric language. It requires learning about mentalization, reflective function, transference, the fuller meaning of splitting, and of projection. Actually, Psychoanalysis, like any theoretical model, must accommodate the latest in scientific research, and it has. Competence in our profession now calls for an acknowledgement of the contributions of neurobiology: of what scientists are teaching about attachment, attunement, right and left hemisphere functioning; the ideas drawn from years of infant and toddler observations in various clinical settings, assessment of attachment styles, or "states of mind" with respect to attachment, in adolescents and adults. It calls for empathy.

However, the working assumption in programs like Thunder Road is that there isn't time for things like depth therapy, for the fuller understanding of clients' histories in the context of attachment histories. Such an approach would mean learning the significant events of a person's life at different stages of development—from 0-5, 5-10, 10-15, and beyond—and holding that information in mind as one sits with the person; it means *knowing* them. Given the number of clients assigned to each caseload, the pace of treatment; the prodigious documentation requirements, and the need to maintain regular contact and consultation with collateral professionals who are lay persons as far as mental health treatment is concerned—a painstaking, nuanced, and focused approached to treatment, as opposed to a diluted approach presided over by a multidisciplinary team, is simply deemed impractical, no matter what clients appear to want; no matter what selectively ignored research has to say, and no matter what is called for by the U.S Department of Health and Human Services. The prescribed models of psychotherapy are therefore the briefer models, which are presumed to defer on a deepening approach. Diversity is proclaimed via the term "individualized treatment", and evolving models are said to incorporate new ideas. But the perspectives are quite limited, actually. They are governed by economics, utilitarian thinking. Diversity and "individualized treatment" are ideas to sell to the consumer of services, and the pitches are thin, disingenuous, and thoroughly soundbitten. It's like when a homogenous social group argues for its diversity by saying something like, "Well, we have people of various backgrounds: Dutch, Norwegian, even Swedish!"

And so the point of this book is to challenge assumptions, to stir those concerned with the state of adolescent treatment, especially that which happens in residential settings; to observe the flaws in a strictly teleological, symptom reduction approach, and observe what scientific research is actually reporting about treatment efficacy. In opposition, some might shake their heads dismissively and raise firmly embedded economic arguments: the lack of money for the type of treatment herein described, regardless of what's most effective. But I'm not calling for a revamping of mental health services, with an appeal for X billion more dollars from state budgets for such a plan. No. This book is clearly about an infrastructure that already exists, and a wrongheaded use of its resources. Unlike private practice settings, many residential or even intensive outpatient providers are not limited by the one visit per week standard that managed care typically reimburses, or the limited-sessions model that more or less compels a brief therapy bias in many settings. I say that given the nature of an extended, intensive treatment—the real opportunity to observe youth closely, on a day-to-day basis, to meet with them multiple times per week over stretches of treatment duration ranging from ninety days to A YEAR (or longer), and to contain the most destructive of acting out behaviors in those time frames—that a thorough, in depth, nuanced, compassionate yet confrontational psychotherapy designed to produce long-term positive results is possible, as long as there is the conviction to support it.

The approach could even integrate the virtues of different orientations, even those of the brief models. It could still aim for that hybrid that Thunder Road founder Randy Snowden described to me. A typical approach might read like the following: if a focus upon acting out patterns of behavior obscures attention to an individual's strengths, or capacities of self, then what's called for is an intervention strategy that draws attention to that event in its entirety. What treatment teams might therefore present is a packaged observation, tailored to an understanding of each individual: empathy for a feeling of distress (or validation); observation of the struggle to sustain or tolerate distress; observation of the efforts to defend against those feelings of distress, and the culminating consequence in which a person's true and positive capacities, as well as their abilities to connect with others, are thwarted, and left under-developed as a result. Sound complicated? It is, but it's not as though these things can't be conveyed in a plain spoken manner by a skilled, empathic therapist, who is tuned in to their own experience, and that of their clients. Most of the kids admitted to Thunder Road, especially those admitted to its long-term track, will never again be afforded such an opportunity to focus their considerable energy around the question of who they really are. I guess I would have liked to continue arguing for this at Thunder Road.

Recently, at that conference in San Diego wherein I'd shared my thoughts about therapist self-disclosure and the intrapsychic defense of splitting, I listened along with hundreds of other professionals to celebrity researchers and clinicians like

Patrick Carnes and Terrance Real speak on the subject of sex addiction. Presenting alongside these prominent figures of the industry were several other speakers, of varying levels of discipline (including one or two interns), from treatment facilities like the Meadows, Sierra Tuscon, and SRI (Sexual Recovery Institute). These facilities are residential and outpatient programs, staffed by licensed and pre-licensed therapists, who are working as therapists, but actively developing their skill-sets, their knowledge and experience, and now sharing their thinking in professional circles, even contributing to professional literature with articles for peer-reviewed journals. In the aftermath of my CEU provider proposal, I learned that Thunder Road had decided to import outside professionals from local agencies to present workshops on subjects relating to adolescent treatment. On the one hand, this seemed a gesture of openness: an indication that Thunder Road was shedding a previously insular reputation, and showing itself to be open to others' ideas. On the other hand, this seemed yet another slap in the face of a knowledgeable and experienced staff; a gesture of utter disregard for its collective hunger for growth opportunities and professional development.

For years, whenever I'd network with other professionals anywhere in the East Bay Area, I'd curry immediate familiarity if referencing Thunder Road. For nearly twenty years I'd heard its name being sounded out within the community where I lived and worked. With this ready visibility and therefore platform from which to spring, why shouldn't Thunder Road take advantage of its resources and reach out to the wider mental health community, just as other well-established providers have done, including some in the Bay Area who are perhaps not as widely known as Thunder Road, and who are no more comprised (in terms of depth) of experienced, trained, and educated professionals? Why shouldn't Thunder Road sponsor serious-minded discussions on topics of substance abuse and the treatment of adolescents in residential settings? Why shouldn't it contribute to literature on these subjects? Why shouldn't its clinical staff feel committed on a long-term basis to a mission that places its efforts at the core of the program, and why shouldn't Thunder Road promote this fact? Why shouldn't it support a rigorous training program, one that challenges therapists at the outset of their careers to be their best? In short, why shouldn't it behave like an institute?

We all know that tighter economies squeeze budgets, but I suppose it comes down to what you're willing to pay for. As a consumer, at least, it should be about knowing *what* you're paying for. For those contemplating a residential or an outpatient setting, one staff facilitating a group of twenty plus people is not sufficient. Actually, a twenty-person deep group is too big regardless of how many facilitators are present in my opinion. Smaller groups are generally more attractive to diffident or anxious individuals, and a standard of no more than eight people participating in a group is one I wholeheartedly support. In my view, psychotherapy or no psychotherapy, the most important ingredients of a residential program are safety and containment, which in concrete terms means a high staff to client ratio. To those contemplating a residential placement, whether a parent, a referral source, or even a motivated young person, I suggest skepticism of programs aiming for the bare minimum. One staff per six or eight kids is not enough for proper supervision. Safety in numbers reduces not only the likelihood of kids acting out with sex, violence, non-violent forms of bullying, or drug-seeking behaviors, but also the likelihood that staff will act out with kids in these areas. Parents and other concerned parties should ask after the training and education of the online and case management staff. Ask, in particular, after the case managers/therapists; ask after the therapeutic services they provide, how much time should a parent expect that a therapist will spend with his or her child per week, and what is a reasonable expectation for regular consultation with a parent, in terms of number of calls per week; aggregate time spent. Above all, ask after what the program is advertising as its core services to its clients.

Voices for Therapeutic Communities

To those who broadly suggest that Therapeutic Communities are abusive, I suggest they consider all sides of the issue. Of course it's wrong for kids to be physically or sexually, or even verbally abused by adults placed in positions of power and trust. It's unacceptable for adults working in this field to develop personal relationships with clients outside of program facilities, or to neglect their needs in other fundamental ways. But are stretches of bench time really the problem? Is the withholding of off-site passes, or of correspondence with outside peers, whether substance-abusing or not, the traumatizing reenactments that concerns us? To those who say that confrontation as a technique, or confrontation group as an activity, is inherently abusive, I say you're wrong. I recall once listening to dissenters argue that kids in group homes and hospital residential programs deserve to have a normal teen experience, or an approximation of it. *What*? Is that what they think these kids had prior to being admitted: a normal experience? Is this what rehabs will advertise in the future? Bring your kids to treatment and have a normal teen experience! Besides, what is a normal teen experience currently: a blunt following breakfast on the way to school? Multiple sex partners by age sixteen? Bullying experiences at lunch or during classes over cyberspace whilst teachers are lecturing? These days, bullying is of topical concern in schools. So should it be in group homes, because frankly the greatest threat to fragile youth in such facilities is not coming from shouting adults, but rather from those kids' peers.

This is not made easier by programs that seem to obsess over filling beds. In pursuit of business, they can take pages from 12-step readings and offer up the maxim, *the newcomer is the most important person,* and focus so much energy around simply getting patients into their buildings. Program leaders may justify this stance, invoking 12-step slogans as well as other precious statements like "everyone deserves a chance at treatment." Maybe that's true, but don't those not creating an unsafe environment deserve a chance also, and isn't that chance being compromised by the diminishing of safety standards, the chance to get clean in a clean and sober environment? So those newcomers enter relentlessly, one after another, sometimes adding a positive influence to the residential community, but just as often disrupting it irredeemably. A solid community, or a solid group, presenting just a minimum threshold of motivation and goodwill, can fulfill much of the promise of the dominant group therapy format: it can provide a powerful, peer-based reality-testing experience. Truly. Alternatively, given a fractured community, one that has been sloppily thrust together like cows in a slaughterhouse, that community—those groups—can become poisonous, regressive stews of collusion, denial, and degeneration, and it is nothing less than painful to observe a kid that is motivated (if naively so) about treatment, yet vulnerable to systemic disorder, get worse in the confines of a residential program. Such a kid is bullied relentlessly in that kind of environment. He or she is triggered towards relapse, feels alone in a crowd, and gives up when their scheming abuser is given "client of the week" status. That's Strength-based treatment for one kid. That's abuse for the other. That's trauma, actually.

But that's the business of adolescent residential treatment, maybe, and the business of treatment rolls on, as any business does. Some kids will stay and take up a bed for upwards of a year, if not longer. Others will enter, AWOL, and later be re-admitted, AWOL again or be dishonorably discharged, go to back to their communities, be re-incarcerated, and then ultimately re-admitted once again a year after their initial admissions, with welcome smiles from the few staff remaining that will recall them from the first time around. Program and community cohesion is left to chance, with the new Therapeutic Community as much mimicking the outside world as contrasting it. Keep coming back. That's an idea of customer service, actually: have the customer return. Once, Thunder Road's program had seemed to contain a fair mix of clients: of gender, race, class; levels of intellectual functioning, levels of motivation; levels of abandonment history; levels of impulsivity; levels of denial to protect from varying levels of pain. What the program seems to have added in numbers are more layers reflecting the shadowy community stew: antisocial personality features, more layers of psychosis.

While seemingly compelled to hire mental health professionals, people trained or training to be therapists, what the program seems to prefer are counselors and case managers of a certain type: those who will energetically go about their jobs and diligently dot their "I"s and cross their "T"s; competently shepherd youth and their families from one point of the program to the next. They will be unfussy and mostly agreeable; focus on teaching skill-sets, but not get lost in a client's psychology. That's a therapist's job. Creatively is valued, but creativity must obey limits. Thunder Road staff, like most in community mental health at the online and case management level, is comprised mostly of youthful figures, those with pets instead of children, rents instead of mortgages, student debt versus medical bills, and second hand vehicles that just about get them between home and work. These worker bee positions are the mental health industry's equivalent of service industry jobs. It's a pity they can't accept tips, though considering the wages that are paid, and more broadly, the stagnant reimbursement rates that are paid to psychotherapists, I wouldn't be surprised if ethical standards around client-to-therapist gift giving receive a thorough make-over in the years to come. If so, those cultural diversity arguments will need to be primed and good to go.

I think administrators, managers, those sets of someones and Star Chambers—they all seem to understand this demographic phenomenon and act accordingly. So customer service, that retail chestnut, is routinely invoked, alongside a kind of philosophical positivism, so as to diminish the seeming power divide between provider and patient; to adhere to a society's demand for equality, even as it asks for "expert" advice. But experts don't work for twenty dollars an hour or less. Experts are behind the scenes, getting paid more, or elsewhere, working privately, and getting paid more. The positions in residential programs are therefore designed as stepping stones for the career oriented, though for what it's worth, the medical benefits, along with the vacation pay packages, were and are pretty good. They cater for burn out—just. Still, the overly qualified or maverick at heart need not apply, and if they do get in the front door, they must be aware of their shelf lives.

Dissent

On these and other issues, I think the management of Thunder Road got tired of either hearing my views directly, or else indirectly through the leaking of opinions shared in private conversations. With interns or full-time therapists whom I supervised, I did my share of proselytizing on program needs. But as much as they are a reflection of my thinking, these written words also represent a composite of all the mutterings and sometimes eloquent statements I've heard told to me over the years, and now coalesced in the service of this book. I sensed management's distrust of my position, particularly in my last year at Thunder Road. There was a belief that I was at least redundant, and perhaps subversive. This shadow cabinet that was my supervision group: it needed to be dissolved, and replaced by a like-group with a leader more consistently fused to the existing direction of the program. Trainings should be outsourced to other agencies with an existing infrastructure for such services. The educating/training of trainees: well, that could be left to the academic institutions, which otherwise held little responsibility for the performance of their students. As for the rest of staff: they would need to soldier on, take more responsibility for their own process; survive, like everyone else has to; like the lower and middle classes have to; like the clients have to. It seems self important to cast myself as a rabble rouser. Let's just say management didn't quite regard me as being on the same page. Actually, I was reading a different book—several different books, in fact. Meanwhile, I think that the elimination of my position had been mooted on numerous occasions, only for my job to be saved by nominal allies of mine, sympathetic advocates who served as buffers between me and the bean counters that pored over the spreadsheets, ever looking for more program fat to trim.

While I bemoan management's position, I also place it in perspective, and therefore do not feel personally victimized by its subsequent treatment of me. Such a reaction would imply that my rights had somehow been violated; that I had an entitlement to remain in the position I had, espousing my opinions, pursuing an agenda that may be in line with many, but clearly wasn't in line with program leadership. Case closed, in so far as my employment was concerned. I had no inalienable right to be the clinical supervisor to trainees and interns at Thunder Road, and by the way, neither do employees of any corporation, non-profit organization, or system of any kind, have a *right* to be supported, understood, mirrored or congratulated. I think it one of the conceits of an individualized society that we think systems ought to support people in these ways. As suggested earlier, gestures of "thanks" are provided from time to time, and I, too, once received an "Employee of the month" award (tellingly, it was while I was IOP coordinator, when I was even more separate from the teamthink).

But these were bonus moments—niceties—to be absorbed and accepted with good grace, but not expected.

My departure was presaged by an episode in the early spring of 2011, though at the same time it also drew attention to a previously unspoken bond I'd achieved with my supervisees. One night I got a call from a manager sympathetic to my position, inquiring whether I was the therapist, as in private practice therapist, of a client concurrently attending Thunder Road's Continuing Care, a department with which I had no role. I couldn't comment for reasons of confidentiality, but I didn't deny the assertion, and meanwhile the client was speaking openly of me as his therapist. I'd taken the case only weeks earlier, having informally consulted with outside colleagues on the matter. I thought there was no problem, despite having had previous contact with the client at the hospital. Well, there was a problem, especially from the point of view of management, which somewhat haughtily reprimanded me for violating Thunder Road policy and pursuing a conflict of interest. Long story short: I disagreed, and the quibble over terms, or the wording of policies, was short-circuited, as the medical director became irritated by my arguments. Ultimately, it was asserted that I should have at least talked to Thunder Road, consulted with the management about the prospect of taking an active Thunder Road client into my practice. Why hadn't I talked about it with them? they asked. They almost sounded hurt.

The bottom line, according to lawyers that I spoke with, and presumably separate lawyers that Thunder Road spoke with, was that I hadn't done anything illegal. Whether I had done anything unethical was a matter of opinion, but the truth was that the client's mother had sought me out, through my private practice contact information, as a therapist for her discharging son on the basis that I would be a reasonable fit given that I was a Thunder Road employee and therefore, in all likelihood, familiar with the needs of youth emerging from adolescent residential treatment. I hadn't solicited the client from within the program, and nor was I *stealing* a client from Thunder Road, as the hospital simply does not provide individual therapy on an outpatient basis. The client had a right to seek out my services, and I had a right to offer them, basically.

The interns, to whom I explained the situation in detail, were offended on my behalf, thinking management was targeting me for ulterior reasons. I actually demurred on these suggestions, and reminded that the lesson for everyone was to not risk isolating from the treatment team. I must have seemed like I was acting like a proper martyr, being gracious in the face tyranny, and so on. I hadn't told anyone within the program about having seen another manager at my CEU training the previous winter, but nonetheless, the therapists, like kids on the long-term track who know what's up whether it's spoken of or not, were convinced of a nefarious plot that predated the episode that led to my suspension. They sensed my vulnerability over the next several months, and seemed to wait for the day when I'd announce my exit, either on my terms or those of the hospital. They meanwhile appealed for that not to happen, pointing out that the role I played allowed for an island of process in a system of stifled or confusing communication. The affection they expressed towards me, or the affirmations they aimed at my purpose at least, touched my heart. The problem, however, was that they'd now see me as one of them, whether I reinforced this fusion or not.

I tried, actually, to create some distance, to restore some space and push back against the false solidarity. I needed to hold my position as a supervisor, despite the seductive warmth of the interns' support. Though the episode had humanized me in some interns' eyes, or dispelled for others my image as an untouchable, I was becoming irreparably separate from management, and that wasn't a situation that could last. I think the truest complaint was actually the one articulated by the medical director on the day prior to my suspension: why hadn't I spoken with them? This time I bit down on my tongue, thinking, *and were you talking to me about preparing others to do my job*? It seems, on reflection, a function of a divide that was long brewing, and finally delivered onto our laps as the unconscious element within a testy set of exchanges about policies, laws, operations manuals, and ethics. We, meaning myself and the Thunder Road management team, had contracts against each other, and we were no longer dealing with them in a consistently responsible way.

An unconscious ending

So months later I sat within the office of the clinical director, speaking to the same two people with my eyes drawn to that white sheet of a window like it was a symbol of all that had been rendered unconscious in them, and in me. Parallel process: what transpired between clients and staff also afflicted the space between colleagues. It should have felt like euthanasia, my departure from Thunder Road. My supervisors might have been kind, yet confrontational. Had they been real with me they might have said something like *Look, we're letting you go because we think you're growing apart from us*. Even something like *we think you have contracts* would have merited grim acceptance on my part. "That's valid," I might have said. But instead they relied on procedure, inflected with sentiment.

An unfinished piece of business after the initial termination meeting was the matter of a farewell gathering—a going away party. I was reluctant at first, feeling jaundiced and thinking the idea cynical: the program was long in the habit of putting smiles on frowning faces, so for them it was at least partly about keeping up appearances. But I am not sentimental in nature. The clinical director was smilingly blunt: "it's not all about you," she rebuked, indicating that many people would want the opportunity to bid a loving farewell. I got the distinct impression she wouldn't be one of them. The other manager was more genuinely solemn. He commented that I'd brought a great deal of value to Thunder Road. I replied that I didn't feel valued by Thunder Road. He said, "I can understand why you'd feel that way," quite skillfully; he neither confirmed nor denied the notion I'd put forth. How empathetic. How therapeutically neutral of him, I thought admiringly.

That night I went home after seeing three or four clients consecutively in my private practice—none of them adolescents, or drug addicts. It was an ordeal compartmentalizing my feelings so as to stay focused, but it didn't get any easier after I left my office. I came home and greeted my wife, whom I'd called earlier to alert as to the situation. She quietly embraced me, put aside all her own feelings about being let go by Thunder Road nearly a decade earlier, and held my hand for an hour or so. I was stoic and monosyllabic as I dissociated with television. Around midnight, I declared that I was ready for bed, and we both plodded to our bedroom. My wife uttered a few words of reassurance as we went through our night-time routine; then, within moments of hitting the sheets, she lapsed into sleep, and I was alone finally, laying in the dark. Had I tried to cry—and I think I did try earlier—then nothing would have happened. Instead, I tried to sleep until a rippling sensation suddenly hit me. It started in my neck and quickly traveled up to my lips. In seconds my shoulders were shaking, a pool was gathering in my eyes, and finally a distraught howl just leapt out of me. The sobbing lasted for minutes, with my body performing contortions as the monstrous emotion worked its way up and down my spine. I no longer fit in. I no longer belonged. By now my wife had awakened, of course, and she was softly stroking my back, and silently holding me. By this time she'd known me for ten years. She knew my moods; she knew how pain traveled through me. Most of all, she'd learned what to do, or rather, what not to do. She stayed present and went on Monads.

About a week passed before I agreed to take part in a farewell gathering. Another three weeks passed before the event finally took place on my last day. That morning I took the intern supervision group out to breakfast, or rather they took me, at my insistence, to Fentons, the locally popular ice cream hangout where we often took staff members for a farewell meal on a last day. Last supper: The mood was melancholic and ritual. The interns weren't in the mood, but put on a smiling face anyway. For me, I pleaded. They knew they were being short-changed by this event, and that this short-changing of their supervision was only partly about me. Management would dispute this, but the fact was that my duties were about to be absorbed into those of an already full-time and plus pair of employees. To suggest that they had sufficient time to perform my role in addition to their existing duties would imply that they had previously been under-used, and that clearly was not the case. Before returning to their jobs, each of the interns stood before the back door of Thunder Road, gave me warm hugs and wished me luck for the future. I kept a dry eye trained over their shoulders, towards a mothballed school of benches stacked in a pile behind the facility's east wing. Ok, so maybe I'm a little sentimental.

The later gathering was all about me. A mock discharge was set-up, in keeping with another Thunder Road tradition, with peers and/or supervisees of mine lined up to make short speeches while I sat in a chair of honor. There were surprise elements, such as a taped message from that silky-voiced, one-time program manager, now living in another state, but still sounding as formidable as ever, and still expressing that she liked me. A written statement sent from a former psychiatrist was another pleasant surprise. It was a short letter, a stylized essay, peering from beyond the Thunder Road grave into my head, and seeking to identify with the complex narcissism that might accompany my leaving: *Now the building will truly shut down.* Those in attendance were just about those whom I'd expected to be there. And business rolled on, with members of the crowd stepping out of the room from time to time, needing to attend to events that were, as ever, happening in the milieu. The mood was heartfelt, if forced, for some in the audience will have known about my leaving, and kept their own contracts on the matter for quite some time.

A buffet of food was generously laid out, and a cake was made by the kitchen staff with the help of three male clients who seemed awkwardly proud standing next to their creation. The man standing over them was one of a handful of people who had been at Thunder Road longer than I had, and who would now outlast me by God knows how long. I must admit I was jealous—jealous that he still had a job at Thunder Road. Yet he was a mysterious character to me, a shadowy talismanic wizard presiding over a generation of Therapeutic Communities. Over the years, he'd seen lots of changes; people arriving and leaving, and had been a member of management through at least two, maybe three different departments. He'd witnessed many ideas, policies, therapeutic visions come and go, and like a cockroach in nuclear winter, had survived everything, kept his head down and ploughed on, exuding the belief that ideas were illusory, and that conflict was the stuff of fools. In his comments to me, he was sage, declaring that Thunder Road was like a rollercoaster, and that everyone gets a ride. His would continue it seemed. Still, he looked at me with a crooked, yet sympathetic grin that carried with it a sad implication: My long rollercoaster ride was over.

REFERENCES

Ainsworth, M. D. S. (1973) "The development of infant-mother attachment", in B.M. Caldwell & H. N. Ricciuti (Eds.), *Review of child development research* (Vol. 3, pp 1-94). Chicago: University of Chicago Press.

American Psychiatric Association (1994) *DSM-IV: Diagnostic and statistical manual of mental disorders*. 4th Ed. Washington D.C.: American Psychiatric Association.

Aposhyan, S. (2004) *Body Mind Psychotherapy: Principle, Techniques, and Practical Applications*. W.W. Norton & Company.

Applebaum, S.A. (1973). Psychological Mindedness: Word, concept, and essence. *International Journal of PsychoAnalysis*, 54, 5-46.

Bader, M. (2009) *Male Sexuality*. Rowman & Littlefield Publishers, Inc.

Balint, M. (1968). *The Basic Fault, Therapeutic Aspects of Regression*. London: Tavistock.

Beattie, M. (1986) *Codependent No More*. Hazelden Publishing.

Beck, A.T, Scott, J., Williams, M.G. (1989). *Cognitive Therapy in Clinical Practice*. Routledge.

Bettman, E. J., Jasperson, R. A. (2009). Adolescents in Residential and Inpatient Treatment: A Review of the Outcome Literature. *Child Youth Care Forum*. 38: 161-183

Bion, W. (1961) *Experiences in Groups*. Tavistock.

Bowen, M. (1976). *Theory in the practice of psychotherapy*. In P. Guerin (Ed.) *Family Therapy: Theory and practice*. New York: Gardner Press.

Bowlby, J. (1969). *Attachment and Loss: Vol. 1. Attachment*. New York: Basic Books.

Bowlby, J. (1973). *Attachment and Loss: Vol. 2. Separation: Anxiety and Anger*. New York: Basic Books.

Bowlby, J. (1980). *Attachment and Loss: Vol. 3. Loss: Sadness and Depression*. New York: Basic Books.

Butler, L. S., McPherson, P.M. (2007). Is Residential Treatment Misunderstood? *Journal of Child and Family Studies*, 16 (4), 465-492. In Bettman, E.J., & Jasperson, R.A. (2009). Adolescents in Residential and Inpatient Treatment: A Review of the Outcome Literature. *Child Youth Care Forum*. 38: 161-183

Buie, D., & Adler, G. (1982) "The definitive treatment of the borderline patient". *International Journal of Psychoanalytic Psychotherapy*, 9, 51-87.

Coates, S.W. (2004). "John Bowlby and Margaret S. Mahler: Their Lives and Theories". *Journal of the American Psychoanalytic Association*. Vol. 52, No. 2: 571-601.

Caligor, E., Yoemans, F., Diamond, F., and Kernberg, O. (2006) "The Interpretive Process in the Psychodynamic Psychotherapy of Borderline Personality." *Journal of the American Psychoanalytic Association*, Vol. 57, 2009, pp. 271-301.

Campbell, J. (1949). *The Hero with a Thousand Faces*. New York. Pantheon books.

Cappas, N., Andres-Hyman, R., Davidson, L. (2005). What Psychotherapists can begin to learn from neuroscience: Seven principles of a brain-based psychotherapy. *Psychotherapy: Theory, Research, Practice, Training*. Vol. 42, No. 3, 374-383.

Cassidy, J. (2001). Truth, Lies, and Intimacy: An attachment perspective. Attachment & Human Development, Vol 3 No. 2, September 2001. P. 121-155.

Cermak, T.L. (1986) *Diagnosing and Treating Codependence*. Johnson Institute. Minneapolis, MN.

Corey, M.S., & Corey, G. (1995) Groups: Process and Practice (4th Ed.) Pacific Grove, Ca. Brooks/Cole.

Cruse, S.W. (1989) *Another Chance: Hope and Health for the Alcoholic Family*. Second Edition. Science and Behavior Books, Inc.

Damasio (October, 2001). Fundamental Feelings. *Nature*, 413,718. In Cappas, N., Andres-Hyman, R., Davidson, L. (2005). What Psychotherapists can begin to learn from neuroscience: Seven principles of a brain-based psychotherapy. *Psychotherapy: Theory, Research, Practice, Training*. Vol. 42, No. 3, 374-383.

de Maat, S., de Jonghe, F., Shoevers, R., & Dekker, J. (2009). The effectiveness of long-term psychoanalytic therapy: a systemic review of empirical studies. Harvard Review of Psychiatry, 17, 1-23. In Shedler, J. (2010) The Efficacy of Psychodynamic Psychotherapy. *American Psychologist*. February-March 2010. American Psychological Association. Vol. 65, No. 2, 98-109

Deleon, G. (2000) *The Therapeutic Community: Theory, Model, & Method*. Springer Publishing Company, Inc. New York City.

Delpit, L. (1996) The Politics of Teaching Literate Discourse. In W. Ayers & P. Ford (Eds.) *City Kids, City Teachers: Reports from the Front Row*. NY: New Press.

Durrant, M. (1993). *Residential Treatment: A cooperative competency-based approach to therapy and program design*. New York: W.W. Norton

Ellis, Albert (1999) *How to make yourself happy and remarkably less disturbable*. Impact Publishers.

Epstein, M., Harniss, M., Robbins, V., Wheeler, L., Cyrulik, S., Kriz, M., & Nelson, R. (2003). Strength-Based approaches to assessment in schools. *Handbook of School Mental Health: Advancing Practice and Research.*

Fenichel, O. (1945) Neurotic Acting Out. *Psychoanalytic Review*, 32: 197-206

Fonagy, P. & Target, M. (1996) Playing with reality: I. "Theory of mind and the normal development of psychic reality". *International Journal of Psychoanalysis*, 77, 217-233.

Fonagy, P., Gergely, G., Jurist, E., & Target, M. (2002). *Affect Regulation, Mentalization, and the Development of the Self.* New York: Other Press.

Fonagy, P. and Bateman, A. (2006) Progress in the Treatment of Borderline Personality Disorder. *The British Journal of Psychiatry*.188:1-3

Foster, M., Nathan, S., Ferry, M. (2010) The experience of drug-dependent adolescents in a therapeutic community. *Drug and Alcohol Review*, 29, 531-539.

Freud, Sigmund (1914g). Errinern, Wiederholen and Durcharbeiten (Weitere Ratschlage zur Technik der Psychoanalyse, II) Internacionale Zeitschrift fur artztliche Psychoanalyse 2, 485-491; Remembering, Repeating, and Working Through. SE, 12. 147-156.

Gorman, J.M., Roose, S.P. (2011). Neurobiology of Fear Memory Reconsolidation and Psychoanalytic Theory. *Journal of The American Psychoanalytic Association*. 59(6) 1201-1220.

Gorski, T. (1989) *Passages Through Recovery: An Action Plan for Preventing Relapse*. Hazelden.

Gottman, J., Silver, N. (1999). *The Seven Principles For Making Marriage Work*. Orion books, Ltd.

Hall, C. (1954). *A Primer in Freudian Psychology*. Meridian Books

Hebb, D.O. (1949). *The Organization of Behavior*. New York: Wiley.

Jellinek, E. M. (1960) *The Disease Concept of Alcoholism. Hillhouse*, New Haven.

Kasl, C. (1992) *Many Roads, One Journey: Moving Beyond the 12 Steps*. Harper Perennial.

Kernberg, O. (1975). *Borderline Conditions and Pathological Narcissism*. New York: Science House.

Klein, M. (1946) Notes on Some Schizoid Mechanisms. *International Journal of Psychoanalysis*, 27: 99-110.
Kohut, H. (1971). *The Analysis of the Self.* New York: International Universities Press.

Kohut, H., Wolf, E.S. (1978). The disorders of the self and their treatment: an outline. *International Journal of Psychoanalysis*, 59, 413-425.

Ledoux, J. (1997). The Emotional Brain. New York. Simon & Schuster. In Cappas, N., Andres-Hyman, R., Davidson, L. (2005). Psychotherapists can begin to learn from neuroscience: Seven principles of a brain-based psychotherapy. *Psychotherapy: Theory, Research, Practice, Training.* Vol. 42, No. 3, 374-383.

Leichsenring, F., Rabung, S., & Leibing, E. (2004). The efficacy of short-term psychodynamic psychotherapy in specific psychiatric disorders: a meta-analysis. *Archives of General Psychiatry*, 61, 1208-1216. In Shedler, J. (2010) The Efficacy of Psychodynamic Psychotherapy. *American Psychologist*. February-March 2010. American Psychological Association. Vol. 65, No. 2, 98-109

Leichsenring, F., Rabung, S. (2008). Effectiveness of long-term psychodynamic psychotherapy: a meta-analysis. *American Journal of Psychiatry*, 160, 1223-1232. In Shedler, J. (2010) The Efficacy of Psychodynamic Psychotherapy. *American Psychologist*. February-March 2010. American Psychological Association. Vol. 65, No. 2, 98-109

Lyons-Ruth, K., Bronfman, E., & Parsons, E. (1999). Atypical attachment in infancy and early childhood among children at developmental risk. *Monographs of the Society for Research in Child Development*, 64(3), 67-96. In Cassidy, J., & Shaver, P. (Eds.) *Handbook Of Attachment: Theory, Research, and Clinical Applications* (2008). The Guilford Press.

Lyons-Ruth, K. (2001). "The emergence of new experiences: Relational improvisation, recognition process, and non-linear change in psychoanalytic therapy". *Psychologist-Psychoanalyst*, 21, 13-17.

Mahler, M., Pine, F., & Bergmann, A. (1975). *The Psychological Birth of the Human Infant: Symbiosis and Individuation*. New York: Basic Books.

Main, M., & Goldwyn, R. (1982-1998) Adult attachment scoring and classification system. Unpublished Manuscript, Department of Psychology, University of California at Berkeley.

Maran, M. (2003). *Dirty*. Harper Collins, HarperSanFrancisco.

Marlatt, G. A, & Gordon, J. R. (1985) *Relapse Prevention: Maintenance Strategies in the Treatment of Addictive Behaviors*. New York. The Guildford Press.

Maroda, K.J. (2005) Show some emotion: completing the cycle of affective communication. In L. Aron & A. Harris (Eds.) Revolutionary connections. *Relational Psychoanalysis. Innovation and expansion*. Vol. II 121-142. Analytic Press.

Masterson, J. F. (1967) *The Psychiatric Dilemma Of Adolescence*. Bruner/Mazel Publishers. New York.

Masterson, J. F. (1972) *Treatment Of The Borderline Adolescent*. Bruner/Mazel Publishers. New York.

Masterson, J. F., Klein, R. (1989) *Psychotherapy of the Disorders of the Self: the Masterson Approach*. New York: Brunner/Mazel.

Masterson, J. F., Klein, R. (1995) *Disorder Of The Self: New Therapeutic Horizons*. Bruner/Mazel. Inc.

Masterson, J. F. (Ed.) (2005) *The Personality Disorders Through the Lens of Attachment Theory and the Neurobiologic Development of the Self*. Zeig, Tucker, & Thiesen, Inc.

McKay, M., Wood, J., Brantley, J. (2007) *The Dialectical Behavior Therapy Skills Workbook: Practical DBT Exercises for Learning Mindfulness, Interpersonal Effectiveness, Emotional Regulation & Distress Tolerance*. New Harbinger Publications, Inc.

Mikulincer, M., & Florian, V. (1997). Are emotional and instrumental supportive interactions beneficial in times of stress? The impact of attachment style. *Anxiety, Stress and Coping: An International Journal*, 10, 109-127. In Cassidy, J., & Shaver, P. (Eds.) *Handbook Of*

Attachment: Theory, Research, and Clinical Applications (2008). The Guilford Press.

Miller, W.R., Rollnick, S. (2002) *Motivational Interviewing: Preparing People for Change* (2nd Ed.) New York. Guilford Press.

Miller, W.R. (1983) Motivational Interviewing with Problem Drinkers. *Behavioral Psychotherapy*, 11, 147-172.

Mock, R., Zempolich, K.A., Titus, J.C., Fisherman, M., Godley, M.D., & Schwebel, R. (2001, December). An overview of the effectiveness of adolescent substance abuse treatment models. *Youth and Society*, 33, 143-168. In Tripodi, S. (2009) A Comprehensive Review: Methodological Rigor of Studies on Residential Centers for Substance-Abusing Adolescents. *Journal of Evidence-Based Social Work*, 6:288-299.

Nerz, A. R. (2013) *Marijuana America: One Man's Quest to Understand America's Dysfunctional Love Affair with Weed.* Abrams Image, New York.

Orcutt, C. (2004) "Trauma in borderline personality disorder" (p. 111-119). In J. F. Masterson & A. R. Lieberman (Eds.), *A Therapist's Guide to Personality Disorders: The Masterson Approach.* Phoenix: Zeig, Tucker & Thiesen.

Orcutt, C. (2012) *Trauma In Personality Disorder: A Clinician's Handbook.* Author House.

Pazaratz, D. (2009) *Residential Treatment Of Adolescents: Integrative Practices and Principles*. Routledge.

Peck, S. M.D. (1978) *The Road Less Traveled.* A Touchstone Book. Simon & Schuster.

Prochaska, J.O., & DiClemente, C.C. (1983). Stages and Processes of Self-Change of Smoking: Towards an Integrative Model of Change. *Journal of Consulting and Clinical Psychology*. 51(3). 390-395.

Prochaska, J., Norcross, J., and DiClemente, C. (1994) *Changing for Good: A Revolutionary Six Stage Program for Overcoming Bad Habits and Moving your Life Positively Forward*. New York. Avon Books.

Rinsley, D. B. (1982). *Borderline and other self disorders*. New York: Aronson.

Rogers, C. (1951). Client-centered therapy: its current practice, implications, and theory. London. Constable.

Ronningstam, E. (2011) "Narcissistic Personality Disorder in DSM V: In support of retaining a significant diagnosis". *Journal of Personality Disorders*, 25(2), 248-259. 2011
Rutan, J.S., & Stone, W.N. (2001). Termination in Group Therapy. In Rutan, J.S. & Stone, W.N. *Psychodynamic Group Therapy* (3rd. Ed.) pp.332-354. New York. Guilford Press.

Schiller D., Monfils, M.H., Raio, C.M., Johnson, D.C., LeDoux, J.E., Phelps, E.A., (2010) Preventing the Return of Fear in Humans Using Reconsolidation Update Mechanisms. *Nature*. Vol. 463, 7.
Schore, A. (1994). *Affect Regulation and the Origin of the Self*. Hillsdale, NJ: Erlbaum.

Schore, A. (2005). A Neuropsychoanalytic Viewpoint: commentary on a paper by Steven H Knoblauch. *Psychoanalytic Dialogues*, 16(5): 829-854.

Seigel, D. J. (1999). *The Developing Mind: Toward a Neurobiology of Interpersonal Experience*. New York: Guilford.

Shavelson, L. (2001) *Hooked: Five Addicts Challenge Our Misguided Drug Rehab System*. The New Press, New York.

Shane, P., Cherry, L., Snowden, R., Gerstel, T. (2003) *Thunder Road Treatment Manual*. Lighthouse Institute Publications.

Shedler, J. (2010) The Efficacy of Psychodynamic Psychotherapy. *American Psychologist*. February-March 2010. American Psychological Association. Vol. 65, No. 2, 98-109.

Short, B. (2005) "From Concrete Truth to Symbolic Reality—Transference and the Language of Change", pp. 61-79. In Masterson, J. F. (Ed.) (2005) *The Personality Disorders Through the Lens of Attachment Theory and the Neurobiologic Development of the Self*. Zeig, Tucker, & Thiesen, Inc.

Skinner, B. F. (1969) *Contingencies of Reinforcement: a theoretical analysis*. New York, Appleton-Century-Crofts.

Spitzer, C., Wilert, C., Grabe, H.J., Rizos, T., Freyberger, H.J. (2004) Dissociation, hemispheric asymmetry and dysfunction of hemispheric interaction: a transcranial magnetic approach. *Journal of Neuropsychiatry and Clinical Neurosciences*. 16, 163-169.

Substance Abuse and Mental Health Services Administration (US); 2000. *Substance Abuse Treatment for Persons with Child Abuse and Neglect Issues. Treatment Improvement Protocol (TIP) Series, No. 36.* Report No.: (SMA) 00-3357.

Taylor, S.E., Klein, L.C., Lewis, B.P., Gruenewald, T.L., Gurung, R.A.R., & Updegraff, J.A. (2000). Biobehavioral responses to stress in females: Tend and befriend, not fight-or-flight. *Psychological Review*, 107(3), 411-429. In Cassidy, J., & Shaver, P. (Eds.) *Handbook Of Attachment: Theory, Research, and Clinical Applications* (2008). The Guilford Press.

Tripodi, S. (2009) A Comprehensive Review: Methodological Rigor of Studies on Residential Centers for Substance-Abusing Adolescents. *Journal of Evidence-Based Social Work*, 6:288-299.

Twelve Steps and Twelve Traditions (1952). New York: Alcoholics Anonymous World Services, Inc.
Volpicelli, J., Szalavitz, M. (2000) *Recovery Options: The Complete Guide*. John Wiley & Sons, Inc.

Weis, R., Wilson, N.L., & Whitemarsh, S.M. (2005) Evaluation of a voluntary, military-style residential treatment program for adolescents with academic and conduct problems. *Journal of Clinical Child & Adolescent Psychology*. 34(4) 692-705. In Bettman, E.J., & Jasperson, R.A (2009) Adolescents in Residential and Inpatient Treatment: A Review of the Outcome Literature. *Child Youth Care Forum*. 39: 161-183

Wheeler, K., Malmquist, J. (1983) Treatment Approaches in Adolescent Chemical Dependency. *Pediatric Clinics of North America*. 34(2) 437-47.

Wilson, D.B., Gottfredson, D.C., Najaka, S.S. (2001) School-Based Prevention of Problem Behaviors: a meta-analysis. *Journal of Quantitative Criminology,* Vol. 17, number 3, 247-272. In Kalke, T., Glanton, A., and Cristalli, M. (2007). Positive Behavior Interventions and Supports: using Strength-based approaches to enhance the culture of care in residential and day treatment education environments. *Child Welfare*. Vol. 86, 151-174.

Winnicott, D. W. (1971). *Playing and Reality*. London: Routledge.
Yalom, Irvin D. (2005) *The Schopenhauer Cure*. Harper Collins Publishers.

Yalom, Irvin D. (1983) *Inpatient Group Psychotherapy*. Basic Books, Inc. Publishers. New York.

Yalom, Irvin D. (1995) *The Theory And Practice Of Group Psychotherapy*. Basic Books, A Division of Harper Collins Publishers.

Yalom, I.D., Leszcz, M. (2005) *The Theory And Practice Of Group Psychotherapy*. Basic Books, A Division of Harper Collins Publishers.

Zetzel, E. R. (1956) Current concepts of transference. *International Journal of Psychoanalysis*, 37, 369.

ENDNOTES

---

[1] According to Websters Dictionary, the term has applications in chemistry, biology, and philosophy and means "alone", or "ultimate unit"; from the Greek *monas*

[2] From the German 'einfuhlungsvermogen', meaning "feeling into".

[3] Applebaum (1973) used this term to describe a capacity to relate actions to thoughts and feelings, which might be further interpreted as the capacity to identify thoughts and feelings within the self, and then attribute behaviors to those thoughts and feelings with some degree of analysis.

[4] A formula of propositional logic is tautological if the formula itself is always true regardless of which valuation is used for the variables. There are many types of tautologies. I believe this popular phrase represents an example of contraposition: if A implies B, then not-B implies not-A.

[5] Founded by Chuck Dederich and described by Volpicelli and Szalavitz (2000) as a "violent cult", Synanon was the prototype TC or "social" model: a rigidly structured treatment program consisting of work activities, group therapy, and "house meetings" (ala contract breaking?) to discuss conflicts. Days begin early and end late, and free time is rare.

[6] The oral "tradition" here indicated has been identified by Deleon (2000), who pointed out the the TC approach has been conveyed orally for the most part. I simply observe that clients mirror this tradition.

[7] Masterson (1985) used this term to describe a real object relationship in which there is a consensus between patient and therapist as to the objective of their work: help the patient get better through insight, control, etc. The term therapeutic alliance is originally attributed to Zetzel (1956). Regardless, it does not simply mean "liking your therapist".

[8] A related concept is projective identification, so-termed by Melanie Klein (1946), referring not only to the attribution of thoughts, feelings to others, but a patient's identification with an analyst. Feelings denied, or dissociated, are induced in the treating professional. A good example at Thunder Road occurred with passively defiant clients, who "frustrated" or "annoyed" staff with their

forgetfulness and general irresponsibility.

[9] Aposhyan (2004) characterizes dissociation as the state of being cut off from some aspect of one's process. Central nervous system dissociation limits ability to perceive, process, respond to current stimuli. Spitzer, Wilert, Grabe, Rizos, and Freyberger (P. 168, 2004), characterize dissociation as, "disruption in the usually integrated functions of consciousness". The term dissociation was originally attributed to French psychiatrist Pierre Janet.

[10] E.M. Jellinik is credited by many as having coined the term "disease model" in reference to alcoholism and addiction. His idea of stages of alcoholism had a major impact on how alcoholism (and addictions in general) was viewed. According to the theory, there are four stages in alcoholism: a pre-symptomatic (no problems) phase; a prodromal stage—featuring blackouts, guilt and increasing drunkenness; a stage of failed attempts at controlling use; and a chronic stage—mental and physical complications, and lengthy binges. Jellinik distinguished the alcoholic from "heavy drinkers" from their inability to control drinking.

[11] These observations recall Jude Cassidy's 2001 article, "Truth, Lies, and Intimacy": a review of attachment literature. Her maxim: a defining feature of a secure narrative is that it is truthful. "Parents can be untruthful about the reality of the child's experience in a variety of ways. They can ignore, withdraw from, or become angry in response to the child's behaviors, and thereby convey that feelings are unacceptable.

[12] At this point, some female readers might object and argue that this is a masculine-centered POV; that girls, women, are often inhibited around anger, and therefore need the help of therapists and communities to facilitate its expression.

[13] A term loosely introduced, it means rewards. Different types of reinforcements are staple features of residential programs: point systems as rewards; privileges for positive behavior (positive reinforcement) or praise; the withholding of privileges until completion of assignments (punishment); pressuring clients to comply with requests until compliance is achieved (negative reinforcement).

[14] Self-disclosure in this context refers only to personal information, versus feelings or thoughts that therapists might express in any given therapeutic exchange. Schore (cited in Masterson, 2003) has suggested that self-revelation (of this latter type) by the therapist is constant, occurring at a right-brain level of communication.

[15] A term with various meanings, philosophical as well as psychological, here it

takes on a distinctive meaning—that of separation—as well as a challenging brief: achieve compatibility with *attachment*, the predominant focus of this text.

[16] Another important term in the behavioral science lexicon, it was rarely used in the residential program; at least, not during the nineties. For reasons rarely discussed, ignoring negative behaviors didn't seem like an option. The belief was that it would not be effective: a priori addicts thrive on secrecy and isolation—in other words, being ignored.

[17] The word *psychodynamic* is an umbrella term, comprised of psychoanalytically-derived therapies based upon Object Relations Theory. According to Hall (1954), the term refers to transformations and exchanges of energy within the personality.

[18] Regardless, consumers of psychotherapy should understand that the relationship is fiduciary, which is a legal term that denotes a special layer of trust and responsibility on the part of the professional, in relationship with the consumer of services. The concept of the fiduciary relationship underlies the legal and ethical principle of confidentiality, and explains why mental health practitioners, unlike retailers, are mandated reporters of child abusers, and must have liability insurance

[19] This view is also influenced by Balint (1968), who offered that a traditional view rooted in linear thinking leads therapists to impose realities, undermining for patients the possibility of creating their own.

[20] Like Maran (2003), Shavelson's book decries the lack of trained therapists working in Therapeutic Communities. However, writing as journalists and not clinicians, they tend to characterize psychotherapeutic interventions in monolithic terms, without attention to the eclectic range of approaches

[21] Codependency: a popularly used term, both inside and outside of treatment circles, it evades precise definition. Cermak (1986) offered five categories for diagnostic consideration, beginning with the statement, "Continued investment of self-esteem in the ability to control both oneself and others in the face of adverse consequences", followed by, "Assumption of responsibility for meeting others' needs to the exclusion of acknowledging one's own".

[22] Maran's *Dirty* (2003) seems to bristle at this kind of characterization, commenting that parent blaming is endorsed by psychoanalysts and is "easy to practice". Actually, there's nothing easy about it. While I wouldn't contest her experience per se, I would offer a contrasting view: kids often reported that their parents were not so much bombarded by criticism as they were simply intolerant of it. As a result, they projected their judgments onto outsiders, and exaggerated that which was directed at them.

[23] This passage borrows from Shavelson (2001) who imagines the efforts of doctors from an opposite standpoint. In his scenario, a doctor listens to the recitation of symptoms, which include relapse. Offended by the continuation of drug-using behavior, a doctor orders a patient from his care, abandoning them

[24] To explain further, there are many who entered therapy—not just those who are mandated—who talk ad nauseum about dropping their defensive strategies, but don't actually do it. Glibness, lack of affect, is a commonplace problem in drug treatment and psychotherapy.

[25] In *The Hero with a Thousand Faces*, Joseph Campbell reviews the cross-cultural phenomenon called the vision quest. He separates adventure into two categories: those undertaken intentionally, and those which are not. For this latter category of adventurer, the will to change is a serendipitous discovery. In both, there is death and resurrection.

[26] While this may be a widely accepted standard, there are no regulations that stipulate limits to size of therapy groups. However, interestingly enough, the standard is incorporated with respect to the training of therapists. Supervision groups of therapist interns or trainees must contain no more than 8 members according to the Board of Behavioral Sciences.

[27] Actually, "discharge" is the term commonly used to parallel this idea of "acting out" feelings

[28] Contrary to this prejudice, psychoanalytic candidates (students of psychoanalysis who are likely experienced therapists already) have been known to charge as little as $10-15/hour

[29] Issues around the alleged harmful effects of drugs like marijuana are largely deferred in this book. However, one can't have worked in rehab over the last 20 years and not become aware of a politicized underground that thinks the demonization of pot is a long-standing government plot with racist undertones. The minstrels of this movement are rap artists, of course, and a history of the legalization cause is reported in Nerz's *Marijuana America: One Man's Quest to Understand America's Dysfunctional Love Affair with Weed.*

[30] Iatrogenic: meaning, treatment-induced pathology.

[31] This term is relevant to previous text concerning impaired reflective function. Psychic equivalence refers to phenomenon wherein mental reality equals external reality. The internal has equal power and status as the external. Staff often referred to this in terms of "concreteness". What was thought by clients was distorted, but characterized as *real*.

[32] To be fair, I found most administrators I worked with to be quite knowledgeable about what was required of therapists by the Board of Behavioral Sciences. They had to know fringe benefits pertaining to the accrual of licensing hours, for example, so as to offer something to offset non-competitive wages

[33] At the Scott's Valley Recovery Camp near Santa Cruz, California, where I visited in the summer of 2012, camp directors explained a similar reward system for kids, as well as a similar controversy owing to the principles of the 12-step program. A kid's free time is an addict's isolation.

[34] Again, this is one area where an industry recommendation is incorporated into standard practice as a requirement. While 8-10 members is considered optimum size for a therapy group, the Board of Behavioral Sciences stipulates that no more than 8 trainees or interns participate in a group supervision for the purpose of accruing licensing hours. A point is being made, I think, about group process: size matters!

[35] Sixties political activist, to whom the following chestnut phrase is often attributed: "If you are not part of the solution, then you are part of the problem"

[36] Avatar: from the Sanskrit *avatara*; from Hindu religion, a god coming down to earth in bodily form; an incarnation; *ava*, meaning down; and *tarati*, he goes, passes beyond.

[37] Referencing the Health Insurance Portability and Accountability Act, legislatively passed in 1996, which established new standards for the maintenance of health records, confidentiality of personal health information (PHI)

[38] Staff at Thunder Road typically viewed rewards for positive behavior as problematic. Giving money wasn't realistic; "token" economies were difficult to regulate. So-called "positive" bookings could lead to nominal gifts, slurpee runs to 7-11, for example. In time, rewards for positive behavior were not as common as reprieves from reassessment packets. Essays would be stricken from the record, bench time halved, etc. If staff couldn't logistically reward the positive, it could at least scale back on punishments and negative reinforcement

[39] Shavelson (2001) appears to extol the Drug Court system, pointing out that its programs achieve success with "hardcore" addicts who have dropped out of, or been discharged from, residential facilities. His reporting indicates that Drug Courts can boast greater rates of program completion, but does this mean that participants' drug use has diminished?

[40] Taylor and colleagues (2000) advance the hypothesis that gender differences occur in response to threat. Whereas "fight-flight" responses are common among males, "tend-befriend" responses are stronger among females. More infant observation studies: Lyons Ruth, Bronfman & Parsons (1999) found significant differences between female and male infants, observing that female infants were more likely than males to continue to approach mothers at reunion after those mothers had exhibited disorganized behavior.

[41] Bader (2009, p. 22) argues that boys have to work harder than girls to feel like separate people. Guilt and longings for closeness are threatening to boys in their quest for masculinity, so the emotional armor of stoicism and self-sufficiency is a perceived solution.

[42] Kasl also weighed in on this issue from a feminist perspective: "A perpetrator or narcissistic person with a well-developed ego needs a much different approach than a depressed person who has been abused and has little ego development" (P. 248, 1992).

[43] I quote Peck (P. 153, 1978) on this question: "To fail to confront when confrontation is required for the nurture of spiritual growth represents a failure to love equally as does thoughtless criticism or condemnation and other forms of active deprivation or caring."

[44] Miller and Rollnick (2002) have latterly described Motivational Interviewing as a "client-centered, directive method for enhancing intrinsic motivation for change by exploring and resolving ambivalence".

[45] It's not clear which report is being referenced by Shavelson, though it's likely that the "Treatment Improvement Protocols" (Shavelson, 2001, P. 269) he indicates refers to TIP report #36, originally published in 2000.

[46] However, the impression recalls Masterson's (1967) now forty five year old assertions about disturbed youth at the Payne Whitney clinic in New York: "We found on review of records that symptoms of anxiety and depression and acting out had indeed diminished. But what was giving them so much trouble five years later, their pathological character traits, had not been treated at all."

[47] In this author's opinion, it seems unclear from McKay, Wood, and Brantley (2007) whether practitioners are meant to confront—that is, draw attention to—negative consequences of destructive behavior (such as self-harming), as the model also advises against afflicted individuals indulging in judgment or self-criticism.

[48] Actually, as long as I can remember, counselors at Thunder Road would address interpersonal aspects of a conflict, with confrontations like "and what

was your part in that?" While some may have issues with such questions, I for one was always a fan of this kind of intervention.

[49] These "quantifiable" objectives were often a source of ridicule within my peer circles. I recall being given an instruction sheet on quantifiable objectives years ago. An example of a "problem" was "tearfulness three times a day resulting in inability to prepare meals for self and children." The objective, which therapists were meant to track, read as follows: "patient will report no more than one episode of tearfulness per day over six months."

[50] Note: level 14 is the level of lock-down. That is, the level at which physical restraints, incarcerations, and isolation rooms are both permitted and common.

[51] Randy Snowden reported that during his tenure (the early nineties), Thunder Road had been "grandfathered in" as a level 11 facility, thus enabling a higher rate of reimbursement. Also, Snowden made almost identical comments regarding forthcoming trends of clients, and he was speaking from the perspective of the late eighties and early nineties.

[52] Ethology, a discipline derived from evolutionary theory, offers that instinctive behaviors reflect the principle of survival of the species. Bowlby (1969, 1973, 1980) argued that attachment behaviors, clinging, following, crying, and smiling, were instinctive behaviors activated in the service of survival. They lead to safety from predators, and help form secure bonds with caregivers.

[53] Citing Clarkin et al (2004a,b) Fonagy and Bateman refer to controlled studies of psychotherapy for Borderline Personality disorder, and point out that equal benefits were found through use of DBT, TFB, and supportive psychotherapy, but that drop-out rates were higher with use of DBT. They cite controlled studies of their own treatment as indicating enduring changes in mood states and interpersonal functioning, as well as improvements in reflective functioning. Meanwhile, Caligor, Diamond, Kernberg, and Yoemans (2009) cite later research (Clarkin et al, 2007) indicating that reflective functioning improved with TFP but is not indicated in controlled studies of DBT or supportive therapy.

[54] This imagined intervention is a paraphrasing drawn from an example in Clarkin, Yoemans, and Kernberg (2006).

ACKNOWLEDGMENTS

My thanks to the following people for giving me their time, recollections, and insights: Thunder Road originals, Randy Snowden and Armando Corpus. From Our Common Ground, Dr. Danielle Van Deventer; Susan Haws and Jeff Geiger from Camp Recovery in Scott's Valley. Thanks to Maggie Lai and Lonny Shavelson for help in finding elusive federal reports about treatment protocols, and thanks again to Don Mathews for his cover art, generosity, and general support. Thanks to the following for critical feedback and/or inspiration: Jeanne McAlister, Letha A. Chunn, Dave Borof, Sean Vitali, Dr. Shelley Nagel, Dr. Ken Seider, Luba Palter, Ayize Jama Everett, Judge Stephen Angelides, The Mechanics Institute of San Francisco, Carol Vigne, Lacey Rainwater, Brian Needleman, Toni Maita, Jonathan Keeley, and Joanne Schurter. Thanks also to Jo, my confidant in the cuts.

Special thanks to Dr. Michael Wachter for his advice, humor, and enthusiasm for this project. This book is dedicated to the staff of Thunder Road. Thanks for remembering.

ABOUT THE AUTHOR

Graeme Daniels is a psychotherapist and author practicing in Contra Costa County, California. He is the author of three novels, *Living Without Blood*, *The Big No,* and *Crystal From The Hills*, the latter about a methamphetamine user also suffering from chronic PTSD. *Working Through Rehab* is his first non-fiction work. Born in the UK, he has lived in California for over thirty years. He can be reached via his website, www.selfinaddiction.com

Made in United States
Troutdale, OR
11/03/2026

56844515R00219